Instant Vortex Air Fryer Oven Cookbook

1000 Foolproof, Quick and Easy Recipes for Delicious and Affordable Homemade Meals

Jean Davis

Copyright© 2021 By Jean Davis All Rights Reserved

This book is copyright protected. It is only for personal use. You cannot amend, distribute, sell, use, quote or paraphrase any part of the content within this book, without the consent of the author or publisher.

Under no circumstances will any blame or legal responsibility be held against the publisher, or author, for any damages, reparation, or monetary loss due to the information contained within this book, either directly or indirectly.

Disclaimer Notice:

Please note the information contained within this document is for educational and entertainment purposes only. All effort has been executed to present accurate, up to date, reliable, complete information. No warranties of any kind are declared or implied. Readers acknowledge that the author is not engaged in the rendering of legal, financial, medical or professional advice. The content within this book has been derived from various sources. Please consult a licensed professional before attempting any techniques outlined in this book.

By reading this document, the reader agrees that under no circumstances is the author responsible for any losses, direct or indirect, that are incurred as a result of the use of the information contained within this document, including, but not limited to, errors, omissions, or inaccuracies.

Table of Content

Introduction 1

Chapter 1 Beginners Guide to The Vortex 3

Step by Step Guide to the Usage of The Vortex 3
Top 6 Instant Vortex Air Fryer Accessories 4

Chapter 2 Cooking with The Instant Vortex Air Fryer 6

Dos and Don'ts 6
Choosing the Right Cooking Mode 7
Tips and Tricks for Air Frying Success 8
Best and Worst Ingredients 8
How to Save Time Cooking 9

Chapter 3 Breakfasts 10

Sweet Banana Bread 10
Low-Fat Buttermilk Biscuits 10
Coffee Cake with Pecan 10
Cheese and Bacon Muffin Sandwiches 10
Baked Fries with Bacon and Eggs 11
Maple Oats and Nuts 11
Parmesan Ham and Egg Cups 11
Cheddar Breakfast Sausage Scones 12
Bell Pepper and Ham Omelet 12
Avocado and Egg Burrito 12
Sausage French Toast Casserole with Maple 13
Corn Frittata with Avocado Dressing 13
Vanilla Banana Bread Pudding 13
Mozzarella Tomato Salsa Rounds 14
Broccoli and Red Pepper Quiche 14
Breakfast Sausage Quiche 14
Cheddar Bacon Casserole 14
Vanilla Pancake with Walnuts 15
Breakfast Raisins Bars 15
Almond, Coconut, and Apple Granola 15
Bell Pepper and Carrot Frittata 15
Baked Avocado with Eggs and Tomato 16
Chicken Breakfast Sausages 16
Garlic Potatoes with Peppers and Onions 16
Brown Rice Quiches with Pimiento 16
Swiss Ham Mustard Pastries 17
Banana Chocolate Bread with Walnuts 17

Half-and-Half Cinnamon Rolls 17
Shrimp and Spinach Frittata 18
Cheddar Hash Brown Casserole 18
Brown Rice Porridge with Dates 18
Vanilla Blueberry Cobbler 18
Baked Eggs with Kale Pesto 19
Blueberries Quesadillas 19
Maple French Toast Casserole 19
Honey Cashew Granola with Cranberries 19
Maple Banana Bread Pudding 20
Spinach and Egg Florentine 20
Cinnamon Rolls with Brown Sugar 20
Asparagus Strata with Havarti Cheese 21
Artichoke and Mushroom Frittata 21
Mushroom and Spinach Frittata 21
Banana Carrot Muffin 22
Whole-Wheat Blueberries Muffins 22
Blueberry Cake with Lemon 22
Vanilla Pancake with Mixed Berries 22
Orange Scones with Blueberries 23
French Toast Sticks with Strawberries 23
Cinnamon Apple Turnovers 23

Chapter 4 Vegan and Vegetarian 24

Stuffed Peppers with Cheese and Basil 24
Garlic Turnip and Zucchini 24
Halloumi Zucchinis and Eggplant 24
Red Chili Okra 24
Garlic Ratatouille 25
Cauliflower with Teriyaki Sauce 25
Onion-Stuffed Mushrooms 25
Mozzarella Walnut Stuffed Mushrooms 25
Tomato-Stuffed Portobello Mushrooms 26
Breaded Zucchini Chips with Parmesan 26
Spinach-Stuffed Beefsteak Tomatoes 26
Parmesan Brussels Sprouts 26
Lemony-Honey Roasted Radishes 27
Potato Shells with Cheddar and Bacon 27
Pepper-Stuffed Portobellos 27
Garlic Bell Peppers with Marjoram 28
Potato and Asparagus Platter 28
Rice and Olives Stuffed Peppers 28
Cheesy Eggplant with Chili Smoked Almonds 29
Butternut Squash with Goat Cheese 29
Smoked Paprika Vegetable with Eggs 29
Double Cheese Roasted Asparagus 30

Chili Tomato with Herbs and Pistachios	30
Tomato and Black Olive Clafoutis	30
Moroccan Roasted Veggies with Labneh	31
Golden Potato, Carrot and Onion	31
Butternut Squash and Parsnip with Thyme	31
Ginger-Pepper Broccoli	32
Roasted Bell Peppers with Burrata and 'Nduja	32
Roasted Veggie Rice with Eggs	32
Air Fried Tofu Sticks	32
Veggie and Oat Meatballs	33
Garlic Eggplant Slices with Parsley	33
Chickpea-Stuffed Bell Peppers	33
Stuffed Bell Peppers with Cream Cheese	34
Carrot, Tofu and Cauliflower Rice	34
Cayenne Green Beans	34
Honey Baby Carrots with Dill	34
Roasted Veggies and Apple Salad	35
Zucchini Quesadilla with Gouda Cheese	35
Parmesan Fennel with Red Pepper	35
Curried Cauliflower with Cashews	36
Roasted Veggie Salad with Lemon	36
Roasted Veggies with Honey-Garlic Glaze	36
Balsamic-Glazed Beets	37
Garlic Tofu with Basil	37
Oregano Eggplants with Chili Anchovy Sauce	37
Buttery Eggplant and Tomato with Freekeh	38
Mozzarella Tomato-Stuffed Squash	38

Chapter 5 Vegetable Sides 39

Garlic Potatoes with Heavy Cream	39
Sesame Green Beans with Sriracha	39
Breaded Asparagus Fries	39
Balsamic Asparagus	39
Garlic Butternut Squash Croquettes	40
Brown Sugar Acorn Squash	40
Cheddar Broccoli Gratin	40
Garlic Zucchini Sticks	40
Roasted Potatoes with Rosemary	41
Lime Sweet Potatoes with Allspice	41
Garlic Broccoli with Parmesan	41
Parmesan Corn on the Cob	41
Garlic-Lime Shishito Peppers	42
Citrus Carrots with Balsamic Glaze	42
Greek Potatoes with Chives	42
Breaded Brussels Sprouts with Paprika	42
Garlic Zucchini Crisps	43
Maple Garlic Brussels Sprouts	43
Garlicky Cabbage with Red Pepper	43
Corn Casserole with Swiss Cheese	43

Chapter 6 Meats 44

Lamb Leg with Root Vegetable	44
Beef Rump with Red Wine Gravy	44
Sherry Lamb Leg and Autumn Vegetable	45
Garlic Pork Belly with Bay Leaves	45
Paprika Lamb Chops with Sage	45
Lamb Shoulder with Lemony Caper Relish	46
Ginger Pork Shoulder in Shaoxing Wine	46
Steak with Brandy Peppercorn Sauce	47
Juicy Bacon and Beef Cheeseburgers	47
Balsamic Italian Sausages and Red Grapes	47
Beef Meatloaf with Roasted Vegetables	48
Rump Roast with Bell Peppers	48
Pork and Pineapple Kebabs	48
Bacon-Wrapped Pork Hot Dogs	49
BBQ Kielbasa Sausage	49
Minted-Balsamic Lamb Chops	49
Dijon Pork Tenderloin	49
Hoisin Pork Butt with Veggies Salad	50
Pork Butt withCoriander-Parsley Sauce	50
Nut-Crusted Pork Rack	51
Lemon Pork Loin Chop with Marjoram	51
Pork Chops with Lime Peach Salsa	51
Lamb Leg with Herb Yogurt Sauce	52
Cider-Bourbon Glazed Pork Loin Roast	52
Mint-Roasted Boneless Lamb Leg	53
Flank Steak and Bell Pepper Fajitas	53
Brown Sugar-Mustard Glazed Ham	53
Pork Chops with Pickapeppa Sauce	53
Citrus Pork Ribs with Oregano	54
Breaded Pork Loin Chops	54
Rosemary-Balsamic Pork Loin Roast	54
Hoisin Roasted Pork Ribs	54
Bourbon Sirloin Steak	55
Colby Pork Sausage with Cauliflower	55
Pork Chop Roast with Worcestershire	55
Thyme Pork Chops with Carrots	55
Pork and Veggie Kebabs	56
Pork Chops and Apple Bake	56
Pork Chops with Sour Cream and Dill Sauce	56
Chuck and Sausage Meatballs	57
Spicy Pepper Steak	57
Beef Ravioli with Parmesan	57
Pork Cutlets with Aloha Salsa	58
Dijon-Honey Pork Tenderloin	58
Beef Meatloaves with Spinach	58
Prosciutto Tart with Asparagus	59
Teriyaki-Glazed Pork Ribs	59
Orange Beef and Broccoli with Sriracha	59
Pork Sausage Ratatouille	60
Vinegary Pork Schnitzel	60

Garlic Pork Leg Roast with Candy Onions 60
Mozzarella Sausage Calzones 61
Mexican Sirloin Steak and Pepper Fajitas 61
Pork Meatballs with Scallions 62
Pork, Squash and Pepper Kebabs 62
Breaded Calf's Liver Strips 62
Pork Tenderloin with Rice 63
Worcestershire Ribeye Steaks with Garlic 63
Pork Loin Chops with Butternut Squash 63

Chapter 7 Fish and Seafood 64

Clam Appetizers 64
Catfish Fillets with Pecan Crust 64
Broiled Lemony Salmon Steak 64
Bacon-Wrapped Herb Rainbow Trout 64
Sea Bass with Asian Chili Dressing 65
Crab Cheese Enchiladas 65
Salmon Fillet with Spinach, and Beans 65
Marinated Catfish Fillet 66
Sherry Tilapia and Mushroom Rice 66
Mackerel with Mango and Chili Salad 66
Fish Fillet with Poblano Sauce 67
Crispy Fish Fillet 67
Mediterranean Baked Fish Fillet 67
Curried Halibut Fillets with Parmesan 67
Breaded Crab Cakes 68
Flounder Fillet and Asparagus Rolls 68
Lemony Shrimp with Arugula 68
Honey Halibut Steaks with Parsley 68
Sea Bass Stuffed with Spice Paste 69
Lemon Tilapia Fillets with Garlic 69
Catfish, Toamto and Onion Kebabs 69
Stuffed Tilapia with Pepper and Cucumber 70
Fish Fillet with Sun-Dried Tomato Pesto 70
Salmon with Cucumber Sauce 70
Paprika Tilapia with Garlic Aioli 71
Shrimp Salad with Caesar Dressing 71
Orange Shrimp with Cayenne 71
Breaded Fish Sticks 72
Dijon Hake Fillets with Garlic Sauce 72
Breaded Catfish Nuggets 72
Cayenne Prawns with Cumin 72
Balsamic Shrimp with Goat Cheese 73
Jumbo Shrimp with Dijon-Mayo Sauce 73
Shrimp and Artichoke Paella 73
Shrimp and Veggie Patties 73
Old Bay Shrimp with Potatoes 74
Cajun Cod Fillets with Lemon Pepper 74
Curried Prawns with Coconut 74
Parmesan Fish Fillets with Tarragon 75
Cajun Catfish Cakes with Parmesan 75

Parsley Shrimp with Lemon 75
Crab Ratatouille with Thyme 75
Shrimp Scampi with Garlic Butter 76
Old Bay Crab Sticks with Mayo Sauce 76
Crab and Fish Cakes 76
Paprika Tiger Shrimp 77
Balsamic Ginger Scallops 77
Lemon Shrimp with Cumin 77
Coconut Curried Fish with Chilies 77
Flounder Fillets with Lemon Pepper 78
Shrimp Kebabs with Cherry Tomatoes 78
Shrimp and Veggie Spring Rolls 78
Hoisin Scallops with Sesame Seeds 79
Curried King Prawns with Cumin 79
Fried Breaded Scallops 79
Lemon Crab Cakes with Mayo 79
Fried Bacon-Wrapped Scallops 80
Garlic Calamari Rings 80
Basil Scallops with Broccoli 80
Fried Scallops with Thyme 80

Chapter 8 Poultry 81

Teriyaki Chicken Thighs 81
Chicken Breast in Mango Sauce 81
Dijon-Rosemary Chicken Breasts 81
Teriyaki Roasted Chicken with Snow Peas 82
Oregano Stuffed Chicken with Feta 82
Chicken Pot Pie 82
Barbecue Drumsticks with Vegetable 83
Simple Chicken Cordon Bleu 83
Balsamic Turkey with Carrots and Snap Peas 83
Cheesy Chicken Tenders with Veggie 84
Marinated Coconut Chicken with Pineapple 84
Chicken Thighs with Mirin 84
Chicken and Pepper Baguette with Mayo 85
Dijon Turkey Breast with Sage 85
Turkey and Mushroom Meatballs 85
Perfect Upside-Down Chicken Nachos 86
Orange-Glazed Whole Chicken 86
Satay Chicken Skewers 86
Sweet-and-Sour Chicken Breasts 87
Turkey Breast with Strawberries 87
Cheddar Turkey Burgers with Mayo 87
Paprika Hens in Wine 88
Chicken Thighs with Cabbage Slaw 88
Vinegary Chicken with Pineapple 88
Dijon Turkey with Carrots 89
Chicken and Veggies with 'Nduja 89
Duck Breast with Potato 89
Garlicky Oregano Chicken with Chipotle Allioli 90
Herb Buttery Turkey Breast 90

Chicken Thighs with Peppers 91
Sesame Balsamic Chicken Breast 91
Garlic Chicken Wings 91
Barbecue Turkey Burgers 91
Chicken, Vegetable and Rice Casserole 92
Whole Duck with Cherry Sauce 92
Chili Chicken Fries 92
Garlic Duck Leg Quarters 93
Balsamic Chicken Breast with Oregano 93
Five-Spice Turkey Thighs 93
Balsamic Duck Breasts with Orange Marmalade ... 93
Garlicky Whole Chicken Bake 94
Maple Turkey Breast with Rosemary 94
Mozzarella Chicken Breasts with Basil 94
Buttery Chicken with Corn 95
Turkey and Cauliflower Meatloaf 95
Paprika Whole Chicken Roast 95
Curried Chicken and Brussels Sprouts 96
Tasty Meat and Vegetable Loaf 96
Peach Chicken with Dark Cherry 96
Turkey Meatloaves with Onion 96
Chicken and Cheese Sandwiches 97
Game Hens with Cucumber Salad 97
Chicken Thighs with Cherry Tomatoes 98
Chicken Kebabs with Corn Salad 98
Turkey Scotch Eggs with Rosemary 99
Turkey-Stuffed Peppers with Cheddar 99
Chicken Gnocchi with Spinach 99
Paprika Hens with Creole Seasoning 100
Chicken Drumsticks with Green Beans 100
Lemon Chicken with Oregano 100

Chapter 9 Pizza 101

Simple Pizza Dough 101
Escarole and Radicchio Pizza with Walnuts 101
Chicken and Butternut Squash Pizza 101
No-Knead Pan Pizza Dough 102
Chorizo Pizza with Piquillo Peppers 102
Pro Dough 102
Garlic Tomato Pizza Sauce 103
Pepperoni Pizza with Mozzarella 103
Mozzarella Meatball Pizza 103
Ham and Pineapple Pizza 104
Zucchini and Summer Squash Pizza 104
Cheese Tomato Pizza with Basil 104
Arugula and Prosciutto Pizza 105
Prosciutto and Fig Pizza 105
Butternut Squash and Arugula Pizza 105
Ricotta Margherita with Basil 106
Double-Cheese Clam Pizza 106
Pear Pizza with Basil 106

Zucchini Pizza with Pistachios 107
Spring Pea Pizza with Ramps 107
Strawberry Pizza 107
Prosciutto and Bacon Pizza 108
Italian Sausage and Bell Pepper Pizza 108
Mushroom and Spinach Pizza 109
Mushroom and Spinach Pizza 109

Chapter 10 Casseroles, Frittatas, and Quiches 110

Cheddar Chicken Sausage Casserole 110
Spinach and Shrimp Frittata 110
Cauliflower and Okra Casserole 110
Corn Casserole with Bell Pepper 110
Asparagus Casserole with Grits 111
Parmesan Green Bean Casserole 111
Kale and Egg Frittata with Feta 111
Swiss Chicken and Ham Casserole 111
Cheddar Pastrami Casserole 112
Beef and Bean Casserole 112
Mushroom and Beef Casserole 112
Spinach and Mushroom Frittata 112
Tomato and Olive Quiche 113
Potato and Chorizo Frittata 113
Mexican Beef and Chile Casserole 113
Chickpea and Spinach Casserole 113
Turkey Casserole with Almond Mayo 114
Cauliflower Casserole with Pecan Butter 114
Chicken and Broccoli Casserole 114
Tilapia and Rockfish Casserole 115
Cheddar and Egg Frittata with Parsley 115
Zucchini and Spinach Frittata 115
Cheddar Broccoli Casserole 115
Peppery Sausage Casserole with Cheddar 116
Cheddar Chicken and Broccoli Divan 116
Cheese and Egg Quiche 116
Cheddar Broccoli and Carrot Quiche 117
Ricotta Pork Gratin with Mustard 117
Asparagus Frittata with Goat Cheese 117

Chapter 11 Wraps and Sandwiches 118

Gochujang Beef and Onion Tacos 118
Chicken and Cabbage Wraps 118
Curried Shrimp and Zucchini Potstickers 118
Cod Fish Tacos with Mango Salsa 119
Avocado and Tomato Wraps 119
Sweet Potato and Spinach Burritos 119
Carrot and Mushroom Spring Rolls 120

Chicken Wraps with Ricotta Cheese	120
Ricotta Spinach and Basil Pockets	120
Cream Cheese and Crab Wontons	121
Cabbage and Prawn Wraps	121
Parmesan Eggplant Hoagies	121
Bacon and Egg Wraps with Salsa	122
Cajun Beef and Bell Pepper Fajitas	122
Mozzarella Chicken Taquitos	122
Turkey and Pepper Hamburger	122
Lamb Hamburgers with Feta Cheese	123
Beef Steak and Bell Pepper Rolls	123
Chickpea and Mushroom Wraps	123
Potato Taquitos with Mexican Cheese	124
Curried Pork Sliders	124
Smoked Paprika Chicken Burgers	124
Pork Momos with Carrot	125
Cheddar Chicken Empanadas	125
Beef Burgers with Seeds	125
Jalapeño Turkey Sliders with Chive Mayo	126
Beef Burgers with Korean Mayo	126
Pork and Cabbage Gyoza	126
Potato Samosas with Mint Chutney	127
Crispy Cream Cheese Wontons	127

Chapter 12 Holiday Specials .. 128

Vanilla Banana Cake	128
Buttermilk Chocolate Cake	128
Mozzarella Rice Arancini	128
Chocolate-Glazed Donut Holes	129
Maple Pecan Tart	129
Pork Egg Rolls with Vinegar Dipping	130
Dill Pickles with Buttermilk Dressing	130
Chocolate Macaroons with Coconut	131
Olive and Basil Stromboli with Garlic	131
Pigs in a Blanket with Sesame Seeds	131
Risotto Croquettes with Tomato Sauce	132
Garlic Nuggets	132
Vanilla Cheese Blintzes	133
Cream-Glazed Cinnamon Rolls	133
Teriyaki-Marinated Shrimp Skewers	133
Asiago Balls	134
Cinnamon Churros	134
Balsamic Cherry Tomatoes	134
Sriracha Shrimp with Mayo	135
Vanilla Butter Cake	135

Chapter 13 Rotisserie Recipes 136

Porchetta with Lemony Sage Rub	136
Dried Fruit Stuffed Pork Loin	136
Spareribs with Paprika Rub	137
Paprika Pulled Pork Butt	137
Chicken Roast with Mustard Paste	138
Mustard Lamb Shoulder	138
Pork Loin Roast with Brown Sugar Brine	138
Sirloin Roast with Porcini-Wine Baste	139
Smoked Paprika Lamb Leg	139
Whiskey-Basted Prime Rib Roast	140
BBQ Chicken with Mustard Rub	140
Orange Honey Glazed Ham	141
Bacon-Wrapped Sirloin Roast	141
Balsamic Chuck Roast	142
Ham with Dijon Bourbon Baste	142
Baby Back Ribs with Paprika Rub	143
Teriyaki Chicken	143
Chicken with Brown Sugar Brine	144
Turkey with Thyme-Sage Brine	144

Chapter 14 Appetizers and Snacks 145

Sausage and Onion Rolls with Mustard	145
Parmesan Cauliflower with Turmeric	145
Pepperoni Pizza Bites with Marinara	145
Cheddar Mushrooms with Pimientos	146
Roasted Mushrooms with Garlic	146
Cheddar Baked Potatoes with Chives	146
Jalapeño Poppers with Cheddar	147
Green Chiles and Cheese Nachos	147
Honey Roasted Grapes with Basil	147
Lemon-Pepper Chicken Wings	147
Cheddar Sausage Balls	148
Sugar Roasted Walnuts	148
Balsamic Prosciutto-Wrapped Pears	148
Breaded Zucchini Tots	148
Ginger Shrimp with Sesame Seeds	149
Tuna Melts with Mayo	149
Paprika Polenta Fries with Chili-Lime Mayo	149
Lemon Ricotta with Capers	150
Fried Pickle Spears with Chili	150
Honey Snack Mix	150
Cumin Tortilla Chips	150
Parmesan Snack Mix	151
Paprika Potato Chips	151
Cinnamon Apple Chips	151
Parmesan Crab Toasts	151
Hush Puppies with Jalapeño	152
Turkey-Wrapped Dates and Almonds	152
Ginger Apple Wedges	152
Avocado Chips with Lime	152
Carrot Chips	153

Mushroom and Sausage Empanadas 153
Old Bay Fried Chicken Wings............................... 153
Deviled Eggs with Mayo 153
Cumin Fried Chickpeas 154
Paprika Nut Mix 154
Garlic Fried Edamame... 154
Nutmeg Apple Chips.. 154
Brie Pear Sandwiches 155
Parmesan Bruschetta with Tomato 155
Sesame Kale Chips 155
Pork and Turkey Sandwiches 155
Italian Rice Balls with Olives................................ 156
Buttermilk-Marinated Chicken Wings 156
Breaded Artichoke Bites 156
Cinnamon Peach Wedges 157
Horseradish Green Tomatoes.............................. 157
BBQ Cheese Chicken Pizza 157
Cheddar Black Bean and Corn Salsa.................. 157
Spinach Calzones with Mushrooms 158
Muffuletta Sliders with Olive Mix.......................... 158

Chapter 15 Desserts 159

Rhubarb with Sloe Gin and Rosemary 159
Apricot Brioche with Croûtes Fraîche.................. 159
Easy Nutmeg Butter Cookies 159
Rice Pudding with Quince Jelly and Blackberry 160
Rum-Plums with Brown Sugar Cream 160
Pumpkin Pudding with Vanilla Wafers 160
Glazed Sweet Bundt Cake 161
Mexican Brownie Squares................................... 161
Honey-Glazed Peach and Plum Kebabs............. 161
Blueberry and Peach Crisp.................................. 162
Vanilla Coconut Cookies with Pecans 162
Chocolate Blueberry Cupcakes 162
Mixed Berry Bake with Almond Topping 163
Peach and Blueberry Galette 163
Cinnamon Apple Fritters 163
Glazed Chocolate Cake....................................... 164
Peach and Apple Crisp with Oatmeal.................. 164
Vanilla Walnuts Tart with Cloves 164
Vanilla Chocolate Chip Cookies 165
Pineapple Sticks with Coconut 165
Vanilla Pound Cake 165
Honey Apple-Peach Crumble 165
Peanut Butter Bread Pudding.............................. 166
Chocolate Cake with Blackberries....................... 166
Sour Cherry Brioche Pudding.............................. 166
Vanilla Ricotta Cake with Lemon 167
Cinnamon Pineapple Rings................................. 167

Vanilla Fudge Pie... 167
Blackberry Cobbler 167
Vanilla Baked Peaches and Blueberries.............. 168
Chocolate Chip Brownies 168
White Chocolate Cookies with Nutmeg 168
Mixed Berry Crisp with Cloves............................. 168
Chocolate S'mores 169
Pecan Pie with Chocolate Chips 169
Apple Bake with Cinnamon 169
Spice Cake with Creamy Frosting 169
Vanilla Chocolate Cake 170
Cinnamon Apple with Apricots 170
Coconut Orange Cake... 170

Chapter 16 Staples 171

Lemon Anchocy Dressing.................................... 171
Teriyaki Sauce 171
Baked White Rice 171
Paprika-Oregano Seasoning 171
Poblano Garlic Sauce.. 171
Shawarma Seasoning 171
Garlic Tomato Sauce 172
Buttery Mushrooms 172
Ginger-Garlic Dipping Sauce 172
Creamy Grits 172

Chapter 17 Dehydrate 173

Dehydrated Pineapple Slices 173
Cinnamon Orange Slices..................................... 173
Peach Fruit Leather 173
Cinnamon Pear Chips 173
Dehydrated Zucchini Chips 173
Candied Bacon.. 173
Dehydrated Onions.. 174
Pork Jerky.. 174
Strawberry Roll Ups... 174
Dried Hot Peppers 174
Beef Jerky.. 174
Dried Mushrooms 175
Kiwi Chips.. 175
Dehydrated Strawberries..................................... 175
Lemon-Pepper Salmon Jerky 175
Smoky Venison Jerky 175

Appendix 1 Measurement Conversion Chart 176
Appendix 2 Air Fryer Cooking Chart.................... 177
Appendix 3 Index 179

Introduction

How I Met My Vortex

The thought of a homemade meal cooked from scratch sounds lovely if only I had time! Who knew that it was possible to become so busy that one would forget to cook or simply be too exhausted to hover over pots that never seem to empty? The traditional lifestyle of cooking fresh foods—straight from the garden to the kitchen—seems like a fantasy in my fast-paced urban lifestyle; I know I am not the only one who feels this way. As many mothers enter the corporate environment and fill up 9-to-5 jobs, no one is left at home to prepare home-cooked meals that simmer for hours in a pot. Even for a foodie like myself, I find it nearly impossible to whip up delicious meals made from scratch while tending to my four children and answering a day's worth of emails in the evenings. For many years, I settled for unhealthy takeout meals that would appease the children and afford me the much needed time to work on other essential tasks. However, these quick and greasy takeout dinners were simply not sustainable in the long run for the health and well-being of my family. I knew that I had to find another convenient alternative that would meet all of my culinary and lifestyle needs.

Christmas came around, and guess what I received from my dear husband? An Instant Vortex Air Fryer oven with a note, "This might be what you were looking for." I did not know what to expect as I unwrapped this elegant and professional kitchen gadget. I realized that it was a modern rendition of an air fryer produced by one of my favorite brands, the Instant Pot. I should have known that any kitchen tool manufactured by Instant Pot would be phenomenal; however, I wanted to find out for myself. The first time I used my Instant Vortex Air Fryer was for a Sunday roast dinner. The Air Fryer assumed the role of kitchen chef, and this allowed me to take time out to read a book while the machine did all the work. This multifunctional appliance gave me the option of air frying, baking, roasting, broiling, reheating, dehydrating, and rotisserie cooking my food to make a fantastic dinner.

Trying it Out

If you are going to make the A-Team, you have to ace the try-outs. I thought about experimenting on something that I cook lot, and that I have perfected cooking conventionally; something that I could run a direct comparison with. I thought about bacon – I confess that I think about bacon a lot!

Normally, I only to cook bacon on the weekend, when I do a big brunch for the fam. We all like our bacon crispy, and not greasy, so I cook it in the oven. Prep. time is around twenty to twenty-five minutes: first, I pre-heat the oven, and then I prepare a try with foil and a rack. For good results, it's a good twenty minutes cooking time. This is OK if I am doing a huge batch, for supper time BLTs, or to crumble on a salad later. But if it's just the four of us for breakfast or brunch, that process is just way too much effort, specially on a Sunday morning!

So, I tried out the Vortex Plus on bacon. The preheating feature is built in. Too easy! I pressed "Airfry" and set the simple timer dial for five minutes. Once pre-heated, the Vortex tells you to "ADD FOOD." That is when you insert the light-weight non-stick, easy-clean tray/s with your bacon on it. It took just two minutes to preheat. Once cooking is finished, the Vortex beeps, and displays "COOL DOWN" for a few seconds. Then it turns itself off, and you can take out the food. Seven minutes: easy start to perfect finish. I have to say, I was impressed. I am not readily impressed. The bacon was perfect. Did anyone in the fam. detect any difference in the flavour? Only to note: "This bacon's really crispy!" There was absolutely no greasiness to the meat either. All the grease dripped down below and collected in the drip tray. Top-notch results. Happy fam. Happy me.

Once the Vortex cooled down, I was able to clean it in my sink, with just a sponge and dish detergent. No fuss. Alternatively, it could have gone straight into the dishwasher. This was such a successful (and tasty!) try-out, that I made 2 trays of bacon, next day, for some quick tasty sandwiches: one tray on the top, and the other tray in the middle. The only difference: I set the timer to ten minutes, and half way through, the Vortex instructed me to turn the food, so I switched the position of the trays. The heating element and fan is at the top, so, naturally, it cooks the top tray quicker than the bottom tray. Both trays of bacon came out perfect and crispy.

Chapter 1 Beginners Guide to The Vortex

Step by Step Guide to the Usage of The Vortex

When you first get your Instant Vortex Air Fryer, it is essential that you do a test run to make sure everything is in working order. It won't take much of your time—approximately 25 minutes—and then you'll know if you're good to go!

Here are the steps to follow the test run and for general cooking:

1. Plug into a 120V power source. The air fryer should not be in Standby mode, and "OFF" should appear on the display. Press the dial button to wake the air fryer.

2. Remove the air fryer basket and place the cooking tray at the bottom of the basket. Look for the indicator arrows on the cooking tray and make sure these arrows point to the back or the front of the air fryer.

3. You can now put the air fryer basket back into the cooking chamber.

4. Press the Air Fry button, followed by Temp—use the dial to set the temperature to 400 degrees Fahrenheit. Press Time and adjust to 20 minutes using the dial.

5. Press start and cooking will begin. "On" will show on the display while the air fryer preheats. You can touch Time or Temp at any time during the cooking process to adjust the time and temperature using the dial.

6. As soon as the air fryer reaches the set temperature, "Add Food" will appear on the display. Since this is a test run, do not add any food.

7. After removing and reinserting the air fryer basket, the display will indicate the cooking time and temperature. It will also read "Cook."

8. Half-way through the selected Smart Program, the air fryer will beep to let you know that it is time to turn the food. You'll see "turn Food" on the display and can proceed to flip or shake the food items in the basket. When you remove the air fryer basket, the Smart Program will pause until 10 seconds after you put the basket back into the cooking chamber. It is only the Air Fry and Roast Smart Programs which will require this step—not all food will need to be turned.

9. Once the time has run out and your food is cooked, the display will indicate 'End' on the display. The fan will continue to blow in order to cool down the air fryer. If you don't remove the tray from the fryer immediately, you'll get a reminder at five, 30, and 60 minutes that the food is ready.

When you're done with this process, and everything runs accordingly to plan, then your Instant Vortex Air Fryer is in working order, and you're ready to use it for whatever culinary delights you can dream up!

Top 6 Instant Vortex Air Fryer Accessories

There are some tools I suggest you add to your kitchen arsenal so that you'll be able to cook anything your heart desires in your Vortex air fryer.

But before you go out looking for accessories, there are a few things you have to keep in mind.

1. Keep the size of the air fryer in mind. For the 4-1 Instant Vortex Air Fryer, I recommend not purchasing any pans or items larger than 8 ½ inches deep by 9 ½ inches wide. A square 8x8 pan will fit perfectly! If you own an Instant Pot, most of the items that are suitable for that appliance will work in the Vortex air fryer—my round springform cake pan meant for my Instant Pot fits absolutely fine in the air fryer.

2. Don't forget the air space. Before buying deep items, keep in mind that there should be space at the top and bottom of the item for air to circulate.

3. Pay attention to the materials. A lot of items claim to be oven-safe, but that is not always the case. The quick heating of the air and the speedy circulation may cause glass dishes to crack or break. Where possible, don't use glass as all but choose stainless steel, aluminum, or ceramic items. If you have to use glass, make sure it's from a reputable brand known for its oven safety.

Okay, let's look at the top six air fryer accessories I recommend.

1. Parchment Liners

Who has time to clean food stuck to the fry basket? Air fryer liners will cut your clean-up process in half. Don't use just any liners. Look for ones with holes in to help air circulate, and even then, you have to make sure the parchment paper is weighed down with something heavy, or the air will pick it up and whirl it around.

2. Baking Pan

You can bake sweet and savory dishes in a baking pan; cake, monkey bread, macaroni, and cheese, etc. The fact that you can cook so many dishes in a baking pan makes it one of those must-have accessories.

3. Grill Pan

Why not push your Instant Vortex Air Fryer's versatility up a notch further by turning it into a grill? With this basic item, you'll be able to make burgers, grill steak, chicken, seafood, and anything else you can toss onto a grill.

4. Cooking Rack With Skewers

A raised cooking rack is essential if you plan on using your air fryer for cooking larger foods. Air fryers work by circulating heat around the food—if you place something down on the surface, the air won't be able to move around it, leaving you with uneven crispness. By using a cooking rack, the food is elevated, and air can circulate freely; the result is an even, crips coating.

5. Silicone Oven Mitts

I suppose you can use traditional oven mitts, but I'd highly recommend getting the silicone kind. They're not bulky, do a better job of protecting you from heat, but most importantly, they have a better grip than fabric mitts. You don't want a basket with hot food slipping and falling on you, your child, or pet. Personally, I see these as essential.

6. Waffle Molds

Do your kids love waffles for breakfast each Saturday morning? The good news is, you can make them some in the air fryer in a fraction of the time it would take you, making it the traditional way. All you need are some air fryer waffle molds, and you're well on your way to winning the parent of the year award.

For those of you who use your air fryer the most out of all your other appliances, you may consider buying a full air fryer accessories pack. They include almost everything you need to ensure your air fryer success. You can also compare different versions to make sure you get one that contains items you think you'll use the most. With your kitchen all kitted out, there will be nothing you can't give a crispy coating.

Chapter 2 Cooking with The Instant Vortex Air Fryer

The air fryer is not a complicated appliance, but there are some tips I picked up that I want to share with you. But, before I do, let's look at things to keep in mind to ensure your safety.

Dos and Don'ts

Although your Instant Vortex Air Fryer comes with built-in safety features, here are some extra steps you can follow to ensure safe use.

1. The air fryer gets really hot while working its air frying magic, so don't touch it. Use oven mitts when you slide out the air fry basket or, better yet, wait for the appliance to cool down completely. Also, keep an eye out for steam escaping from the vents; you don't want to burn your hands or face.

2. You shouldn't let anyone with physical or mental disabilities use the air fryer without constant supervision. The same goes if a person has no idea to use an Instant Vortex Air Fryer; make sure you're there that they're not doing something wrong or dangerous.

3. Always place your air fryer out of reach of children. Make sure not to let the cord dangle from the countertop where a toddler can grab it and pull the warm appliance on to themselves.

4. Do not use your air fryer if you notice that its power cord is damaged.

5. Air Fryers are indoor appliances, so don't use it outside.

6. Never place your air fryer near a hot gas or an electric burner. It should be stable and secure on a dry, flat surface.

7. Make sure the air fry basket is locked in place before you use your fryer.

8. Don't tip the air fry basket to remove the food. The liquid inside may splash on you and cause burns.

Choosing the Right Cooking Mode

All cooking programs are essentially the same. The only difference is the temperature the mode heats to, as well as the cooking time. In the beginning, I didn't know this, and, unfortunately, the manual doesn't tell you. The different programs are only there for your convenience—you don't have to set the time and temperature manually; you just press one button.

Smart Programs

Here are some pre-sets to choose from to make your cooking as easy as possible.

Smart Program	Time Range	Temperature Range
Air Fry	1-60 minutes	180-400 °F
Roast	1-60 minutes	180-400 °F
Bake	1-60 minutes	180-400 °F
Reheat	1-60 minutes	120-360 °F
Broil*	1-40 minutes	400 °F
Dehydrate*	1-72 hours	96-175 °F

* You will only find the Broil and Dehydrate functions on the Vortex Plus 6 models, but I add them here to give you a better idea of the difference between the models.

Tips and Tricks for Air Frying Success

If you want your food to be extra crispy or you just want to ensure that none of your recipes flop, here are nine of my tips and tricks to help you succeed.

1. Use a kitchen spray bottle filled with oil to coat food. You'll end up using less than a teaspoon of oil, which makes it even healthier. It's also easier to cover more delicate foods this way. Extra-light olive oil should be your first choice since it has a higher smoking point and a milder taste than extra-virgin olive oil.

2. When cooking high-fat foods, empty some of the oil part way through cooking to avoid any smoking caused by excess fat.

3. Switch your Instant Vortex Air Fryer on four to five minutes before use.

4. Don't overfill the air fry basket. You should leave space for air to flow between the food. This will ensure everything is cooked evenly. I usually cook in batches when I have to make food for a lot of people, and I always stick to filling the basket only 2/3.

5. For food you want to crumb, always use the right order of breading. You'll first coat the food in flour, then dunk in egg, and lastly, roll in the bread crumbs. If you set up a dredging station beforehand—that means setting up the bowls in the correct order—it will take you less time to crumb your food. Another hint I can give you is to spray oil on food with crumbs gently. You don't want the breading to be too wet and fall off. Furthermore, the fan in the air fryer is mighty and if you don't press the crumbs onto the food firmly, it will get blown off.

6. When you cook food from frozen, you will need to adjust the cooking time. Check for doneness before removing from the air fryer.

7. As mentioned earlier, some food will need to be turned halfway through the cooking process. If you don't, then your food will not be crispy all around or cooked evenly.

8. Forget about your microwave and use your air fryer instead. A lot of the time, a microwave will leave your food soggy, but the air fryer will restore it to its former crunchy glory.

9. For extra crunch, spray your food with a second layer of oil.

Best and Worst Ingredients

I know it's obvious that you can air fry the foods that you always enjoyed deep-fried. It may even end up tasting better! But since the Instant Vortex Air Fryer is more than just a simple air fryer, you should experiment not only with the ingredients you air fry but also with the various mods.

Here are some things you need to keep in mind when it comes to ingredients.

The Best

- You can cook all vegetables in your air fryer. Cover it generously in batter and pop it in the air fryer. Crumbed beans with a tomato salsa is one of my favorite appetizers to serve to guests.

- You can cook meat, fish, and poultry in your air fryer any way you like—grill, roast, or fry; what are you in the mood for?

- Baking frozen foods in your air fryer will give it extra crunch than a standard convection oven would.

- If you fancy yourself a baker, you'd be happy to know that there won't be any temperature fluctuations in the air fryer. So, no more flopped souffle, cakes, or muffins.

The Worst

The Instant Vortex Air Fryer is not meant for wet ingredients. The fan is mighty, and soups and sauces will just end up splattered all over. The same goes for food covered in wet batter. You'll end up with a ruined recipe and a big mess to clean.

Also, consider if the food you plan on making requires a lot of stirring. Pasta, for instance, will not cook well in an air fryer since it requires not only a lot of liquid to cook but also regular stirring.

How to Save Time Cooking

The Instant Vortex Air Fryer will already cut your cooking time in half, but there are ways that you can get out of the kitchen even quicker. I enjoy cooking mouth-watering meals, but some days I want to get in and out as quickly as possible to spend time with my friends and family.

Here are some things I do to save time in the kitchen.

- Prepare ingredients. This is also known as mise en place. It is where you dice, cut, marinate, and prep all your ingredients before you start cooking.

- Don't deviate from the recipe. I know there are times when you feel you know what to do next and forget to check the recipe. If you're new to the kitchen, there is a big chance that you'll end up using too much or little of something, and you'll end up doing something wrong. It will take extra time to fix your mistake or, worst-case scenario, start from scratch.

- Take your meat out of the fridge a few minutes before cooking. Room temperature meat will cook more evenly, and it may shorten the cooking time with a few minutes.

Chapter 3 Breakfasts

Sweet Banana Bread

Prep time: 10 minutes | Cook time: 40 minutes | Serves 6

2 ripe bananas
1 egg
½ cup skim milk
2 tablespoons honey
1 tablespoon vegetable oil
1 cup unbleached flour
¾ cup chopped trail mix
1 teaspoon baking powder
Salt, to taste

1. Process the bananas, egg, milk, honey, and oil in a blender or food processor until smooth and transfer to a mixing bowl.
2. Add the flour and trail mix, stirring to mix well. Add the baking powder and stir just enough to blend it into the batter. Add salt, to taste. Pour the mixture into an oiled or nonstick loaf pan.
3. Select Bake. Set temperature to 400ºF (205ºC) and set time to 40 minutes. Select Start to begin preheating.
4. Once preheated, slide the pan into the oven.
5. When done, a toothpick inserted in the center will come out clean.
6. Serve.

Low-Fat Buttermilk Biscuits

Prep time: 10 minutes | Cook time: 15 minutes | Makes 12 biscuits

2 cups unbleached flour
1 tablespoon baking powder
½ teaspoon baking soda
Salt, to taste
3 tablespoons margarine, at room temperature
1 cup low-fat buttermilk
Vegetable oil

Combine the flour, baking powder, baking soda, and salt in a medium bowl.
Cut in the margarine with 2 knives or a pastry blender until the mixture is crumbly.
Stir in the buttermilk, adding just enough so the dough will stay together when pinched.
Knead the dough on a floured surface for one minute, then pat or roll out the dough to ¾ inch thick. Cut out biscuit rounds with a 2½-inch biscuit cutter. Place the rounds on an oiled or nonstick baking sheet.
Select Bake. Set temperature to 400ºF (205ºC) and set time to 15 minutes. Select Start to begin preheating.
Once preheated, slide the baking sheet into the oven.
When done, the biscuits will be golden brown.
Serve.

Coffee Cake with Pecan

Prep time: 10 minutes | Cook time: 40 minutes | Serves 6

For the Cake:
2 cups unbleached flour
2 teaspoons baking powder
2 tablespoons vegetable oil
1 egg
1¼ cups skim milk

For the Topping:
½ cup brown sugar
1 tablespoon margarine, at room temperature
1 teaspoon ground cinnamon
¼ teaspoon grated nutmeg
¼ cup chopped pecans
Salt, to taste

1. Combine the ingredients for the cake in a medium bowl and mix thoroughly. Pour the batter into an oiled square baking (cake) pan and set aside.
2. Combine the topping ingredients in a small bowl, mashing the margarine into the dry ingredients with a fork until the mixture is crumbly. Sprinkle evenly on top of the batter.
3. Select Bake. Set temperature to 375ºF (190ºC) and set time to 40 minutes. Select Start to begin preheating.
4. Once preheated, slide the pan into the oven.
5. When done, a toothpick inserted in the center will come out clean. Cool and cut into squares.

Cheese and Bacon Muffin Sandwiches

Prep time: 5 minutes | Cook time: 8 minutes | Serves 4

4 English muffins, split
8 slices Canadian bacon
4 slices cheese
Cooking spray

1. Make the sandwiches: Top each of 4 muffin halves with 2 slices of Canadian bacon, 1 slice of cheese, and finish with the remaining muffin half.
2. Put the sandwiches in the perforated pan and spritz the tops with cooking spray.
3. Select Bake. Set temperature to 370ºF (188ºC) and set time to 8 minutes. Press Start to begin preheating.
4. Once preheated, place the pan into the oven. Flip the sandwiches halfway through the cooking time.
5. When cooking is complete, remove the pan from the oven. Divide the sandwiches among four plates and serve warm.

Baked Fries with Bacon and Eggs
Prep time: 10 minutes | Cook time: 23 minutes | Serves 4

2 medium Yukon gold potatoes, peeled and cut into ¼-inch cubes (about 3 cups)
1 medium onion, chopped
⅓ cup diced red or green bell pepper
1 tablespoon vegetable oil
½ teaspoon kosher salt, divided
¼ teaspoon freshly ground black pepper, divided
12 ounces (340 g) thick-sliced bacon, cut into ¼-inch pieces
4 large eggs

1. Put the potatoes, onion, and bell pepper on a sheet pan. Drizzle with the oil, ¼ teaspoon of salt, and ⅛ teaspoon of pepper and toss to coat. Spread the vegetables out in a single layer as much as possible. Scatter the bacon pieces evenly over the top.
2. Select Bake. Set temperature to 375ºF (190ºC) and set time to 20 minutes. Select Start to begin preheating.
3. Once preheated, slide the pan into the oven.
4. After 10 minutes, remove the pan from the oven and stir the potato mixture. Return to the oven and bake for another 10 minutes, or until the potatoes are tender inside and beginning to crisp on the outside, and the bacon is becoming crisp.
5. Remove the pan from the oven. Using a large spoon, create four circular openings in the potato mixture. Gently crack an egg into each opening; season the eggs with the remaining ¼ teaspoon of salt and ⅛ teaspoon of pepper. Return the pan to the oven and bake for 3 minutes for very runny yolks or up to 8 minutes for firm yolks.
6. Use a spatula to transfer the eggs from the pan to four separate plates, then scoop out the home fries to serve on the side.

Maple Oats and Nuts
Prep time: 15 minutes | Cook time: 35 minutes | Makes 7 to 8 cups

3 cups old-fashioned rolled oats (use gluten-free if necessary)
¾ cup shredded sweetened coconut
¾ cup raw cashews
¾ cup chopped raw walnuts
½ cup pumpkin seeds
¼ cup sesame seeds (optional)
¼ cup dark brown sugar
½ cup maple syrup
¼ cup oil (coconut, grapeseed, safflower, or other neutral-flavored oil with a high smoke point)
1 teaspoon ground cinnamon
1 teaspoon vanilla extract
¾ teaspoon kosher salt
1 cup raisins

1. In a large bowl, stir together the oats, coconut, cashews, walnuts, pumpkin seeds, sesame seeds (if using), and brown sugar.
2. In a small bowl, stir together the maple syrup, oil, cinnamon, vanilla, and salt. Add the wet maple syrup mixture to the oat-nut mixture and stir to mix well. Divide the nut mixture between two rimmed baking sheets and spread it in an even layer.
3. Select Bake. Set temperature to 275ºF (135ºC) and set time to 35 minutes. Select Start to begin preheating.
4. Once preheated, slide the baking sheets into the oven. Stir the nut mixture once or twice during the cooking time.
5. When done, the oats and nuts will be golden brown.
6. Transfer the hot mixture to a large bowl and immediately stir in the raisins. Cool to room temperature before serving or storing.

Parmesan Ham and Egg Cups
Prep time: 5 minutes | Cook time: 12 minutes | Serves 6

Nonstick cooking spray
6 thin slices ham
6 large eggs
Kosher salt, to taste
Freshly ground black pepper, to taste
2 tablespoons finely grated Parmesan cheese

1. Spray the cups of a 6-cup muffin tin with cooking spray. Press a slice of ham into each cup, smoothing out the sides as much as possible. The ham should extend over the top of the cup by ¼ to ½ inch. Crack an egg into each cup and season with salt and pepper. Top each yolk with 1 teaspoon of the cheese.
2. Select Bake. Set temperature to 375ºF (190ºC) and set time to 10 minutes. Select Start to begin preheating.
3. Once preheated, slide the muffin tin into the oven.
4. After 5 minutes, slide out the muffin tin and check the eggs. They should just be starting to firm up and turn opaque. Rotate the muffin tin if the eggs are cooking unevenly.
5. Cook for another 5 minutes and check again; if the egg whites are cooked through, remove the tin from the oven. The total cook time is about 12 minutes for fully cooked whites and runny yolks; if you prefer the yolks more done, cook for an additional minute or two.
6. When the eggs are cooked as desired, remove the muffin tin and let cool for a couple of minutes. Run a thin knife around the ham and use a spoon to remove the cups.

When you eat crap, you feel crap. -Chapter 3 Breakfasts |11

Cheddar Breakfast Sausage Scones
Prep time: 10 minutes | Cook time: 20 minutes | Serves 6

1½ cups all-purpose flour
2 teaspoons baking powder
½ teaspoon kosher salt
3 tablespoons unsalted butter, very cold
1 cup coarsely grated sharp Cheddar cheese
2 or 3 scallions, finely chopped
8 ounces (227 g) breakfast sausage, cooked and coarsely chopped
1 large egg, beaten, divided
½ cup heavy (whipping) cream

1. Line a sheet pan with a silicone baking mat.
2. In a large bowl, whisk together the flour, baking powder, and salt. Using the large holes of a cheese grater, grate the butter into the flour mixture and stir to combine. Mix in the cheese, scallions, and sausage.
3. Pour 1 tablespoon of the beaten egg into a small bowl and set aside. Whisk the cream into the remaining egg. Add the egg mixture to the flour and butter mixture. The dough should hold together but be shaggy rather than moist.
4. Transfer the dough to a lightly floured work surface. Gather it together into a rectangle. Fold the dough into thirds and press together. Repeat.
5. Form the dough into a smooth 6-inch disk. Cut the disk into 6 wedges, and carefully transfer them to the prepared pan.
6. Brush the scones with the reserved egg.
7. Select Bake. Set temperature to 400ºF (205ºC) and set time to 20 minutes. Select Start to begin preheating.
8. Once preheated, slide the pan into the oven.
9. When done, the scones will be golden brown.
10. Cool on the pan for about 10 minutes. Serve warm or at room temperature.

Bell Pepper and Ham Omelet
Prep time: 5 minutes | Cook time: 20 minutes | Serves 2

¼ cup chopped bell pepper, green or red
¼ cup chopped onion
¼ cup diced ham
1 teaspoon butter
4 large eggs
2 tablespoons milk
⅛ teaspoon salt
¾ cup shredded sharp Cheddar cheese

1. Put the bell pepper, onion, ham, and butter in a baking pan and mix well.
2. Select Air Fry. Set temperature to 390ºF (199ºC) and set time to 5 minutes. Press Start to begin preheating.
3. Once the oven has preheated, place the pan into the oven.
4. After 1 minute, remove the pan from the oven. Stir the mixture. Return the pan to the oven and continue to cook for another 4 minutes.
5. When done, the veggies should be softened.
6. Whisk together the eggs, milk, and salt in a bowl. Pour the egg mixture over the veggie mixture.
7. Select Bake. Set temperature to 360ºF (182ºC) and set time to 15 minutes. place the pan into the oven.
8. After 14 minutes, remove the pan from the oven. Scatter the omelet with the shredded cheese. Return the pan to the oven and continue to cook for another 1 minute.
9. When cooking is complete, the top will be lightly golden browned, the eggs will be set and the cheese will be melted.
10. Let the omelet cool for 5 minutes before serving.

Avocado and Egg Burrito
Prep time: 10 minutes | Cook time: 4 minutes | Serves 4

4 low-sodium whole-wheat flour tortillas
Filling:
1 hard-boiled egg, chopped
2 hard-boiled egg whites, chopped
1 ripe avocado, peeled, pitted, and chopped
1 red bell pepper, chopped
1 (1.2-ounce / 34-g) slice low-sodium, low-fat American cheese, torn into pieces
3 tablespoons low-sodium salsa, plus additional for serving (optional)

Special Equipment:
4 toothpicks (optional) soaked in water for at least 30 minutes

1. Make the filling: Combine the egg, egg whites, avocado, red bell pepper, cheese, and salsa in a medium bowl and stir until blended.
2. Assemble the burritos: Arrange the tortillas on a clean work surface and place ¼ of the prepared filling in the middle of each tortilla, leaving about 1½-inch on each end unfilled. Fold in the opposite sides of each tortilla and roll up. Secure with toothpicks through the center, if needed.
3. Transfer the burritos to the perforated pan.
4. Select Air Fry. Set temperature to 390ºF (199ºC) and set time to 4 minutes. Press Start to begin preheating.
5. Once the oven has preheated, place the pan into the oven.
6. When cooking is complete, the burritos should be crisp and golden brown.
7. Allow to cool for 5 minutes and serve with salsa, if desired.

Sausage French Toast Casserole with Maple

Prep time: 5 minutes | Cook time: 45 minutes | Serves 4

6 fresh breakfast sausage links
4 large eggs
1½ cups whole milk
½ teaspoon kosher salt
5 tablespoons pure maple syrup, divided
5 or 6 thick slices of stale bread, cut into 1-inch cubes

1. Put the sausage links in a baking pan.
2. Select Bake. Set temperature to 375ºF (190ºC) and set time to 15 minutes. Select Start to begin preheating.
3. Once preheated, slide the pan into the oven.
4. When done, the sausage links will be lightly browned. They may not be cooked all the way through, but they will cook again. You just want to render some of their fat.
5. Meanwhile, in a medium bowl, whisk the eggs until completely mixed. Add the milk, salt, and 1 tablespoon of maple syrup and whisk to combine. Add the bread cubes and gently stir to coat with the egg mixture. Let sit for 2 to 3 minutes to let the bread absorb some of the custard, then gently stir again.
6. After the sausages have browned, remove from the oven. Transfer the sausages to a plate. If there is more than a thin coat of fat on the bottom of the pan, pour out the excess.
7. Pour the bread mixture into the pan, then top with the sausage links.
8. Select Bake. Set temperature to 350ºF (180ºC) and set time to 30 minutes. Slide the pan into the oven. When done, the sausages will be browned and a knife inserted into the center of the casserole will come out clean.
9. Serve with the remaining 4 tablespoons of maple syrup.

Corn Frittata with Avocado Dressing

Prep time: 10 minutes | Cook time: 20 minutes | Serves 2 or 3

½ cup cherry tomatoes, halved
Kosher salt and freshly ground black pepper, to taste
6 large eggs, lightly beaten
½ cup fresh corn kernels
¼ cup milk
1 tablespoon finely chopped fresh dill
½ cup shredded Monterey Jack cheese
Avocado Dressing:
1 ripe avocado, pitted and peeled
2 tablespoons fresh lime juice
¼ cup olive oil
1 scallion, finely chopped
8 fresh basil leaves, finely chopped

1. Put the tomato halves in a colander and lightly season with salt. Set aside for 10 minutes to drain well. Pour the tomatoes into a large bowl and fold in the eggs, corn, milk, and dill. Sprinkle with salt and pepper and stir until mixed.
2. Pour the egg mixture into a baking pan.
3. Select Bake. Set temperature to 300ºF (150ºC) and set time to 15 minutes. Press Start to begin preheating.
4. Once the oven has preheated, place the pan into the oven.
5. When done, remove the pan from the oven. Scatter the cheese on top.
6. Select Bake. Set temperature to 315ºF (157ºC) and set time to 5 minutes. Return the pan to the oven.
7. Meanwhile, make the avocado dressing: Mash the avocado with the lime juice in a medium bowl until smooth. Mix in the olive oil, scallion, and basil and stir until well incorporated.
8. When cooking is complete, the frittata will be puffy and set. Let the frittata cool for 5 minutes and serve alongside the avocado dressing.

Vanilla Banana Bread Pudding

Prep time: 10 minutes | Cook time: 16 minutes | Serves 4

2 medium ripe bananas, mashed
½ cup low-fat milk
2 tablespoons maple syrup
2 tablespoons peanut butter
1 teaspoon vanilla extract
1 teaspoon ground cinnamon
2 slices whole-grain bread, cut into bite-sized cubes
¼ cup quick oats
Cooking spray

1. Spritz a baking dish lightly with cooking spray.
2. Mix the bananas, milk, maple syrup, peanut butter, vanilla, and cinnamon in a large mixing bowl and stir until well incorporated.
3. Add the bread cubes to the banana mixture and stir until thoroughly coated. Fold in the oats and stir to combine.
4. Transfer the mixture to the baking dish. Wrap the baking dish in aluminum foil.
5. Select Air Fry. Set temperature to 350ºF (180ºC) and set time to 16 minutes. Press Start to begin preheating.
6. Once the oven has preheated, place the pan into the oven.
7. After 10 minutes, remove the baking dish from the oven. Remove the foil. Return the baking dish to the oven and continue to cook another 6 minutes.
8. When done, the pudding should be set.
9. Let the pudding cool for 5 minutes before serving.

Mozzarella Tomato Salsa Rounds

Prep time: 5 minutes | Cook time: 6 minutes | Makes 12 slices

1 French baguette, cut to make 12 1-inch slices (rounds)
¼ cup olive oil
1 cup tomato salsa
½ cup shredded low-fat Mozzarella
2 tablespoons finely chopped fresh cilantro

1. Brush both sides of each round with olive oil.
2. Spread one side of each slice with salsa and sprinkle each with Mozzarella. Place the rounds in an oiled or nonstick square baking (cake) pan.
3. Select Broil. Set temperature to 400ºF (205ºC) and set time to 6 minutes. Select Start to begin preheating.
4. Once preheated, slide the pan into the oven.
5. When done, the cheese will be melted and the rounds will be lightly browned. Garnish with the chopped cilantro and serve.

Broccoli and Red Pepper Quiche

Prep time: 5 minutes | Cook time: 10 minutes | Serves 4

1 cup broccoli florets
¾ cup chopped roasted red peppers
1¼ cups grated Fontina cheese
6 eggs
¾ cup heavy cream
½ teaspoon salt
Freshly ground black pepper, to taste
Cooking spray

1. Spritz a baking pan with cooking spray
2. Add the broccoli florets and roasted red peppers to the pan and scatter the grated Fontina cheese on top.
3. In a bowl, beat together the eggs and heavy cream. Sprinkle with salt and pepper. Pour the egg mixture over the top of the cheese. Wrap the pan in foil.
4. Select Air Fry. Set temperature to 325ºF (163ºC) and set time to 10 minutes. Press Start to begin preheating.
5. Once preheated, place the pan into the oven.
6. After 8 minutes, remove the pan from the oven. Remove the foil. Return the pan to the oven and continue to cook another 2 minutes.
7. When cooked, the quiche should be golden brown.
8. Rest for 5 minutes before cutting into wedges and serve warm.

Breakfast Sausage Quiche

Prep time: 5 minutes | Cook time: 25 minutes | Serves 4

12 large eggs
1 cup heavy cream
Salt and black pepper, to taste
12 ounces (340 g) sugar-free breakfast sausage
2 cups shredded Cheddar cheese
Cooking spray

1. Coat a casserole dish with cooking spray.
2. Beat together the eggs, heavy cream, salt and pepper in a large bowl until creamy. Stir in the breakfast sausage and Cheddar cheese.
3. Pour the sausage mixture into the prepared casserole dish.
4. Select Bake. Set temperature to 375ºF (190ºC) and set time to 25 minutes. Press Start to begin preheating.
5. Once the oven has preheated, place the dish into the oven.
6. When done, the top of the quiche should be golden brown and the eggs will be set.
7. Remove from the oven and let sit for 5 to 10 minutes before serving.

Cheddar Bacon Casserole

Prep time: 10 minutes | Cook time: 16 minutes | Serves 4

6 slices bacon
6 eggs
Salt and pepper, to taste
Cooking spray
½ cup chopped green bell pepper
½ cup chopped onion
¾ cup shredded Cheddar cheese

1. Place the bacon in a skillet over medium-high heat and cook each side for about 4 minutes until evenly crisp. Remove from the heat to a paper towel-lined plate to drain. Crumble it into small pieces and set aside.
2. Whisk the eggs with the salt and pepper in a medium bowl.
3. Spritz a baking pan with cooking spray.
4. Place the whisked eggs, crumbled bacon, green bell pepper, and onion in the prepared pan.
5. Select Bake. Set temperature to 400ºF (205ºC) and set time to 8 minutes. Press Start to begin preheating.
6. Once preheated, place the pan into the oven.
7. After 6 minutes, remove the pan from the oven. Scatter the Cheddar cheese all over. Return the pan to the oven and continue to cook another 2 minutes.
8. When cooking is complete, let sit for 5 minutes and serve on plates.

Vanilla Pancake with Walnuts

Prep time: 10 minutes | Cook time: 20 minutes | Serves 4

3 tablespoons melted butter, divided
1 cup flour
2 tablespoons sugar
1½ teaspoons baking powder
¼ teaspoon salt
1 egg, beaten
¾ cup milk
1 teaspoon pure vanilla extract
½ cup roughly chopped walnuts
Maple syrup or fresh sliced fruit, for serving

1. Grease a baking pan with 1 tablespoon of melted butter.
2. Mix together the flour, sugar, baking powder, and salt in a medium bowl. Add the beaten egg, milk, the remaining 2 tablespoons of melted butter, and vanilla and stir until the batter is sticky but slightly lumpy.
3. Slowly pour the batter into the greased baking pan and scatter with the walnuts.
4. Select Bake. Set temperature to 330ºF (166ºC) and set time to 20 minutes. Press Start to begin preheating.
5. Once preheated, place the pan into the oven.
6. When cooked, the pancake should be golden brown and cooked through.
7. Let the pancake rest for 5 minutes and serve topped with the maple syrup or fresh fruit, if desired.

Breakfast Raisins Bars

Prep time: 15 minutes | Cook time: 35 minutes | Makes 6 bars

1 cup unsweetened applesauce
1 carrot, peeled and grated
½ cup raisins
1 egg
1 tablespoon vegetable oil
2 tablespoons molasses
2 tablespoons brown sugar
¼ cup chopped walnuts
2 cups rolled oats
2 tablespoons sesame seeds
1 teaspoon ground cinnamon
¼ teaspoon grated nutmeg
¼ teaspoon ground ginger
Salt, to taste

1. Combine all the ingredients in a bowl, stirring well to blend. Press the mixture into an oiled or nonstick square baking (cake) pan.
2. Select Bake. Set temperature to 375ºF (190ºC) and set time to 35 minutes. Select Start to begin preheating.
3. Once preheated, slide the pan into the oven.
4. When done, the mixture will be golden brown. Cool and cut into squares.

Almond, Coconut, and Apple Granola

Prep time: 10 minutes | Cook time: 12 minutes | Serves 6

3 cups gluten-free old-fashioned rolled oats
1 cup slivered almonds
1 cup unsweetened coconut chips
½ cup honey or pure maple syrup
⅓ cup packed light brown sugar
¼ cup vegetable oil
1 teaspoon ground cinnamon
¼ teaspoon kosher salt
2 cups chopped dried apples

1. In a large bowl, combine the oats, almonds, coconut, honey, brown sugar, oil, cinnamon, and salt and mix well. Spread the mixture in an even layer on a sheet pan.
2. Select Bake. Set temperature to 325ºF (163ºC) and set time to 12 minutes. Select Start to begin preheating.
3. Once preheated, slide the pan into the oven.
4. Bake for 6 minutes. Remove the pan and stir the granola. Return to the oven and continue baking until the nuts and oats are golden brown and crisp, another 6 minutes.
5. Let cool, then stir in the apples.

Bell Pepper and Carrot Frittata

Prep time: 10 minutes | Cook time: 12 minutes | Serves 4

½ cup chopped red bell pepper
⅓ cup grated carrot
⅓ cup minced onion
1 teaspoon olive oil
1 egg
6 egg whites
⅓ cup 2% milk
1 tablespoon shredded Parmesan cheese

1. Mix together the red bell pepper, carrot, onion, and olive oil in a baking pan and stir to combine.
2. Select Bake. Set temperature to 350ºF (180ºC) and set time to 12 minutes. Press Start to begin preheating.
3. Once preheated, place the pan into the oven.
4. After 3 minutes, remove the pan from the oven. Stir the vegetables. Return the pan to the oven and continue cooking.
5. Meantime, whisk together the egg, egg whites, and milk in a medium bowl until creamy.
6. After 3 minutes, remove the pan from the oven. Pour the egg mixture over the top and scatter with the Parmesan cheese. Return the pan to the oven and continue cooking for additional 6 minutes.
7. When cooking is complete, the eggs will be set and the top will be golden around the edges.
8. Allow the frittata to cool for 5 minutes before slicing and serving.

When you eat crap, you feel crap. -Chapter 3 Breakfasts

Baked Avocado with Eggs and Tomato
Prep time: 5 minutes | Cook time: 11 minutes | Serves 2

1 large avocado, halved and pitted
2 large eggs
2 tomato slices, divided
½ cup nonfat Cottage cheese, divided
½ teaspoon fresh cilantro, for garnish

1. Line the sheet pan with the aluminium foil.
2. Slice a thin piece from the bottom of each avocado half so they sit flat. Remove a small amount from each avocado half to make a bigger hole to hold the egg.
3. Arrange the avocado halves on the pan, hollow-side up. Break 1 egg into each half. Top each half with 1 tomato slice and ¼ cup of the Cottage cheese.
4. Select Bake. Set temperature to 400ºF (205ºC) and set time to 11 minutes. Press Start to begin preheating.
5. Once the unit has preheated, place the pan into the oven.
6. When cooking is complete, remove the pan from the oven. Garnish with the fresh cilantro and serve.

Chicken Breakfast Sausages
Prep time: 15 minutes | Cook time: 10 minutes | Makes 8 patties

1 Granny Smith apple, peeled and finely chopped
2 tablespoons apple juice
2 garlic cloves, minced
1 egg white
⅓ cup minced onion
3 tablespoons ground almonds
⅛ teaspoon freshly ground black pepper
1 pound (454 g) ground chicken breast

1. Combine all the ingredients except the chicken in a medium mixing bowl and stir well.
2. Add the chicken breast to the apple mixture and mix with your hands until well incorporated.
3. Divide the mixture into 8 equal portions and shape into patties. Arrange the patties in the perforated pan.
4. Select Air Fry. Set temperature to 330ºF (166ºC) and set time to 10 minutes. Press Start to begin preheating.
5. Once the oven has preheated, place the pan into the oven.
6. When done, a meat thermometer inserted in the center of the chicken should reach at least 165ºF (74ºC).
7. Remove from the oven to a plate. Let the chicken cool for 5 minutes and serve warm.

Garlic Potatoes with Peppers and Onions
Prep time: 10 minutes | Cook time: 35 minutes | Serves 4

1 pound (454 g) red potatoes, cut into ½-inch dices
1 large red bell pepper, cut into ½-inch dices
1 large green bell pepper, cut into ½-inch dices
1 medium onion, cut into ½-inch dices
1½ tablespoons extra-virgin olive oil
1¼ teaspoons kosher salt
¾ teaspoon sweet paprika
¾ teaspoon garlic powder
Freshly ground black pepper, to taste

1. Mix together the potatoes, bell peppers, onion, oil, salt, paprika, garlic powder, and black pepper in a large mixing and toss to coat.
2. Transfer the potato mixture to the perforated pan.
3. Select Air Fry. Set temperature to 350ºF (180ºC) and set time to 35 minutes. Press Start to begin preheating.
4. Once preheated, place the pan into the oven. Stir the potato mixture three times during cooking.
5. When done, the potatoes should be nicely browned.
6. Remove from the oven to a plate and serve warm.

Brown Rice Quiches with Pimiento
Prep time: 10 minutes | Cook time: 14 minutes | Serves 6

4 ounces (113 g) diced green chilies
3 cups cooked brown rice
1 cup shredded reduced-fat Cheddar cheese, divided
½ cup egg whites
⅓ cup fat-free milk
¼ cup diced pimiento
½ teaspoon cumin
1 small eggplant, cubed
1 bunch fresh cilantro, finely chopped
Cooking spray

1. Spritz a 12-cup muffin pan with cooking spray.
2. In a large bowl, stir together all the ingredients, except for ½ cup of the cheese.
3. Scoop the mixture evenly into the muffin cups and sprinkle the remaining ½ cup of the cheese on top.
4. Select Bake. Set temperature to 400ºF (205ºC) and set time to 14 minutes. Press Start to begin preheating.
5. Once the unit has preheated, place the pan into the oven.
6. When cooking is complete, remove the pan and check the quiches. They should be set.
7. Carefully transfer the quiches to a platter and serve immediately.

Swiss Ham Mustard Pastries

Prep time: 10 minutes | Cook time: 20 minutes | Serves 4

¾ cup diced ham
½ cup shredded Gruyère or other Swiss-style cheese
2 tablespoons cream cheese, softened
1 tablespoon Dijon mustard
1 sheet frozen puff pastry, thawed
1 large egg, beaten
2 tablespoons finely grated Parmesan cheese

1. Line a sheet pan with a silicone baking mat.
2. In a medium bowl, stir together the ham, shredded cheese, cream cheese, and mustard.
3. Lightly flour a cutting board. Unfold the puff pastry sheet onto the board. Using a rolling pin, gently roll the dough to smooth out the folds, sealing any tears. Cut the dough into four squares.
4. Scoop a quarter of the ham mixture into the center of each puff pastry square and spread it evenly in a triangle shape over half the pastry, leaving a ½-inch border around the edges. Fold the pastry diagonally over the filling to form triangles. With a fork, crimp the edges to seal them. Place the pastries on the prepared pan, spacing them evenly.
5. Cut two or three small slits into the top of each turnover. Brush with the egg and sprinkle the Parmesan on top.
6. Select Bake. Set temperature to 350ºF (180ºC) and set time to 20 minutes. Select Start to begin preheating.
7. Once preheated, slide the pan into the oven.
8. Bake for 10 minutes, then remove from the oven. Check the pastries; if they are browning unevenly, rotate the pan. Return the pan to the oven and continue baking for another 10 minutes, or until the turnovers are golden brown.
9. Let cool for about 10 minutes before serving (the filling will be very hot).

Banana Chocolate Bread with Walnuts

Prep time: 10 minutes | Cook time: 30 minutes | Serves 4

¼ cup cocoa powder
6 tablespoons plus 2 teaspoons all-purpose flour, divided
½ teaspoon kosher salt
¼ teaspoon baking soda
1½ ripe bananas
1 large egg, whisked
¼ cup vegetable oil
½ cup sugar
3 tablespoons buttermilk or plain yogurt (not Greek)
½ teaspoon vanilla extract
6 tablespoons chopped white chocolate
6 tablespoons chopped walnuts

1. Mix together the cocoa powder, 6 tablespoons of the flour, salt, and baking soda in a medium bowl.
2. Mash the bananas with a fork in another medium bowl until smooth. Fold in the egg, oil, sugar, buttermilk, and vanilla, and whisk until thoroughly combined. Add the wet mixture to the dry mixture and stir until well incorporated.
3. Combine the white chocolate, walnuts, and the remaining 2 tablespoons of flour in a third bowl and toss to coat. Add this mixture to the batter and stir until well incorporated. Pour the batter into a baking pan and smooth the top with a spatula.
4. Select Bake. Set temperature to 310ºF (154ºC) and set time to 30 minutes. Press Start to begin preheating.
5. Once the oven has preheated, place the pan into the oven.
6. When done, a toothpick inserted into the center of the bread should come out clean.
7. Remove from the oven and allow to cool on a wire rack for 10 minutes before serving.

Half-and-Half Cinnamon Rolls

Prep time: 10 minutes | Cook time: 15 minutes | Makes 12 rolls and ½ cup icing

Cinnamon Mixture:
3 tablespoons dark brown sugar
3 tablespoons chopped pecans
2 tablespoons margarine
1 teaspoon ground cinnamon
Salt, to taste

Icing:
1 cup confectioners' sugar, sifted
1 tablespoon fat-free half-and-half
½ teaspoon vanilla extract
Salt, to taste

1. Make the buttermilk biscuit dough.
2. Roll out or pat the dough to ½ inch thick. In a small bowl, combine the cinnamon mixture ingredients. Spread the dough evenly with the cinnamon mixture and roll up like a jelly roll. With a sharp knife, cut the roll into 1-inch slices. Place on an oiled or nonstick baking sheet.
3. Select Bake. Set temperature to 400ºF (205ºC) and set time to 15 minutes. Select Start to begin preheating.
4. Once preheated, slide the pan into the oven.
5. When done, the rolls will be lightly browned. Let cool before frosting.
6. Combine the icing ingredients in a small bowl, adding more half-and-half or confectioners' sugar until the consistency is like thick cream. Drizzle over the tops of the cinnamon rolls and serve.

When you eat crap, you feel crap. -Chapter 3 Breakfasts

Shrimp and Spinach Frittata

Prep time: 15 minutes | Cook time: 16 minutes | Serves 4

4 eggs
Pinch salt
½ cup cooked rice
½ cup chopped cooked shrimp
½ cup baby spinach
½ cup grated Monterey Jack cheese
Nonstick cooking spray

1. Spritz a baking pan with nonstick cooking spray.
2. Whisk the eggs and salt in a small bowl until frothy.
3. Place the cooked rice, shrimp, and baby spinach in the baking pan. Pour in the whisked eggs and scatter the cheese on top.
4. Select Bake. Set temperature to 320ºF (160ºC) and set time to 16 minutes. Press Start to begin preheating.
5. Once the oven has preheated, place the pan into the oven.
6. When cooking is complete, the frittata should be golden and puffy.
7. Let the frittata cool for 5 minutes before slicing to serve.

Cheddar Hash Brown Casserole

Prep time: 15 minutes | Cook time: 30 minutes | Serves 4

3½ cups frozen hash browns, thawed
1 teaspoon salt
1 teaspoon freshly ground black pepper
3 tablespoons butter, melted
1 (10.5-ounce / 298-g) can cream of chicken soup
½ cup sour cream
1 cup minced onion
½ cup shredded sharp Cheddar cheese
Cooking spray

1. Put the hash browns in a large bowl and season with salt and black pepper. Add the melted butter, cream of chicken soup, and sour cream and stir until well incorporated. Mix in the minced onion and cheese and stir well.
2. Spray a baking pan with cooking spray.
3. Spread the hash brown mixture evenly into the baking pan.
4. Select Bake. Set temperature to 325ºF (163ºC) and set time to 30 minutes. Press Start to begin preheating.
5. Once the oven has preheated, place the pan into the oven.
6. When cooked, the hash brown mixture will be browned.
7. Cool for 5 minutes before serving.

Brown Rice Porridge with Dates

Prep time: 5 minutes | Cook time: 23 minutes | Serves 1 or 2

½ cup cooked brown rice
1 cup canned coconut milk
¼ cup unsweetened shredded coconut
¼ cup packed dark brown sugar
4 large Medjool dates, pitted and roughly chopped
½ teaspoon kosher salt
¼ teaspoon ground cardamom
Heavy cream, for serving (optional)

1. Place all the ingredients except the heavy cream in a baking pan and stir until blended.
2. Select Bake. Set temperature to 375ºF (190ºC) and set time to 23 minutes. Press Start to begin preheating.
3. Once the oven has preheated, place the pan into the oven. Stir the porridge halfway through the cooking time.
4. When cooked, the porridge will be thick and creamy.
5. Remove from the oven and ladle the porridge into bowls.
6. Serve hot with a drizzle of the cream, if desired.

Vanilla Blueberry Cobbler

Prep time: 5 minutes | Cook time: 15 minutes | Serves 4

¾ teaspoon baking powder
⅓ cup whole-wheat pastry flour
Dash sea salt
⅓ cup unsweetened nondairy milk
2 tablespoons maple syrup
½ teaspoon vanilla
Cooking spray
½ cup blueberries
¼ cup granola
Nondairy yogurt, for topping (optional)

1. Spritz a baking pan with cooking spray.
2. Mix together the baking powder, flour, and salt in a medium bowl. Add the milk, maple syrup, and vanilla and whisk to combine.
3. Scrape the mixture into the prepared pan. Scatter the blueberries and granola on top.
4. Select Bake. Set temperature to 347ºF (175ºC) and set time to 15 minutes. Press Start to begin preheating.
5. Once preheated, place the pan into the oven.
6. When done, the top should begin to brown and a knife inserted in the center should come out clean.
7. Let the cobbler cool for 5 minutes and serve with a drizzle of nondairy yogurt.

Baked Eggs with Kale Pesto

Prep time: 5 minutes | Cook time: 11 minutes | Serves 2

1 cup roughly chopped kale leaves, stems and center ribs removed
¼ cup grated pecorino cheese
¼ cup olive oil
1 garlic clove, peeled
3 tablespoons whole almonds
Kosher salt and freshly ground black pepper, to taste
4 large eggs
2 tablespoons heavy cream
3 tablespoons chopped pitted mixed olives

1. Place the kale, pecorino, olive oil, garlic, almonds, salt, and pepper in a small blender and blitz until well incorporated.
2. One at a time, crack the eggs in a baking pan. Drizzle the kale pesto on top of the egg whites. Top the yolks with the cream and swirl together the yolks and the pesto.
3. Select Bake. Set temperature to 300ºF (150ºC) and set time to 11 minutes. Press Start to begin preheating.
4. Once preheated, place the pan into the oven.
5. When cooked, the top should begin to brown and the eggs should be set.
6. Allow the eggs to cool for 5 minutes. Scatter the olives on top and serve warm.

Blueberries Quesadillas

Prep time: 5 minutes | Cook time: 4 minutes | Serves 2

¼ cup nonfat Ricotta cheese
¼ cup plain nonfat Greek yogurt
2 tablespoons finely ground flaxseeds
1 tablespoon granulated stevia
½ teaspoon cinnamon
¼ teaspoon vanilla extract
2 (8-inch) low-carb whole-wheat tortillas
½ cup fresh blueberries, divided

1. Line the sheet pan with the aluminum foil.
2. In a small bowl, whisk together the Ricotta cheese, yogurt, flaxseeds, stevia, cinnamon and vanilla.
3. Place the tortillas on the sheet pan. Spread half of the yogurt mixture on each tortilla, almost to the edges. Top each tortilla with ¼ cup of blueberries. Fold the tortillas in half.
4. Select Bake. Set temperature to 400ºF (205ºC) and set time to 4 minutes. Press Start to begin preheating.
5. Once the unit has preheated, place the pan into the oven.
6. When cooking is complete, remove the pan from the oven. Serve immediately.

Maple French Toast Casserole

Prep time: 5 minutes | Cook time: 12 minutes | Serves 6

3 large eggs, beaten
1 cup whole milk
1 tablespoon pure maple syrup
1 teaspoon vanilla extract
¼ teaspoon cinnamon
¼ teaspoon kosher salt
3 cups stale bread cubes
1 tablespoon unsalted butter, at room temperature

1. In a medium bowl, whisk together the eggs, milk, maple syrup, vanilla extract, cinnamon and salt. Stir in the bread cubes to coat well.
2. Grease the bottom of the sheet pan with the butter. Spread the bread mixture into the pan in an even layer.
3. Select Roast. Set temperature to 350ºF (180ºC) and set time to 12 minutes. Press Start to begin preheating.
4. Once the unit has preheated, place the pan into the oven.
5. After about 10 minutes, remove the pan and check the casserole. The top should be browned and the middle of the casserole just set. If more time is needed, return the pan to the oven and continue cooking.
6. When cooking is complete, serve warm.

Honey Cashew Granola with Cranberries

Prep time: 5 minutes | Cook time: 12 minutes | Serves 6

3 cups old-fashioned rolled oats
2 cups raw cashews
1 cup unsweetened coconut chips
½ cup honey
¼ cup vegetable oil
⅓ cup packed light brown sugar
¼ teaspoon kosher salt
1 cup dried cranberries

1. In a large bowl, stir together all the ingredients, except for the cranberries. Spread the mixture on the sheet pan in an even layer.
2. Select Bake. Set temperature to 325ºF (163ºC) and set time to 12 minutes. Press Start to begin preheating.
3. Once the unit has preheated, place the pan into the oven.
4. After 5 to 6 minutes, remove the pan and stir the granola. Return the pan to the oven and continue cooking.
5. When cooking is complete, remove the pan. Let the granola cool to room temperature. Stir in the cranberries before serving.

Maple Banana Bread Pudding

Prep time: 10 minutes | Cook time: 18 minutes | Serves 4

2 medium ripe bananas, mashed
½ cup low-fat milk
2 tablespoons maple syrup
2 tablespoons peanut butter
1 teaspoon vanilla extract
1 teaspoon ground cinnamon
2 slices whole-grain bread, torn into bite-sized pieces
¼ cup quick oats
Cooking spray

1. Spritz the sheet pan with cooking spray.
2. In a large bowl, combine the bananas, milk, maple syrup, peanut butter, vanilla extract and cinnamon. Use an immersion blender to mix until well combined.
3. Stir in the bread pieces to coat well. Add the oats and stir until everything is combined.
4. Transfer the mixture to the sheet pan. Cover with the aluminum foil.
5. Select Air Fry. Set temperature to 375ºF (190ºC) and set time to 18 minutes. Press Start to begin preheating.
6. Once the unit has preheated, place the pan into the oven.
7. After 10 minutes, remove the foil and continue to cook for 8 minutes.
8. Serve immediately.

Spinach and Egg Florentine

Prep time: 10 minutes | Cook time: 15 minutes | Serves 4

3 cups frozen spinach, thawed and drained
2 tablespoons heavy cream
¼ teaspoon kosher salt
⅛ teaspoon freshly ground black pepper
4 ounces (113 g) Ricotta cheese
2 garlic cloves, minced
½ cup panko bread crumbs
3 tablespoons grated Parmesan cheese
2 teaspoons unsalted butter, melted
4 large eggs

1. In a medium bowl, whisk together the spinach, heavy cream, salt, pepper, Ricotta cheese and garlic.
2. In a small bowl, whisk together the bread crumbs, Parmesan cheese and butter. Set aside.
3. Spoon the spinach mixture on the sheet pan and form four even circles.
4. Select Roast. Set temperature to 375ºF (190ºC) and set time to 15 minutes. Press Start to begin preheating.
5. Once the unit has preheated, place the pan into the oven.
6. After 8 minutes, remove the pan from the oven. The spinach should be bubbling. With the back of a large spoon, make indentations in the spinach for the eggs. Crack the eggs into the indentations and sprinkle the panko mixture over the surface of the eggs. Return the pan to the oven to continue cooking.
7. When cooking is complete, remove the pan from the oven. Serve hot.

Cinnamon Rolls with Brown Sugar

Prep time: 5 minutes | Cook time: 25 minutes | Makes 18 rolls

⅓ cup light brown sugar
2 teaspoons cinnamon
1 (9-by-9-inch) frozen puff pastry sheet, thawed
All-purpose flour, for dusting
6 teaspoons unsalted butter, melted, divided

1. In a small bowl, stir together the brown sugar and cinnamon.
2. On a clean work surface, lightly dust with the flour and lay the puff pastry sheet. Using a rolling pin, press the folds together and roll the dough out in one direction so that it measures about 9 by 11 inches. Cut it in half to form two squat rectangles of about 5½ by 9 inches.
3. Brush 2 teaspoons of the butter over each pastry half. Sprinkle with 2 tablespoons of the cinnamon sugar. Pat it down lightly with the palm of your hand to help it adhere to the butter.
4. Starting with the 9-inch side of one rectangle. Using your hands, carefully roll the dough into a cylinder. Repeat with the other rectangle. To make slicing easier, refrigerate the rolls for 10 to 20 minutes.
5. Using a sharp knife, slice each roll into nine 1-inch pieces. Transfer the rolls to the center of the sheet pan. They should be very close to each other, but not quite touching. Drizzle the remaining 2 teaspoons of the butter over the rolls and sprinkle with the remaining cinnamon sugar.
6. Select Bake. Set temperature to 350ºF (180ºC) and set time to 25 minutes. Press Start to begin preheating.
7. Once the unit has preheated, place the pan into the oven.
8. When cooking is complete, remove the pan and check the rolls. They should be puffed up and golden brown.
9. Let the rolls rest for 5 minutes and transfer them to a wire rack to cool completely. Serve.

Asparagus Strata with Havarti Cheese
Prep time: 10 minutes | Cook time: 17 minutes | Serves 4

6 asparagus spears, cut into 2-inch pieces
1 tablespoon water
2 slices whole-wheat bread, cut into ½-inch cubes
4 eggs
3 tablespoons whole milk
2 tablespoons chopped flat-leaf parsley
½ cup grated Havarti or Swiss cheese
Pinch salt
Freshly ground black pepper, to taste
Cooking spray

1. Add the asparagus spears and 1 tablespoon of water in a baking pan.
2. Select Bake. Set temperature to 330ºF (166ºC) and set time to 4 minutes. Press Start to begin preheating.
3. Once preheated, place the pan into the oven.
4. When cooking is complete, the asparagus spears will be crisp-tender.
5. Remove the asparagus from the pan and drain on paper towels.
6. Spritz the pan with cooking spray. Place the bread and asparagus in the pan.
7. Whisk together the eggs and milk in a medium mixing bowl until creamy. Fold in the parsley, cheese, salt, and pepper and stir to combine. Pour this mixture into the baking pan.
8. Select Bake and set time to 13 minutes. Place the pan back to the oven. When done, the eggs will be set and the top will be lightly browned.
9. Let cool for 5 minutes before slicing and serving.

Artichoke and Mushroom Frittata
Prep time: 10 minutes | Cook time: 15 minutes | Serves 6

8 eggs
½ teaspoon kosher salt
¼ cup whole milk
¾ cup shredded Mozzarella cheese, divided
2 tablespoons unsalted butter, melted
1 cup coarsely chopped artichoke hearts
¼ cup chopped onion
½ cup mushrooms
¼ cup grated Parmesan cheese
¼ teaspoon freshly ground black pepper

1. In a medium bowl, whisk together the eggs and salt. Let rest for a minute or two, then pour in the milk and whisk again. Stir in ½ cup of the Mozzarella cheese.
2. Grease the sheet pan with the butter. Stir in the artichoke hearts and onion and toss to coat with the butter.
3. Select Roast. Set temperature to 375ºF (190ºC) and set time to 12 minutes. Press Start to begin preheating.
4. Once the unit has preheated, place the pan into the oven.
5. After 5 minutes, remove the pan. Spread the mushrooms over the vegetables. Pour the egg mixture on top. Stir gently just to distribute the vegetables evenly. Return the pan to the oven and continue cooking for 5 to 7 minutes, or until the edges are set. The center will still be quite liquid.
6. Select Broil. Set temperature to 400ºF (205ºC) and set time to 3 minutes. Place the pan into the oven.
7. After 1 minute, remove the pan and sprinkle the remaining ¼ cup of the Mozzarella and Parmesan cheese over the frittata. Return the pan to the oven and continue cooking for 2 minutes.
8. When cooking is complete, the cheese should be melted with the top completely set but not browned. Sprinkle the black pepper on top and serve.

Mushroom and Spinach Frittata
Prep time: 10 minutes | Cook time: 22 minutes | Serves 2

4 large eggs
4 ounces (113 g) baby bella mushrooms, chopped
1 cup baby spinach, chopped
½ cup shredded Cheddar cheese
⅓ cup chopped leek, white part only
¼ cup halved grape tomatoes
1 tablespoon 2% milk
¼ teaspoon dried oregano
¼ teaspoon garlic powder
½ teaspoon kosher salt
Freshly ground black pepper, to taste
Cooking spray

1. Lightly spritz a baking dish with cooking spray.
2. Whisk the eggs in a large bowl until frothy. Add the mushrooms, baby spinach, cheese, leek, tomatoes, milk, oregano, garlic powder, salt, and pepper and stir until well blended. Pour the mixture into the prepared baking dish.
3. Select Bake. Set temperature to 300ºF (150ºC) and set time to 22 minutes. Press Start to begin preheating.
4. Once the oven has preheated, place the dish into the oven.
5. When cooked, the center will be puffed up and the top will be golden brown.
6. Let the frittata cool for 5 minutes before slicing to serve.

Banana Carrot Muffin

Prep time: 10 minutes | Cook time: 20 minutes | Serves 12

1½ cups whole-wheat flour
1 cup grated carrot
1 cup mashed banana
½ cup bran
½ cup low-fat buttermilk
2 tablespoons agave nectar
2 teaspoons baking powder
1 teaspoon vanilla
1 teaspoon baking soda
½ teaspoon nutmeg
Pinch cloves
2 egg whites

1. Line a muffin pan with 12 paper liners.
2. In a large bowl, stir together all the ingredients. Mix well, but do not over beat.
3. Scoop the mixture into the muffin cups.
4. Select Bake. Set temperature to 400ºF (205ºC) and set time to 20 minutes. Press Start to begin preheating.
5. Once the unit has preheated, place the pan into the oven.
6. When cooking is complete, remove the pan and let rest for 5 minutes.
7. Serve warm or at room temperature.

Whole-Wheat Blueberries Muffins

Prep time: 5 minutes | Cook time: 25 minutes | Makes 8 muffins

½ cup unsweetened applesauce
½ cup plant-based milk
½ cup maple syrup
1 teaspoon vanilla extract
2 cups whole-wheat flour
½ teaspoon baking soda
1 cup blueberries
Cooking spray

1. Spritz a 8-cup muffin pan with cooking spray.
2. In a large bowl, stir together the applesauce, milk, maple syrup and vanilla extract. Whisk in the flour and baking soda until no dry flour is left and the batter is smooth. Gently mix in the blueberries until they are evenly distributed throughout the batter.
3. Spoon the batter into the muffin cups, three-quarters full.
4. Select Bake. Set temperature to 375ºF (190ºC) and set time to 25 minutes. Press Start to begin preheating.
5. Once preheated, place the pan into the oven.
6. When cooking is complete, remove the pan and check the muffins. You can stick a knife into the center of a muffin and it should come out clean.
7. Let rest for 5 minutes before serving.

Blueberry Cake with Lemon

Prep time: 5 minutes | Cook time: 10 minutes | Serves 8

1½ cups Bisquick
¼ cup granulated sugar
2 large eggs, beaten
¾ cup whole milk
1 teaspoon vanilla extract
½ teaspoon lemon zest
Cooking spray
2 cups blueberries

1. Stir together the Bisquick and sugar in a medium bowl. Stir together the eggs, milk, vanilla and lemon zest. Add the wet ingredients to the dry ingredients and stir until well combined.
2. Spritz the sheet pan with cooking spray and line with the parchment paper, pressing it into place. Spray the parchment paper with cooking spray. Pour the batter on the pan and spread it out evenly. Sprinkle the blueberries evenly over the top.
3. Select Bake. Set temperature to 375ºF (190ºC) and set time to 10 minutes. Press Start to begin preheating.
4. Once the unit has preheated, place the pan into the oven.
5. When cooking is complete, the cake should be pulling away from the edges of the pan and the top should be just starting to turn golden brown.
6. Let the cake rest for a minute before cutting into 16 squares. Serve immediately.

Vanilla Pancake with Mixed Berries

Prep time: 10 minutes | Cook time: 14 minutes | Serves 4

1 tablespoon unsalted butter, at room temperature
1 egg
2 egg whites
½ cup 2% milk
½ cup whole-wheat pastry flour
1 teaspoon pure vanilla extract
1 cup sliced fresh strawberries
½ cup fresh raspberries
½ cup fresh blueberries

1. Grease a baking pan with the butter.
2. Using a hand mixer, beat together the egg, egg whites, milk, pastry flour, and vanilla in a medium mixing bowl until well incorporated.
3. Pour the batter into the pan.
4. Select Bake. Set temperature to 330ºF (166ºC) and set time to 14 minutes. Press Start to begin preheating.
5. Once the oven has preheated, place the pan into the oven.
6. When cooked, the pancake should puff up in the center and the edges should be golden brown
7. Allow the pancake to cool for 5 minutes and serve topped with the berries.

Chapter 3 Breakfasts - When you eat crap, you feel crap.

Orange Scones with Blueberries
Prep time: 5 minutes | Cook time: 20 minutes | Serves 14

½ cup low-fat buttermilk
¾ cup orange juice
Zest of 1 orange
2¼ cups whole-wheat pastry flour
⅓ cup agave nectar
¼ cup canola oil
1 teaspoon baking soda
1 teaspoon cream of tartar
1 cup fresh blueberries

1. In a small bowl, stir together the buttermilk, orange juice and orange zest.
2. In a large bowl, whisk together the flour, agave nectar, canola oil, baking soda and cream of tartar.
3. Add the buttermilk mixture and blueberries to the bowl with the flour mixture. Mix gently by hand until well combined.
4. Transfer the batter onto a lightly floured baking sheet. Pat into a circle about ¾ inch thick and 8 inches across. Use a knife to cut the circle into 14 wedges, cutting almost all the way through.
5. Select Bake. Set temperature to 375ºF (190ºC) and set time to 20 minutes. Press Start to begin preheating.
6. Once the unit has preheated, place the baking sheet into the oven.
7. When cooking is complete, remove the baking sheet and check the scones. They should be lightly browned.
8. Let rest for 5 minutes and cut completely through the wedges before serving.

French Toast Sticks with Strawberries
Prep time: 5 minutes | Cook time: 12 minutes | Serves 4

3 slices low-sodium whole-wheat bread, each cut into 4 strips
1 tablespoon unsalted butter, melted
1 tablespoon 2 percent milk
1 tablespoon sugar
1 egg, beaten
1 egg white
1 cup sliced fresh strawberries
1 tablespoon freshly squeezed lemon juice

1. Arrange the bread strips on a plate and drizzle with the melted butter.
2. In a bowl, whisk together the milk, sugar, egg and egg white.
3. Dredge the bread strips into the egg mixture and place on a wire rack to let the batter drip off. Arrange half the coated bread strips on the sheet pan.
4. Select Air Fry. Set temperature to 380ºF (193ºC) and set time to 6 minutes. Press Start to begin preheating.
5. Once preheated, place the pan into the oven.
6. After 3 minutes, remove the pan from the oven. Use tongs to turn the strips over. Rotate the pan and return the pan to the oven to continue cooking.
7. When cooking is complete, the strips should be golden brown.
8. In a small bowl, mash the strawberries with a fork and stir in the lemon juice. Serve the French toast sticks with the strawberry sauce.

Cinnamon Apple Turnovers
Prep time: 10 minutes | Cook time: 20 minutes | Serves 4

1 cup diced apple
1 tablespoon brown sugar
1 teaspoon freshly squeezed lemon juice
1 teaspoon all-purpose flour, plus more for dusting
¼ teaspoon cinnamon
⅛ teaspoon allspice
½ package frozen puff pastry, thawed
1 large egg, beaten
2 teaspoons granulated sugar

1. Whisk together the apple, brown sugar, lemon juice, flour, cinnamon and allspice in a medium bowl.
2. On a clean work surface, lightly dust with the flour and lay the puff pastry sheet. Using a rolling pin, gently roll the dough to smooth out the folds, seal any tears and form it into a square. Cut the dough into four squares.
3. Spoon a quarter of the apple mixture into the center of each puff pastry square and spread it evenly in a triangle shape over half the pastry, leaving a border of about ½ inch around the edges of the pastry. Fold the pastry diagonally over the filling to form triangles. With a fork, crimp the edges to seal them. Place the turnovers on the sheet pan, spacing them evenly.
4. Cut two or three small slits in the top of each turnover. Brush with the egg. Sprinkle evenly with the granulated sugar.
5. Select Bake. Set temperature to 350ºF (180ºC) and set time to 20 minutes. Press Start to begin preheating.
6. Once the unit has preheated, place the pan into the oven.
7. After 10 to 12 minutes, remove the pan from the oven. Check the pastries. If they are browned unevenly, rotate the pan. Return the pan to the oven and continue cooking.
8. When cooking is complete, remove the pan from the oven. The turnovers should be golden brown and the filling bubbling. Let cool for about 10 minutes before serving.

When you eat crap, you feel crap. -Chapter 3 Breakfasts

Chapter 4 Vegan and Vegetarian

Stuffed Peppers with Cheese and Basil
Prep time: 10 minutes | Cook time: 40 minutes | Serves 6

6 medium bell peppers
A little extra-virgin olive oil
5½ ounces (156 g) ricotta (fresh rather than ultra-pasteurized, if possible)
10½ ounces (297 g) soft goat cheese
1 cup finely grated Parmesan cheese
Sea salt flakes and freshly ground black pepper, to taste
1 cup basil leaves, torn
1 large egg
1 garlic clove, crushed
1 tablespoon toasted pine nuts (optional)

1. Halve the peppers, deseed them, brush them with olive oil, and put them into a gratin dish from which they can be served.
2. Drain the ricotta and the goat cheese. Mix together all three cheeses with seasoning, the basil, egg, and garlic, gently mashing. Add the pine nuts if you are using them.
3. Spoon the mixture into the pepper halves and transfer the stuffed peppers to a baking pan.
4. Select Bake. Set temperature to 375ºF (190ºC) and set time to 40 minutes. Select Start to begin preheating.
5. Once preheated, slide the pan into the oven. When done, the filling should be golden and souffléd and the peppers completely tender when pierced with a sharp knife. If they're not ready, return them to the oven for an extra 5 to 10 minutes, then test again.

Garlic Turnip and Zucchini
Prep time: 5 minutes | Cook time: 18 minutes | Serves 4

3 turnips, sliced
1 large zucchini, sliced
1 large red onion, cut into rings
2 cloves garlic, crushed
1 tablespoon olive oil
Salt and black pepper, to taste

1. Put the turnips, zucchini, red onion, and garlic in a baking pan. Drizzle the olive oil over the top and sprinkle with the salt and pepper.
2. Select Bake. Set temperature to 330ºF (166ºC) and set time to 18 minutes. Press Start to begin preheating.
3. Once preheated, place the pan into the oven.
4. When cooking is complete, the vegetables should be tender. Remove from the oven and serve on a plate.

Halloumi Zucchinis and Eggplant
Prep time: 5 minutes | Cook time: 14 minutes | Serves 2

2 zucchinis, cut into even chunks
1 large eggplant, peeled, cut into chunks
1 large carrot, cut into chunks
6 ounces (170 g) halloumi cheese, cubed
2 teaspoons olive oil
Salt and black pepper, to taste
1 teaspoon dried mixed herbs

1. Combine the zucchinis, eggplant, carrot, cheese, olive oil, salt, and pepper in a large bowl and toss to coat well.
2. Spread the mixture evenly in the perforated pan.
3. Select Air Fry. Set temperature to 340ºF (171ºC) and set time to 14 minutes. Press Start to begin preheating.
4. Once preheated, place the pan into the oven. Stir the mixture once during cooking.
5. When cooking is complete, they should be crispy and golden. Remove from the oven and serve topped with mixed herbs.

Red Chili Okra
Prep time: 5 minutes | Cook time: 10 minutes | Serves 4

3 tablespoons sour cream
2 tablespoons flour
2 tablespoons semolina
½ teaspoon red chili powder
Salt and black pepper, to taste
1 pound (454 g) okra, halved
Cooking spray

1. Spray the perforated pan with cooking spray. Set aside.
2. In a shallow bowl, place the sour cream. In another shallow bowl, thoroughly combine the flour, semolina, red chili powder, salt, and pepper.
3. Dredge the okra in the sour cream, then roll in the flour mixture until evenly coated. Transfer the okra to the perforated pan.
4. Select Air Fry. Set temperature to 400ºF (205ºC) and set time to 10 minutes. Press Start to begin preheating.
5. Once preheated, place the pan into the oven. Flip the okra halfway through the cooking time.
6. When cooking is complete, the okra should be golden brown and crispy. Remove the pan from the oven. Cool for 5 minutes before serving.

Garlic Ratatouille

Prep time: 15 minutes | Cook time: 16 minutes | Serves 2

2 Roma tomatoes, thinly sliced
1 zucchini, thinly sliced
2 yellow bell peppers, sliced
2 garlic cloves, minced
2 tablespoons olive oil
2 tablespoons herbes de Provence
1 tablespoon vinegar
Salt and black pepper, to taste

1. Place the tomatoes, zucchini, bell peppers, garlic, olive oil, herbes de Provence, and vinegar in a large bowl and toss until the vegetables are evenly coated. Sprinkle with salt and pepper and toss again. Pour the vegetable mixture into a baking dish.
2. Select Roast. Set temperature to 390°F (199°C) and set time to 16 minutes. Press Start to begin preheating.
3. Once preheated, place the baking dish into the oven. Stir the vegetables halfway through.
4. When cooking is complete, the vegetables should be tender.
5. Let the vegetable mixture stand for 5 minutes in the oven before removing and serving.

Cauliflower with Teriyaki Sauce

Prep time: 5 minutes | Cook time: 14 minutes | Serves 4

½ cup soy sauce
⅓ cup water
1 tablespoon brown sugar
1 teaspoon sesame oil
1 teaspoon cornstarch
2 cloves garlic, chopped
½ teaspoon chili powder
1 big cauliflower head, cut into florets

1. Make the teriyaki sauce: In a small bowl, whisk together the soy sauce, water, brown sugar, sesame oil, cornstarch, garlic, and chili powder until well combined.
2. Place the cauliflower florets in a large bowl and drizzle the top with the prepared teriyaki sauce and toss to coat well.
3. Put the cauliflower florets in the perforated pan.
4. Select Air Fry. Set temperature to 340°F (171°C) and set time to 14 minutes. Press Start to begin preheating.
5. Once preheated, place the pan into the oven. Stir the cauliflower halfway through.
6. When cooking is complete, the cauliflower should be crisp-tender.
7. Let the cauliflower cool for 5 minutes before serving.

Onion-Stuffed Mushrooms

Prep time: 5 minutes | Cook time: 12 minutes | Serves 2

18 medium-sized white mushrooms
1 small onion, peeled and chopped
4 garlic cloves, peeled and minced
2 tablespoons olive oil
2 teaspoons cumin powder
A pinch ground allspice
Fine sea salt and freshly ground black pepper, to taste

1. On a clean work surface, remove the mushroom stems. Using a spoon, scoop out the mushroom gills and discard.
2. Thoroughly combine the onion, garlic, olive oil, cumin powder, allspice, salt, and pepper in a mixing bowl. Stuff the mushrooms evenly with the mixture.
3. Place the stuffed mushrooms in the perforated pan.
4. Select Roast. Set temperature to 345°F (174°C) and set time to 12 minutes. Press Start to begin preheating.
5. Once preheated, place the pan into the oven.
6. When cooking is complete, the mushroom should be browned.
7. Cool for 5 minutes before serving.

Mozzarella Walnut Stuffed Mushrooms

Prep time: 5 minutes | Cook time: 10 minutes | Serves 4

4 large portobello mushrooms
1 tablespoon canola oil
½ cup shredded Mozzarella cheese
⅓ cup minced walnuts
2 tablespoons chopped fresh parsley
Cooking spray

1. Spritz the perforated pan with cooking spray.
2. On a clean work surface, remove the mushroom stems. Scoop out the gills with a spoon and discard. Coat the mushrooms with canola oil. Top each mushroom evenly with the shredded Mozzarella cheese, followed by the minced walnuts.
3. Arrange the mushrooms in the perforated pan.
4. Select Roast. Set temperature to 350°F (180°C) and set time to 10 minutes. Press Start to begin preheating.
5. Once preheated, place the pan into the oven.
6. When cooking is complete, the mushroom should be golden brown.
7. Transfer the mushrooms to a plate and sprinkle the parsley on top for garnish before serving.

Keep going. -Chapter 4 Vegan and Vegetarian

Tomato-Stuffed Portobello Mushrooms

Prep time: 5 minutes | Cook time: 8 minutes | Serves 4

4 portobello mushrooms, stem removed
1 tablespoon olive oil
1 tomato, diced
½ green bell pepper, diced
½ small red onion, diced
½ teaspoon garlic powder
Salt and black pepper, to taste
½ cup grated Mozzarella cheese

1. Using a spoon to scoop out the gills of the mushrooms and discard them. Brush the mushrooms with the olive oil.
2. In a mixing bowl, stir together the remaining ingredients except the Mozzarella cheese. Using a spoon to stuff each mushroom with the filling and scatter the Mozzarella cheese on top.
3. Arrange the mushrooms in the perforated pan.
4. Select Roast. Set temperature to 330ºF (166ºC) and set time to 8 minutes. Press Start to begin preheating.
5. Once preheated, place the pan into the oven.
6. When cooking is complete, the cheese should be melted.
7. Serve warm.

Breaded Zucchini Chips with Parmesan

Prep time: 5 minutes | Cook time: 14 minutes | Serves 4

2 egg whites
Salt and black pepper, to taste
½ cup seasoned bread crumbs
2 tablespoons grated Parmesan cheese
¼ teaspoon garlic powder
2 medium zucchini, sliced
Cooking spray

1. Spritz the perforated pan with cooking spray.
2. In a bowl, beat the egg whites with salt and pepper. In a separate bowl, thoroughly combine the bread crumbs, Parmesan cheese, and garlic powder.
3. Dredge the zucchini slices in the egg white, then coat in the bread crumb mixture.
4. Arrange the zucchini slices in the perforated pan.
5. Select Air Fry. Set temperature to 400ºF (205ºC) and set time to 14 minutes. Press Start to begin preheating.
6. Once preheated, place the pan into the oven. Flip the zucchini halfway through.
7. When cooking is complete, the zucchini should be tender.
8. Remove from the oven to a plate and serve.

Spinach-Stuffed Beefsteak Tomatoes

Prep time: 10 minutes | Cook time: 18 minutes | Serves 4

4 medium beefsteak tomatoes, rinsed
½ cup grated carrot
1 medium onion, chopped
1 garlic clove, minced
2 teaspoons olive oil
2 cups fresh baby spinach
¼ cup crumbled low-sodium feta cheese
½ teaspoon dried basil

1. On your cutting board, cut a thin slice off the top of each tomato. Scoop out a ¼- to ½-inch-thick tomato pulp and place the tomatoes upside down on paper towels to drain. Set aside.
2. Stir together the carrot, onion, garlic, and olive oil in a baking pan.
3. Select Bake. Set temperature to 350ºF (180ºC) and set time to 5 minutes. Press Start to begin preheating.
4. Once preheated, place the pan into the oven. Stir the vegetables halfway through.
5. When cooking is complete, the carrot should be crisp-tender.
6. Remove the pan from the oven and stir in the spinach, feta cheese, and basil.
7. Spoon ¼ of the vegetable mixture into each tomato and transfer the stuffed tomatoes to the oven. Set time to 13 minutes on Bake.
8. When cooking is complete, the filling should be hot and the tomatoes should be lightly caramelized.
9. Let the tomatoes cool for 5 minutes and serve.

Parmesan Brussels Sprouts

Prep time: 10 minutes | Cook time: 20 minutes | Serves 4

1 pound (454 g) fresh Brussels sprouts, trimmed
1 tablespoon olive oil
½ teaspoon salt
⅛ teaspoon pepper
¼ cup grated Parmesan cheese

1. In a large bowl, combine the Brussels sprouts with olive oil, salt, and pepper and toss until evenly coated.
2. Spread the Brussels sprouts evenly in the perforated pan.
3. Select Air Fry. Set temperature to 330ºF (166ºC) and set time to 20 minutes. Press Start to begin preheating.
4. Once preheated, place the pan into the oven. Stir the Brussels sprouts twice during cooking.
5. When cooking is complete, the Brussels sprouts should be golden brown and crisp. Remove the pan from the oven. Sprinkle the grated Parmesan cheese on top and serve warm.

Lemony-Honey Roasted Radishes

Prep time: 10 minutes | Cook time: 17 minutes | Serves 4

1 pound (454 g) radishes, with green leaves attached
1 tablespoon extra-virgin olive oil
1 tablespoon white balsamic vinegar
1 preserved lemon, flesh discarded, rind cut into shreds, plus 2 tablespoons brine from the jar, plus more if needed
1 tablespoon unsalted butter
Sea salt flakes and freshly ground black pepper, to taste
1½ tablespoons clear honey
Leaves from 6 mint sprigs, torn

1. Wash the radishes well and remove their leaves.
2. Halve the radishes lengthwise. Put them in a baking pan with the olive oil, white balsamic, half the preserved lemon brine, and all the butter. Season.
3. Select Bake. Set temperature to 400°F (205°C) and set time to 17 minutes. Select Start to begin preheating.
4. Once preheated, slide the pan into the oven.
5. After 7 minutes, add the remaining tablespoon of brine and the honey. Shake the pan around and return to the oven for a final 10 minutes.
6. Transfer to a warmed serving dish and mix in the reserved radish leaves; they will wilt in the heat. Stir in the shredded preserved lemon rind and taste for seasoning. Scatter on the mint leaves and serve.

Potato Shells with Cheddar and Bacon

Prep time: 5 minutes | Cook time: 8 minutes | Serves 4

4 tablespoons shredded reduced-fat Cheddar cheese
4 slices lean turkey bacon, cooked and crumbled
4 potato shells
4 tablespoons nonfat sour cream
4 teaspoons chopped fresh or frozen chives
Salt and freshly ground black pepper, to taste

1. Sprinkle 1 tablespoon Cheddar cheese and 1 tablespoon crumbled bacon into each potato shell. Place the shells on a broiling rack with a pan underneath.
2. Select Broil. Set temperature to 400°F (205°C) and set time to 8 minutes. Select Start to begin preheating.
3. Once preheated, slide the pan into the oven.
4. When done, the cheese will be melted and the shells lightly browned. Spoon 1 tablespoon sour cream into each shell and sprinkle with 1 teaspoon chives. Add salt and pepper to taste.

Pepper-Stuffed Portobellos

Prep time: 15 minutes | Cook time: 15 minutes | Serves 4

4 tablespoons sherry vinegar or white wine vinegar
6 garlic cloves, minced, divided
1 tablespoon fresh thyme leaves
1 teaspoon Dijon mustard
1 teaspoon kosher salt, divided
¼ cup plus 3¼ teaspoons extra-virgin olive oil, divided
8 portobello mushroom caps, each about 3 inches across, patted dry
1 small red or yellow bell pepper, thinly sliced
1 small green bell pepper, thinly sliced
1 small onion, thinly sliced
¼ teaspoon red pepper flakes
Freshly ground black pepper, to taste
4 ounces (113 g) shredded Fontina cheese

1. Stir together the vinegar, 4 minced garlic cloves, thyme, mustard, and ½ teaspoon of kosher salt in a small bowl. Slowly pour in ¼ cup of olive oil, whisking constantly, or until an emulsion is formed. Reserve 2 tablespoons of the marinade and set aside.
2. Put the mushrooms in a resealable plastic bag and pour in the marinade. Seal and shake the bag, coating the mushrooms in the marinade. Transfer the mushrooms to the sheet pan, gill-side down.
3. Put the remaining 2 minced garlic cloves, bell peppers, onion, red pepper flakes, remaining ½ teaspoon of salt, and black pepper in a medium bowl. Drizzle with the remaining 3¼ teaspoons of olive oil and toss well. Transfer the bell pepper mixture to the sheet pan.
4. Select Roast. Set temperature to 375°F (190°C) and set time to 12 minutes. Press Start to begin preheating.
5. Once preheated, place the pan into the oven.
6. After 7 minutes, remove the pan and stir the peppers and flip the mushrooms. Return the pan to the oven and continue cooking for 5 minutes.
7. Remove the pan from the oven and place the pepper mixture onto a cutting board and coarsely chop.
8. Brush both sides of the mushrooms with the reserved 2 tablespoons marinade. Stuff the caps evenly with the pepper mixture. Scatter the cheese on top.
9. Select Broil. Set temperature to 400°F (205°C) and set time to 3 minutes. Place the pan into the oven.
10. When done, the mushrooms should be tender and the cheese should be melted.
11. Serve warm.

Keep going. -Chapter 4 Vegan and Vegetarian

Garlic Bell Peppers with Marjoram

Prep time: 10 minutes | Cook time: 22 minutes | Serves 4

1 green bell pepper, sliced into 1-inch strips
1 red bell pepper, sliced into 1-inch strips
1 orange bell pepper, sliced into 1-inch strips
1 yellow bell pepper, sliced into 1-inch strips
2 tablespoons olive oil, divided
½ teaspoon dried marjoram
Pinch salt
Freshly ground black pepper, to taste
1 head garlic

1. Toss the bell peppers with 1 tablespoon of olive oil in a large bowl until well coated. Season with the marjoram, salt, and pepper. Toss again and set aside.
2. Cut off the top of a head of garlic. Place the garlic cloves on a large square of aluminum foil. Drizzle the top with the remaining 1 tablespoon of olive oil and wrap the garlic cloves in foil.
3. Transfer the garlic to the perforated pan.
4. Select Roast. Set temperature to 330ºF (166ºC) and set time to 15 minutes. Press Start to begin preheating.
5. Once preheated, place the pan into the oven.
6. After 15 minutes, remove the perforated pan from the oven and add the bell peppers. Return to the oven and set time to 7 minutes.
7. When cooking is complete or until the garlic is soft and the bell peppers are tender.
8. Transfer the cooked bell peppers to a plate. Remove the garlic and unwrap the foil. Let the garlic rest for a few minutes. Once cooled, squeeze the roasted garlic cloves out of their skins and add them to the plate of bell peppers. Stir well and serve immediately.

Potato and Asparagus Platter

Prep time: 5 minutes | Cook time: 26 minutes | Serves 5

4 medium potatoes, cut into wedges
Cooking spray
1 bunch asparagus, trimmed
2 tablespoons olive oil
Salt and pepper, to taste
Cheese Sauce:
¼ cup crumbled cottage cheese
¼ cup buttermilk
1 tablespoon whole-grain mustard
Salt and black pepper, to taste

1. Spritz the perforated pan with cooking spray.
2. Put the potatoes in the perforated pan.
3. Select Roast. Set temperature to 400ºF (205ºC) and set time to 20 minutes. Press Start to begin preheating.
4. Once preheated, place the pan into the oven. Stir the potatoes halfway through.
5. When cooking is complete, the potatoes should be golden brown.
6. Remove the potatoes from the oven to a platter. Cover the potatoes with foil to keep warm. Set aside.
7. Place the asparagus in the perforated pan and drizzle with the olive oil. Sprinkle with salt and pepper.
8. Select Roast. Set temperature to 400ºF (205ºC) and set time to 6 minutes. Place the pan into the oven. Stir the asparagus halfway through.
9. When cooking is complete, the asparagus should be crispy.
10. Meanwhile, make the cheese sauce by stirring together the cottage cheese, buttermilk, and mustard in a small bowl. Season as needed with salt and pepper.
11. Transfer the asparagus to the platter of potatoes and drizzle with the cheese sauce. Serve immediately.

Rice and Olives Stuffed Peppers

Prep time: 5 minutes | Cook time: 16 to 17 minutes | Serves 4

4 red bell peppers, tops sliced off
2 cups cooked rice
1 cup crumbled feta cheese
1 onion, chopped
¼ cup sliced kalamata olives
¾ cup tomato sauce
1 tablespoon Greek seasoning
Salt and black pepper, to taste
2 tablespoons chopped fresh dill, for serving

1. Microwave the red bell peppers for 1 to 2 minutes until tender.
2. When ready, transfer the red bell peppers to a plate to cool.
3. Mix the cooked rice, feta cheese, onion, kalamata olives, tomato sauce, Greek seasoning, salt, and pepper in a medium bowl and stir until well combined.
4. Divide the rice mixture among the red bell peppers and transfer to a greased baking dish.
5. Select Bake. Set temperature to 360ºF (182ºC) and set time to 15 minutes. Press Start to begin preheating.
6. Once preheated, place the baking dish into the oven.
7. When cooking is complete, the rice should be heated through and the vegetables should be soft.
8. Remove from the oven and serve with the dill sprinkled on top.

28|Chapter 4 Vegan and Vegetarian - Keep going.

Cheesy Eggplant with Chili Smoked Almonds

Prep time: 10 minutes | Cook time: 45 minutes | Serves 6

3¾ pounds (1.7 kg) globe eggplants
5 tablespoons extra-virgin olive oil
2 teaspoons harissa
Sea salt flakes and freshly ground black pepper, to taste
2 garlic cloves, finely grated
Juice of ½ lemon, or to taste
3½ ounces (99 g) goat curd or soft creamy goat cheese
1 tablespoon smoked almonds, roughly chopped (you want quite big bits)
2 red Fresno chilies, halved, seeded, and very thinly sliced
Leaves from 1 rosemary sprig, chopped
Warm flatbread or toasted sourdough bread, to serve

1. Put the eggplants in a baking pan and brush lightly with some of the olive oil. Pierce each a few times with the tines of a fork.
2. Select Bake. Set temperature to 400ºF (205ºC) and set time to 45 minutes. Select Start to begin preheating.
3. Once preheated, slide the pan into the oven.
4. When done, the eggplants will be completely soft and look a bit deflated.
5. Leave until cool enough to handle, then slit the skins and scoop the flesh out into a bowl. Chop the flesh. Mash, and add about 3½ tablespoons of the oil, the harissa, salt, pepper, garlic, and lemon juice to taste. Put this into a warmed serving bowl and scatter the goat cheese on top.
6. Heat the remaining extra-virgin olive oil in a frying pan and quickly fry the smoked almonds, chilies, and rosemary together. Pour this over the roast eggplants and serve with bread.

Butternut Squash with Goat Cheese

Prep time: 5 minutes | Cook time: 20 minutes | Serves 2

1 pound (454 g) butternut squash, cut into wedges
2 tablespoons olive oil
1 tablespoon dried rosemary
Salt, to salt
1 cup crumbled goat cheese
1 tablespoon maple syrup

1. Toss the squash wedges with the olive oil, rosemary, and salt in a large bowl until well coated.
2. Transfer the squash wedges to the perforated pan, spreading them out in as even a layer as possible.
3. Select Air Fry. Set temperature to 350ºF (180ºC) and set time to 20 minutes. Press Start to begin preheating.
4. Once preheated, place the pan into the oven.
5. After 10 minutes, remove from the oven and flip the squash. Return the pan to the oven and continue cooking for 10 minutes.
6. When cooking is complete, the squash should be golden brown. Remove the pan from the oven. Sprinkle the goat cheese on top and serve drizzled with the maple syrup.

Smoked Paprika Vegetable with Eggs

Prep time: 15 minutes | Cook time: 46 minutes | Serves 4

4 zucchini
1 pound (454 g) small waxy potatoes, scrubbed and quartered
⅔ pound (302 g) cherry tomatoes
12 scallions, trimmed
3 tablespoons extra-virgin olive oil
Sea salt flakes and freshly ground black pepper, to taste
Leaves from 3 thyme sprigs, plus 5 whole thyme sprigs
½ teaspoon crushed red pepper (optional)
¾ tablespoon smoked paprika, plus more to serve
4 garlic cloves, finely grated
½ pound (227 g) string beans, stem ends removed
6 to 8 extra-large eggs
Greek yogurt, to serve (optional)

1. Trim the ends from the zucchini and cut them into ¼in thick slices. Put all the vegetables except the string beans into a baking pan in a single layer. Add 2 tablespoons of the olive oil, the seasoning, thyme, crushed red pepper, smoked paprika, and garlic. Toss everything together.
2. Select Bake. Set temperature to 400ºF (205ºC) and set time to 46 minutes. Select Start to begin preheating.
3. Once preheated, slide the pan into the oven. Stir the vegetables over a couple of times.
4. After 30 minutes, toss the string beans with the remaining oil and scatter them on top of the other vegetables. Return to the oven for 8 minutes.
5. Break the eggs on top, season, and return the casserole or pan to the oven for a final 8 minutes or so. The eggs should be cooked.
6. Serve straight from the pan, sprinkling the eggs with a little more paprika, if you like. If you've made it very spicy and I often do a bowl of Greek yogurt on the side is good.

Double Cheese Roasted Asparagus

Prep time: 5 minutes | Cook time: 10 minutes | Serves 4

⅔ pound (302 g) asparagus spears, of medium thickness
Extra-virgin olive oil
Sea salt flakes and freshly ground black pepper, to taste
4½ ounces (127 g) ricotta cheese (fresh rather than ultra-pasteurized, if possible)
Pecorino cheese, or Parmesan cheese, shaved

1. Trim the woody ends from the asparagus spears, put them on an sheet pan with a slight lip, and drizzle with olive oil. Season with salt.
2. Select Bake. Set temperature to 400ºF (205ºC) and set time to 10 minutes. Select Start to begin preheating.
3. Once preheated, slide the pan into the oven.
4. When done, the asparagus spears will be tender.
5. Put the asparagus on a serving plate. Scatter the ricotta in nuggets over the top, followed by the shaved pecorino or Parmesan cheese. Season with salt and pepper, pour on more olive oil, and serve immediately.

Chili Tomato with Herbs and Pistachios

Prep time: 15 minutes | Cook time: 30 minutes | Serves

1⅔ pounds (756 g) plum tomatoes, halved lengthwise
4 tablespoons extra-virgin olive oil
3 teaspoons crushed red pepper
2 teaspoons fennel seeds
Sea salt flakes and freshly ground black pepper, to taste
4 teaspoons clear honey
1 cup Greek yogurt, or more, depending on the size of your serving plate
1 cup crumbled Feta cheese
1 garlic clove, finely grated
⅓ cup dill, chopped, any thick stalks removed
Scant 1 cup mint leaves
1 tablespoon chopped shelled unsalted pistachio nuts

1. Put all the tomatoes into a baking pan in which they can lie in a single layer; if they are too close to each other, they will steam instead of roasting. Spoon 3 tablespoons of the oil over them, then turn them over with your hands so they get well coated. Leave them cut sides up.
2. Put the crushed red pepper and fennel seeds into a mortar and bash them. You won't break the fennel seeds down, but you'll crush them a bit. Sprinkle these over the tomatoes and season. Mix the honey with the remaining olive oil and spoon a little over each tomato.
3. Select Bake. Set temperature to 400ºF (205ºC) and set time to 30 minutes. Select Start to begin preheating.
4. Once preheated, slide the pan into the oven.
5. Keep an eye on them; you may find they need a little longer, but don't overcook them. They get to a point when they completely collapse and even though they're delicious at this stage, they've lost all their shape and you don't want that here.
6. Stir the yogurt, Feta, and garlic together and season. Put the yogurt mixture on a serving plate and pile the roast tomatoes on top. Sprinkle the herbs and pistachios all over the dish and serve.

Tomato and Black Olive Clafoutis

Prep time: 15 minutes | Cook time: 55 minutes | Serves 6

1 pound (454 g) mixed cherry and plum tomatoes, halved or quartered, depending on size
1½ tablespoons extra-virgin olive oil
Sea salt flakes and freshly ground black pepper, to taste
4 large eggs, plus 2 large egg yolks
⅓ cup all-purpose flour
Scant 1 cup milk
1¼ cups heavy cream
Generous ½ cup finely grated Parmesan cheese
1 garlic clove, finely grated
2 tablespoons chopped pitted black olives
7 ounces (198 g) soft goat cheese, crumbled
⅓ cup basil leaves, torn

1. Put the tomatoes into a gratin dish with the olive oil and season them. Turn them over so the surfaces are all coated in a little oil.
2. Select Bake. Set temperature to 400ºF (205ºC) and set time to 25 minutes. Select Start to begin preheating.
3. Once preheated, slide the dish into the oven.
4. When done, the tomatoes will be soft and slightly shrunken. Take out of the oven and leave to sit on a work surface.
5. Reduce the oven temperature to 375ºF (190ºC).
6. Put the eggs, egg yolks, flour, milk, and cream into a food processor, season well, and whizz. Stir in the Parmesan and garlic.
7. Scatter the olives over the tomatoes and crumble on the goat cheese.
8. Pour the batter over the tomatoes, olives, and cheese and bake for 30 minutes, until the custard is puffed, golden, and just set in the middle. Leave it for 5 minutes to settle: it will sink a little once it has sat for a while. Scatter over the basil and serve.

30|Chapter 4 Vegan and Vegetarian - Keep going.

Moroccan Roasted Veggies with Labneh

Prep time: 20 minutes | Cook time: 40 minutes | Serves 6

For the Labneh:
¾ cup Greek yogurt
Sea salt flakes and freshly ground black pepper, to taste

For the Vegetables:
4½ pounds (2 kg) winter squash or pumpkin
3 onions, cut into thick wedges
2 pounds (907 g) cauliflower florets
1 pound (454 g) creamer potatoes, scrubbed and quartered
2 to 3 red Fresno chilies, halved, seeded, and thinly sliced
1¼-inch fresh ginger, peeled and finely grated
½ tablespoon ground cumin
1 tablespoon harissa
7 tablespoons extra-virgin olive oil
2 (15-ounce / 425-g) cans of chickpeas, drained and rinsed
4 garlic cloves, finely sliced
½ pound (227 g) cherry tomatoes
Juice of ½ lemon
½ cup chopped cilantro leaves, to serve
3 preserved lemons, rind only, shredded, to serve
Couscous, to serve (optional)

1. Start the labneh the day before. Put the yogurt into a piece of cheesecloth or a brand new all-purpose kitchen cloth set in a sieve over a bowl. Stir in some salt and pepper. Pull the fabric up round the yogurt to make a "bag." Put the whole thing, including the bowl to catch the liquid that drains out in the refrigerator for 24 hours. Give it a gentle squeeze every so often. You'll get a firm yogurt "cheese."
2. Cut the squash into wedges and remove the seeds. Divide between 2 baking pans, then do the same with the onions, cauliflower, and potatoes. The vegetables need to be able to lie in a single layer, with room to add the tomatoes later. Season, add the chilies, ginger, cumin, and harissa, and drizzle everything with 5 tablespoons of the olive oil. Turn the vegetables so they get covered in the flavorings and oil.
3. Select Bake. Set temperature to 400ºF (205ºC) and set time to 40 minutes. Select Start to begin preheating.
4. Once preheated, slide the pans into the oven.
5. After 20 minutes, stir in the chickpeas and garlic, add the tomatoes, and drizzle with the rest of the olive oil.
6. Bake for a final 20 minutes, or until the vegetables are tender and slightly charred in places. Check the seasoning.
7. Transfer the vegetables to a warmed platter or shallow bowl. Squeeze over the lemon juice and scatter with the cilantro and shredded preserved lemon rind. Serve the vegetables and labneh on their own, the dish already contains a starch in the potatoes or with couscous.

Golden Potato, Carrot and Onion

Prep time: 10 minutes | Cook time: 38 minutes | Serves 4

2 cups peeled and shredded potatoes
½ cup peeled and shredded carrots
¼ cup shredded onion
1 teaspoon salt
1 teaspoon dried rosemary
1 teaspoon dried cumin
3 tablespoons vegetable oil
Salt and freshly ground black pepper, to taste

1. Mix all the ingredients together in an ovenproof baking dish. Adjust the seasonings to taste. Cover the dish with aluminum foil.
2. Select Bake. Set temperature to 400ºF (205ºC) and set time to 30 minutes. Select Start to begin preheating.
3. Once preheated, slide the baking dish into the oven. When done, the vegetables will be tender. Remove the cover.
4. Select Broil. Set temperature to 400ºF (205ºC) and set time to 8 minutes. Slide the pan into the oven. When done, the top will be browned.

Butternut Squash and Parsnip with Thyme

Prep time: 5 minutes | Cook time: 16 minutes | Serves 2

1 parsnip, sliced
1 cup sliced butternut squash
1 small red onion, cut into wedges
½ chopped celery stalk
1 tablespoon chopped fresh thyme
2 teaspoons olive oil
Salt and black pepper, to taste

1. Toss all the ingredients in a large bowl until the vegetables are well coated.
2. Transfer the vegetables to the perforated pan.
3. Select Air Fry. Set temperature to 380ºF (193ºC) and set time to 16 minutes. Press Start to begin preheating.
4. Once preheated, place the pan into the oven. Stir the vegetables halfway through the cooking time.
5. When cooking is complete, the vegetables should be golden brown and tender. Remove from the oven and serve warm.

Keep going. -Chapter 4 Vegan and Vegetarian

Ginger-Pepper Broccoli

Prep time: 5 minutes | Cook time: 10 minutes | Serves 2

12 ounces (340 g) broccoli florets
2 tablespoons Asian hot chili oil
1 teaspoon ground Sichuan peppercorns (or black pepper)
2 garlic cloves, finely chopped
1 (2-inch) piece fresh ginger, peeled and finely chopped
Kosher salt and freshly ground black pepper

1. Toss the broccoli florets with the chili oil, Sichuan peppercorns, garlic, ginger, salt, and pepper in a mixing bowl until thoroughly coated.
2. Transfer the broccoli florets to the perforated pan.
3. Select Air Fry. Set temperature to 375°F (190°C) and set time to 10 minutes. Press Start to begin preheating.
4. Once preheated, place the pan into the oven. Stir the broccoli florets halfway through the cooking time.
5. When cooking is complete, the broccoli florets should be lightly browned and tender. Remove the broccoli from the oven and serve on a plate.

Roasted Bell Peppers with Burrata and 'Nduja

Prep time: 5 minutes | Cook time: 30 minutes | Serves 4

6 red bell peppers
A little extra-virgin olive oil
Sea salt flakes and freshly ground black pepper, to taste
2¼ ounces (64 g) 'nduja
1 pound (454 g) burrata
Ciabatta, to serve

1. Halve the peppers, seed them, and put them into a baking pan. Brush them with olive oil and season.
2. Select Bake. Set temperature to 400°F (205°C) and set time to 30 minutes. Select Start to begin preheating.
3. Once preheated, slide the pan into the oven.
4. After 20 minutes, break the 'nduja into chunks and divide it among the peppers, putting it inside them. Bake for a final 10 minutes.
5. When they're cooked, the pepper skins should be slightly blistered and a little charred in places. Leave them until they're cool enough to handle, then tear them or leave them whole—whichever you prefer—and divide them among 4 plates. Drain the burrata, tear it, and serve it alongside the peppers and 'nduja. Serve some ciabatta on the side.

Roasted Veggie Rice with Eggs

Prep time: 5 minutes | Cook time: 12 minutes | Serves 4

2 teaspoons melted butter
1 cup chopped mushrooms
1 cup cooked rice
1 cup peas
1 carrot, chopped
1 red onion, chopped
1 garlic clove, minced
Salt and black pepper, to taste
2 hard-boiled eggs, grated
1 tablespoon soy sauce

1. Coat a baking dish with melted butter.
2. Stir together the mushrooms, cooked rice, peas, carrot, onion, garlic, salt, and pepper in a large bowl until well mixed. Pour the mixture into the prepared baking dish.
3. Select Roast. Set temperature to 380°F (193°C) and set time to 12 minutes. Press Start to begin preheating.
4. Once preheated, place the baking dish into the oven.
5. When cooking is complete, remove from the oven. Divide the mixture among four plates. Serve warm with a sprinkle of grated eggs and a drizzle of soy sauce.

Air Fried Tofu Sticks

Prep time: 5 minutes | Cook time: 14 minutes | Serves 4

2 tablespoons olive oil, divided
½ cup flour
½ cup crushed cornflakes
Salt and black pepper, to taste
14 ounces (397 g) firm tofu, cut into ½-inch-thick strips

1. Grease the perforated pan with 1 tablespoon of olive oil.
2. Combine the flour, cornflakes, salt, and pepper on a plate.
3. Dredge the tofu strips in the flour mixture until they are completely coated. Transfer the tofu strips to the greased pan.
4. Drizzle the remaining 1 tablespoon of olive oil over the top of tofu strips.
5. Select Air Fry. Set temperature to 360°F (182°C) and set time to 14 minutes. Press Start to begin preheating.
6. Once preheated, place the pan into the oven. Flip the tofu strips halfway through the cooking time.
7. When cooking is complete, the tofu strips should be crispy. Remove from the oven and serve warm.

Veggie and Oat Meatballs

Prep time: 15 minutes | Cook time: 18 minutes | Serves 3

½ cup grated carrots
½ cup sweet onions
2 tablespoons olive oil
1 cup rolled oats
½ cup roasted cashews
2 cups cooked chickpeas
Juice of 1 lemon
2 tablespoons soy sauce
1 tablespoon flax meal
1 teaspoon garlic powder
1 teaspoon cumin
½ teaspoon turmeric

1. Mix the carrots, onions, and olive oil in a baking dish and stir to combine.
2. Select Roast. Set temperature to 350ºF (180ºC) and set time to 6 minutes. Press Start to begin preheating.
3. Once preheated, place the baking dish into the oven. Stir the vegetables halfway through.
4. When cooking is complete, the vegetables should be tender.
5. Meanwhile, put the oats and cashews in a food processor or blender and pulse until coarsely ground. Transfer the mixture to a large bowl. Add the chickpeas, lemon juice, and soy sauce to the food processor and pulse until smooth. Transfer the chickpea mixture to the bowl of oat and cashew mixture.
6. Remove the carrots and onions from the oven to the bowl of chickpea mixture. Add the flax meal, garlic powder, cumin, and turmeric and stir to incorporate.
7. Scoop tablespoon-sized portions of the veggie mixture and roll them into balls with your hands. Transfer the balls to the perforated pan.
8. Increase the temperature to 370ºF (188ºC) and set time to 12 minutes on Bake. Place the pan into the oven. Flip the balls halfway through the cooking time.
9. When cooking is complete, the balls should be golden brown.
10. Serve warm.

Garlic Eggplant Slices with Parsley

Prep time: 5 minutes | Cook time: 12 minutes | Serves 4

1 cup flour
4 eggs
Salt, to taste
2 cups bread crumbs
1 teaspoon Italian seasoning
2 eggplants, sliced
2 garlic cloves, sliced
2 tablespoons chopped parsley
Cooking spray

1. Spritz the perforated pan with cooking spray. Set aside.
2. On a plate, place the flour. In a shallow bowl, whisk the eggs with salt. In another shallow bowl, combine the bread crumbs and Italian seasoning.
3. Dredge the eggplant slices, one at a time, in the flour, then in the whisked eggs, finally in the bread crumb mixture to coat well.
4. Lay the coated eggplant slices in the perforated pan.
5. Select Air Fry. Set temperature to 390ºF (199ºC) and set time to 12 minutes. Press Start to begin preheating.
6. Once preheated, place the pan into the oven. Flip the eggplant slices halfway through the cooking time.
7. When cooking is complete, the eggplant slices should be golden brown and crispy. Transfer the eggplant slices to a plate and sprinkle the garlic and parsley on top before serving.

Chickpea-Stuffed Bell Peppers

Prep time: 10 minutes | Cook time: 18 minutes | Serves 4

4 medium red, green, or yellow bell peppers, halved and deseeded
4 tablespoons extra-virgin olive oil, divided
½ teaspoon kosher salt, divided
1 (15-ounce / 425-g) can chickpeas
1½ cups cooked white rice
½ cup diced roasted red peppers
¼ cup chopped parsley
½ small onion, finely chopped
3 garlic cloves, minced
½ teaspoon cumin
¼ teaspoon freshly ground black pepper
¾ cup panko bread crumbs

1. Brush the peppers inside and out with 1 tablespoon of olive oil. Season the insides with ¼ teaspoon of kosher salt. Arrange the peppers on the sheet pan, cut side up.
2. Place the chickpeas with their liquid into a large bowl. Lightly mash the beans with a potato masher. Sprinkle with the remaining ¼ teaspoon of kosher salt and 1 tablespoon of olive oil. Add the rice, red peppers, parsley, onion, garlic, cumin, and black pepper to the bowl and stir to incorporate.
3. Divide the mixture among the bell pepper halves.
4. Stir together the remaining 2 tablespoons of olive oil and panko in a small bowl. Top the pepper halves with the panko mixture.
5. Select Roast. Set temperature to 375ºF (190ºC) and set time to 18 minutes. Press Start to begin preheating.
6. Once preheated, place the pan into the oven.
7. When done, the peppers should be slightly wrinkled, and the panko should be golden brown.
8. Remove from the oven and serve on a plate.

Keep going. -Chapter 4 Vegan and Vegetarian

Stuffed Bell Peppers with Cream Cheese

Prep time: 5 minutes | Cook time: 15 minutes | Serves 2

2 bell peppers, tops and seeds removed
Salt and pepper, to taste
⅔ cup cream cheese
2 tablespoons mayonnaise
1 tablespoon chopped fresh celery stalks
Cooking spray

1. Spritz the perforated pan with cooking spray.
2. Place the peppers in the perforated pan.
3. Select Roast. Set temperature to 400ºF (205ºC) and set time to 10 minutes. Press Start to begin preheating.
4. Once preheated, place the pan into the oven. Flip the peppers halfway through.
5. When cooking is complete, the peppers should be crisp-tender.
6. Remove from the oven to a plate and season with salt and pepper.
7. Mix the cream cheese, mayo, and celery in a small bowl and stir to incorporate. Evenly stuff the roasted peppers with the cream cheese mixture with a spoon. Serve immediately.

Carrot, Tofu and Cauliflower Rice

Prep time: 10 minutes | Cook time: 22 minutes | Serves 4

½ block tofu, crumbled
1 cup diced carrot
½ cup diced onions
Cauliflower:
3 cups cauliflower rice
½ cup chopped broccoli
½ cup frozen peas
2 tablespoons soy sauce
1 tablespoon minced ginger
2 garlic cloves, minced
1 tablespoon rice vinegar
1½ teaspoons toasted sesame oil
2 tablespoons soy sauce
1 teaspoon turmeric

1. Mix the tofu, carrot, onions, soy sauce, and turmeric in a baking dish and stir until well incorporated.
2. Select Roast. Set temperature to 370ºF (188ºC) and set time to 10 minutes. Press Start to begin preheating.
3. Once preheated, place the baking dish into the oven. Flip the tofu and carrot halfway through the cooking time.
4. When cooking is complete, the tofu should be crisp.
5. Meanwhile, in a large bowl, combine all the ingredients for the cauliflower and toss well.
6. Remove the dish from the oven and add the cauliflower mixture to the tofu and stir to combine.
7. Return the baking dish to the oven and set time to 12 minutes on Roast. Place the baking dish into the oven
8. When cooking is complete, the vegetables should be tender.
9. Cool for 5 minutes before serving.

Cayenne Green Beans

Prep time: 5 minutes | Cook time: 15 minutes | Serves 4

½ cup flour
2 eggs
1 cup panko bread crumbs
½ cup grated Parmesan cheese
1 teaspoon cayenne pepper
Salt and black pepper, to taste
1½ pounds (680 g) green beans

1. In a bowl, place the flour. In a separate bowl, lightly beat the eggs. In a separate shallow bowl, thoroughly combine the bread crumbs, cheese, cayenne pepper, salt, and pepper.
2. Dip the green beans in the flour, then in the beaten eggs, finally in the bread crumb mixture to coat well. Transfer the green beans to the perforated pan.
3. Select Air Fry. Set temperature to 400ºF (205ºC) and set time to 15 minutes. Press Start to begin preheating.
4. Once preheated, place the pan into the oven. Stir the green beans halfway through the cooking time.
5. When cooking is complete, remove from the oven to a bowl and serve.

Honey Baby Carrots with Dill

Prep time: 5 minutes | Cook time: 12 minutes | Serves 4

1 pound (454 g) baby carrots
2 tablespoons olive oil
1 tablespoon honey
1 teaspoon dried dill
Salt and black pepper, to taste

1. Place the carrots in a large bowl. Add the olive oil, honey, dill, salt, and pepper and toss to coat well.
2. Transfer the carrots to the perforated pan.
3. Select Roast. Set temperature to 350ºF (180ºC) and set time to 12 minutes. Press Start to begin preheating.
4. Once preheated, place the pan into the oven. Stir the carrots once during cooking.
5. When cooking is complete, the carrots should be crisp-tender. Remove from the oven and serve warm.

Roasted Veggies and Apple Salad

Prep time: 15 minutes | Cook time: 30 minutes | Serves 4

For the Salad:

¾ pound (340 g) young carrots
3 tablespoons extra-virgin olive oil
Sea salt flakes and freshly ground black pepper, to taste
1¼ cups cooked Puy lentils
1 red Fresno chili and 1 green chili, halved, seeded, and very finely shredded
2 preserved lemons, rind only, finely shredded, plus 2 teaspoons brine from the jar
1 large or 2 medium tart apples
Juice of ½ lemon
Leaves from 10 mint sprigs, torn
¼ cup cilantro leaves

For the Dressing:

2 tablespoons white balsamic vinegar
⅓ cup extra-virgin olive oil
1 fat garlic clove, finely grated
½-inch fresh ginger, peeled and finely grated
¼ teaspoon clear honey

1. Trim the carrots, but leave a bit of green tuft. If you can't find young carrots, halve or quarter larger ones lengthwise. Don't peel them, just wash them well. Place in a single layer in a baking pan. Add the olive oil, salt, and pepper, then toss to ensure the carrots are coated.
2. Select Bake. Set temperature to 400ºF (205ºC) and set time to 30 minutes. Select Start to begin preheating.
3. Once preheated, slide the pan into the oven.
4. When done, the carrots will be tender. Be careful not to overcook them.
5. Make the dressing by putting the vinegar in a bowl and whisking in all the other ingredients with a fork. Season.
6. Put the lentils into a broad shallow serving bowl with half the chili and one-third of the preserved lemon. Season a little, then toss with about one-third of the dressing.
7. Halve and core the apple or apples (there's no need to peel them) and cut into matchsticks. Throw into a large mixing bowl with the lemon juice and add the carrots. Add the rest of the preserved lemons and chili, along with two-thirds of the herbs and the remaining dressing.
8. Throw the rest of the mint and cilantro into the lentils. Put the carrot and apple mixture on top, you should still be able to see the lentils around the sides and serve.

Zucchini Quesadilla with Gouda Cheese

Prep time: 5 minutes | Cook time: 10 minutes | Serves 1

1 teaspoon olive oil
2 flour tortillas
¼ zucchini, sliced
¼ yellow bell pepper, sliced
¼ cup shredded Gouda cheese
1 tablespoon chopped cilantro
½ green onion, sliced

1. Coat the perforated pan with 1 teaspoon of olive oil.
2. Arrange a flour tortilla in the perforated pan and scatter the top with zucchini, bell pepper, Gouda cheese, cilantro, and green onion. Place the other flour tortilla on top.
3. Select Air Fry. Set temperature to 390ºF (199ºC) and set time to 10 minutes. Press Start to begin preheating.
4. Once preheated, place the pan into the oven.
5. When cooking is complete, the tortillas should be lightly browned and the vegetables should be tender. Remove from the oven and cool for 5 minutes before slicing into wedges.

Parmesan Fennel with Red Pepper

Prep time: 10 minutes | Cook time: 30 minutes | Serves 6 to 8

4 fennel bulbs
3 tablespoons extra-virgin olive oil
2 garlic cloves, finely grated
3 teaspoons fennel seeds, coarsely crushed in a mortar
3 teaspoons crushed red pepper
Sea salt flakes and freshly ground black pepper, to taste
½ cup finely grated Parmesan cheese

1. Trim the tips of the fennel bulbs, halve the bulbs and remove any thicker or discolored outer leaves. Cut each half into ¾-in thick wedges, keeping them intact at the base. Toss in a bowl with the olive oil, garlic, fennel seeds, crushed red pepper, any reserved fennel fronds, and plenty of seasoning. Put into a gratin dish and cover tightly with foil.
2. Select Bake. Set temperature to 400ºF (205ºC) and set time to 30 minutes. Select Start to begin preheating.
3. Once preheated, slide the pan into the oven.
4. Bake for about 20 minutes, then remove the foil, sprinkle on the Parmesan, and return to the oven for a final 10 minutes, or until the fennel is tender (check it by piercing a piece with a sharp knife) and the top is golden.

Keep going. -Chapter 4 Vegan and Vegetarian

Curried Cauliflower with Cashews

Prep time: 5 minutes | Cook time: 12 minutes | Serves 2

4 cups cauliflower florets (about half a large head)
1 tablespoon olive oil
1 teaspoon curry powder
Yogurt Sauce:
¼ cup plain yogurt
2 tablespoons sour cream
1 teaspoon honey
1 teaspoon lemon juice
Pinch cayenne pepper
Salt, to taste
½ cup toasted, chopped cashews, for garnish
Salt, to taste
1 tablespoon chopped fresh cilantro, plus leaves for garnish

1. In a large mixing bowl, toss the cauliflower florets with the olive oil, curry powder, and salt.
2. Place the cauliflower florets in the perforated pan.
3. Select Air Fry. Set temperature to 400ºF (205ºC) and set time to 12 minutes. Press Start to begin preheating.
4. Once preheated, place the pan into the oven. Stir the cauliflower florets twice during cooking.
5. When cooking is complete, the cauliflower should be golden brown.
6. Meanwhile, mix all the ingredients for the yogurt sauce in a small bowl and whisk to combine.
7. Remove the cauliflower from the oven and drizzle with the yogurt sauce. Scatter the toasted cashews and cilantro on top and serve immediately.

Roasted Veggie Salad with Lemon

Prep time: 5 minutes | Cook time: 20 minutes | Serves 2

1 potato, chopped
1 carrot, sliced diagonally
1 cup cherry tomatoes
½ small beetroot, sliced
¼ onion, sliced
½ teaspoon turmeric
½ teaspoon cumin
¼ teaspoon sea salt
2 tablespoons olive oil, divided
A handful of arugula
A handful of baby spinach
Juice of 1 lemon
3 tablespoons canned chickpeas, for serving
Parmesan shavings, for serving

1. Combine the potato, carrot, cherry tomatoes, beetroot, onion, turmeric, cumin, salt, and 1 tablespoon of olive oil in a large bowl and toss until well coated.
2. Arrange the veggies in the perforated pan.
3. Select Roast. Set temperature to 370ºF (188ºC) and set time to 20 minutes. Press Start to begin preheating.
4. Once preheated, place the pan into the oven. Stir the vegetables halfway through.
5. When cooking is complete, the potatoes should be golden brown.
6. Let the veggies cool for 5 to 10 minutes in the oven.
7. Put the arugula, baby spinach, lemon juice, and remaining 1 tablespoon of olive oil in a salad bowl and stir to combine. Mix in the roasted veggies and toss well.
8. Scatter the chickpeas and Parmesan shavings on top and serve immediately.

Roasted Veggies with Honey-Garlic Glaze

Prep time: 15 minutes | Cook time: 20 minutes | Makes 3 cups

Glaze:
2 tablespoons raw honey
2 teaspoons minced garlic
¼ teaspoon dried marjoram
¼ teaspoon dried basil
¼ teaspoon dried oregano
⅛ teaspoon dried sage
⅛ teaspoon dried rosemary
⅛ teaspoon dried thyme
½ teaspoon salt
¼ teaspoon ground black pepper
Veggies:
3 to 4 medium red potatoes, cut into 1- to 2-inch pieces
1 small zucchini, cut into 1- to 2-inch pieces
1 small carrot, sliced into ¼-inch rounds
1 (10.5-ounce / 298-g) package cherry tomatoes, halved
1 cup sliced mushrooms
3 tablespoons olive oil

1. Combine the honey, garlic, marjoram, basil, oregano, sage, rosemary, thyme, salt, and pepper in a small bowl and stir to mix well. Set aside.
2. Place the red potatoes, zucchini, carrot, cherry tomatoes, and mushroom in a large bowl. Drizzle with the olive oil and toss to coat.
3. Pour the veggies into the perforated pan.
4. Select Roast. Set temperature to 380ºF (193ºC) and set time to 15 minutes. Press Start to begin preheating.
5. Once preheated, place the pan into the oven. Stir the veggies halfway through.
6. When cooking is complete, the vegetables should be tender.
7. When ready, transfer the roasted veggies to the large bowl. Pour the honey mixture over the veggies, tossing to coat.
8. Spread out the veggies in a baking pan and place in the oven.
9. Increase the temperature to 390ºF (199ºC) and set time to 5 minutes on Roast. Place the pan into the oven.
10. When cooking is complete, the veggies should be tender and glazed. Serve warm.

Balsamic-Glazed Beets

Prep time: 5 minutes | Cook time: 10 minutes | Serves 2

Beet:
2 beets, cubed
2 tablespoons olive oil
2 springs rosemary, chopped
Salt and black pepper, to taste

Balsamic Glaze:
⅓ cup balsamic vinegar
1 tablespoon honey

1. Combine the beets, olive oil, rosemary, salt, and pepper in a mixing bowl and toss until the beets are completely coated.
2. Place the beets in the perforated pan.
3. Select Air Fry. Set temperature to 400°F (205°C) and set time to 10 minutes. Press Start to begin preheating.
4. Once preheated, place the pan into the oven. Stir the vegetables halfway through.
5. When cooking is complete, the beets should be crisp and browned at the edges.
6. Meanwhile, make the balsamic glaze: Place the balsamic vinegar and honey in a small saucepan and bring to a boil over medium heat. When the sauce boils, reduce the heat to medium-low heat and simmer until the liquid is reduced by half.
7. When ready, remove the beets from the oven to a platter. Pour the balsamic glaze over the top and serve immediately.

Garlic Tofu with Basil

Prep time: 5 minutes | Cook time: 10 minutes | Serves 2

1 tablespoon soy sauce
1 tablespoon water
⅓ teaspoon garlic powder
⅓ teaspoon onion powder
⅓ teaspoon dried oregano
⅓ teaspoon dried basil
Black pepper, to taste
6 ounces (170 g) extra firm tofu, pressed and cubed

1. In a large mixing bowl, whisk together the soy sauce, water, garlic powder, onion powder, oregano, basil, and black pepper. Add the tofu cubes, stirring to coat, and let them marinate for 10 minutes.
2. Arrange the tofu in the perforated pan.
3. Select Bake. Set temperature to 390°F (199°C) and set time to 10 minutes. Press Start to begin preheating.
4. Once preheated, place the pan into the oven. Flip the tofu halfway through the cooking time.
5. When cooking is complete, the tofu should be crisp.
6. Remove from the oven to a plate and serve.

Oregano Eggplants with Chili Anchovy Sauce

Prep time: 15 minutes | Cook time: 40 minutes | Serves 4

For the Eggplants:
4¾ pounds (2.2 kg) globe eggplants
4 tablespoons extra-virgin olive oil
Leaves from 3 oregano sprigs, torn
Sea salt flakes and freshly ground black pepper, to taste
Juice of ½ lemon
Good crusty bread, to serve

For the Sauce:
Leaves from 2 rosemary sprigs
2 garlic cloves, chopped
14 anchovies, drained of oil
Juice of 1 lemon, or to taste
4 tablespoons extra-virgin olive oil
1 red Fresno chili, halved, seeded, and chopped, plus more if you want it hotter

1. Halve the eggplants and cut a cross-hatched pattern in the flesh of each one, without cutting all the way through to the skin. Put them on to a rimmed baking sheet—line it with parchment paper or foil if you want and smear the olive oil evenly all over the cut surfaces. Toss in the oregano, too, and salt and pepper. Turn the eggplants over with your hands, making sure the seasoning and some of the herb leaves go into the flesh.
2. Select Bake. Set temperature to 400°F (205°C) and set time to 40 minutes. Select Start to begin preheating.
3. Once preheated, slide the baking sheet into the oven.
4. When done, the eggplants will be completely tender right through and golden. Squeeze the lemon juice over the top.
5. To make the sauce, pound the rosemary and garlic in a mortar, then add the anchovies and crush to a paste. Gradually add the lemon juice and then the olive oil, a little at a time, grinding as you go. You aren't making a mayonnaise—so don't expect this to emulsify, you'll be left with a lumpy "sauce"—but the pounding melds all the elements together. Add the chili and set aside. The longer the sauce sits with the chili, the hotter it will become.
6. Serve the eggplants with the sauce, either on the side or spooned over the top. You need good bread with this, to mop up all the juices.

Keep going. -Chapter 4 Vegan and Vegetarian

Buttery Eggplant and Tomato with Freekeh

Prep time: 20 minutes | Cook time: 30 minutes | Serves 4

For the Vegetables and Freekeh:
- 2¼ pounds (1 kg) baby eggplants
- 2¼ pounds (1 kg) plum tomatoes
- 7 tablespoons unsalted butter
- 12 garlic cloves, thickly sliced
- Sea salt flakes and freshly ground black pepper, to taste
- A little light brown sugar (optional, only if your tomatoes aren't sweet)
- Scant 2 cups cooked freekeh
- Plain yogurt, to serve
- Good bread, to serve

For the Koch-Kocha:
- ½ green bell pepper, halved, seeded, and roughly chopped
- 4 cups cilantro leaves
- 1 red Fresno chili and 1 green chili, halved and deseeded
- 1¼-inch fresh ginger, peeled and finely grated
- Juice of 1 lime
- ½ tablespoon cider vinegar or white wine vinegar
- 1 garlic clove, finely grated
- 1 teaspoon ground cumin
- 1 teaspoon ground cardamom
- ¼ teaspoon grains of paradise, crushed
- ½ teaspoon ajwain, crushed
- 7 tablespoons extra-virgin olive oil

1. Pierce each eggplant with the tip of a knife, you don't have to remove the tops and cut the tomatoes in half. Put them into a baking pan in a single layer.
2. Melt the butter in a saucepan and add the garlic. Cook over a low heat for a few minutes, then pour the butter all over the vegetables, turning them over. Season and sprinkle each tomato half with a little sugar if they aren't very sweet; if you have great tomatoes you won't need it.
3. Select Bake. Set temperature to 400ºF (205ºC) and set time to 40 minutes. Select Start to begin preheating.
4. Once preheated, slide the pan into the oven. Flip the eggplants halfway through the cooking time.
5. For the koch-kocha sauce, simply put everything into a food processor and whizz until smooth.
6. After 30 minutes, add the freekeh to the baking pan, pushing it down under the vegetables. Return to the oven for a final 10 minutes, or until the tomatoes are caramelized, the eggplants are tender right through, and the freekeh has become slightly sticky at the edges. Serve the dish with the sauce, a big bowl of plain yogurt, and good bread.

Mozzarella Tomato-Stuffed Squash

Prep time: 5 minutes | Cook time: 30 minutes | Serves 4

- 1 pound (454 g) butternut squash, ends trimmed
- 2 teaspoons olive oil, divided
- 6 grape tomatoes, halved
- 1 poblano pepper, cut into strips
- Salt and black pepper, to taste
- ¼ cup grated Mozzarella cheese

1. Using a large knife, cut the squash in half lengthwise on a flat work surface. This recipe just needs half of the squash. Scoop out the flesh to make room for the stuffing. Coat the squash half with 1 teaspoon of olive oil.
2. Put the squash half in the perforated pan.
3. Select Bake. Set temperature to 350ºF (180ºC) and set time to 15 minutes. Press Start to begin preheating.
4. Once preheated, place the pan into the oven. Flip the squash halfway through.
5. When cooking is complete, the squash should be tender.
6. Meanwhile, thoroughly combine the tomatoes, poblano pepper, remaining 1 teaspoon of olive oil, salt, and pepper in a bowl.
7. Remove the pan from the oven and spoon the tomato mixture into the squash. Return to the oven.
8. Select Roast. Set time to 15 minutes. Place the pan into the oven
9. After 12 minutes, remove the pan from the oven. Scatter the Mozzarella cheese on top. Return the pan to the oven and continue cooking.
10. When cooking is complete, the tomatoes should be soft and the cheese should be melted.
11. Cool for 5 minutes before serving.

Chapter 5 Vegetable Sides

Garlic Potatoes with Heavy Cream

Prep time: 5 minutes | Cook time: 15 to 20 minutes | Serves 4

2 cup sliced frozen potatoes, thawed
3 cloves garlic, minced
Pinch salt
Freshly ground black pepper, to taste
¾ cup heavy cream

1. Toss the potatoes with the garlic, salt, and black pepper in a baking pan until evenly coated. Pour the heavy cream over the top.
2. Select Bake. Set temperature to 380ºF (193ºC) and set time to 15 minutes. Press Start to begin preheating.
3. Once preheated, place the pan into the oven.
4. When cooking is complete, the potatoes should be tender and the top golden brown. Check for doneness and bake for another 5 minutes if needed. Remove from the oven and serve hot.

Sesame Green Beans with Sriracha

Prep time: 5 minutes | Cook time: 8 minutes | Serves 4

1 tablespoon reduced-sodium soy sauce or tamari
½ tablespoon Sriracha sauce
4 teaspoons toasted sesame oil, divided
12 ounces (340 g) trimmed green beans
½ tablespoon toasted sesame seeds

1. Whisk together the soy sauce, Sriracha sauce, and 1 teaspoon of sesame oil in a small bowl until smooth. Set aside.
2. Toss the green beans with the remaining sesame oil in a large bowl until evenly coated.
3. Place the green beans in the perforated pan in a single layer.
4. Select Air Fry. Set temperature to 375ºF (190ºC) and set time to 8 minutes. Press Start to begin preheating.
5. Once preheated, place the pan into the oven. Stir the green beans halfway through the cooking time.
6. When cooking is complete, the green beans should be lightly charred and tender. Remove from the oven to a platter. Pour the prepared sauce over the top of green beans and toss well. Serve sprinkled with the toasted sesame seeds.

Breaded Asparagus Fries

Prep time: 15 minutes | Cook time: 6 minutes | Serves 4

2 egg whites
¼ cup water
¼ cup plus 2 tablespoons grated Parmesan cheese, divided
¾ cup panko bread crumbs
¼ teaspoon salt
12 ounces (340 g) fresh asparagus spears, woody ends trimmed
Cooking spray

1. In a shallow dish, whisk together the egg whites and water until slightly foamy. In a separate shallow dish, thoroughly combine ¼ cup of Parmesan cheese, bread crumbs, and salt.
2. Dip the asparagus in the egg white, then roll in the cheese mixture to coat well.
3. Place the asparagus in the perforated pan in a single layer, leaving space between each spear. Spritz the asparagus with cooking spray.
4. Select Air Fry. Set temperature to 390ºF (199ºC) and set time to 6 minutes. Press Start to begin preheating.
5. Once preheated, place the pan into the oven.
6. When cooking is complete, the asparagus should be golden brown and crisp. Remove the pan from the oven. Sprinkle with the remaining 2 tablespoons of cheese and serve hot.

Balsamic Asparagus

Prep time: 5 minutes | Cook time: 10 minutes | Serves 4

1 pound (454 g) asparagus, woody ends trimmed
2 tablespoons olive oil
1 tablespoon balsamic vinegar
2 teaspoons minced garlic
Salt and freshly ground black pepper, to taste

1. In a large shallow bowl, toss the asparagus with the olive oil, balsamic vinegar, garlic, salt, and pepper until thoroughly coated. Put the asparagus in the perforated pan.
2. Select Roast. Set temperature to 400ºF (205ºC) and set time to 10 minutes. Press Start to begin preheating.
3. Once preheated, place the pan into the oven. Flip the asparagus with tongs halfway through the cooking time.
4. When cooking is complete, the asparagus should be crispy. Remove the pan from the oven and serve warm.

Garlic Butternut Squash Croquettes

Prep time: 5 minutes | Cook time: 17 minutes | Serves 4

⅓ butternut squash, peeled and grated
⅓ cup all-purpose flour
2 eggs, whisked
4 cloves garlic, minced
1½ tablespoons olive oil
1 teaspoon fine sea salt
⅓ teaspoon freshly ground black pepper, or more to taste
⅓ teaspoon dried sage
A pinch of ground allspice

1. Line the perforated pan with parchment paper. Set aside.
2. In a mixing bowl, stir together all the ingredients until well combined.
3. Make the squash croquettes: Use a small cookie scoop to drop tablespoonfuls of the squash mixture onto a lightly floured surface and shape into balls with your hands. Transfer them to the perforated pan.
4. Select Air Fry. Set temperature to 345°F (174°C) and set time to 17 minutes. Press Start to begin preheating.
5. Once preheated, place the pan into the oven.
6. When cooking is complete, the squash croquettes should be golden brown. Remove from the oven to a plate and serve warm.

Brown Sugar Acorn Squash

Prep time: 5 minutes | Cook time: 15 minutes | Serves 2

1 medium acorn squash, halved crosswise and deseeded
1 teaspoon coconut oil
1 teaspoon light brown sugar
Few dashes of ground cinnamon
Few dashes of ground nutmeg

1. On a clean work surface, rub the cut sides of the acorn squash with coconut oil. Scatter with the brown sugar, cinnamon, and nutmeg.
2. Put the squash halves in the perforated pan, cut-side up.
3. Select Air Fry. Set temperature to 325°F (163°C) and set time to 15 minutes. Press Start to begin preheating.
4. Once preheated, place the pan into the oven.
5. When cooking is complete, the squash halves should be just tender when pierced in the center with a paring knife. Remove the pan from the oven. Rest for 5 to 10 minutes and serve warm.

Cheddar Broccoli Gratin

Prep time: 5 minutes | Cook time: 14 minutes | Serves 2

⅓ cup fat-free milk
1 tablespoon all-purpose or gluten-free flour
½ tablespoon olive oil
½ teaspoon ground sage
¼ teaspoon kosher salt
⅛ teaspoon freshly ground black pepper
2 cups roughly chopped broccoli florets
6 tablespoons shredded Cheddar cheese
2 tablespoons panko bread crumbs
1 tablespoon grated Parmesan cheese
Olive oil spray

1. Spritz a baking dish with olive oil spray.
2. Mix the milk, flour, olive oil, sage, salt, and pepper in a medium bowl and whisk to combine. Stir in the broccoli florets, Cheddar cheese, bread crumbs, and Parmesan cheese and toss to coat.
3. Pour the broccoli mixture into the prepared baking dish.
4. Select Bake. Set temperature to 330°F (166°C) and set time to 14 minutes. Press Start to begin preheating.
5. Once preheated, place the baking dish into the oven.
6. When cooking is complete, the top should be golden brown and the broccoli should be tender. Remove from the oven and serve immediately.

Garlic Zucchini Sticks

Prep time: 5 minutes | Cook time: 14 minutes | Serves 4

2 small zucchini, cut into 2-inch × ½-inch sticks
3 tablespoons chickpea flour
2 teaspoons arrowroot (or cornstarch)
½ teaspoon garlic granules
¼ teaspoon sea salt
⅛ teaspoon freshly ground black pepper
1 tablespoon water
Cooking spray

1. Combine the zucchini sticks with the chickpea flour, arrowroot, garlic granules, salt, and pepper in a medium bowl and toss to coat. Add the water and stir to mix well.
2. Spritz the perforated pan with cooking spray and spread out the zucchini sticks in the pan. Mist the zucchini sticks with cooking spray.
3. Select Air Fry. Set temperature to 392°F (200°C) and set time to 14 minutes. Press Start to begin preheating.
4. Once preheated, place the pan into the oven. Stir the sticks halfway through the cooking time.
5. When cooking is complete, the zucchini sticks should be crispy and nicely browned. Remove from the oven and serve warm.

Roasted Potatoes with Rosemary

Prep time: 5 minutes | Cook time: 20 minutes | Serves 4

1½ pounds (680 g) small red potatoes, cut into 1-inch cubes
2 tablespoons olive oil
2 tablespoons minced fresh rosemary
1 tablespoon minced garlic
1 teaspoon salt, plus additional as needed
½ teaspoon freshly ground black pepper, plus additional as needed

1. Toss the potato cubes with the olive oil, rosemary, garlic, salt, and pepper in a large bowl until thoroughly coated.
2. Arrange the potato cubes in the perforated pan in a single layer.
3. Select Roast. Set temperature to 400ºF (205ºC) and set time to 20 minutes. Press Start to begin preheating.
4. Once preheated, place the pan into the oven. Stir the potatoes a few times during cooking for even cooking.
5. When cooking is complete, the potatoes should be tender. Remove from the oven to a plate. Taste and add additional salt and pepper as needed.

Lime Sweet Potatoes with Allspice

Prep time: 5 minutes | Cook time: 22 minutes | Serves 4

5 garnet sweet potatoes, peeled and diced
1½ tablespoons fresh lime juice
1 tablespoon butter, melted
2 teaspoons tamarind paste
1½ teaspoon ground allspice
⅓ teaspoon white pepper
½ teaspoon turmeric powder
A few drops liquid stevia

1. In a large mixing bowl, combine all the ingredients and toss until the sweet potatoes are evenly coated. Place the sweet potatoes in the perforated pan.
2. Select Air Fry. Set temperature to 400ºF (205ºC) and set time to 22 minutes. Press Start to begin preheating.
3. Once preheated, place the pan into the oven. Stir the potatoes twice during cooking.
4. When cooking is complete, the potatoes should be crispy on the outside and soft on the inside. Let the potatoes cool for 5 minutes before serving.

Garlic Broccoli with Parmesan

Prep time: 5 minutes | Cook time: 4 minutes | Serves 4

1 pound (454 g) broccoli florets
1 medium shallot, minced
2 tablespoons olive oil
2 tablespoons unsalted butter, melted
2 teaspoons minced garlic
¼ cup grated Parmesan cheese

1. Combine the broccoli florets with the shallot, olive oil, butter, garlic, and Parmesan cheese in a medium bowl and toss until the broccoli florets are thoroughly coated.
2. Place the broccoli florets in the perforated pan in a single layer.
3. Select Roast. Set temperature to 360ºF (182ºC) and set time to 4 minutes. Press Start to begin preheating.
4. Once preheated, place the pan into the oven.
5. When cooking is complete, the broccoli florets should be crisp-tender. Remove from the oven and serve warm.

Parmesan Corn on the Cob

Prep time: 10 minutes | Cook time: 15 minutes | Serves 4

2 tablespoon olive oil, divided
2 tablespoons grated Parmesan cheese
1 teaspoon garlic powder
1 teaspoon chili powder
1 teaspoon ground cumin
1 teaspoon paprika
1 teaspoon salt
¼ teaspoon cayenne pepper (optional)
4 ears fresh corn, shucked

1. Grease the perforated pan with 1 tablespoon of olive oil. Set aside.
2. Combine the Parmesan cheese, garlic powder, chili powder, cumin, paprika, salt, and cayenne pepper (if desired) in a small bowl and stir to mix well.
3. Lightly coat the ears of corn with the remaining 1 tablespoon of olive oil. Rub the cheese mixture all over the ears of corn until completely coated.
4. Arrange the ears of corn in the greased pan in a single layer.
5. Select Air Fry. Set temperature to 400ºF (205ºC) and set time to 15 minutes. Press Start to begin preheating.
6. Once preheated, place the pan into the oven. Flip the ears of corn halfway through the cooking time.
7. When cooking is complete, they should be lightly browned. Remove from the oven and let them cool for 5 minutes before serving.

Garlic-Lime Shishito Peppers

Prep time: 5 minutes | Cook time: 9 minutes | Serves 3

½ pound (227 g) shishito peppers, rinsed
Cooking spray
Sauce:
1 tablespoon tamari or shoyu
2 teaspoons fresh lime juice
2 large garlic cloves, minced

1. Spritz the perforated pan with cooking spray.
2. Place the shishito peppers in the perforated pan and spritz them with cooking spray.
3. Select Roast. Set temperature to 392ºF (200ºC) and set time to 9 minutes. Press Start to begin preheating.
4. Once preheated, place the pan into the oven.
5. Meanwhile, whisk together all the ingredients for the sauce in a large bowl. Set aside.
6. After 3 minutes, remove the pan from the oven. Flip the peppers and spritz them with cooking spray. Return to the oven and continue cooking.
7. After another 3 minutes, remove the pan from the oven. Flip the peppers and spray with cooking spray. Return to the oven and continue roasting for 3 minutes more, or until the peppers are blistered and nicely browned.
8. When cooking is complete, remove the peppers from the oven to the bowl of sauce. Toss to coat well and serve immediately.

Citrus Carrots with Balsamic Glaze

Prep time: 5 minutes | Cook time: 18 minutes | Serves 3

3 medium-size carrots, cut into 2-inch × ½-inch sticks
1 tablespoon orange juice
2 teaspoons balsamic vinegar
1 teaspoon maple syrup
1 teaspoon avocado oil
½ teaspoon dried rosemary
¼ teaspoon sea salt
¼ teaspoon lemon zest

1. Put the carrots in a baking pan and sprinkle with the orange juice, balsamic vinegar, maple syrup, avocado oil, rosemary, sea salt, finished by the lemon zest. Toss well.
2. Select Roast. Set temperature to 392ºF (200ºC) and set time to 18 minutes. Press Start to begin preheating.
3. Once preheated, place the pan into the oven. Stir the carrots several times during the cooking process.
4. When cooking is complete, the carrots should be nicely glazed and tender. Remove from the oven and serve hot.

Greek Potatoes with Chives

Prep time: 5 minutes | Cook time: 35 minutes | Serves 4

4 (7-ounce / 198-g) russet potatoes, rinsed
Olive oil spray
½ teaspoon kosher salt, divided
½ cup 2% plain Greek yogurt
¼ cup minced fresh chives
Freshly ground black pepper, to taste

1. Pat the potatoes dry and pierce them all over with a fork. Spritz the potatoes with olive oil spray. Sprinkle with ¼ teaspoon of the salt.
2. Transfer the potatoes to the perforated pan.
3. Select Bake. Set temperature to 400ºF (205ºC) and set time to 35 minutes. Press Start to begin preheating.
4. Once preheated, place the pan into the oven.
5. When cooking is complete, the potatoes should be fork-tender. Remove from the oven and split open the potatoes. Top with the yogurt, chives, the remaining ¼ teaspoon of salt, and finish with the black pepper. Serve immediately.

Breaded Brussels Sprouts with Paprika

Prep time: 5 minutes | Cook time: 15 minutes | Serves 4

1 pound (454 g) Brussels sprouts, halved
1 cup bread crumbs
2 tablespoons grated Grana Padano cheese
1 tablespoon paprika
2 tablespoons canola oil
1 tablespoon chopped sage

1. Line the perforated pan with parchment paper. Set aside.
2. In a small bowl, thoroughly mix the bread crumbs, cheese, and paprika. In a large bowl, place the Brussels sprouts and drizzle the canola oil over the top. Sprinkle with the bread crumb mixture and toss to coat.
3. Transfer the Brussels sprouts to the prepared pan.
4. Select Roast. Set temperature to 400ºF (205ºC) and set time to 15 minutes. Press Start to begin preheating.
5. Once preheated, place the pan into the oven. Stir the Brussels a few times during cooking.
6. When cooking is complete, the Brussels sprouts should be lightly browned and crisp. Transfer the Brussels sprouts to a plate and sprinkle the sage on top before serving.

Garlic Zucchini Crisps
Prep time: 5 minutes | Cook time: 14 minutes | Serves 4

2 zucchini, sliced into ¼- to ½-inch-thick rounds (about 2 cups)
¼ teaspoon garlic granules
⅛ teaspoon sea salt
Freshly ground black pepper, to taste (optional)
Cooking spray

1. Spritz the perforated pan with cooking spray.
2. Put the zucchini rounds in the perforated pan, spreading them out as much as possible. Top with a sprinkle of garlic granules, sea salt, and black pepper (if desired). Spritz the zucchini rounds with cooking spray.
3. Select Roast. Set temperature to 392ºF (200ºC) and set time to 14 minutes. Press Start to begin preheating.
4. Once preheated, place the pan into the oven. Flip the zucchini rounds halfway through.
5. When cooking is complete, the zucchini rounds should be crisp-tender. Remove from the oven. Let them rest for 5 minutes and serve.

Maple Garlic Brussels Sprouts
Prep time: 10 minutes | Cook time: 11 minutes | Serves 4

2½ cups trimmed Brussels sprouts
Sauce:
1½ teaspoons mellow white miso
1½ tablespoons maple syrup
1 teaspoon toasted sesame oil
1 teaspoons tamari or shoyu
1 teaspoon grated fresh ginger
2 large garlic cloves, finely minced
¼ to ½ teaspoon red chili flakes
Cooking spray

1. Spritz the perforated pan with cooking spray.
2. Arrange the Brussels sprouts in the perforated pan and spray them with cooking spray.
3. Select Air Fry. Set temperature to 392ºF (200ºC) and set time to 11 minutes. Press Start to begin preheating.
4. Once preheated, place the pan into the oven.
5. After 6 minutes, remove the pan from the oven. Flip the Brussels sprouts and spritz with cooking spray again. Return to the oven and continue cooking for 5 minutes more.
6. Meanwhile, make the sauce: Stir together the miso and maple syrup in a medium bowl. Add the sesame oil, tamari, ginger, garlic, and red chili flakes and whisk to combine.
7. When cooking is complete, the Brussels sprouts should be crisp-tender. Transfer the Brussels sprouts to the bowl of sauce, tossing to coat well. If you prefer a saltier taste, you can add additional ½ teaspoon tamari to the sauce. Serve immediately.

Garlicky Cabbage with Red Pepper
Prep time: 5 minutes | Cook time: 7 minutes | Serves 4

1 head cabbage, sliced into 1-inch-thick ribbons
1 tablespoon olive oil
1 teaspoon garlic powder
1 teaspoon red pepper flakes
1 teaspoon salt
1 teaspoon freshly ground black pepper

1. Toss the cabbage with the olive oil, garlic powder, red pepper flakes, salt, and pepper in a large mixing bowl until well coated.
2. Transfer the cabbage to the perforated pan.
3. Select Roast. Set temperature to 350ºF (180ºC) and set time to 7 minutes. Press Start to begin preheating.
4. Once preheated, place the pan into the oven. Flip the cabbage with tongs halfway through the cooking time.
5. When cooking is complete, the cabbage should be crisp. Remove from the oven to a plate and serve warm.

Corn Casserole with Swiss Cheese
Prep time: 5 minutes | Cook time: 15 minutes | Serves 4

2 cups frozen yellow corn
1 egg, beaten
3 tablespoons flour
½ cup grated Swiss or Havarti cheese
½ cup light cream
¼ cup milk
Pinch salt
Freshly ground black pepper, to taste
2 tablespoons butter, cut into cubes
Nonstick cooking spray

1. Spritz a baking pan with nonstick cooking spray.
2. Stir together the remaining ingredients except the butter in a medium bowl until well incorporated. Transfer the mixture to the prepared baking pan and scatter with the butter cubes.
3. Select Bake. Set temperature to 320ºF (160ºC) and set time to 15 minutes. Press Start to begin preheating.
4. Once preheated, place the pan into the oven.
5. When cooking is complete, the top should be golden brown and a toothpick inserted in the center should come out clean. Remove the pan from the oven. Let the casserole cool for 5 minutes before slicing into wedges and serving.

Chapter 6 Meats

Lamb Leg with Root Vegetable
Prep time: 10 minutes | Cook time: 1 hour | Serves 6 to 8

2¼ cups finely grated pecorino cheese
6 garlic cloves, finely grated
Sea salt flakes and freshly ground black pepper, to taste
3 tablespoons extra-virgin olive oil, plus more if needed
⅓ cup basil leaves, plus more to serve (optional)
4 pound (1.8 kg) leg of lamb
2 medium red onions, cut into wedges
1⅓ pounds (605 g) small waxy potatoes, scrubbed, then halved or quartered, depending on size
¾ pound (340 g) red and yellow cherry tomatoes, halved or quartered
Generous 1 cup white wine

1. Put the cheese, garlic, and some salt into a mortar and pound to a rough purée, gradually adding the olive oil. Tear the basil leaves, add them to the mortar, and pound them, too.
2. Place the leg of lamb in a baking pan. Make deep incisions all over it and push the paste from the mortar down into them. You can also loosen the meat around the bone to make a pocket and push the paste into that, too. Season all over and put into the oven.
3. Select Bake. Set temperature to 400ºF (205ºC) and set time to 1 hour. Select Start to begin preheating.
4. Once preheated, slide the pan into the oven.
5. After 15 minutes, reduce the temperature to 375ºF (190ºC). Add the onions, potatoes, and tomatoes to the baking pan, toss them in the fat in the pan, adding a little more oil if it's needed to moisten them, then season and bake for a final 45 minutes, adding the wine after 20 minutes. The lamb will be pink. If you prefer it more well done, cook it for a little longer.
6. Remove the lamb to a plate, cover with foil, insulate well (I use old towels or tea towels), and leave to rest for 15 minutes. If the potatoes are tender, cover them and keep warm in a low oven while the lamb rests; if they're still a bit firm, increase the oven temperature to 400ºF (205ºC), return the vegetables to the oven, uncovered, and cook until they're ready.
7. Serve the lamb with the potatoes, tomatoes, and onions, scattered with a few basil leaves, if you like.

Beef Rump with Red Wine Gravy
Prep time: 15 minutes | Cook time: 2 hours | Serves 6 to 8

For the Roast:
1 (3- to 3½-pound / 1.4- to 1.6-kg) boneless rump roast, at room temperature
1 tablespoon olive oil
4 garlic cloves, peeled and halved
1½ tablespoons Italian seasoning
1 teaspoon kosher salt
1 teaspoon freshly ground black pepper

For the Red Wine Gravy:
2 tablespoons unsalted butter
3 tablespoons all-purpose flour
¾ cup beef broth
½ cup red wine
Kosher salt, to taste
Freshly ground black pepper, to taste

Make the Roast
1. Brush the roast all over with the olive oil. With the tip of a sharp knife, cut eight slits into the roast and insert a garlic clove half into each slit. Sprinkle the Italian seasoning, salt, and pepper all over the roast and place the roast directly on a rimmed baking sheet, fat-side up.
2. Select Bake. Set temperature to 350ºF (180ºC) and set time to 20 minutes. Select Start to begin preheating.
3. Once preheated, slide the pan into the oven.
4. When done, the outside of the meat will be browned.
5. Lower the temperature to 200ºF (93ºC) and bake for 1 hour 30 minutes more, until the internal temperature is 135ºF (57ºC) to 140ºF (60ºC). Remove the roast from the oven, tent loosely with aluminum foil, and let rest for 10 minutes.

Make the Red Wine Gravy
1. While the roast rests, carefully remove the pan with the drippings from the oven and reserve.
2. In a medium saucepan over medium-high heat, melt the butter.
3. Add the flour and cook for 3 to 5 minutes, whisking constantly, until the mixture turns golden brown and becomes thick and smooth.
4. Add the pan drippings, beef broth, and red wine. Cook over medium-high heat for 8 to 10 minutes, stirring frequently, until the sauce thickens to the desired consistency. Carve the roast thinly and serve with the gravy.

Sherry Lamb Leg and Autumn Vegetable

Prep time: 10 minutes | Cook time: 3 hours | Serves 8

8 garlic cloves, plus 1 head of garlic, cloves separated
Sea salt flakes and freshly ground black pepper, to taste
Large pinch of saffron threads (optional)
Leaves from 8 thyme sprigs, plus 4 whole thyme sprigs
½ cup extra-virgin olive oil
4½ pounds (2 kg) leg of lamb
1 large onion, cut into wedges
⅔ pound (302 g) thin bunched carrots, or, if you can only find thick ones, halve or quarter them lengthwise
1 pound (454 g) waxy potatoes, scrubbed and sliced (no need to peel)
1¾ cups amontillado sherry, plus more if needed

1. Crush the 8 cloves of garlic in a mortar and pestle with some sea salt flakes (the salt flakes act as an abrasive). Grind in the saffron, if using; it will add its flavor, and of course its gorgeous color, but the dish is just as delicious without. Add the thyme leaves, pepper, and olive oil, to make a loose paste.
2. Make incisions all over the lamb with a knife and slightly loosen the meat around the bone end, too. Push the garlic and herb paste down into these incisions, into the space around the bone and all over the roast. Put into a large baking pan; you will need to add all the vegetables later, too, so there has to be room for them as well. Season all over.
3. Select Bake. Set temperature to 400°F (205°C) and set time to 3 hours. Select Start to begin preheating.
4. Once preheated, slide the pan into the oven.
5. After 30 minutes, remove the pan from the oven. Put the onion, carrots, the rest of the garlic cloves, potatoes, and thyme sprigs under and around the lamb. Bring the sherry to just under a boil, then pour it over. Cover tightly with a double layer of foil, or the lid, and return to the oven.
6. Reduce the temperature to 350°F (180°C). Bake for 2½ hours, turning the lamb over about 3 times and checking on the sherry, too. Most of it will be absorbed during cooking, but don't let it get dry. If there are a lot of juices, remove the foil or uncover the pot 45 minutes before the end of cooking time, so they can reduce. The lamb should be cooked to softness, if it isn't, cook it for a little longer, and the vegetables completely tender. Serve the lamb with the vegetables and the sherry juices.

Garlic Pork Belly with Bay Leaves

Prep time: 10 minutes | Cook time: 30 minutes | Serves 4

1 pound (454 g) pork belly, cut into three thick chunks
6 garlic cloves
2 bay leaves
2 tablespoons soy sauce
1 teaspoon kosher salt
1 teaspoon ground black pepper
3 cups water
Cooking spray

1. Put all the ingredients in a pressure cooker, then put the lid on and cook on high for 15 minutes.
2. Natural release the pressure and release any remaining pressure, transfer the tender pork belly on a clean work surface. Allow to cool under room temperature until you can handle.
3. Generously Spritz the perforated pan with cooking spray.
4. Cut each chunk into two slices, then put the pork slices in the pan.
5. Select Air Fry. Set temperature to 400°F (205°C) and set time to 15 minutes. Press Start to begin preheating.
6. Once preheated, place the pan into the oven.
7. After 7 minutes, remove the pan from the oven. Flip the pork. Return the pan to the oven and continue cooking.
8. When cooking is complete, the pork fat should be crispy.
9. Serve immediately.

Paprika Lamb Chops with Sage

Prep time: 5 minutes | Cook time: 25 minutes | Serves 4

1 cup all-purpose flour
2 teaspoons dried sage leaves
2 teaspoons garlic powder
1 tablespoon mild paprika
1 tablespoon salt
4 (6-ounce / 170-g) bone-in lamb shoulder chops, fat trimmed
Cooking spray

1. Spritz the perforated pan with cooking spray.
2. Combine the flour, sage leaves, garlic powder, paprika, and salt in a large bowl. Stir to mix well. Dunk in the lamb chops and toss to coat well.
3. Arrange the lamb chops in the pan and spritz with cooking spray.
4. Select Air Fry. Set temperature to 375°F (190°C) and set time to 25 minutes. Press Start to begin preheating.
5. Once preheated, place the pan into the oven. Flip the chops halfway through.
6. When cooking is complete, the chops should be golden brown and reaches your desired doneness.
7. Serve immediately.

Lamb Shoulder with Lemony Caper Relish

Prep time: 20 minutes | Cook time: 4 hours | Serves 6

For the Lamb:
2 tablespoons lemon thyme leaves, plus another dozen whole sprigs
6 rosemary sprigs, leaves removed and chopped, plus another dozen whole sprigs
1 tablespoon dried oregano
1 tablespoon sea salt flakes
Freshly ground black pepper, to taste
2 tablespoons extra-virgin olive oil
4½ pounds (2 kg) lamb shoulder on the bone
1 head of garlic, cloves separated
Juice of 1 lemon
1 cup dry white wine
2 tablespoons honey (a floral or herbal type, such as lavender or thyme)

For the Relish:
2 unwaxed lemons
¼ cup extra-virgin olive oil
2 tablespoons honey
1 tablespoon white balsamic vinegar
2 tablespoons lemon juice, or to taste
2 tablespoons capers, drained, rinsed, and patted dry
½ small garlic clove, finely grated
Leaves from 12 mint sprigs, torn

1. Put all the herb leaves (not the whole sprigs,) and the dried oregano in a mortar with the salt, pepper, and olive oil and grind everything together. Score the lamb fat without cutting into the meat, and rub the herb mixture all over it, pushing it down into the slashes. Scatter the herb sprigs and all the garlic cloves in a baking pan that will hold the lamb snugly. Set the lamb on top; the garlic and the herbs must be underneath, or they will burn. Squeeze the lemon juice over, then pour half the wine into the pan. Cover with a double layer of foil, sealing it tightly around the edges.
2. Select Bake. Set temperature to 300ºF (150ºC) and set time to 4 hours. Select Start to begin preheating.
3. Once preheated, slide the pan into the oven.
4. Check every so often to see whether you need to add any more wine (just enough to keep the pan moist). The meat is ready when it is falling off the bone. When there are just 30 minutes cooking time left, drizzle the honey on top. Once it's cooked, lay some towels over the foil and leave the lamb to rest for 15 minutes.
5. To make the relish, remove the lemon zest from 1 lemon with a zester, then roughly chop the zest. Peel the white pith away from the same lemon, then remove all the peel and pith from the other. Remove the flesh from both: using a very sharp knife, cut between each segment and carefully ease it out. Chop the flesh into little pieces and put it in a bowl with the zest, olive oil, honey, vinegar, and lemon juice. Add the capers to the bowl with the garlic. Stir and taste for balance: remember this will be served with fatty lamb that can take a relish that's assertive and quite acidic. Just when you are about to serve, add the mint leaves (they turn black if they sit in acid for too long).

Ginger Pork Shoulder in Shaoxing Wine

Prep time: 10 minutes | Cook time: 15 minutes | Serves 4

¼ cup honey
1 teaspoon Chinese five-spice powder
1 tablespoon Shaoxing wine (rice cooking wine)
1 tablespoon hoisin sauce
2 teaspoons minced garlic
2 teaspoons minced fresh ginger
2 tablespoons soy sauce
1 tablespoon sugar
1 pound (454 g) fatty pork shoulder, cut into long, 1-inch-thick pieces
Cooking spray

1. Combine all the ingredients, except for the pork should, in a microwave-safe bowl. Stir to mix well. Microwave until the honey has dissolved. Stir periodically.
2. Pierce the pork pieces generously with a fork, then put the pork in a large bowl. Pour in half of the honey mixture. Set the remaining sauce aside until ready to serve.
3. Press the pork pieces into the mixture to coat and wrap the bowl in plastic and refrigerate to marinate for at least 8 hours.
4. Spritz the perforated pan with cooking spray.
5. Discard the marinade and transfer the pork pieces in the perforated pan.
6. Select Air Fry. Set temperature to 400ºF (205ºC) and set time to 15 minutes. Press Start to begin preheating.
7. Once preheated, place the pan into the oven. Flip the pork halfway through.
8. When cooking is complete, the pork should be well browned.
9. Meanwhile, microwave the remaining marinade on high for a minute or until it has a thick consistency. Stir periodically.
10. Remove the pork from the oven and allow to cool for 10 minutes before serving with the thickened marinade.

Steak with Brandy Peppercorn Sauce
Prep time: 10 minutes | Cook time: 21 minutes | Serves 4

2 pounds (907 g) steak, such as top loin, strip, or rib eye, about ½ to 1 inch thick
Kosher salt, to taste
Freshly ground black pepper, to taste
3 tablespoons olive oil
3 garlic cloves, skin on and smashed
1 medium shallot, finely chopped
¼ cup brandy
1 cup beef broth
3 tablespoons cracked peppercorns
¼ cup heavy (whipping) cream
¼ cup chopped fresh flat-leaf parsley

1. Season the steak with salt and pepper and place it on a baking pan.
2. Select Broil. Set temperature to 400ºF (205ºC) and set time to 10 minutes. Select Start to begin preheating.
3. Once preheated, slide the pan into the oven.
4. After 5 minutes, turn the steak and cook for about 5 minutes more for medium (reduce the time slightly for medium-rare or increase the time slightly for medium-well).
5. Remove the steak from the oven, tent loosely with aluminum foil, and let rest for about 10 minutes.
6. While the steak rests, in a medium heavy-bottomed skillet or cast-iron pan over medium heat, heat the olive oil.
7. Add the garlic and shallot. Cook for 2 minutes, stirring.
8. Stir in the brandy and cook for 2 to 3 minutes, stirring and scraping up any browned bits from the bottom of the pan.
9. Add the beef broth and peppercorns. Continue to cook for 5 to 7 minutes, stirring, until the sauce is reduced by about half.
10. Stir in the heavy cream. Continue to cook for about 2 minutes more, stirring, until the sauce is thick. Stir in the parsley. Serve the steak with the sauce spooned over the top.

Juicy Bacon and Beef Cheeseburgers
Prep time: 10 minutes | Cook time: 18 minutes | Serves 4

1½ pounds (680 g) ground beef
1 tablespoon Worcestershire sauce
1 teaspoon kosher salt
½ teaspoon freshly ground black pepper
½ teaspoon garlic powder
¾ cup grated sharp Cheddar cheese
4 bacon slices, halved crosswise so you have 8 short strips
4 hamburger buns
Burger fixings as desired: sliced tomatoes, pickles, onions, ketchup, mustard, relish, mayonnaise, etc., for serving

1. Line a baking sheet with aluminum foil and place a wire rack on top.
2. In a medium bowl, mix together the ground beef, Worcestershire sauce, salt, pepper, and garlic powder. Shape the mixture into 8 very thin patties. Top 4 patties with Cheddar, dividing the cheese equally, and top each with 1 of the remaining 4 patties. Press the patties together, sealing the cheese inside. The patties should be equal sizes, about ½ inch thick and 4 to 5 inches across. Place the patties on the wire rack on top of the baking sheet.
3. Arrange the bacon slices on the rack around the patties.
4. Select Bake. Set temperature to 400ºF (205ºC) and set time to 18 minutes. Select Start to begin preheating.
5. Once preheated, slide the baking sheet into the oven.
6. When done, the burgers will be cooked through and the bacon will be browned and crisp.
7. Remove the patties immediately and place them on the buns.
8. Pat the bacon strips with a paper towel to remove excess fat and lay 2 pieces on top of each burger. Garnish as desired and serve immediately.

Balsamic Italian Sausages and Red Grapes
Prep time: 10 minutes | Cook time: 20 minutes | Serves 6

2 pounds (905 g) seedless red grapes
3 shallots, sliced
2 teaspoons fresh thyme
2 tablespoons olive oil
½ teaspoon kosher salt
Freshly ground black pepper, to taste
6 links (about 1½ pounds / 680 g) hot Italian sausage
3 tablespoons balsamic vinegar

1. Place the grapes in a large bowl. Add the shallots, thyme, olive oil, salt, and pepper. Gently toss. Place the grapes in a baking pan. Arrange the sausage links evenly in the pan.
2. Select Roast. Set temperature to 375ºF (190ºC) and set time to 20 minutes. Press Start to begin preheating.
3. Once preheated, place the pan into the oven.
4. After 10 minutes, remove the pan. Turn over the sausages and sprinkle the vinegar over the sausages and grapes. Gently toss the grapes and move them to one side of the pan. Return the pan to the oven and continue cooking.
5. When cooking is complete, the grapes should be very soft and the sausages browned. Serve immediately.

Fall seven times, stand up eight. -Chapter 6 Meats

Beef Meatloaf with Roasted Vegetables

Prep time: 15 minutes | Cook time: 45 minutes | Serves 4

1½ pounds (680 g) ground beef
¼ cup finely diced onion
1 large egg, lightly beaten
½ cup dried bread crumbs, or panko bread crumbs
2 tablespoons tomato paste
2 tablespoons Worcestershire sauce
1½ teaspoons kosher salt, divided
1 teaspoon freshly ground black pepper, divided
2 cups small Brussels sprouts, halved
1 large red onion, halved and sliced
2 cups small new potatoes, halved or quartered
2 tablespoons olive oil

1. Line one or two rimmed baking sheets with aluminum foil or parchment paper.
2. In a medium bowl, mix together the ground beef, onion, egg, bread crumbs, tomato paste, Worcestershire sauce, 1 teaspoon of salt, and ½ teaspoon of pepper until well combined. Form the mixture into a loaf on the prepared sheet.
3. In a large bowl, toss together the Brussels sprouts, red onion, potatoes, olive oil, and the remaining ½ teaspoon of salt and ½ teaspoon of pepper. Arrange the vegetables either around the meatloaf or on a separate baking sheet.
4. Select Bake. Set temperature to 350ºF (180ºC) and set time to 45 minutes. Select Start to begin preheating.
5. Once preheated, slide the baking sheet into the oven.
6. When done, the vegetables will be tender and browned and the meat will be cooked through. Remove from the oven, tent the meatloaf loosely with foil, and let stand for 10 minutes before serving.

Rump Roast with Bell Peppers

Prep time: 10 minutes | Cook time: 40 minutes | Serves 6 to 8

2 red bell peppers, stemmed, seeded, and cut into 1-inch-wide strips
2 yellow bell peppers, stemmed, seeded, and cut into 1-inch-wide strips
2 green bell peppers, stemmed, seeded, and cut into 1-inch-wide strips
6 garlic cloves, peeled and left whole
4 tablespoons olive oil, divided
2 teaspoons kosher salt, divided
1½ teaspoons freshly ground black pepper, divided
1 (3- to 3½-pound / 1.4- to 1.6-kg) boneless rump roast, at room temperature
1 tablespoon chopped fresh thyme leaves

1. In a baking dish, toss together the red, yellow, and green bell peppers, garlic, 2 tablespoons of olive oil, ½ teaspoon of salt, and ½ teaspoon of pepper. Spread the peppers out to the sides of the pan, leaving space in the middle for the roast.
2. Rub the remaining 2 tablespoons of olive oil all over the roast and season it with the remaining 1½ teaspoons of salt and 1 teaspoon of pepper.
3. Select Bake. Set temperature to 375ºF (190ºC) and set time to 40 minutes. Select Start to begin preheating.
4. Once preheated, slide the baking dish into the oven.
5. When done, the outside of the roast will be browned and it will be cooked to an internal temperature of 135ºF (57ºC).
6. Remove the roast from the oven, tent loosely with aluminum foil, and let rest for 10 minutes. Carve the roast thinly and serve hot, with the roasted peppers and garlic alongside, garnished with the thyme.

Pork and Pineapple Kebabs

Prep time: 10 minutes | Cook time: 12 minutes | Serves 4

¼ teaspoon kosher salt or ⅛ teaspoon fine salt
1 medium pork tenderloin (about 1 pound / 454 g) cut into 1½-inch chunks
1 green bell pepper, seeded and cut into 1-inch pieces
1 red bell pepper, seeded and cut into 1-inch pieces
2 cups fresh pineapple chunks
¾ cup Teriyaki Sauce or store-bought variety, divided

Special Equipment:
12 (9- to 12-inch) wooden skewers, soaked in water for about 30 minutes

1. Sprinkle the pork cubes with the salt.
2. Thread the pork, bell peppers, and pineapple onto a skewer. Repeat until all skewers are complete. Brush the skewers generously with about half of the Teriyaki Sauce. Place them on the sheet pan.
3. Select Roast. Set temperature to 375ºF (190ºC) and set time to 10 minutes. Press Start to begin preheating.
4. Once the unit has preheated, place the pan into the oven.
5. After about 5 minutes, remove the pan from the oven. Turn over the skewers and brush with the remaining half of Teriyaki Sauce. Transfer the pan back to the oven and continue cooking until the vegetables are tender and browned in places and the pork is browned and cooked through.
6. Remove the pan from the oven and serve.

Bacon-Wrapped Pork Hot Dogs

Prep time: 5 minutes | Cook time: 10 minutes | Serves 5

10 thin slices of bacon
5 pork hot dogs, halved
1 teaspoon cayenne pepper
Sauce:
¼ cup mayonnaise
4 tablespoons low-carb ketchup
1 teaspoon rice vinegar
1 teaspoon chili powder

1. Arrange the slices of bacon on a clean work surface. One by one, place the halved hot dog on one end of each slice, season with cayenne pepper and wrap the hot dog with the bacon slices and secure with toothpicks as needed.
2. Place wrapped hot dogs in the perforated pan.
3. Select Air Fry. Set temperature to 390ºF (199ºC) and set time to 10 minutes. Press Start to begin preheating.
4. Once preheated, place the pan into the oven. Flip the bacon-wrapped hot dogs halfway through.
5. When cooking is complete, the bacon should be crispy and browned.
6. Make the sauce: Stir all the ingredients for the sauce in a small bowl. Wrap the bowl in plastic and set in the refrigerator until ready to serve.
7. Transfer the hot dogs to a platter and serve hot with the sauce.

BBQ Kielbasa Sausage

Prep time: 15 minutes | Cook time: 10 minutes | Serves 2 to 4

¾ pound (340 g) kielbasa sausage, cut into ½-inch slices
1 (8-ounce / 227-g) can pineapple chunks in juice, drained
1 cup bell pepper chunks
1 tablespoon barbecue seasoning
1 tablespoon soy sauce
Cooking spray

1. Spritz the perforated pan with cooking spray.
2. Combine all the ingredients in a large bowl. Toss to mix well.
3. Pour the sausage mixture in the perforated pan.
4. Select Air Fry. Set temperature to 390ºF (199ºC) and set time to 10 minutes. Press Start to begin preheating.
5. Once preheated, place the pan into the oven.
6. After 5 minutes, remove the pan from the oven. Stir the sausage mixture. Return the pan to the oven and continue cooking.
7. When cooking is complete, the sausage should be lightly browned and the bell pepper and pineapple should be soft.
8. Serve immediately.

Minted-Balsamic Lamb Chops

Prep time: 5 minutes | Cook time: 15 minutes | Serves 4

4 lean lamb chops, fat trimmed, approximately ¾ inch thick
1 tablespoon balsamic vinegar

Mint Mixture:
4 tablespoons finely chopped fresh mint
2 tablespoons nonfat yogurt
1 tablespoon olive oil
Salt and freshly ground black pepper, to taste

1. Combine the mint mixture ingredients in a small bowl, stirring well to blend. Set aside. Place the lamp chops on a broiling rack with a pan underneath.
2. Select Broil. Set temperature to 400ºF (205ºC) and set time to 15 minutes. Select Start to begin preheating.
3. Once preheated, slide the pan into the oven.
4. Broil the lamb chops for 10 minutes, or until they are slightly pink. Remove from the oven and brush one side liberally with balsamic vinegar. Turn the chops over with tongs and spread with the mint mixture, using all of the mixture.
5. Broil again for 5 minutes, or until lightly browned.

Dijon Pork Tenderloin

Prep time: 5 minutes | Cook time: 10 minutes | Serves 6

2 large egg whites
1½ tablespoons Dijon mustard
2 cups crushed pretzel crumbs
1½ pounds (680 g) pork tenderloin, cut into ¼-pound (113-g) sections
Cooking spray

1. Spritz the perforated pan with cooking spray.
2. Whisk the egg whites with Dijon mustard in a bowl until bubbly. Pour the pretzel crumbs in a separate bowl.
3. Dredge the pork tenderloin in the egg white mixture and press to coat. Shake the excess off and roll the tenderloin over the pretzel crumbs.
4. Arrange the well-coated pork tenderloin in the pan and spritz with cooking spray.
5. Select Air Fry. Set temperature to 350ºF (180ºC) and set time to 10 minutes. Press Start to begin preheating.
6. Once preheated, place the pan into the oven.
7. After 5 minutes, remove the pan from the oven. Flip the pork. Return the pan to the oven and continue cooking.
8. When cooking is complete, the pork should be golden brown and crispy.
9. Serve immediately.

Hoisin Pork Butt with Veggies Salad

Prep time: 20 minutes | Cook time: 4½ minutes | Serves 6

For the Pork:
- 4½ pounds (2 kg) boned pork butt
- ½ cup soy sauce
- ½ cup clear honey
- ½ cup hoisin sauce
- ½ cup amontillado sherry
- 2 teaspoons five spice powder
- 1¼-inch fresh ginger, peeled and finely grated

To Serve:
- Boiled rice, or soft white bread rolls
- Radish and Cucumber
- Salad, to serve
- Crisp lettuce leaves

For the Salad:
- 3 tablespoons unseasoned rice vinegar
- 3 teaspoons superfine sugar
- Pinch of fine sea salt
- ¾-inch fresh ginger, peeled and finely grated
- 1 large garlic clove, very finely chopped or grated
- 1 cucumber, chilled
- ⅔ pound (302 g) radishes (a mixture of colors if possible), quartered, or cut into eighths if they're big
- 1 teaspoon toasted sesame oil
- 1 teaspoon toasted sesame seeds (a mixture of white and black, if you like)

1. Remove the skin from the pork and discard. Leave the fat on.
2. Mix together all the other ingredients for the pork in a small bowl to make a marinade. Put this with the pork in a large plastic food storage bag. Marinate in the refrigerator for 24 to 48 hours, turning the meat over every so often.
3. Bring the pork to room temperature by removing it from the refrigerator for at least 1 hour before you are going to cook it.
4. Put the pork into a baking pan in which it will fit snugly (if there is a lot of room around it, the juices and the marinade will just run off and burn) and pour the marinade into a saucepan.
5. Select Bake. Set temperature to 275ºF (135ºC) and set time to 4½ hours. Select Start to begin preheating.
6. Once preheated, slide the pan into the oven.
7. When done, the meat will be soft and melting.
8. Bring the marinade to a boil, then remove from the heat. Now ladle some of the marinade over the pork and return to the oven. Keep adding more of the marinade and basting the pork every 10 minutes for the next hour. Turn it over every time you do this. The pork should end up dark and glossy. If the roast starts to get too dark on the outside, cover it with foil.
9. To make the salad, mix the vinegar, sugar, salt, ginger, and garlic together. Peel the cucumber in stripes. Halve it along its length and scoop out the seeds, then cut it into 1½in lengths. Bash these with a mallet or a rolling pin. Put the cucumber into a serving bowl with the dressing and place in the refrigerator for 20 minutes. When you're ready to eat, add the radishes and the sesame oil and toss everything together. Scatter the sesame seeds on top.
10. Serve the pork with boiled rice, or in soft white bread rolls, with the radish and cucumber salad, and with crisp lettuce leaves.

Pork Butt withCoriander-Parsley Sauce

Prep time: 1 hour 15 minutes | Cook time: 30 minutes | Serves 4

- 1 teaspoon golden flaxseeds meal
- 1 egg white, well whisked
- 1 tablespoon soy sauce
- 1 teaspoon lemon juice, preferably freshly squeezed
- 1 tablespoon olive oil
- 1 pound (454 g) pork butt, cut into pieces 2-inches long
- Salt and ground black pepper, to taste

Garlicky Coriander-Parsley Sauce:
- 3 garlic cloves, minced
- ⅓ cup fresh coriander leaves
- ⅓ cup fresh parsley leaves
- 1 teaspoon lemon juice
- ½ tablespoon salt
- ⅓ cup extra-virgin olive oil

1. Combine the flaxseeds meal, egg white, soy sauce, lemon juice, salt, black pepper, and olive oil in a large bowl. Dunk the pork strips in and press to submerge.
2. Wrap the bowl in plastic and refrigerate to marinate for at least an hour.
3. Arrange the marinated pork strips in the perforated pan.
4. Select Air Fry. Set temperature to 380ºF (193ºC) and set time to 30 minutes. Press Start to begin preheating.
5. Once preheated, place the pan into the oven.
6. After 15 minutes, remove the pan from the oven. Flip the pork. Return the pan to the oven and continue cooking.
7. When cooking is complete, the pork should be well browned.
8. Meanwhile, combine the ingredients for the sauce in a small bowl. Stir to mix well. Arrange the bowl in the refrigerator to chill until ready to serve.
9. Serve the air fried pork strips with the chilled sauce.

Nut-Crusted Pork Rack

Prep time: 5 minutes | Cook time: 35 minutes | Serves 2

1 clove garlic, minced
2 tablespoons olive oil
1 pound (454 g) rack of pork
1 cup chopped macadamia nuts
1 tablespoon bread crumbs
1 tablespoon rosemary, chopped
1 egg
Salt and ground black pepper, to taste

1. Combine the garlic and olive oil in a small bowl. Stir to mix well.
2. On a clean work surface, rub the pork rack with the garlic oil and sprinkle with salt and black pepper on both sides.
3. Combine the macadamia nuts, bread crumbs, and rosemary in a shallow dish. Whisk the egg in a large bowl.
4. Dredge the pork in the egg, then roll the pork over the macadamia nut mixture to coat well. Shake the excess off.
5. Arrange the pork in the perforated pan.
6. Select Air Fry. Set temperature to 350ºF (180ºC) and set time to 30 minutes. Press Start to begin preheating.
7. Once preheated, place the pan into the oven.
8. After 30 minutes, remove the pan from the oven. Flip the pork rack. Return the pan to the oven and increase temperature to 390ºF (199ºC) and set time to 5 minutes. Keep cooking.
9. When cooking is complete, the pork should be browned.
10. Serve immediately.

Lemon Pork Loin Chop with Marjoram

Prep time: 15 minutes | Cook time: 15 minutes | Serves 4

4 thin boneless pork loin chops
2 tablespoons lemon juice
½ cup flour
¼ teaspoon marjoram
1 teaspoon salt
1 cup panko bread crumbs
2 eggs
Lemon wedges, for serving
Cooking spray

1. On a clean work surface, drizzle the pork chops with lemon juice on both sides.
2. Combine the flour with marjoram and salt on a shallow plate. Pour the bread crumbs on a separate shallow dish. Beat the eggs in a large bowl.
3. Dredge the pork chops in the flour, then dunk in the beaten eggs to coat well. Shake the excess off and roll over the bread crumbs. Arrange the pork chops in the perforated pan and spritz with cooking spray.
4. Select Air Fry. Set temperature to 400ºF (205ºC) and set time to 15 minutes. Press Start to begin preheating.
5. Once preheated, place the pan into the oven.
6. After 7 minutes, remove the pan from the oven. Flip the pork. Return the pan to the oven and continue cooking.
7. When cooking is complete, the pork should be crispy and golden.
8. Squeeze the lemon wedges over the fried chops and serve immediately.

Pork Chops with Lime Peach Salsa

Prep time: 15 minutes | Cook time: 25 minutes | Serves 4

For the Pork Chops:
3 tablespoons low-sodium soy sauce
2 tablespoons ketchup
2 tablespoons light brown sugar
1 tablespoon olive oil
1 garlic clove, minced
1 teaspoon red wine vinegar, or white wine vinegar
4 (7-ounce / 198-g) bone-in pork chops

For the Salsa:
½ medium red bell pepper, seeded and diced
1 to 2 red or green jalapeño peppers, or serrano peppers, diced
2 garlic cloves, minced
4 medium peaches, peeled, pitted, and diced
¼ cup freshly squeezed lime juice
½ teaspoon kosher salt
Fresh cilantro leaves, for garnish

Make the Pork Chops
1. In a small bowl, stir together the soy sauce, ketchup, brown sugar, olive oil, garlic, and vinegar. Rub the mixture all over the pork chops, reserving any excess mixture for later.
2. Arrange the chops on a rimmed baking sheet in a single layer.
3. Select Bake. Set temperature to 400ºF (205ºC) and set time to 20 minutes. Select Start to begin preheating.
4. Once preheated, slide the pan into the oven.
5. After 10 minutes, spoon the reserved rub mixture over the top and bake for 10 minutes more.
6. Select Broil and cook for 5 minutes more, until the tops are golden brown. Serve immediately, topped with a spoonful of the salsa and garnished with cilantro.

Make the Salsa
7. While the pork chops roast, combine the red bell pepper, jalapeño, garlic, and peaches in a medium bowl. Toss to combine.
8. Add the lime juice and salt and toss to coat the mixture well.

Lamb Leg with Herb Yogurt Sauce

Prep time: 20 minutes | Cook time: 30 minutes | Serves 8

For the Lamb:

1½ tablespoons cumin seeds
2 teaspoons coriander seeds
1 onion, chopped
Finely grated zest and juice of 1 lime, plus lime wedges to serve
⅔ cup plain yogurt
Leaves from 8 mint sprigs, plus mint leaves to serve
Scant 2 cups cilantro leaves and stalks, plus cilantro leaves to serve
6 garlic cloves, chopped
1 red Fresno chili, seeded if you want, chopped
1-inch fresh ginger, peeled and chopped
½ teaspoon sea salt flakes
½ teaspoon freshly ground black pepper
5 pounds (2.3 kg) of lamb (pre-boned weight), boned and butterflied by your butcher

For the Sauce:

1 cup Greek yogurt
Leaves from 8 mint sprigs
2 cups cilantro leaves
5 tablespoons extra-virgin olive oil
2 garlic cloves, chopped
1 scallion, trimmed and chopped
Finely grated zest of 1 lime
2 tablespoons lime juice
3 tablespoons mayonnaise
Sea salt flakes and freshly ground black pepper, to taste

1. Toast the cumin and coriander seeds in a dry frying pan over medium heat for about 2 minutes. Let them cool, then put them in a food processor with the onion, lime zest and juice, yogurt, mint and cilantro, garlic, chili, and ginger, salt and pepper. Whizz until you have a paste.
2. Put the lamb in a dish, or a large plastic food storage bag, with the marinade, making sure the marinade covers the flesh as well as the fatty side. Cover with plastic wrap, or seal the bag, then refrigerate for about 6 hours. Bring the meat to room temperature.
3. Lift the lamb out of the marinade, shaking it off. Spread the meat out in a baking pan, fatty side up.
4. Select Bake. Set temperature to 400ºF (205ºC) and set time to 30 minutes. Select Start to begin preheating.
5. Once preheated, slide the pan into the oven.
6. After 15 minutes, reduce the oven temperature to 375ºF (190ºC) and cook for another 15 minutes. The lamb will be pink.
7. Remove from the oven, cover with foil, insulate with kitchen towels or old towels, and leave to rest for 15 minutes.
8. To make the sauce, just put all the ingredients into a clean food processor bowl and blend. Taste for seasoning.
9. Slice the meat and arrange it on a warmed platter, spooning over any juices that have come out of it, and scatter with mint and cilantro leaves and some sea salt flakes. Serve immediately, with lime wedges and the yogurt sauce.

Cider-Bourbon Glazed Pork Loin Roast

Prep time: 10 minutes | Cook time: 1¼ hours | Serves 6

3 tablespoons olive oil, divided
1 onion, finely diced
Kosher salt, to taste
1 Granny Smith apple, peeled and finely diced
2 tablespoons chopped fresh sage leaves
Freshly ground black pepper, to taste
1 (2-pound / 907-g) boneless pork loin roast, butterflied and pounded to an even 1-inch thickness
3 tablespoons olive oil
½ cup bourbon
2 cups apple cider
1 tablespoon dark brown sugar

1. In a large skillet over medium-high heat, heat 2 tablespoons of olive oil.
2. Add the onion and a pinch of salt. Cook for 3 minutes, stirring.
3. Add the apple and continue to cook for 3 minutes more, stirring.
4. Stir in the sage and remove from the heat. Taste and season with salt and pepper, if needed.
5. Season the pork loin generously with salt and pepper. Brush the remaining 1 tablespoon of olive oil all over the outside of the roast.
6. Spoon the apple mixture over the pork loin, covering the pork in an even layer. Gently roll the meat around the stuffing and secure with toothpicks or kitchen twine and place in a baking dish.
7. Return the skillet to medium heat and carefully add the bourbon and apple cider. Cook for 2 minutes, stirring and scraping up any browned bits from the bottom of the skillet. Pour ¼ cup of the bourbon mixture over the pork.
8. Select Roast. Set temperature to 375ºF (190ºC) and set time to 1 hour. Select Start to begin preheating.
9. Once preheated, put the skillet in the oven. Pour another ¼ cup of the bourbon mixture over the pork every 20 minutes.
10. After basting with the glaze for a third time, whisk the brown sugar into the bourbon mixture until it dissolves.
11. When the pork is done, transfer it to a cutting board, tent loosely with aluminum foil, and let rest for at least 10 minutes. To serve, cut into 1-inch-thick slices and spoon the sweetened glaze over the top.

Mint-Roasted Boneless Lamb Leg

Prep time: 10 minutes | Cook time: 30 minutes | Serves 8

2 tablespoons olive oil
6 garlic cloves, minced
¼ cup chopped fresh mint leaves
1 tablespoon chopped fresh flat-leaf parsley leaves
1 teaspoon kosher salt
¾ teaspoon freshly ground black pepper
1 (3- to 3½-pound / 1.4- to 1.6-kg) boneless leg of lamb, at room temperature

1. In a small bowl, stir together the olive oil, garlic, mint, parsley, salt, and pepper. Rub the herb mixture all over the meat. Place the meat in a shallow baking pan.
2. Select Bake. Set temperature to 400ºF (205ºC) and set time to 30 minutes. Select Start to begin preheating.
3. Once preheated, slide the pan into the oven.
4. When done, the meat will be reach the desired internal temperature to 130ºF (54ºC) for medium-rare, 140ºF (60ºC) for medium, and 145ºF (63ºC) for medium-well.
5. Remove the roast from the oven, tent with aluminum foil, and let rest for at least 15 minutes.
6. To serve, carve the meat thinly across the grain and serve with the pan juices drizzled over the top.

Flank Steak and Bell Pepper Fajitas

Prep time: 15 minutes | Cook time: 30 minutes | Serves 4 to 6

1 tablespoon chili powder
1½ teaspoons sweet paprika
½ teaspoon onion powder
¼ teaspoon garlic powder
¼ teaspoon ground cumin
⅛ teaspoon cayenne pepper
1 teaspoon sugar
½ teaspoon kosher salt
1 large red onion, sliced
2 bell peppers, any color, stemmed, seeded, and cut into strips
1 pound (454 g) flank steak, cut into thin strips
2 tablespoons vegetable oil
Juice of 1 lime
2 tablespoons chopped fresh cilantro
8 flour tortillas, warmed

1. In a small bowl, stir together the chili powder, paprika, onion powder, garlic powder, cumin, cayenne, sugar, and salt.
2. Arrange the red onion, bell peppers, and steak in a single layer on a baking pan (or use two baking sheets if needed). Drizzle the vegetable oil over everything and toss to coat well.
3. Sprinkle the spice mixture over the top and toss again to distribute. Spread the meat and vegetables into a single layer again.
4. Select Bake. Set temperature to 400ºF (205ºC) and set time to 30 minutes. Select Start to begin preheating.
5. Once preheated, slide the pan into the oven.
6. When done, the peppers and onion will be tender and browned and the meat will be sizzling.
7. Transfer the meat and vegetables to a serving platter and squeeze the lime juice over the top. Garnish with the cilantro and serve with the tortillas and any desired toppings.

Brown Sugar-Mustard Glazed Ham

Prep time: 5 minutes | Cook time: 1½ hours | Serves 14 to 16

1 (10- to 12-pound / 4.5- to 5.4-kg) bone-in spiral-sliced ham
1 cup brown sugar
2 tablespoons honey
2 tablespoons Dijon mustard
2 tablespoons apple cider vinegar

1. Place the ham in a shallow baking pan.
2. Select Bake. Set temperature to 325ºF (163ºC) and set time to 1½ hours. Select Start to begin preheating.
3. Once preheated, slide the pan into the oven.
4. In a small bowl, stir together the brown sugar, honey, mustard, and vinegar.
5. After 1 hour, spoon the brown sugar mixture all over the ham. Return the ham to the oven and bake for 30 minutes more, until heated through and the glaze is bubbling and browned.

Pork Chops with Pickapeppa Sauce

Prep time: 10 minutes | Cook time: 16 minutes | Serves 2

½ to ¾ pound (227- to 340-g) boneless lean pork sirloin chops
Seasoning Mixture:
½ teaspoon ground cumin
¼ teaspoon turmeric
Pinch of ground cardamom
Pinch of grated nutmeg
1 teaspoon vegetable oil
1 teaspoon Pickapeppa sauce

1. Combine the seasoning mixture ingredients in a small bowl and brush on both sides of the chops. Place the chops on the broiling rack with a pan underneath.
2. Select Broil. Set temperature to 400ºF (205ºC) and set time to 16 minutes. Select Start to begin preheating.
3. Once preheated, slide the pan into the oven.
4. After 8 minutes, remove the chops, turn, and brush with the mixture. Broil again for 8 minutes, or until the chops are done to your preference.

Citrus Pork Ribs with Oregano

Prep time: 10 minutes | Cook time: 25 minutes | Serves 6

2½ pounds (1.1 kg) boneless country-style pork ribs, cut into 2-inch pieces
3 tablespoons olive brine
1 tablespoon minced fresh oregano leaves
⅓ cup orange juice
1 teaspoon ground cumin
1 tablespoon minced garlic
1 teaspoon salt
1 teaspoon ground black pepper
Cooking spray

1. Combine all the ingredients in a large bowl. Toss to coat the pork ribs well. Wrap the bowl in plastic and refrigerate for at least an hour to marinate.
2. Spritz the perforated pan with cooking spray.
3. Arrange the marinated pork ribs in the pan and spritz with cooking spray.
4. Select Air Fry. Set temperature to 400ºF (205ºC) and set time to 25 minutes. Press Start to begin preheating.
5. Once preheated, place the pan into the oven. Flip the ribs halfway through.
6. When cooking is complete, the ribs should be well browned.
7. Serve immediately.

Breaded Pork Loin Chops

Prep time: 5 minutes | Cook time: 10 minutes | Serves 4

⅔ cup all-purpose flour
2 large egg whites
1 cup panko bread crumbs
4 (4-ounce / 113-g) center-cut boneless pork loin chops (about ½ inch thick)
Cooking spray

1. Pour the flour in a bowl. Whisk the egg whites in a separate bowl. Spread the bread crumbs on a large plate.
2. Dredge the pork loin chops in the flour first, press to coat well, then shake the excess off and dunk the chops in the eggs whites, and then roll the chops over the bread crumbs. Shake the excess off.
3. Arrange the pork chops in the perforated pan and spritz with cooking spray.
4. Select Air Fry. Set temperature to 375ºF (190ºC) and set time to 10 minutes. Press Start to begin preheating.
5. Once preheated, place the pan into the oven.
6. After 5 minutes, remove the pan from the oven. Flip the pork chops. Return the pan to the oven and continue cooking.
7. When cooking is complete, the pork chops should be crunchy and lightly browned.
8. Serve immediately.

Rosemary-Balsamic Pork Loin Roast

Prep time: 10 minutes | Cook time: 35 minutes | Serves 4

¼ cup olive oil
3 tablespoons balsamic vinegar
5 garlic cloves, minced
½ cup chopped fresh rosemary leaves
1 teaspoon kosher salt
½ teaspoon freshly ground black pepper
1 (2-pound / 907-g) boneless pork loin roast

1. In a small bowl, stir together the olive oil, vinegar, garlic, rosemary, salt, and pepper. Rub the mixture all over the pork loin and place it in a baking dish.
2. Select Bake. Set temperature to 400ºF (205ºC) and set time to 18 minutes. Select Start to begin preheating.
3. Once preheated, slide the pan into the oven.
4. When done, lower the temperature to 350ºF (180ºC) and continue to roast the pork for 20 to 30 minutes more, until the internal temperature is around 145ºF (63ºC). Remove from the oven, tent loosely with aluminum foil, and let rest for 10 minutes before slicing and serving.

Hoisin Roasted Pork Ribs

Prep time: 10 minutes | Cook time: 1 hour | Serves 4 to 6

2 pounds (907 g) baby back pork ribs
⅓ cup hoisin sauce
2 tablespoons soy sauce
2 tablespoons light brown sugar
1 tablespoon minced peeled fresh ginger
2 garlic cloves, minced
1 tablespoon toasted sesame oil
¼ teaspoon ground cinnamon
¼ teaspoon ground fennel
¼ teaspoon cayenne pepper
¼ teaspoon freshly ground black pepper

1. Place the ribs in a large baking pan. Pierce the meat with a fork.
2. In a small bowl, whisk the hoisin sauce, soy sauce, brown sugar, ginger, garlic, sesame oil, cinnamon, fennel, cayenne, and pepper. Brush the mixture over the meat. Reserve any extra marinade for basting.
3. Select Bake. Set temperature to 350ºF (180ºC) and set time to 1 hour. Select Start to begin preheating.
4. Once preheated, slide the pan into the oven. Baste the ribs with the reserved seasoning mixture every 20 minutes.
5. Cut between the bones to separate the ribs and serve immediately.

Bourbon Sirloin Steak

Prep time: 5 minutes | Cook time: 14 minutes | Serves 2

2 (6- to 8-ounce / 170- to 227-g) sirloin steaks, ¾ inch thick
Brushing Mixture:
¼ cup bourbon
1 teaspoon garlic powder
1 tablespoon olive oil
1 teaspoon soy sauce

1. Combine the brushing mixture ingredients in a small bowl. Brush the steaks on both sides with the mixture and place on the broiling rack with a pan underneath.
2. Select Broil. Set temperature to 400ºF (205ºC) and set time to 14 minutes. Select Start to begin preheating.
3. Once preheated, slide the pan into the oven.
4. After 4 minutes, remove from the oven, turn with tongs, brush the top and sides, and broil again for 4 minutes, or until done to your preference. To use the brushing mixture as a sauce or gravy, pour the mixture into a baking pan.
5. Broil the mixture for 6 minutes, or until it begins to bubble.

Colby Pork Sausage with Cauliflower

Prep time: 5 minutes | Cook time: 27 minutes | Serves 6

1 pound (454 g) cauliflower, chopped
6 pork sausages, chopped
½ onion, sliced
3 eggs, beaten
⅓ cup Colby cheese
1 teaspoon cumin powder
½ teaspoon tarragon
½ teaspoon sea salt
½ teaspoon ground black pepper
Cooking spray

1. Spritz the baking pan with cooking spray.
2. In a saucepan over medium heat, boil the cauliflower until tender. Place the boiled cauliflower in a food processor and pulse until puréed. Transfer to a large bowl and combine with remaining ingredients until well blended.
3. Pour the cauliflower and sausage mixture into the pan.
4. Select Bake. Set temperature to 365ºF (185ºC) and set time to 27 minutes. Press Start to begin preheating.
5. Once preheated, place the pan into the oven.
6. When cooking is complete, the sausage should be lightly browned.
7. Divide the mixture among six serving dishes and serve warm.

Pork Chop Roast with Worcestershire

Prep time: 5 minutes | Cook time: 20 minutes | Serves 2

2 (10-ounce / 284-g) bone-in, center cut pork chops, 1-inch thick
2 teaspoons Worcestershire sauce
Salt and ground black pepper, to taste
Cooking spray

1. Rub the Worcestershire sauce on both sides of pork chops.
2. Season with salt and pepper to taste.
3. Spritz the perforated pan with cooking spray and place the chops in the perforated pan side by side.
4. Select Roast. Set temperature to 350ºF (180ºC) and set time to 20 minutes. Press Start to begin preheating.
5. Once preheated, place the pan into the oven.
6. After 10 minutes, remove the pan from the oven. Flip the pork chops with tongs. Return the pan to the oven and continue cooking.
7. When cooking is complete, the pork should be well browned on both sides.
8. Let rest for 5 minutes before serving.

Thyme Pork Chops with Carrots

Prep time: 10 minutes | Cook time: 15 minutes | Serves 4

2 carrots, cut into sticks
1 cup mushrooms, sliced
2 garlic cloves, minced
2 tablespoons olive oil
1 pound (454 g) boneless pork chops
1 teaspoon dried oregano
1 teaspoon dried thyme
1 teaspoon cayenne pepper
Salt and ground black pepper, to taste
Cooking spray

1. In a mixing bowl, toss together the carrots, mushrooms, garlic, olive oil and salt until well combined.
2. Add the pork chops to a different bowl and season with oregano, thyme, cayenne pepper, salt and black pepper.
3. Lower the vegetable mixture in the greased pan. Place the seasoned pork chops on top.
4. Select Air Fry. Set temperature to 360ºF (182ºC) and set time to 15 minutes. Press Start to begin preheating.
5. Once preheated, place the pan into the oven.
6. After 7 minutes, remove the pan from the oven. Flip the pork and stir the vegetables. Return the pan to the oven and continue cooking.
7. When cooking is complete, the pork chops should be browned and the vegetables should be tender.
8. Transfer the pork chops to the serving dishes and let cool for 5 minutes. Serve warm with vegetable on the side.

Fall seven times, stand up eight.

Pork and Veggie Kebabs

Prep time: 25 minutes | Cook time: 15 minutes | Serves 4

1 pound (454 g) pork tenderloin, cubed
1 teaspoon smoked paprika
Salt and ground black pepper, to taste
1 green bell pepper, cut into chunks
1 zucchini, cut into chunks
1 red onion, sliced
1 tablespoon oregano
Cooking spray

Special Equipment:
Small bamboo skewers, soaked in water for 20 minutes to keep them from burning while cooking

1. Spritz the perforated pan with cooking spray.
2. Add the pork to a bowl and season with the smoked paprika, salt and black pepper. Thread the seasoned pork cubes and vegetables alternately onto the soaked skewers. Arrange the skewers in the pan.
3. Select Air Fry. Set temperature to 350ºF (180ºC) and set time to 15 minutes. Press Start to begin preheating.
4. Once preheated, place the pan into the oven.
5. After 7 minutes, remove the pan from the oven. Flip the pork skewers. Return the pan to the oven and continue cooking.
6. When cooking is complete, the pork should be browned and vegetables are tender.
7. Transfer the skewers to the serving dishes and sprinkle with oregano. Serve hot.

Pork Chops and Apple Bake

Prep time: 10 minutes | Cook time: 45 minutes | Serves 4

2 apples, peeled, cored, and sliced
1 teaspoon ground cinnamon, divided
4 boneless pork chops (½-inch thick)
Salt and freshly ground black pepper, to taste
3 tablespoons brown sugar
¾ cup water
1 tablespoon olive oil

1. Layer apples in bottom of a baking pan. Sprinkle with ½ teaspoon of cinnamon.
2. Trim fat from pork chops. Lay on top of the apple slices. Sprinkle with salt and pepper.
3. In a small bowl, combine the brown sugar, water, and remaining cinnamon. Pour the mixture over the chops. Drizzle chops with 1 tablespoon of olive oil.
4. Select Bake. Set temperature to 375ºF (190ºC) and set time to 45 minutes. Press Start to begin preheating.
5. Once preheated, place the pan into the oven.
6. When cooking is complete, an instant-read thermometer inserted in the pork should register 165ºF (74ºC).
7. Allow to rest for 3 minutes before serving.

Pork Chops with Sour Cream and Dill Sauce

Prep time: 5 minutes | Cook time: 4 minutes | Serves 4 to 6

½ cup flour
1½ teaspoons salt
Freshly ground black pepper, to taste
2 eggs
½ cup milk
1½ cups toasted bread crumbs
1 teaspoon paprika
6 boneless, center cut pork chops (about 1½ pounds / 680 g) fat trimmed, pound to ½-inch thick
2 tablespoons olive oil
3 tablespoons melted butter
Lemon wedges, for serving

Sour Cream and Dill Sauce:
1 cup chicken stock
1½ tablespoons cornstarch
⅓ cup sour cream
1½ tablespoons chopped fresh dill
Salt and ground black pepper, to taste

1. Combine the flour with salt and black pepper in a large bowl. Stir to mix well. Whisk the egg with milk in a second bowl. Stir the bread crumbs and paprika in a third bowl.
2. Dredge the pork chops in the flour bowl, then in the egg milk, and then into the bread crumbs bowl. Press to coat well. Shake the excess off.
3. Arrange the pork chop in the perforated pan, then brush with olive oil and butter on all sides.
4. Select Air Fry. Set temperature to 400ºF (205ºC) and set time to 4 minutes. Press Start to begin preheating.
5. Once preheated, place the pan into the oven.
6. After 2 minutes, remove the pan from the oven. Flip the pork. Return the pan to the oven and continue cooking.
7. When cooking is complete, the pork chop should be golden brown and crispy.
8. Meanwhile, combine the chicken stock and cornstarch in a small saucepan and bring to a boil over medium-high heat. Simmer for 2 more minutes.
9. Turn off the heat, then mix in the sour cream, fresh dill, salt, and black pepper.
10. Remove the schnitzels from the oven to a plate and baste with sour cream and dill sauce. Squeeze the lemon wedges over and slice to serve.

Chuck and Sausage Meatballs

Prep time: 15 minutes | Cook time: 24 minutes | Serves 4

1 large egg
¼ cup whole milk
24 saltines, crushed but not pulverized
1 pound (454 g) ground chuck
1 pound (454 g) Italian sausage, casings removed
4 tablespoons grated Parmesan cheese, divided
1 teaspoon kosher salt
4 sub rolls, split
1 cup Marinara sauce
¾ cup shredded Mozzarella cheese

1. In a large bowl, whisk the egg into the milk, then stir in the crackers. Let sit for 5 minutes to hydrate.
2. With your hands, break the ground chuck and sausage into the milk mixture, alternating beef and sausage. When you've added half of the meat, sprinkle 2 tablespoons of the grated Parmesan and the salt over it, then continue breaking up the meat until it's all in the bowl. Gently mix everything together. Try not to overwork the meat, but get it all combined.
3. Form the mixture into balls about the size of a golf ball. You should get about 24 meatballs. Flatten the balls slightly to prevent them from rolling, then place them on a baking pan, about 2 inches apart.
4. Select Roast. Set temperature to 400°F (205°C) and set time to 20 minutes. Press Start to begin preheating.
5. Once preheated, place the pan into the oven.
6. After 10 minutes, remove the pan from the oven and turn over the meatballs. Return the pan to the oven and continue cooking.
7. When cooking is complete, remove the pan from the oven. Place the meatballs on a rack. Wipe off the baking pan.
8. Open the rolls, cut-side up, on the baking pan. Place 3 to 4 meatballs on the base of each roll, and top each sandwich with ¼ cup of marinara sauce. Divide the Mozzarella among the top halves of the buns and sprinkle the remaining Parmesan cheese over the Mozzarella.
9. Select Broil. Set temperature to 400°F (205°C) and set time to 4 minutes.
10. Place the pan into the oven. Check the sandwiches after 2 minutes; the Mozzarella cheese should be melted and bubbling slightly.
11. When cooking is complete, remove the pan from the oven. Close the sandwiches and serve.

Spicy Pepper Steak

Prep time: 10 minutes | Cook time: 12 minutes | Serves 2

½ to ¾ pound (227- to 340-g) pepper steaks, cut into 3 × 4-inch strips
Spicy Mixture:
1 tablespoon olive oil
1 tablespoon brown mustard
1 teaspoon chili powder
1 teaspoon garlic powder
1 teaspoon hot sauce
1 tablespoon barbecue sauce or salsa
Salt and freshly ground black pepper, to taste

1. Blend the spicy mixture ingredients in a small bowl and brush both sides of the beef strips.
2. Roll up the strips lengthwise and fasten with toothpicks near each end. Place the beef rolls in an oiled or nonstick square baking (cake) pan.
3. Select Broil. Set temperature to 400°F (205°C) and set time to 12 minutes. Select Start to begin preheating.
4. Once preheated, slide the pan into the oven.
5. After 6 minutes, remove from the oven, and turn with tongs. Brush with the spicy mixture and broil again for 6 minutes, or until done to your preference.

Beef Ravioli with Parmesan

Prep time: 10 minutes | Cook time: 12 minutes | Serves 4

1 (20-ounce / 567-g) package frozen cheese ravioli
1 teaspoon kosher salt
1¼ cups water
6 ounces (170 g) cooked ground beef
2½ cups Marinara sauce
¼ cup grated Parmesan cheese, for garnish

1. Place the ravioli in an even layer on a baking pan. Stir the salt into the water until dissolved and pour it over the ravioli.
2. Select Bake. Set temperature to 400°F (205°C) and set time to 12 minutes. Press Start to begin preheating.
3. Once preheated, place the pan into the oven.
4. While the ravioli is cooking, mix the ground beef into the marinara sauce in a medium bowl.
5. After 6 minutes, remove the pan from the oven. Blot off any remaining water, or drain the ravioli and return them to the pan. Pour the meat sauce over the ravioli. Return the pan to the oven and continue cooking.
6. When cooking is complete, remove the pan from the oven. The ravioli should be tender and sauce heated through. Gently stir the ingredients. Serve the ravioli with the Parmesan cheese, if desired.

Pork Cutlets with Aloha Salsa
Prep time: 20 minutes | Cook time: 7 minutes | Serves 4

2 eggs
2 tablespoons milk
¼ cup all-purpose flour
¼ cup panko bread crumbs
4 teaspoons sesame seeds
Aloha Salsa:
1 cup fresh pineapple, chopped in small pieces
¼ cup red bell pepper, chopped
½ teaspoon ground cinnamon
1 teaspoon soy sauce
1 pound (454 g) boneless, thin pork cutlets (½-inch thick)
¼ cup cornstarch
Salt and ground lemon pepper, to taste
Cooking spray
¼ cup red onion, finely chopped
⅛ teaspoon crushed red pepper
⅛ teaspoon ground black pepper

1. In a medium bowl, stir together all ingredients for salsa. Cover and refrigerate while cooking the pork.
2. Beat together eggs and milk in a large bowl. In another bowl, mix the flour, panko, and sesame seeds. Pour the cornstarch in a shallow dish.
3. Sprinkle pork cutlets with lemon pepper and salt. Dip pork cutlets in cornstarch, egg mixture, and then panko coating. Spritz both sides with cooking spray.
4. Select Air Fry. Set temperature to 400ºF (205ºC) and set time to 7 minutes. Press Start to begin preheating.
5. Once preheated, place the pan into the oven.
6. After 3 minutes, remove the pan from the oven. Flip the cutlets with tongs. Return the pan to the oven and continue cooking.
7. When cooking is complete, the pork should be crispy and golden brown on both sides.
8. Serve the fried cutlets with the Aloha salsa on the side.

Dijon-Honey Pork Tenderloin
Prep time: 15 minutes | Cook time: 18 minutes | Serves 4

3 tablespoons Dijon mustard
3 tablespoons honey
1 teaspoon dried rosemary
1 tablespoon olive oil
1 pound (454 g) pork tenderloin, rinsed and drained
Salt and freshly ground black pepper, to taste

1. In a small bowl, combine the Dijon mustard, honey, and rosemary. Stir to combine.
2. Rub the pork tenderloin with salt and pepper on all sides on a clean work surface.
3. Heat the olive oil in an oven-safe skillet over high heat. Sear the pork loin on all sides in the skillet for 6 minutes or until golden brown. Flip the pork halfway through.
4. Remove from the heat and spread honey-mustard mixture evenly to coat the pork loin. Transfer the pork to a sheet pan.
5. Select Bake. Set temperature to 400ºF (205ºC) and set time to 18 minutes. Press Start to begin preheating.
6. Once preheated, place the pan into the oven.
7. When cooking is complete, an instant-read thermometer inserted in the pork should register at least 145ºF (63ºC).
8. Remove from the oven and allow to rest for 3 minutes. Slice the pork into ½-inch slices and serve.

Beef Meatloaves with Spinach
Prep time: 15 minutes | Cook time: 45 minutes | Serves 2

1 large egg, beaten
1 cup frozen spinach
⅓ cup almond meal
¼ cup chopped onion
¼ cup plain Greek milk
¼ teaspoon salt
¼ teaspoon dried sage
2 teaspoons olive oil, divided
Freshly ground black pepper, to taste
½ pound (227 g) extra-lean ground beef
¼ cup tomato paste
1 tablespoon granulated stevia
¼ teaspoon Worcestershire sauce
Cooking spray

1. Coat a shallow baking pan with cooking spray.
2. In a large bowl, combine the beaten egg, spinach, almond meal, onion, milk, salt, sage, 1 teaspoon of olive oil, and pepper.
3. Crumble the beef over the spinach mixture. Mix well to combine. Divide the meat mixture in half. Shape each half into a loaf. Place the loaves in the prepared pan.
4. In a small bowl, whisk together the tomato paste, stevia, Worcestershire sauce, and remaining 1 teaspoon of olive oil. Spoon half of the sauce over each meatloaf.
5. Select Bake. set temperature to 350ºF (180ºC) and set time to 40 minutes. Press Start to begin preheating.
6. Once preheated, place the pan into the oven.
7. When cooking is complete, an instant-read thermometer inserted in the center of the meatloaves should read at least 165ºF (74ºC).
8. Serve immediately.

Prosciutto Tart with Asparagus
Prep time: 10 minutes | Cook time: 25 minutes | Serves 4

All-purpose flour, for dusting
1 sheet (½ package) frozen puff pastry, thawed
½ cup grated Parmesan cheese
1 pound (454 g) (or more) asparagus, trimmed
8 ounces (227 g) thinly sliced prosciutto, sliced into ribbons about ½-inch wide
2 teaspoons aged balsamic vinegar

1. On a lightly floured cutting board, unwrap and unfold the puff pastry and roll it lightly with a rolling pin so as to press the folds together. Place it on the sheet pan.
2. Roll about ½ inch of the pastry edges up to form a ridge around the perimeter. Crimp the corners together to create a solid rim around the pastry. Using a fork, pierce the bottom of the pastry all over. Scatter the cheese over the bottom of the pastry.
3. Arrange the asparagus spears on top of the cheese in a single layer with 4 or 5 spears pointing one way, the next few pointing the opposite direction. You may need to trim them so they fit within the border of the pastry shell. Lay the prosciutto on top more or less evenly.
4. Select Bake. Set temperature to 375ºF (190ºC) and set time to 25 minutes. Press Start to begin preheating.
5. Once the unit has preheated, place the pan into the oven.
6. After about 15 minutes, check the tart, rotating the pan if the crust is not browning evenly and continue cooking until the pastry is golden brown and the edges of the prosciutto pieces are browned.
7. Remove the pan from the oven. Allow to cool for 5 minutes before slicing.
8. Drizzle with the balsamic vinegar just before serving.

Teriyaki-Glazed Pork Ribs
Prep time: 5 minutes | Cook time: 30 minutes | Serves 4

¼ cup soy sauce
¼ cup honey
1 teaspoon garlic powder
1 teaspoon ground dried ginger
4 (8-ounce / 227-g) boneless country-style pork ribs
Cooking spray

1. Spritz the perforated pan with cooking spray.
2. Make the teriyaki sauce: combine the soy sauce, honey, garlic powder, and ginger in a bowl. Stir to mix well.
3. Brush the ribs with half of the teriyaki sauce, then arrange the ribs in the pan. Spritz with cooking spray.
4. Select Air Fry. Set temperature to 350ºF (180ºC) and set time to 30 minutes. Press Start to begin preheating.
5. Once preheated, place the pan into the oven.
6. After 15 minutes, remove the pan from the oven. Flip the ribs and brush with remaining teriyaki sauce. Return the pan to the oven and continue cooking.
7. When cooking is complete, the internal temperature of the ribs should reach at least 145ºF (63ºC).
8. Serve immediately.

Orange Beef and Broccoli with Sriracha
Prep time: 10 minutes | Cook time: 15 minutes | Serves 4

12 ounces (340 g) broccoli, cut into florets (about 4 cups)
1 pound (454 g) flat iron steak, cut into thin strips
½ teaspoon kosher salt
¾ cup soy sauce
1 teaspoon Sriracha sauce
3 tablespoons freshly squeezed orange juice
1 teaspoon cornstarch
1 medium onion, thinly sliced

1. Line a baking pan with aluminum foil. Place the broccoli on top and sprinkle with 3 tablespoons of water. Seal the broccoli in the foil in a single layer.
2. Select Roast. Set temperature to 375ºF (190ºC) and set time to 6 minutes. Press Start to begin preheating.
3. Once preheated, place the pan into the oven.
4. While the broccoli steams, sprinkle the steak with the salt. In a small bowl, whisk together the soy sauce, Sriracha, orange juice, and cornstarch. Place the onion and beef in a large bowl.
5. When cooking is complete, remove the pan from the oven. Open the packet of broccoli and use tongs to transfer the broccoli to the bowl with the beef and onion, discarding the foil and remaining water. Pour the sauce over the beef and vegetables and toss to coat. Place the mixture in the baking pan.
6. Select Roast. Set temperature to 375ºF (190ºC) and set time to 9 minutes.
7. Place the pan into the oven.
8. After about 4 minutes, remove the pan from the oven and gently toss the ingredients. Return the pan to oven and continue cooking.
9. When cooking is complete, the sauce should be thickened, the vegetables tender, and the beef barely pink in the center. Serve warm.

Pork Sausage Ratatouille
Prep time: 10 minutes | Cook time: 25 minutes | Serves 4

4 pork sausages
Ratatouille:
2 zucchinis, sliced
1 eggplant, sliced
15 ounces (425 g) tomatoes, sliced
1 red bell pepper, sliced
1 medium red onion, sliced
1 cup canned butter beans, drained
1 tablespoon balsamic vinegar
2 garlic cloves, minced
1 red chili, chopped
2 tablespoons fresh thyme, chopped
2 tablespoons olive oil

1. Place the sausages in the perforated pan.
2. Select Air Fry. Set temperature to 390ºF (199ºC) and set time to 10 minutes. Press Start to begin preheating.
3. Once preheated, place the pan into the oven.
4. After 7 minutes, remove the pan from the oven. Flip the sausages. Return the pan to the oven and continue cooking.
5. When cooking is complete, the sausages should be lightly browned.
6. Meanwhile, make the ratatouille: arrange the vegetable slices on the prepared pan alternatively, then add the remaining ingredients on top.
7. Transfer the air fried sausage to a plate, then place the pan into the oven.
8. Select Bake. Set time to 15 minutes and bake until the vegetables are tender. Give the vegetables a stir halfway through the baking.
9. Serve the ratatouille with the sausage on top.

Vinegary Pork Schnitzel
Prep time: 5 minutes | Cook time: 14 minutes | Serves 2

½ cup pork rinds
½ tablespoon fresh parsley
½ teaspoon fennel seed
½ teaspoon mustard
⅓ tablespoon cider vinegar
1 teaspoon garlic salt
⅓ teaspoon ground black pepper
2 eggs
2 pork schnitzel, halved
Cooking spray

1. Spritz the perforated pan with cooking spray.
2. Put the pork rinds, parsley, fennel seeds, and mustard in a food processor. Pour in the vinegar and sprinkle with salt and ground black pepper. Pulse until well combined and smooth.
3. Pour the pork rind mixture in a large bowl. Whisk the eggs in a separate bowl.
4. Dunk the pork schnitzel in the whisked eggs, then dunk in the pork rind mixture to coat well. Shake the excess off.
5. Arrange the schnitzel in the pan and spritz with cooking spray.
6. Select Air Fry. Set temperature to 350ºF (180ºC) and set time to 14 minutes. Press Start to begin preheating.
7. Once preheated, place the pan into the oven.
8. After 7 minutes, remove the pan from the oven. Flip the schnitzel. Return the pan to the oven and continue cooking.
9. When cooking is complete, the schnitzel should be golden and crispy.
10. Serve immediately.

Garlic Pork Leg Roast with Candy Onions
Prep time: 10 minutes | Cook time: 52 minutes | Serves 4

2 teaspoons sesame oil
1 teaspoon dried sage, crushed
1 teaspoon cayenne pepper
1 rosemary sprig, chopped
1 thyme sprig, chopped
Sea salt and ground black pepper, to taste
2 pounds (907 g) pork leg roast, scored
½ pound (227 g) candy onions, sliced
4 cloves garlic, finely chopped
2 chili peppers, minced

1. In a mixing bowl, combine the sesame oil, sage, cayenne pepper, rosemary, thyme, salt and black pepper until well mixed. In another bowl, place the pork leg and brush with the seasoning mixture.
2. Place the seasoned pork leg in a baking pan. Select Air Fry. Set temperature to 400ºF (205ºC) and set time to 40 minutes. Press Start to begin preheating.
3. Once preheated, place the pan into the oven.
4. After 20 minutes, remove the pan from the oven. Flip the pork leg. Return the pan to the oven and continue cooking.
5. After another 20 minutes, add the candy onions, garlic, and chili peppers to the pan and air fry for another 12 minutes.
6. When cooking is complete, the pork leg should be browned.
7. Transfer the pork leg to a plate. Let cool for 5 minutes and slice. Spread the juices left in the pan over the pork and serve warm with the candy onions.

Mozzarella Sausage Calzones
Prep time: 10 minutes | Cook time: 27 minutes | Serves 4

2 links Italian sausages (about ½ pound / 227 g)
1 pound (454 g) pizza dough, thawed
3 tablespoons olive oil, divided
¼ cup Marinara sauce
½ cup roasted mushrooms
1 cup shredded Mozzarella cheese

1. Place the sausages in a baking pan.
2. Select Roast. Set temperature to 375ºF (190ºC) and set time to 12 minutes. Press Start to begin preheating.
3. Once preheated, place the pan into the oven.
4. After 6 minutes, remove the pan from the oven and turn over the sausages. Return the pan to the oven and continue cooking.
5. While the sausages cook, divide the pizza dough into 4 equal pieces. One at a time, place a piece of dough onto a square of parchment paper 9 inches in diameter. Brush the dough on both sides with ¾ teaspoon of olive oil, then top the dough with another piece of parchment. Press the dough into a 7-inch circle. Remove the top piece of parchment and set aside. Repeat with the remaining pieces of dough.
6. When cooking is complete, remove the pan from the oven. Place the sausages on a cutting board. Let them cool for several minutes, then slice into ¼-inch rounds and cut each round into 4 pieces.
7. One at a time, spread a tablespoon of marinara sauce over half of a dough circle, leaving a ½-inch border at the edges. Cover with a quarter of the sausage pieces and add a quarter of the mushrooms. Sprinkle with ¼ cup of cheese. Pull the other side of the dough over the filling and pinch the edges together to seal. Transfer from the parchment to the baking pan. Repeat with the other rounds of dough, sauce, sausage, mushrooms, and cheese.
8. Brush the tops of the calzones with 1 tablespoon of olive oil.
9. Select Roast. Set temperature to 400ºF (205ºC) and set time to 15 minutes.
10. Place the pan into the oven.
11. After 6 minutes, remove the pan from the oven. The calzones should be golden brown. Turn over the calzones and brush the tops with the remaining olive oil. Return the pan to the oven and continue cooking.
12. When cooking is complete, the crust should be a deep golden brown on both sides. Remove the pan from the oven. The center should be molten; let cool for several minutes before serving.

Mexican Sirloin Steak and Pepper Fajitas
Prep time: 10 minutes | Cook time: 15 minutes | Serves 4

8 (6-inch) flour tortillas
1 pound (454 g) top sirloin steak, sliced ¼-inch thick
1 red bell pepper, deseeded and sliced ½-inch thick
1 green bell pepper, deseeded and sliced ½-inch thick
1 jalapeño, deseeded and sliced thin
1 medium onion, sliced ½-inch thick
2 tablespoons vegetable oil
2 tablespoons Mexican seasoning
1 teaspoon kosher salt
2 tablespoons salsa
1 small avocado, sliced

1. Line a baking pan with aluminum foil. Place the tortillas on the foil in two stacks and wrap in the foil.
2. Select Roast. Set temperature to 325ºF (163ºC) and set time to 6 minutes. Press Start to begin preheating.
3. Once preheated, place the pan into the oven. After 3 minutes, remove the pan from the oven and flip the packet of tortillas over. Return the pan to the oven and continue cooking.
4. While the tortillas warm, place the steak, bell peppers, jalapeño, and onion in a large bowl and drizzle the oil over. Sprinkle with the Mexican seasoning and salt, and toss to coat.
5. When cooking is complete, remove the pan from the oven and place the packet of tortillas on top of the oven to keep warm. Place the beef and peppers mixture on the baking pan, spreading out into a single layer as much as possible.
6. Select Roast. Set temperature to 375ºF (190ºC) and set time to 9 minutes.
7. Place the pan into the oven.
8. After about 5 minutes, remove the pan from the oven and stir the ingredients. Return the pan to the oven and continue cooking.
9. When cooking is complete, the vegetables will be soft and browned in places, and the beef will be browned on the outside and barely pink inside. Remove the pan from the oven. Unwrap the tortillas and spoon the fajita mixture into the tortillas. Serve with salsa and avocado slices.

Fall seven times, stand up eight. -Chapter 6 Meats | 61

Pork Meatballs with Scallions

Prep time: 5 minutes | Cook time: 15 minutes | Serves 4

1 pound (454 g) ground pork
2 cloves garlic, finely minced
1 cup scallions, finely chopped
1½ tablespoons Worcestershire sauce
½ teaspoon freshly grated ginger root
1 teaspoon turmeric powder
1 tablespoon oyster sauce
1 small sliced red chili, for garnish
Cooking spray

1. Spritz the perforated pan with cooking spray.
2. Combine all the ingredients, except for the red chili in a large bowl. Toss to mix well.
3. Shape the mixture into equally sized balls, then arrange them in the perforated pan and spritz with cooking spray.
4. Select Air Fry. Set temperature to 350ºF (180ºC) and set time to 15 minutes. Press Start to begin preheating.
5. Once preheated, place the pan into the oven.
6. After 7 minutes, remove the pan from the oven. Flip the balls. Return the pan to the oven and continue cooking.
7. When cooking is complete, the balls should be lightly browned.
8. Serve the pork meatballs with red chili on top.

Pork, Squash and Pepper Kebabs

Prep time: 20 minutes | Cook time: 8 minutes | Serves 4

For the Pork:
1 pound (454 g) pork steak, cut in cubes
1 tablespoon white wine vinegar
3 tablespoons steak sauce
¼ cup soy sauce
1 teaspoon powdered chili
1 teaspoon red chili flakes
2 teaspoons smoked paprika
1 teaspoon garlic salt

For the Vegetable:
1 green squash, deseeded and cut in cubes
1 yellow squash, deseeded and cut in cubes
1 red pepper, cut in cubes
1 green pepper, cut in cubes
Salt and ground black pepper, to taste
Cooking spray

Special Equipment:
4 bamboo skewers, soaked in water for at least 30 minutes

1. Combine the ingredients for the pork in a large bowl. Press the pork to dunk in the marinade. Wrap the bowl in plastic and refrigerate for at least an hour.
2. Spritz the perforated pan with cooking spray.
3. Remove the pork from the marinade and run the skewers through the pork and vegetables alternatively. Sprinkle with salt and pepper to taste.
4. Arrange the skewers in the pan and spritz with cooking spray.
5. Select Air Fry. Set temperature to 380ºF (193ºC) and set time to 8 minutes. Press Start to begin preheating.
6. Once preheated, place the pan into the oven.
7. After 4 minutes, remove the pan from the oven. Flip the skewers. Return the pan to the oven and continue cooking.
8. When cooking is complete, the pork should be browned and the vegetables should be lightly charred and tender.
9. Serve immediately.

Breaded Calf's Liver Strips

Prep time: 15 minutes | Cook time: 4 to 5 minutes | Serves 4

1 pound (454 g) sliced calf's liver, cut into about ½-inch-wide strips
Salt and ground black pepper, to taste
2 eggs
2 tablespoons milk
½ cup whole wheat flour
1½ cups panko bread crumbs
½ cup plain bread crumbs
½ teaspoon salt
¼ teaspoon ground black pepper
Cooking spray

1. Sprinkle the liver strips with salt and pepper.
2. Beat together the egg and milk in a bowl. Place wheat flour in a shallow dish. In a second shallow dish, mix panko, plain bread crumbs, ½ teaspoon salt, and ¼ teaspoon pepper.
3. Dip liver strips in flour, egg wash, and then bread crumbs, pressing in coating slightly to make crumbs stick.
4. Spritz the perforated pan with cooking spray. Place strips in a single layer in the perforated pan.
5. Select Air Fry. Set temperature to 400ºF (205ºC) and set time to 4 minutes. Press Start to begin preheating.
6. Once preheated, place the pan into the oven.
7. After 2 minutes, remove the pan from the oven. Flip the strips with tongs. Return the pan to the oven and continue cooking.
8. When cooking is complete, the liver strips should be crispy and golden.
9. Serve immediately.

Pork Tenderloin with Rice
Prep time: 10 minutes | Cook time: 12 minutes | Serves 4

3 scallions, diced (about ½ cup)
½ red bell pepper, diced (about ½ cup)
2 teaspoons sesame oil
½ pound (227 g) pork tenderloin, diced
½ cup frozen peas, thawed
½ cup roasted mushrooms
½ cup soy sauce
2 cups cooked rice
1 egg, beaten

1. Place the scallions and red pepper on a baking pan. Drizzle with the sesame oil and toss the vegetables to coat them in the oil.
2. Select Roast. Set temperature to 375ºF (190ºC) and set time to 12 minutes. Press Start to begin preheating.
3. Once preheated, place the pan into the oven.
4. While the vegetables are cooking, place the pork in a large bowl. Add the peas, mushrooms, soy sauce, and rice and toss to coat the ingredients with the sauce.
5. After about 4 minutes, remove the pan from the oven. Place the pork mixture on the pan and stir the scallions and peppers into the pork and rice. Return the pan to the oven and continue cooking.
6. After another 6 minutes, remove the pan from the oven. Move the rice mixture to the sides to create an empty circle in the middle of the pan. Pour the egg in the circle. Return the pan to the oven and continue cooking.
7. When cooking is complete, remove the pan from the oven and stir the egg to scramble it. Stir the egg into the fried rice mixture. Serve immediately.

Worcestershire Ribeye Steaks with Garlic
Prep time: 15 minutes | Cook time: 10 to 12 minutes | Serves 2 to 4

2 (8-ounce / 227-g) boneless ribeye steaks
4 teaspoons Worcestershire sauce
½ teaspoon garlic powder
Salt and ground black pepper, to taste
4 teaspoons olive oil

1. Brush the steaks with Worcestershire sauce on both sides. Sprinkle with garlic powder and coarsely ground black pepper. Drizzle the steaks with olive oil. Allow steaks to marinate for 30 minutes.
2. Transfer the steaks in the perforated pan.
3. Select Roast. Set temperature to 400ºF (205ºC) and set time to 4 minutes. Press Start to begin preheating.
4. Once preheated, place the pan into the oven.
5. After 2 minutes, remove the pan from the oven. Flip the steaks. Return the pan to the oven and continue cooking.
6. When cooking is complete, the steaks should be well browned.
7. Remove the steaks from the perforated pan and let sit for 5 minutes. Salt and serve.

Pork Loin Chops with Butternut Squash
Prep time: 15 minutes | Cook time: 13 minutes | Serves 4

4 boneless pork loin chops, ¾- to 1-inch thick
1 teaspoon kosher salt, divided
2 tablespoons Dijon mustard
2 tablespoons brown sugar
1 pound (454 g) butternut squash, cut into 1-inch cubes
1 large apple, peeled and cut into 12 to 16 wedges
1 medium onion, thinly sliced
½ teaspoon dried thyme
¼ teaspoon freshly ground black pepper
1 tablespoon unsalted butter, melted
½ cup chicken stock

1. Sprinkle the pork chops on both sides with ½ teaspoon of kosher salt. In a small bowl, whisk together the mustard and brown sugar. Baste about half of the mixture on one side of the pork chops. Place the chops, basted-side up, on a baking pan.
2. Place the squash in a large bowl. Add the apple, onion, thyme, remaining kosher salt, pepper, and butter and toss to coat. Arrange the squash-fruit mixture around the chops on the pan. Pour the chicken stock over the mixture, avoiding the chops.
3. Select Roast. Set temperature to 350ºF (180ºC) and set time to 13 minutes. Press Start to begin preheating.
4. Once preheated, place the pan into the oven.
5. After about 7 minutes, remove the pan from the oven. Gently toss the squash mixture and turn over the chops. Baste the chops with the remaining mustard mixture. Return the pan to the oven and continue cooking.
6. When cooking is complete, the pork chops should register at least 145ºF (63ºC) in the center on a meat thermometer, and the squash and apples should be tender. If necessary, continue cooking for up to 3 minutes more.
7. Remove the pan from the oven. Spoon the squash and apples onto four plates, and place a pork chop on top. Serve immediately.

Chapter 7 Fish and Seafood

Clam Appetizers

Prep time: 10 minutes | Cook time: 15 minutes | Makes 12 appetizers

1 (6-ounce / 170-g) can minced clams, well drained
1 cup multigrain bread crumbs
1 tablespoon minced onion
1 teaspoon garlic powder
1 teaspoon Worcestershire sauce
1 tablespoon chopped fresh parsley
2 tablespoons olive oil
Salt and freshly ground black pepper, to taste
Lemon wedges

1. Combine all the ingredients in a medium bowl and fill 12 scrubbed clamshells or small baking dishes with equal portions of the mixture. Place in an oiled or nonstick square (cake) pan.
2. Select Bake. Set temperature to 400ºF (205ºC) and set time to 15 minutes. Select Start to begin preheating.
3. Once preheated, slide the pan into the oven.
4. When done, the clam will be lightly browned.

Catfish Fillets with Pecan Crust

Prep time: 5 minutes | Cook time: 12 minutes | Serves 4

½ cup pecan meal
1 teaspoon fine sea salt
¼ teaspoon ground black pepper
For Garnish (Optional):
Fresh oregano
4 (4-ounce / 113-g) catfish fillets
Avocado oil spray

Pecan halves

1. Spray the perforated pan with avocado oil spray.
2. Combine the pecan meal, sea salt, and black pepper in a large bowl. Dredge each catfish fillet in the meal mixture, turning until well coated. Spritz the fillets with avocado oil spray, then transfer to the perforated pan.
3. Select Air Fry. Set temperature to 375ºF (190ºC) and set time to 12 minutes. Press Start to begin preheating.
4. Once preheated, place the pan into the oven. Flip the fillets halfway through the cooking time.
5. When cooking is complete, the fish should be cooked through and no longer translucent. Remove from the oven and sprinkle the oregano sprigs and pecan halves on top for garnish, if desired. Serve immediately.

Broiled Lemony Salmon Steak

Prep time: 10 minutes | Cook time: 20 minutes | Serves 2

2 (6-ounce / 170-g) salmon steaks
Brushing Mixture:
2 tablespoons lemon juice
2 tablespoons olive oil
1 tablespoon soy sauce
1 teaspoon dried dill or dill weed
½ teaspoon garlic powder
1 teaspoon soy sauce

1. Combine the brushing mixture ingredients in a small bowl and brush the salmon steak tops, skin side down, liberally, reserving the remaining mixture. Let the steaks sit at room temperature for 10 minutes, then place on a broiling rack with a pan underneath.
2. Select Broil. Set temperature to 400ºF (205ºC) and set time to 20 minutes. Select Start to begin preheating.
3. Once preheated, slide the pan into the oven.
4. After 15 minutes, remove from the oven, and brush the steaks with the remaining mixture. Broil again for 5 minutes, or until the meat flakes easily with a fork.

Bacon-Wrapped Herb Rainbow Trout

Prep time: 10 minutes | Cook time: 20 minutes | Serves 4

4 (8- to 10-ounce / 227- to 283-g) rainbow trout, butterflied and boned
2 teaspoons kosher salt, divided
1 tablespoon extra-virgin olive oil, divided
1 tablespoon freshly squeezed lemon juice, divided
2 tablespoons chopped fresh parsley, divided
2 tablespoons chopped fresh chives, divided
8 thin bacon slices
Lemon wedges, for serving

1. Lightly oil a sheet pan.
2. Sprinkle the inside and outside of each trout with the salt. Brush the inside with the oil and drizzle with the lemon juice. Scatter the parsley and chives on one side of each butterflied trout. Fold the trout closed and wrap each one with two slices of bacon. Transfer to the sheet pan.
3. Select Bake. Set temperature to 400ºF (205ºC) and set time to 20 minutes. Select Start to begin preheating.
4. Once preheated, slide the pan into the oven. Flip the trout halfway through the cooking time.
5. When done, the bacon will be crisp.
6. Serve with lemon wedges.

Sea Bass with Asian Chili Dressing
Prep time: 15 minutes | Cook time: 20 minutes | Serves 6

For the Fish:
1 red Fresno chili, halved, seeded, and chopped
1¼-inch fresh ginger, peeled and finely grated
3 garlic cloves, finely grated
¾ cup cilantro leaves, roughly chopped, plus ¼ cup Cilantro leaves to serve
Finely grated zest of 2 limes, plus the juice of ½ lime, plus Lime wedges to serve
Sea salt flakes
2 tablespoons peanut oil
2 (2-pound / 907-g) sea bass (branzino), gutted, scaled and washed
6 scallions, trimmed and roughly chopped

For the Dressing:
Juice of 1 lime
2 tablespoons superfine sugar
⅓ cup fish sauce
1 red Fresno chili, halved, seeded, and very thinly sliced

1. Put a double layer of parchment paper into a baking pan.
2. Put the chili, ginger, garlic, the ¾ cup of cilantro, and the lime zest into a mortar with some salt and pound them together, adding 1 tablespoon of the oil, until you have a rough paste. Add the lime juice.
3. Put the fish on the parchment paper. Make 4 slits in both sides of each fish, without cutting through the bone, and push the paste into them. Stuff the fish with the scallions. Rub the rest of the oil over the fish on both sides and season with salt.
4. Select Bake. Set temperature to 400ºF (205ºC) and set time to 20 minutes. Select Start to begin preheating.
5. Once preheated, slide the pan into the oven.
6. When done, the flesh near the bone at the thickest part should be opaque, not translucent.
7. Make the dressing by mixing together the lime juice, sugar, fish sauce, and chili. Serve the fish with the dressing on the side, or spoon it over the top. Scatter with the ¼ cup cilantro leaves and serve with lime wedges.

Crab Cheese Enchiladas
Prep time: 10 minutes | Cook time: 25 minutes | Serves 4

8 (6-inch) corn tortillas
Nonstick cooking spray or vegetable oil, for brushing
2 cups mild tomatillo salsa or green enchilada sauce
½ cup heavy (whipping) cream
8 ounces (227 g) lump crab meat, picked through to remove any shells
3 or 4 scallions, chopped
8 ounces (227 g) Monterey Jack cheese, shredded

1. Spray the tortillas on both sides with cooking spray or brush lightly with oil. Arrange on a sheet pan, overlapping as little as possible.
2. Select Bake. Set temperature to 350ºF (180ºC) and set time to 5 minutes. Select Start to begin preheating.
3. Once preheated, slide the pan into the oven.
4. When done, the tortillas will be warm and flexible.
5. Meanwhile, stir together the salsa and cream in a shallow, microwave-safe bowl and heat in the microwave until very warm, about 45 seconds.
6. Pour a quarter of the salsa mixture into a baking pan. Place a tortilla in the sauce, turning it over to coat thoroughly. Spoon a heaping tablespoon of crab down the middle of the tortilla, then top with a teaspoon of scallions and a heaping tablespoon of cheese. Roll up the tortilla and place it seam-side down at one end of the pan. Repeat with the remaining tortillas, forming a row of enchiladas in the pan. Spoon most or all of the remaining sauce over the enchiladas so they are nicely coated but not drowning. Sprinkle the remaining cheese over the top.
7. Bake for 18 to 20 minutes, until the cheese is melted and the sauce is bubbling.

Salmon Fillet with Spinach, and Beans
Prep time: 10 minutes | Cook time: 35 minutes | Serves 4

2 tablespoons olive oil, divided
1 garlic clove, thinly sliced
1 (9- to 10-ounce / 255- to 283-g) bag baby spinach
1 (15-ounce / 425-g) can cannellini or navy beans, rinsed and drained
1½ teaspoons kosher salt, divided
½ teaspoon ground cumin
½ teaspoon ground coriander
¼ teaspoon red pepper flakes
4 (6-ounce / 170-g) skinless salmon fillets

1. Heat 1 tablespoon of oil in a large, oven-safe skillet over medium-high heat. Add the garlic and cook, stirring, until fragrant, about 30 seconds. Add the spinach a handful at a time and cook, tossing, until slightly wilted, adding more as you have room. Stir in the beans, ¾ teaspoon of salt, cumin, coriander, and red pepper flakes.
2. Season the salmon with the remaining ¾ teaspoon of salt. Place the fillets in a single layer on top of the spinach mixture and drizzle with the remaining 1 tablespoon of oil.
3. Select Bake. Set temperature to 300ºF (150ºC) and set time to 35 minutes. Select Start to begin preheating.
4. Once preheated, put the skillet in the oven.
5. When done, the salmon will be opaque in the center.

Marinated Catfish Fillet

Prep time: 10 minutes | Cook time: 15 minutes | Serves 4

4 (6-ounce / 170-g) catfish fillets
Marinade Ingredients:
1 tablespoon olive oil
1 tablespoon lemon juice
¼ dry white wine
1 tablespoon garlic powder
1 tablespoon soy sauce

1. Combine the marinade ingredients in an ovenproof baking dish. Add the fillets and let stand for 10 minutes, spooning the marinade over the fillets every 2 minutes.
2. Select Broil. Set temperature to 400°F (205°C) and set time to 15 minutes. Select Start to begin preheating.
3. Once preheated, place the baking dish in the oven.
4. When done, the fish will flake easily with a fork.

Sherry Tilapia and Mushroom Rice

Prep time: 15 minutes | Cook time: 25 minutes | Serves 4

4 tablespoons unsalted butter
12 ounces (340 g) cremini or white button mushrooms, trimmed and sliced
4 to 6 scallions, chopped
1 teaspoon kosher salt, divided
2 tablespoons all-purpose flour
¾ cup dry sherry or dry white wine
¾ cup low-sodium vegetable or fish broth
3 tablespoons heavy (whipping) cream
1 tablespoon chopped fresh parsley, divided
2 cups cooked white or brown rice
4 (6-ounce / 170-g) tilapia fillets
⅛ teaspoon freshly ground black pepper

1. In a large cast-iron or other oven-safe skillet, melt the butter over medium heat until foaming. Sauté the mushrooms and scallions until the mushrooms are soft. Stir in ½ teaspoon of salt and the flour. Cook for 1 minute, stirring constantly. Gradually stir in the sherry. Let the sauce simmer for 3 to 5 minutes, until some of the alcohol evaporates. Add the broth, cream, and 1½ teaspoons of parsley and bring back to a simmer.
2. Stir the rice into the sauce. Place the fish fillets in a single layer on top of the rice and sauce. Sprinkle the fish with the remaining ½ teaspoon of salt and the pepper, then spoon a little of the sauce over the fillets.
3. Select Bake. Set temperature to 325°F (163°C) and set time to 20 minutes. Select Start to begin preheating.
4. Once preheated, put the skillet in the oven.
5. When done, the fish will flake with a fork.
6. To serve, spoon some rice onto each plate and top with a fillet. Sprinkle with the remaining 1½ teaspoons of parsley.

Mackerel with Mango and Chili Salad

Prep time: 15 minutes | Cook time: 20 minutes | Serves 4

For the Fish:
2 garlic cloves, finely grated
1½in fresh ginger, peeled and finely grated
¾ teaspoon ground turmeric
1½ teaspoons ground cumin
½ teaspoon ground fenugreek
2½ tablespoons tamarind paste
¼ cup lime juice, plus more to serve, plus lime wedges to serve
1 tablespoon light brown sugar
2 tablespoons peanut oil
Sea salt flakes and freshly ground black pepper, to taste
4 whole Boston mackerel, gutted and washed
Rice, or warmed naan bread and plain yogurt, to serve

For the Salad:
2 just-ripe or slightly under-ripe mangoes
Juice of 2 limes
1 red Fresno chlli and 1 green chilli, halved, seeded, and very finely shredded
½ cup cilantro leaves and stalks (make sure the stalks aren't too long or thick)

1. Mix together the garlic, ginger, and all the spices for the mackerel, adding the lime juice, sugar, oil, and seasoning. Spread this all over each fish, inside and out. Cover and put in the refrigerator for about 15 minutes.
2. Now make the salad. Peel the mangoes and cut off the 'cheeks' (the fleshy bits that lie alongside the stone). Cut the cheeks into neat slices.
3. Put the mango slices in a serving bowl and add the lime juice, chilies, some salt, and the cilantro, and toss.
4. Line a baking pan with foil or parchment paper and put the mackerel in it.
5. Select Bake. Set temperature to 400°F (205°C) and set time to 20 minutes. Select Start to begin preheating.
6. Once preheated, slide the pan into the oven.
7. When done, squeeze some lime juice over the fish and serve with rice, or warmed naan bread and yogurt, lime wedges, and the mango and chili salad.

Fish Fillet with Poblano Sauce

Prep time: 10 minutes | Cook time: 20 minutes | Makes 4 fillets

4 (5-ounce / 142-g) thin fish fillets—perch, scrod, catfish, or flounder
1 tablespoon olive oil

Poblano Sauce:
1 poblano chili, seeded and chopped
1 bell pepper, seeded and chopped
2 tablespoons chopped onion
5 garlic cloves, peeled
1 tablespoon flour
1 cup fat-free half-and-half
Salt, to taste

1. Brush the fillets with olive oil and transfer to an oiled or nonstick square baking (cake) pan. Set aside.
2. Combine the poblano sauce ingredients and process in a blender or food processor until smooth. Spoon the poblano sauce over the fillets, covering them well.
3. Select Bake. Set temperature to 350ºF (180ºC) and set time to 20 minutes. Select Start to begin preheating.
4. Once preheated, slide the pan into the oven.
5. When done, the fish will flake easily with a fork.

Crispy Fish Fillet

Prep time: 10 minutes | Cook time: 14 minutes | Serves 4

4 (6-ounce / 170-g) fish fillets, approximately ¼- to ½-inch thick
2 tablespoons vegetable oil

Coating Ingredients:
1 cup cornmeal
1 teaspoon garlic powder
1 teaspoon ground cumin
1 teaspoon paprika
Salt, to taste

1. Combine the coating ingredients in a small bowl, blending well. Transfer to a large plate, spreading evenly over the surface. Brush the fillets with vegetable oil and press both sides of each fillet into the coating.
2. Place the fillets in an oiled or nonstick square baking (cake) pan, laying them flat.
3. Select Broil. Set temperature to 400ºF (205ºC) and set time to 14 minutes. Select Start to begin preheating.
4. Once preheated, slide the pan into the oven.
5. Broil for 7 minutes, then remove the pan from the oven and carefully turn the fillets with a spatula. Broil for another 7 minutes, or until the fish flakes easily with a fork and the coating is crisped to your preference. Serve immediately.

Mediterranean Baked Fish Fillet

Prep time: 10 minutes | Cook time: 25 minutes | Serves 4

4 (6-ounce / 170-g) fish fillets (red snapper, cod, whiting, sole, or mackerel)

Mixture Ingredients:
1 tablespoon olive oil
2 tablespoons tomato paste
3 plum tomatoes, chopped
2 garlic cloves, minced
2 tablespoons capers
2 tablespoons pitted and chopped black olives
2 tablespoons chopped fresh basil leaves
2 tablespoons chopped fresh parsley

1. Combine the baking mixture ingredients in a small bowl. Set aside.
2. Layer the fillets in an oiled or nonstick square baking (cake) pan, overlapping them if necessary, and spoon the baking mixture over the fish.
3. Select Bake. Set temperature to 350ºF (180ºC) and set time to 25 minutes. Select Start to begin preheating.
4. Once preheated, slide the pan into the oven.
5. When done, the fish will flake easily with a fork.

Curried Halibut Fillets with Parmesan

Prep time: 5 minutes | Cook time: 10 minutes | Serves 4

2 medium-sized halibut fillets
Dash of tabasco sauce
1 teaspoon curry powder
½ teaspoon ground coriander
½ teaspoon hot paprika
Kosher salt and freshly cracked mixed peppercorns, to taste
2 eggs
1½ tablespoons olive oil
½ cup grated Parmesan cheese

1. On a clean work surface, drizzle the halibut fillets with the tabasco sauce. Sprinkle with the curry powder, coriander, hot paprika, salt, and cracked mixed peppercorns. Set aside.
2. In a shallow bowl, beat the eggs until frothy. In another shallow bowl, combine the olive oil and Parmesan cheese.
3. One at a time, dredge the halibut fillets in the beaten eggs, shaking off any excess, then roll them over the Parmesan cheese until evenly coated.
4. Arrange the halibut fillets in the perforated pan in a single layer.
5. Select Roast. Set temperature to 365ºF (185ºC) and set time to 10 minutes. Press Start to begin preheating.
6. Once preheated, place the pan into the oven.
7. When cooking is complete, the fish should be golden brown and crisp. Cool for 5 minutes before serving.

Breaded Crab Cakes
Prep time: 10 minutes | Cook time: 30 minutes | Serves 6

1 pound (454 g) fresh lump crab meat, drained and chopped
1 cup bread crumbs
½ cup plain nonfat yogurt
1 tablespoon olive oil
2 tablespoons capers
1 tablespoon garlic powder
1 teaspoon hot sauce
1 egg, beaten
1 tablespoon Worcestershire sauce
Salt and freshly ground black pepper, to taste

1. Combine all the ingredients in a bowl. Shape the mixture into patties approximately 2½ inches wide, adding more bread crumbs if the mixture is too wet and sticky and more yogurt if the mixture is too dry and crumbly. Place the patties in an oiled or nonstick square (cake) pan.
2. Select Bake. Set temperature to 350°F (180°C) and set time to 25 minutes. Select Start to begin preheating.
3. Once preheated, slide the pan into the oven, uncovered.
4. After 25 minutes, select Broil. Set temperature to 400°F (205°C) and set time to 5 minutes.
5. When done, the patties will be golden brown.

Flounder Fillet and Asparagus Rolls
Prep time: 10 minutes | Cook time: 30 minutes | Serves 4

1 dozen asparagus stalks, tough stem part cut off
4 (6-ounce / 170-g) flounder fillets
4 tablespoons chopped scallions
4 tablespoons shredded carrots
4 tablespoons finely chopped Almonds
1 teaspoon dried dill weed
Salt and freshly ground black pepper, to taste
1 lemon, cut into wedges

1. Place 3 asparagus stalks lengthwise on a flounder fillet. Add 1 tablespoon scallions, 1 tablespoon carrots, 1 tablespoon almonds, and a sprinkling of dill. Season to taste with salt and pepper and roll the fillet together so that the long edges overlap. Secure the edges with toothpicks or tie with cotton string. Carefully place the rolled fillet in an oiled or nonstick square baking (cake) pan. Repeat the process for the remaining ingredients. Cover the pan with aluminum foil.
2. Select Bake. Set temperature to 400°F (205°C) and set time to 20 minutes. Select Start to begin preheating.
3. Once preheated, slide the pan into the oven, covered.
4. When done, the asparagus will be tender. Remove the cover.
5. Select Broil. Set temperature to 400°F (205°C) and set time to 10 minutes. Slide the pan into the oven. When done, the fish will be lightly browned.
6. Remove and discard the toothpicks or string. Serve the rolled fillets with lemon wedges.

Lemony Shrimp with Arugula
Prep time: 10 minutes | Cook time: 10 minutes | Serves 4

4 tablespoons unsalted butter, melted
2 tablespoons extra-virgin olive oil
1 teaspoon kosher salt
6 garlic cloves, minced
¼ cup chopped fresh parsley, divided
2 pounds (907 g) large shrimp, peeled and deveined
2 tablespoons freshly squeezed lemon juice
1 (9- to 10-ounce / 255- to 283-g) bag arugula

1. In a baking pan, add the butter, oil, salt, garlic, and half the parsley. Stir well. Add the shrimp and toss to coat, then arrange the shrimp in a single layer.
2. Select Bake. Set temperature to 375°F (190°C) and set time to 5 minutes. Select Start to begin preheating.
3. Once preheated, slide the pan into the oven.
4. When done, the shrimp will be opaque and pink.
5. Remove the pan from the oven. Add the lemon juice, arugula, and remaining parsley. Toss well to wilt the arugula. Serve immediately.

Honey Halibut Steaks with Parsley
Prep time: 5 minutes | Cook time: 10 minutes | Serves 4

1 pound (454 g) halibut steaks
¼ cup vegetable oil
2½ tablespoons Worcester sauce
2 tablespoons honey
2 tablespoons vermouth
1 tablespoon freshly squeezed lemon juice
1 tablespoon fresh parsley leaves, coarsely chopped
Salt and pepper, to taste
1 teaspoon dried basil

1. Put all the ingredients in a large mixing dish and gently stir until the fish is coated evenly. Transfer the fish to the perforated pan.
2. Select Roast. Set temperature to 390°F (199°C) and set time to 10 minutes. Press Start to begin preheating.
3. Once preheated, place the pan into the oven. Flip the fish halfway through cooking time.
4. When cooking is complete, the fish should reach an internal temperature of at least 145°F (63°C) on a meat thermometer. Remove from the oven and let the fish cool for 5 minutes before serving.

Sea Bass Stuffed with Spice Paste

Prep time: 20 minutes | Cook time: 20 minutes | Serves 6 to 8

For the Spice Paste:
1½-inch fresh ginger, peeled and finely grated
2 garlic cloves, finely grated
Scant ¼ teaspoon cayenne pepper
Juice of ½ small lemon
2 tablespoons extra-virgin olive oil
Sea salt flakes and freshly ground black pepper, to taste

For the Stuffing:
9 tablespoons unsalted butter, softened
Generous ¼ cup almond flour
½ cup raisins, soaked in boiling water for 15 minutes, then Drained and patted dry
2 slices of crystallized ginger, very finely chopped
2 preserved lemons, flesh and rind finely chopped, pips removed
1 garlic clove, finely grated
2 tablespoons chopped cilantro leaves

For the Fish:
2 (2-pound / 907-g) sea bass (branzino), gutted, scaled and washed
A little extra-virgin olive oil
1 unwaxed lemon, finely sliced, plus lemon wedges to serve
Couscous, to serve

1. Make the spice paste by mixing everything together in a bowl. Make the stuffing in the same way in a separate bowl, adding plenty of seasoning to both mixtures.
2. Wash the fish to get rid of any blood (it's bitter) and pat dry with paper towels. Put a double layer of parchment into a baking pan big enough for the fish. Brush the center—where the fish will lie—with olive oil.
3. Make diagonal slashes in the fish on each side, cutting down to the bone but not through it. Push the spice paste inside the slits on both sides of each fish. Carefully stuff the butter mixture inside, pushing it up into the heads to get all of it in (you're not going to eat the heads, but you will be able to get the stuffing out of it). Put the fish on to the oiled parchment paper. Lay the lemon slices inside and on top, then drizzle with olive oil and season.
4. Select Bake. Set temperature to 400ºF (205ºC) and set time to 20 minutes. Select Start to begin preheating.
5. Once preheated, slide the pan into the oven.
6. When done, the flesh near the bone in the thickest part of the fish should be opaque.
7. Serve with lemon wedges and a bowl of couscous tossed with some chopped pistachios, lemon juice, and finely grated lemon zest.

Lemon Tilapia Fillets with Garlic

Prep time: 10 minutes | Cook time: 12 minutes | Serves 4

1 tablespoon olive oil
1 tablespoon lemon juice
1 teaspoon minced garlic
½ teaspoon chili powder
4 tilapia fillets

1. Line a baking pan with parchment paper.
2. In a shallow bowl, stir together the olive oil, lemon juice, garlic, and chili powder to make a marinade. Put the tilapia fillets in the bowl, turning to coat evenly.
3. Place the fillets in the baking pan in a single layer.
4. Select Air Fry. Set temperature to 375ºF (190ºC) and set time to 12 minutes. Press Start to begin preheating.
5. Once preheated, slide the pan into the oven.
6. When cooked, the fish will flake apart with a fork. Remove from the oven to a plate and serve hot.

Catfish, Toamto and Onion Kebabs

Prep time: 10 minutes | Cook time: 20 minutes | Serves 4

4 (5-ounce / 142-g) catfish fillets
4 (9-inch) metal skewers
2 plum tomatoes, quartered
1 onion, cut into 1 × 1-inch pieces

Marinade:
3 tablespoons lemon juice
3 tablespoons tomato juice
2 garlic cloves, minced
2 tablespoons olive oil
1 teaspoon soy sauce

1. Combine the marinade ingredients in a small bowl. Set aside.
2. Cut the fillets into 2 by 3-inch strips and place in a shallow glass or ceramic dish. Add the marinade and refrigerate, covered, for at least 20 minutes. Remove the strips from the marinade, roll, and skewer, alternating the rolled strips with the tomatoes and onion.
3. Brush the kebabs with marinade, reserving the remaining marinade for brushing again later. Place the skewers on a broiling rack with a pan underneath.
4. Select Broil. Set temperature to 400ºF (205ºC) and set time to 20 minutes. Select Start to begin preheating.
5. Once preheated, slide the pan into the oven.
6. Broil for 10 minutes, then remove the pan from the oven and carefully turn the skewers. Brush the kebabs with the marinade and broil again for 10 minutes, or until browned.

Stuffed Tilapia with Pepper and Cucumber

Prep time: 15 minutes | Cook time: 20 minutes | Makes 6 tilapia rolls

6 (5-ounce / 142-g) tilapia fillets
2 tablespoons olive oil
Filling:
1 cucumber, peeled, seeds scooped out and discarded, and chopped
½ cup chopped roasted peppers, drained
2 tablespoons lemon juice
2 tablespoons chopped fresh parsley or cilantro
1 teaspoon garlic powder
1 teaspoon paprika
Salt and freshly ground black pepper, to taste
Dip Mixture:
1 cup nonfat sour cream
2 tablespoons low-fat mayonnaise
3 tablespoons Dijon mustard
1 teaspoon Worcestershire sauce
1 teaspoon dried dill

1. Combine the filling ingredients in a bowl, adjusting the seasonings to taste.
2. Spoon equal portions of filling in the centers of the tilapia filets. Roll up the fillets, starting at the smallest end. Secure each roll with toothpicks and place the rolls in an oiled or nonstick baking pan. Carefully brush the fillets with oil and place them in an oiled or nonstick square baking (cake) pan.
3. Select Broil. Set temperature to 400ºF (205ºC) and set time to 20 minutes. Select Start to begin preheating.
4. Once preheated, slide the pan into the oven.
5. When done, the fillets will be lightly browned.
6. Combine the dip mixture ingredients in a small bowl and serve with the fish.

Fish Fillet with Sun-Dried Tomato Pesto

Prep time: 10 minutes | Cook time: 31 minutes | Serves 4

4 (6-ounce / 170-g) fish fillets (trout, catfish, flounder, or tilapia)
1 tablespoon reduced-fat mayonnaise
2 tablespoons chopped fresh cilantro Olive oil
Tomato Sauce:
¼ cup chopped sun-dried tomatoes
2 tablespoons chopped fresh basil
⅔ cup dry white wine
2 tablespoons grated Parmesan cheese
2 tablespoons olive oil
1 tablespoon pine nuts
2 garlic cloves
Salt and freshly ground black pepper, to taste

1. Process the tomato sauce ingredients in a blender or food processor until smooth.
2. Layer the fish fillets in an oiled or nonstick square baking (cake) pan. Spoon the sauce over the fish, spreading evenly.
3. Select Bake. Set temperature to 400ºF (205ºC) and set time to 25 minutes. Select Start to begin preheating.
4. Once preheated, slide the pan into the oven, uncovered.
5. When done, the fish will flake easily with a fork. Remove from the oven, spread the mayonnaise on top of the fish, and garnish with the cilantro.
6. Select Broil. Set temperature to 400ºF (205ºC) and set time to 6 minutes. Slide the pan into the oven. When done, the fish will be lightly browned.

Salmon with Cucumber Sauce

Prep time: 15 minutes | Cook time: 20 minutes | Serves 2

2 (6-ounce / 170-g) salmon steaks
2 tablespoons fresh watercress, rinsed, drained, and chopped (for serving hot)
1 lemon, cut into small wedges (for serving hot)
Poaching Liquid:
1 cup dry white wine
2 bay leaves
1 tablespoon mustard seed
Salt and freshly ground black pepper, to taste
Cucumber Sauce:
1 cucumber, peeled, halved, seeds scooped out with a teaspoon and discarded, and finely chopped
½ teaspoon white vinegar
½ teaspoon honey
¼ teaspoon salt
½ cup plain fat-free yogurt
½ cup fat-free or reduced-fat sour cream
1 tablespoon finely chopped fresh dill or 1 teaspoon dried dill weed

1. Combine the poaching liquid ingredients with 1 cup water in a small bowl and set aside.
2. Place the salmon steaks in an oiled or nonstick square baking (cake) pan and pour enough poaching liquid over the steaks to barely cover them. Adjust the seasonings to taste.
3. Select Bake. Set temperature to 350ºF (180ºC) and set time to 20 minutes. Select Start to begin preheating.
4. Once preheated, slide the pan into the oven.
5. When done, the fish will feel springy to the touch. Remove the bay leaves and serve the fish hot with watercress and lemon or cold with cucumber sauce.

Paprika Tilapia with Garlic Aioli

Prep time: 5 minutes | Cook time: 15 minutes | Serves 4

Tilapia:
- 4 tilapia fillets
- 1 tablespoon extra-virgin olive oil
- 1 teaspoon garlic powder
- 1 teaspoon paprika
- 1 teaspoon dried basil
- A pinch of lemon-pepper seasoning

Garlic Aioli:
- 2 garlic cloves, minced
- 1 tablespoon mayonnaise
- Juice of ½ lemon
- 1 teaspoon extra-virgin olive oil
- Salt and pepper, to taste

1. On a clean work surface, brush both sides of each fillet with the olive oil. Sprinkle with the garlic powder, paprika, basil, and lemon-pepper seasoning. Place the fillets in the perforated pan.
2. Select Bake. Set temperature to 400ºF (205ºC) and set time to 15 minutes. Press Start to begin preheating.
3. Once preheated, place the pan into the oven. Flip the fillets halfway through.
4. Meanwhile, make the garlic aioli: Whisk together the garlic, mayo, lemon juice, olive oil, salt, and pepper in a small bowl until smooth.
5. When cooking is complete, the fish should flake apart with a fork and no longer translucent in the center. Remove the fish from the oven and serve with the garlic aioli on the side.

Shrimp Salad with Caesar Dressing

Prep time: 10 minutes | Cook time: 15 minutes | Serves 4

- ½ baguette, cut into 1-inch cubes (about 2½ cups)
- 4 tablespoons extra-virgin olive oil, divided
- ¼ teaspoon granulated garlic
- ¼ teaspoon kosher salt
- ¾ cup Caesar dressing, divided
- 2 romaine lettuce hearts, cut in half lengthwise and ends trimmed
- 1 pound (454 g) medium shrimp, peeled and deveined
- 2 ounces (57 g) Parmesan cheese, coarsely grated

1. Make the croutons: Put the bread cubes in a medium bowl and drizzle 3 tablespoons of olive oil over top. Season with granulated garlic and salt and toss to coat. Transfer to the perforated pan in a single layer.
2. Select Air Fry. Set temperature to 400ºF (205ºC) and set time to 4 minutes. Press Start to begin preheating.
3. Once the oven has preheated, place the pan into the oven. Toss the croutons halfway through the cooking time.
4. When done, remove the perforated pan from the oven and set aside.
5. Brush 2 tablespoons of Caesar dressing on the cut side of the lettuce. Set aside.
6. Toss the shrimp with the ¼ cup of Caesar dressing in a large bowl until well coated. Set aside.
7. Coat the sheet pan with the remaining 1 tablespoon of olive oil. Arrange the romaine halves on the coated pan, cut side down. Brush the tops with the remaining 2 tablespoons of Caesar dressing.
8. Select Roast. Set temperature to 375ºF (190ºC) and set time to 10 minutes. Place the pan into the oven.
9. After 5 minutes, remove the pan from the oven and flip the romaine halves. Spoon the shrimp around the lettuce. Return the pan to the oven and continue cooking.
10. When done, remove the sheet pan from the oven. If they are not quite cooked through, roast for another 1 minute.
11. On each of four plates, put a romaine half. Divide the shrimp among the plates and top with croutons and grated Parmesan cheese. Serve immediately.

Orange Shrimp with Cayenne

Prep time: 40 minutes | Cook time: 12 minutes | Serves 4

- ⅓ cup orange juice
- 3 teaspoons minced garlic
- 1 teaspoon Old Bay seasoning
- ¼ to ½ teaspoon cayenne pepper
- 1 pound (454 g) medium shrimp, thawed, deveined, peeled, with tails off, and patted dry
- Cooking spray

1. Stir together the orange juice, garlic, Old Bay seasoning, and cayenne pepper in a medium bowl. Add the shrimp to the bowl and toss to coat well.
2. Cover the bowl with plastic wrap and marinate in the refrigerator for 30 minutes.
3. Spritz the perforated pan with cooking spray. Place the shrimp in the pan and spray with cooking spray.
4. Select Air Fry. Set temperature to 400ºF (205ºC) and set time to 12 minutes. Press Start to begin preheating.
5. Once preheated, place the pan into the oven. Flip the shrimp halfway through the cooking time.
6. When cooked, the shrimp should be opaque and crisp. Remove from the oven and serve hot.

Breaded Fish Sticks

Prep time: 10 minutes | Cook time: 8 minutes | Makes 8 fish sticks

8 ounces (227 g) fish fillets (pollock or cod) cut into ½×3-inch strips
Salt, to taste (optional)
½ cup plain bread crumbs
Cooking spray

1. Season the fish strips with salt to taste, if desired.
2. Place the bread crumbs on a plate. Roll the fish strips in the bread crumbs to coat. Spritz the fish strips with cooking spray.
3. Arrange the fish strips in the perforated pan in a single layer.
4. Select Air Fry. Set temperature to 390ºF (199ºC) and set time to 8 minutes. Press Start to begin preheating.
5. Once preheated, place the pan into the oven.
6. When cooking is complete, they should be golden brown. Remove from the oven and cool for 5 minutes before serving.

Dijon Hake Fillets with Garlic Sauce

Prep time: 5 minutes | Cook time: 10 minutes | Serves 3

Fish:
6 tablespoons mayonnaise
1 tablespoon fresh lime juice
1 teaspoon Dijon mustard
1 cup grated Parmesan cheese
Salt, to taste
¼ teaspoon ground black pepper, or more to taste
3 hake fillets, patted dry
Nonstick cooking spray

Garlic Sauce:
¼ cup plain Greek yogurt
2 tablespoons olive oil
2 cloves garlic, minced
½ teaspoon minced tarragon leaves

1. Mix the mayo, lime juice, and mustard in a shallow bowl and whisk to combine. In another shallow bowl, stir together the grated Parmesan cheese, salt, and pepper.
2. Dredge each fillet in the mayo mixture, then roll them in the cheese mixture until they are evenly coated on both sides.
3. Spray the perforated pan with nonstick cooking spray. Place the fillets in the pan.
4. Select Air Fry. Set temperature to 395ºF (202ºC) and set time to 10 minutes. Press Start to begin preheating.
5. Once preheated, place the pan into the oven. Flip the fillets halfway through the cooking time.
6. Meanwhile, in a small bowl, whisk all the ingredients for the sauce until well incorporated.
7. When cooking is complete, the fish should flake apart with a fork. Remove the fillets from the oven and serve warm alongside the sauce.

Breaded Catfish Nuggets

Prep time: 10 minutes | Cook time: 7 to 8 minutes | Serves 4

2 medium catfish fillets, cut into chunks (approximately 1 × 2 inch)
Salt and pepper, to taste
2 eggs
2 tablespoons skim milk
½ cup cornstarch
1 cup panko bread crumbs
Cooking spray

1. In a medium bowl, season the fish chunks with salt and pepper to taste.
2. In a small bowl, beat together the eggs with milk until well combined.
3. Place the cornstarch and bread crumbs into separate shallow dishes.
4. Dredge the fish chunks one at a time in the cornstarch, coating well on both sides, then dip in the egg mixture, shaking off any excess, finally press well into the bread crumbs. Spritz the fish chunks with cooking spray.
5. Arrange the fish chunks in the perforated pan in a single layer.
6. Select Air Fry. Set temperature to 390ºF (199ºC) and set time to 8 minutes. Press Start to begin preheating.
7. Once preheated, place the pan into the oven. Flip the fish chunks halfway through the cooking time.
8. When cooking is complete, they should be no longer translucent in the center and golden brown. Remove the fish chunks from the oven to a plate. Serve warm.

Cayenne Prawns with Cumin

Prep time: 10 minutes | Cook time: 8 minutes | Serves 2

8 prawns, cleaned
Salt and black pepper, to taste
½ teaspoon ground cayenne pepper
½ teaspoon garlic powder
½ teaspoon ground cumin
½ teaspoon red chili flakes
Cooking spray

1. Spritz the perforated pan with cooking spray.
2. Toss the remaining ingredients in a large bowl until the prawns are well coated.
3. Spread the coated prawns evenly in the perforated pan and spray them with cooking spray.
4. Select Air Fry. Set temperature to 340ºF (171ºC) and set time to 8 minutes. Press Start to begin preheating.
5. Once preheated, place the pan into the oven. Flip the prawns halfway through the cooking time.
6. When cooking is complete, the prawns should be pink. Remove the prawns from the oven to a plate.

Balsamic Shrimp with Goat Cheese

Prep time: 15 minutes | Cook time: 8 minutes | Serves 2

1 pound (454 g) shrimp, deveined
1½ tablespoons olive oil
1½ tablespoons balsamic vinegar
1 tablespoon coconut aminos
½ tablespoon fresh parsley, roughly chopped
Sea salt flakes, to taste
1 teaspoon Dijon mustard
½ teaspoon smoked cayenne pepper
½ teaspoon garlic powder
Salt and ground black peppercorns, to taste
1 cup shredded goat cheese

1. Except for the cheese, stir together all the ingredients in a large bowl until the shrimp are evenly coated.
2. Place the shrimp in the perforated pan.
3. Select Roast. Set temperature to 385ºF (196ºC) and set time to 8 minutes. Press Start to begin preheating.
4. Once preheated, place the pan into the oven.
5. When cooking is complete, the shrimp should be pink and cooked through. Remove from the oven and serve with the shredded goat cheese sprinkled on top.

Shrimp and Artichoke Paella

Prep time: 5 minutes | Cook time: 16 minutes | Serves 4

1 (10-ounce / 284-g) package frozen cooked rice, thawed
1 (6-ounce / 170-g) jar artichoke hearts, drained and chopped
¼ cup vegetable broth
½ teaspoon dried thyme
½ teaspoon turmeric
1 cup frozen cooked small shrimp
½ cup frozen baby peas
1 tomato, diced

1. Mix together the cooked rice, chopped artichoke hearts, vegetable broth, thyme, and turmeric in a baking pan and stir to combine.
2. Select Bake. Set temperature to 340ºF (171ºC) and set time to 16 minutes. Press Start to begin preheating.
3. Once preheated, place the pan into the oven.
4. After 9 minutes, remove from the oven and add the shrimp, baby peas, and diced tomato to the baking pan. Mix well. Return the pan to the oven and continue cooking for 7 minutes more, or until the shrimp are done and the paella is bubbling.
5. When cooking is complete, remove the pan from the oven. Cool for 5 minutes before serving.

Jumbo Shrimp with Dijon-Mayo Sauce

Prep time: 5 minutes | Cook time: 7 minutes | Serves 4

Shrimp:
12 jumbo shrimp
½ teaspoon garlic salt
¼ teaspoon freshly cracked mixed peppercorns

Sauce:
4 tablespoons mayonnaise
1 teaspoon grated lemon rind
1 teaspoon Dijon mustard
1 teaspoon chipotle powder
½ teaspoon cumin powder

1. In a medium bowl, season the shrimp with garlic salt and cracked mixed peppercorns.
2. Place the shrimp in the perforated pan.
3. Select Air Fry. Set temperature to 395ºF (202ºC) and set time to 7 minutes. Press Start to begin preheating.
4. Once preheated, place the pan into the oven.
5. After 5 minutes, remove from the oven and flip the shrimp. Return the pan to the oven and continue cooking for 2 minutes more, or until they are pink and no longer opaque.
6. Meanwhile, stir together all the ingredients for the sauce in a small bowl until well mixed.
7. When cooking is complete, remove the shrimp from the oven and serve alongside the sauce.

Shrimp and Veggie Patties

Prep time: 15 minutes | Cook time: 12 minutes | Serves 4

½ pound (227 g) raw shrimp, shelled, deveined, and chopped finely
2 cups cooked sushi rice
¼ cup chopped red bell pepper
¼ cup chopped celery
¼ cup chopped green onion
2 teaspoons Worcestershire sauce
½ teaspoon salt
½ teaspoon garlic powder
½ teaspoon Old Bay seasoning
½ cup plain bread crumbs
Cooking spray

1. Put all the ingredients except the bread crumbs and oil in a large bowl and stir to incorporate.
2. Scoop out the shrimp mixture and shape into 8 equal-sized patties with your hands, no more than ½-inch thick. Roll the patties in the bread crumbs on a plate and spray both sides with cooking spray. Place the patties in the perforated pan.
3. Select Air Fry. Set temperature to 390ºF (199ºC) and set time to 12 minutes. Press Start to begin preheating.
4. Once preheated, place the pan into the oven. Flip the patties halfway through the cooking time.
5. When cooking is complete, the outside should be crispy brown. Remove the pan from the oven. Divide the patties among four plates and serve warm.

Old Bay Shrimp with Potatoes

Prep time: 10 minutes | Cook time: 15 minutes | Serves 4

1 pound (454 g) small red potatoes, halved
2 ears corn, shucked and cut into rounds, 1 to 1½ inches thick
2 tablespoons Old Bay or similar seasoning
½ cup unsalted butter, melted
1 (12- to 13-ounce / 340- to 369-g) package kielbasa or other smoked sausages
3 garlic cloves, minced
1 pound (454 g) medium shrimp, peeled and deveined

1. Place the potatoes and corn in a large bowl.
2. Stir together the butter and Old Bay seasoning in a small bowl. Drizzle half the butter mixture over the potatoes and corn, tossing to coat. Spread out the vegetables on a sheet pan.
3. Select Roast. Set temperature to 350°F (180°C) and set time to 15 minutes. Press Start to begin preheating.
4. Once the oven has preheated, place the pan into the oven.
5. Meanwhile, cut the sausages into 2-inch lengths, then cut each piece in half lengthwise. Put the sausages and shrimp in a medium bowl and set aside.
6. Add the garlic to the bowl of remaining butter mixture and stir well.
7. After 10 minutes, remove the sheet pan and pour the vegetables into the large bowl. Drizzle with the garlic butter and toss until well coated. Arrange the vegetables, sausages, and shrimp on the sheet pan.
8. Return to the oven and continue cooking. After 5 minutes, check the shrimp for doneness. The shrimp should be pink and opaque. If they are not quite cooked through, roast for an additional 1 minute.
9. When done, remove from the oven and serve on a plate.

Cajun Cod Fillets with Lemon Pepper

Prep time: 5 minutes | Cook time: 12 minutes | Makes 2 cod fillets

1 tablespoon Cajun seasoning
1 teaspoon salt
½ teaspoon lemon pepper
½ teaspoon freshly ground black pepper
2 (8-ounce / 227-g) cod fillets, cut to fit into the perforated pan
Cooking spray
2 tablespoons unsalted butter, melted
1 lemon, cut into 4 wedges

1. Spritz the perforated pan with cooking spray.
2. Thoroughly combine the Cajun seasoning, salt, lemon pepper, and black pepper in a small bowl. Rub this mixture all over the cod fillets until completely coated.
3. Put the fillets in the perforated pan and brush the melted butter over both sides of each fillet.
4. Select Bake. Set temperature to 360°F (182°C) and set time to 12 minutes. Press Start to begin preheating.
5. Once preheated, place the pan into the oven. Flip the fillets halfway through the cooking time.
6. When cooking is complete, the fish should flake apart with a fork. Remove the fillets from the oven and serve with fresh lemon wedges.

Curried Prawns with Coconut

Prep time: 15 minutes | Cook time: 8 minutes | Serves 4

12 prawns, cleaned and deveined
1 teaspoon fresh lemon juice
½ teaspoon cumin powder
Salt and ground black pepper, to taste
1 medium egg
⅓ cup beer
½ cup flour, divided
1 tablespoon curry powder
1 teaspoon baking powder
½ teaspoon grated fresh ginger
1 cup flaked coconut

1. In a large bowl, toss the prawns with the lemon juice, cumin powder, salt, and pepper until well coated. Set aside.
2. In a shallow bowl, whisk together the egg, beer, ¼ cup of flour, curry powder, baking powder, and ginger until combined.
3. In a separate shallow bowl, put the remaining ¼ cup of flour, and on a plate, place the flaked coconut.
4. Dip the prawns in the flour, then in the egg mixture, finally roll in the flaked coconut to coat well. Transfer the prawns to a baking sheet.
5. Select Air Fry. Set temperature to 350°F (180°C) and set time to 8 minutes. Press Start to begin preheating.
6. Once preheated, place the baking sheet into the oven.
7. After 5 minutes, remove from the oven and flip the prawns. Return to the oven and continue cooking for 3 minutes more.
8. When cooking is complete, remove from the oven and serve warm.

Parmesan Fish Fillets with Tarragon
Prep time: 8 minutes | Cook time: 17 minutes | Serves 4

⅓ cup grated Parmesan cheese	2 eggs, beaten
½ teaspoon fennel seed	4 (4-ounce / 113-g) fish fillets, halved
½ teaspoon tarragon	2 tablespoons dry white wine
⅓ teaspoon mixed peppercorns	1 teaspoon seasoned salt

1. Place the grated Parmesan cheese, fennel seed, tarragon, and mixed peppercorns in a food processor and pulse for about 20 seconds until well combined. Transfer the cheese mixture to a shallow dish.
2. Place the beaten eggs in another shallow dish.
3. Drizzle the dry white wine over the top of fish fillets. Dredge each fillet in the beaten eggs on both sides, shaking off any excess, then roll them in the cheese mixture until fully coated. Season with the salt.
4. Arrange the fillets in the perforated pan.
5. Select Air Fry. Set temperature to 345ºF (174ºC) and set time to 17 minutes. Press Start to begin preheating.
6. Once preheated, place the pan into the oven. Flip the fillets once halfway through the cooking time.
7. When cooking is complete, the fish should be cooked through no longer translucent. Remove from the oven and cool for 5 minutes before serving.

Cajun Catfish Cakes with Parmesan
Prep time: 5 minutes | Cook time: 15 minutes | Serves 4

2 catfish fillets	½ cup buttermilk
3 ounces (85 g) butter	1 teaspoon baking powder
1 cup shredded Parmesan cheese	1 teaspoon baking soda
1 cup shredded Swiss cheese	1 teaspoon Cajun seasoning

1. Bring a pot of salted water to a boil. Add the catfish fillets to the boiling water and let them boil for 5 minutes until they become opaque.
2. Remove the fillets from the pot to a mixing bowl and flake them into small pieces with a fork.
3. Add the remaining ingredients to the bowl of fish and stir until well incorporated.
4. Divide the fish mixture into 12 equal portions and shape each portion into a patty. Place the patties in the perforated pan.
5. Select Air Fry. Set temperature to 380ºF (193ºC) and set time to 15 minutes. Press Start to begin preheating.
6. Once preheated, place the pan into the oven. Flip the patties halfway through the cooking time.
7. When cooking is complete, the patties should be golden brown and cooked through. Remove from the oven. Let the patties sit for 5 minutes and serve.

Parsley Shrimp with Lemon
Prep time: 10 minutes | Cook time: 8 minutes | Serves 4

1 pound (454 g) shrimp, deveined	2 cloves garlic, finely minced
4 tablespoons olive oil	1 teaspoon crushed red pepper flakes, or more to taste
1½ tablespoons lemon juice	Garlic pepper, to taste
1½ tablespoons fresh parsley, roughly chopped	Sea salt flakes, to taste

1. Toss all the ingredients in a large bowl until the shrimp are coated on all sides.
2. Arrange the shrimp in the perforated pan.
3. Select Air Fry. Set temperature to 385ºF (196ºC) and set time to 8 minutes. Press Start to begin preheating.
4. Once preheated, place the pan into the oven.
5. When cooking is complete, the shrimp should be pink and cooked through. Remove from the oven and serve warm.

Crab Ratatouille with Thyme
Prep time: 15 minutes | Cook time: 13 minutes | Serves 4

1½ cups peeled and cubed eggplant	½ teaspoon dried basil
2 large tomatoes, chopped	½ teaspoon dried thyme
1 red bell pepper, chopped	Pinch salt
1 onion, chopped	Freshly ground black pepper, to taste
1 tablespoon olive oil	1½ cups cooked crab meat

1. In a metal bowl, stir together the eggplant, tomatoes, bell pepper, onion, olive oil, basil and thyme. Season with salt and pepper.
2. Select Roast. Set temperature to 400ºF (205ºC) and set time to 13 minutes. Press Start to begin preheating.
3. Once preheated, place the metal bowl into the oven.
4. After 9 minutes, remove the bowl from the oven. Add the crab meat and stir well and continue roasting for another 4 minutes, or until the vegetables are softened and the ratatouille is bubbling.
5. When cooking is complete, remove from the oven and serve warm.

Shrimp Scampi with Garlic Butter

Prep time: 5 minutes | Cook time: 8 minutes | Serves 4

Sauce:
¼ cup unsalted butter
2 tablespoons fish stock or chicken broth
2 cloves garlic, minced
2 tablespoons chopped fresh basil leaves
1 tablespoon lemon juice
1 tablespoon chopped fresh parsley, plus more for garnish
1 teaspoon red pepper flakes

Shrimp:
1 pound (454 g) large shrimp, peeled and deveined, tails removed
Fresh basil sprigs, for garnish

1. Put all the ingredients for the sauce in a baking pan and stir to incorporate.
2. Select Air Fry. Set temperature to 350ºF (180ºC) and set time to 8 minutes. Press Start to begin preheating.
3. Once preheated, place the baking pan into the oven.
4. After 3 minutes, remove from the oven and add the shrimp to the baking pan, flipping to coat in the sauce. Return the pan to the oven and continue cooking for 5 minutes until the shrimp are pink and opaque. Stir the shrimp twice during cooking.
5. When cooking is complete, remove the pan from the oven. Serve garnished with the parsley and basil sprigs.

Old Bay Crab Sticks with Mayo Sauce

Prep time: 5 minutes | Cook time: 12 minutes | Serves 4

Crab Sticks:
2 eggs
1 cup flour
⅓ cup panko bread crumbs
1 tablespoon Old Bay seasoning
1 pound (454 g) crab sticks
Cooking spray

Mayo Sauce:
½ cup mayonnaise
1 lime, juiced
2 garlic cloves, minced

1. In a bowl, beat the eggs. In a shallow bowl, place the flour. In another shallow bowl, thoroughly combine the panko bread crumbs and Old Bay seasoning.
2. Dredge the crab sticks in the flour, shaking off any excess, then in the beaten eggs, finally press them in the bread crumb mixture to coat well.
3. Arrange the crab sticks in the perforated pan and spray with cooking spray.
4. Select Air Fry. Set temperature to 390ºF (199ºC) and set time to 12 minutes. Press Start to begin preheating.
5. Once preheated, place the pan into the oven. Flip the crab sticks halfway through the cooking time.
6. Meanwhile, make the sauce by whisking together the mayo, lime juice, and garlic in a small bowl.
7. When cooking is complete, remove the pan from the oven. Serve the crab sticks with the mayo sauce on the side.

Crab and Fish Cakes

Prep time: 20 minutes | Cook time: 12 minutes | Serves 4

8 ounces (227 g) imitation crab meat
4 ounces (113 g) leftover cooked fish (such as cod, pollock, or haddock)
2 tablespoons minced celery
2 tablespoons minced green onion
2 tablespoons light mayonnaise
1 tablespoon plus 2 teaspoons Worcestershire sauce
¾ cup crushed saltine cracker crumbs
2 teaspoons dried parsley flakes
1 teaspoon prepared yellow mustard
½ teaspoon garlic powder
½ teaspoon dried dill weed, crushed
½ teaspoon Old Bay seasoning
½ cup panko bread crumbs
Cooking spray

1. Pulse the crab meat and fish in a food processor until finely chopped.
2. Transfer the meat mixture to a large bowl, along with the celery, green onion, mayo, Worcestershire sauce, cracker crumbs, parsley flakes, mustard, garlic powder, dill weed, and Old Bay seasoning. Stir to mix well.
3. Scoop out the meat mixture and form into 8 equal-sized patties with your hands.
4. Place the panko bread crumbs on a plate. Roll the patties in the bread crumbs until they are evenly coated on both sides. Put the patties in the perforated pan and spritz them with cooking spray.
5. Select Bake. Set temperature to 390ºF (199ºC) and set time to 12 minutes. Press Start to begin preheating.
6. Once preheated, place the pan into the oven. Flip the patties halfway through the cooking time.
7. When cooking is complete, they should be golden brown and cooked through. Remove the pan from the oven. Divide the patties among four plates and serve.

Paprika Tiger Shrimp

Prep time: 5 minutes | Cook time: 10 minutes | Serves 4

1 pound (454 g) tiger shrimp
2 tablespoons olive oil
½ tablespoon Old Bay seasoning
¼ tablespoon smoked paprika
¼ teaspoon cayenne pepper
A pinch of sea salt

1. Toss all the ingredients in a large bowl until the shrimp are evenly coated.
2. Arrange the shrimp in the perforated pan.
3. Select Air Fry. Set temperature to 380°F (193°C) and set time to 10 minutes. Press Start to begin preheating.
4. Once preheated, place the pan into the oven.
5. When cooking is complete, the shrimp should be pink and cooked through. Remove from the oven and serve hot.

Balsamic Ginger Scallops

Prep time: 10 minutes | Cook time: 12 minutes | Serves 2

⅓ cup shallots, chopped
1½ tablespoons olive oil
1½ tablespoons coconut aminos
1 tablespoon Mediterranean seasoning mix
½ tablespoon balsamic vinegar
½ teaspoon ginger, grated
1 clove garlic, chopped
1 pound (454 g) scallops, cleaned
Cooking spray
Belgian endive, for garnish

1. Place all the ingredients except the scallops and Belgian endive in a small skillet over medium heat and stir to combine. Let this mixture simmer for about 2 minutes.
2. Remove the mixture from the skillet to a large bowl and set aside to cool.
3. Add the scallops, coating them all over, then transfer to the refrigerator to marinate for at least 2 hours.
4. When ready, place the scallops in the perforated pan in a single layer and spray with cooking spray.
5. Select Air Fry. Set temperature to 345°F (174°C) and set time to 10 minutes. Press Start to begin preheating.
6. Once preheated, place the pan into the oven. Flip the scallops halfway through the cooking time.
7. When cooking is complete, the scallops should be tender and opaque. Remove from the oven and serve garnished with the Belgian endive.

Lemon Shrimp with Cumin

Prep time: 10 minutes | Cook time: 5 minutes | Serves 4

18 shrimp, shelled and deveined
2 garlic cloves, peeled and minced
2 tablespoons extra-virgin olive oil
2 tablespoons freshly squeezed lemon juice
½ cup fresh parsley, coarsely chopped
1 teaspoon onion powder
1 teaspoon lemon-pepper seasoning
½ teaspoon hot paprika
½ teaspoon salt
¼ teaspoon cumin powder

1. Toss all the ingredients in a mixing bowl until the shrimp are well coated.
2. Cover and allow to marinate in the refrigerator for 30 minutes.
3. When ready, transfer the shrimp to the perforated pan.
4. Select Air Fry. Set temperature to 400°F (205°C) and set time to 5 minutes. Press Start to begin preheating.
5. Once preheated, place the pan into the oven.
6. When cooking is complete, the shrimp should be pink on the outside and opaque in the center. Remove from the oven and serve warm.

Coconut Curried Fish with Chilies

Prep time: 10 minutes | Cook time: 22 minutes | Serves 4

2 tablespoons sunflower oil, divided
1 pound (454 g) fish, chopped
1 ripe tomato, pureéd
2 red chilies, chopped
1 shallot, minced
1 garlic clove, minced
1 cup coconut milk
1 tablespoon coriander powder
1 teaspoon red curry paste
½ teaspoon fenugreek seeds
Salt and white pepper, to taste

1. Coat the perforated pan with 1 tablespoon of sunflower oil. Place the fish in the perforated pan.
2. Select Air Fry. Set temperature to 380°F (193°C) and set time to 10 minutes. Press Start to begin preheating.
3. Once preheated, place the pan into the oven. Flip the fish halfway through the cooking time.
4. When cooking is complete, transfer the cooked fish to a baking pan greased with the remaining 1 tablespoon of sunflower oil. Stir in the remaining ingredients.
5. Select Air Fry. Set temperature to 350°F (180°C) and set time to 12 minutes. Place the pan into the oven.
6. When cooking is complete, they should be heated through. Cool for 5 to 8 minutes before serving.

Flounder Fillets with Lemon Pepper

Prep time: 8 minutes | Cook time: 12 minutes | Serves 2

2 flounder fillets, patted dry
1 egg
½ teaspoon Worcestershire sauce
¼ cup almond flour
¼ cup coconut flour
½ teaspoon coarse sea salt
½ teaspoon lemon pepper
¼ teaspoon chili powder
Cooking spray

1. In a shallow bowl, beat together the egg with Worcestershire sauce until well incorporated.
2. In another bowl, thoroughly combine the almond flour, coconut flour, sea salt, lemon pepper, and chili powder.
3. Dredge the fillets in the egg mixture, shaking off any excess, then roll in the flour mixture to coat well.
4. Spritz the perforated pan with cooking spray. Place the fillets in the pan.
5. Select Bake. Set temperature to 390°F (199°C) and set time to 12 minutes. Press Start to begin preheating.
6. Once preheated, place the pan into the oven.
7. After 7 minutes, remove from the oven and flip the fillets and spray with cooking spray. Return the pan to the oven and continue cooking for 5 minutes, or until the fish is flaky.
8. When cooking is complete, remove from the oven and serve warm.

Shrimp Kebabs with Cherry Tomatoes

Prep time: 15 minutes | Cook time: 5 minutes | Serves 4

1½ pounds (680 g) jumbo shrimp, cleaned, shelled and deveined
1 pound (454 g) cherry tomatoes
2 tablespoons butter, melted
1 tablespoons Sriracha sauce
Sea salt and ground black pepper, to taste
1 teaspoon dried parsley flakes
½ teaspoon dried basil
½ teaspoon dried oregano
½ teaspoon mustard seeds
½ teaspoon marjoram

Special Equipment:
4 to 6 wooden skewers, soaked in water for 30 minutes

1. Put all the ingredients in a large bowl and toss to coat well.
2. Make the kebabs: Thread, alternating jumbo shrimp and cherry tomatoes, onto the wooden skewers. Place the kebabs in the perforated pan.
3. Select Air Fry. Set temperature to 400°F (205°C) and set time to 5 minutes. Press Start to begin preheating.
4. Once preheated, place the pan into the oven.
5. When cooking is complete, the shrimp should be pink and the cherry tomatoes should be softened. Remove from the oven. Let the shrimp and cherry tomato kebabs cool for 5 minutes and serve hot.

Shrimp and Veggie Spring Rolls

Prep time: 10 minutes | Cook time: 20 minutes | Serves 4

1 tablespoon olive oil
2 teaspoons minced garlic
1 cup matchstick cut carrots
2 cups finely sliced cabbage
2 (4-ounce / 113-g) cans tiny shrimp, drained
4 teaspoons soy sauce
Salt and freshly ground black pepper, to taste
16 square spring roll wrappers
Cooking spray

1. Spray the perforated pan with cooking spray. Set aside.
2. Heat the olive oil in a medium skillet over medium heat until it shimmers.
3. Add the garlic to the skillet and cook for 30 seconds. Stir in the cabbage and carrots and sauté for about 5 minutes, stirring occasionally, or until the vegetables are lightly tender.
4. Fold in the shrimp and soy sauce and sprinkle with salt and pepper, then stir to combine. Sauté for another 2 minutes, or until the moisture is evaporated. Remove from the heat and set aside to cool.
5. Put a spring roll wrapper on a work surface and spoon 1 tablespoon of the shrimp mixture onto the lower end of the wrapper.
6. Roll the wrapper away from you halfway, and then fold in the right and left sides, like an envelope. Continue to roll to the very end, using a little water to seal the edge. Repeat with the remaining wrappers and filling.
7. Place the spring rolls in the perforated pan in a single layer, leaving space between each spring roll. Mist them lightly with cooking spray.
8. Select Air Fry. Set temperature to 375°F (190°C) and set time to 10 minutes. Press Start to begin preheating.
9. Once preheated, place the pan into the oven. Flip the rolls halfway through the cooking time.
10. When cooking is complete, the spring rolls will be heated through and start to brown. If necessary, continue cooking for 5 minutes more. Remove from the oven and cool for a few minutes before serving.

Hoisin Scallops with Sesame Seeds
Prep time: 10 minutes | Cook time: 8 minutes | Serves 4

1 pound (454 g) sea scallops
3 tablespoons hoisin sauce
½ cup toasted sesame seeds
6 ounces (170 g) snow peas, trimmed
3 teaspoons vegetable oil, divided
1 teaspoon soy sauce
1 teaspoon sesame oil
1 cup roasted mushrooms

1. Brush the scallops with the hoisin sauce. Put the sesame seeds in a shallow dish. Roll the scallops in the sesame seeds until evenly coated.
2. Combine the snow peas with 1 teaspoon of vegetable oil, the sesame oil, and soy sauce in a medium bowl and toss to coat.
3. Grease the sheet pan with the remaining 2 teaspoons of vegetable oil. Put the scallops in the middle of the pan and arrange the snow peas around the scallops in a single layer.
4. Select Roast. Set temperature to 375°F (190°C) and set time to 8 minutes. Press Start to begin preheating.
5. Once the oven has preheated, place the pan into the oven.
6. After 5 minutes, remove the pan and flip the scallops. Fold in the mushrooms and stir well. Return the pan to the oven and continue cooking.
7. When done, remove the pan from the oven and cool for 5 minutes. Serve warm.

Curried King Prawns with Cumin
Prep time: 10 minutes | Cook time: 8 minutes | Serves 2

12 king prawns, rinsed
1 tablespoon coconut oil
Salt and ground black pepper, to taste
1 teaspoon onion powder
1 teaspoon garlic paste
1 teaspoon curry powder
½ teaspoon piri piri powder
½ teaspoon cumin powder

1. Combine all the ingredients in a large bowl and toss until the prawns are completely coated. Place the prawns in the perforated pan.
2. Select Air Fry. Set temperature to 360°F (182°C) and set time to 8 minutes. Press Start to begin preheating.
3. Once preheated, place the pan into the oven. Flip the prawns halfway through the cooking time.
4. When cooking is complete, the prawns will turn pink. Remove from the oven and serve hot.

Fried Breaded Scallops
Prep time: 5 minutes | Cook time: 7 minutes | Serves 4

1 egg
3 tablespoons flour
1 cup bread crumbs
1 pound (454 g) fresh scallops
2 tablespoons olive oil
Salt and black pepper, to taste

1. In a bowl, lightly beat the egg. Place the flour and bread crumbs into separate shallow dishes.
2. Dredge the scallops in the flour and shake off any excess. Dip the flour-coated scallops in the beaten egg and roll in the bread crumbs.
3. Brush the scallops generously with olive oil and season with salt and pepper, to taste. Transfer the scallops to the perforated pan.
4. Select Air Fry. Set temperature to 360°F (182°C) and set time to 7 minutes. Press Start to begin preheating.
5. Once preheated, place the pan into the oven. Flip the scallops halfway through the cooking time.
6. When cooking is complete, the scallops should reach an internal temperature of just 145°F (63°C) on a meat thermometer. Remove the pan from the oven. Let the scallops cool for 5 minutes and serve.

Lemon Crab Cakes with Mayo
Prep time: 5 minutes | Cook time: 10 minutes | Serves 4

8 ounces (227 g) jumbo lump crab meat
1 egg, beaten
Juice of ½ lemon
⅓ cup bread crumbs
¼ cup diced green bell pepper
¼ cup diced red bell pepper
¼ cup mayonnaise
1 tablespoon Old Bay seasoning
1 teaspoon flour
Cooking spray

1. Make the crab cakes: Place all the ingredients except the flour and oil in a large bowl and stir until well incorporated.
2. Divide the crab mixture into four equal portions and shape each portion into a patty with your hands. Top each patty with a sprinkle of ¼ teaspoon of flour.
3. Arrange the crab cakes in the perforated pan and spritz them with cooking spray.
4. Select Air Fry. Set temperature to 375°F (190°C) and set time to 10 minutes. Press Start to begin preheating.
5. Once preheated, place the pan into the oven. Flip the crab cakes halfway through.
6. When cooking is complete, the cakes should be cooked through. Remove the pan from the oven. Divide the crab cakes among four plates and serve.

Fried Bacon-Wrapped Scallops

Prep time: 5 minutes | Cook time: 10 minutes | Serves 4

8 slices bacon, cut in half
16 sea scallops, patted dry
Cooking spray
Salt and freshly ground
black pepper, to taste
16 toothpicks, soaked in water for at least 30 minutes

1. On a clean work surface, wrap half of a slice of bacon around each scallop and secure with a toothpick.
2. Lay the bacon-wrapped scallops in the perforated pan in a single layer.
3. Spritz the scallops with cooking spray and sprinkle the salt and pepper to season.
4. Select Air Fry. Set temperature to 370°F (188°C) and set time to 10 minutes. Press Start to begin preheating.
5. Once preheated, place the pan into the oven. Flip the scallops halfway through the cooking time.
6. When cooking is complete, the bacon should be cooked through and the scallops should be firm. Remove the scallops from the oven to a plate Serve warm.

Garlic Calamari Rings

Prep time: 5 minutes | Cook time: 12 minutes | Serves 4

2 large eggs
2 garlic cloves, minced
½ cup cornstarch
1 cup bread crumbs
1 pound (454 g) calamari rings
Cooking spray
1 lemon, sliced

1. In a small bowl, whisk the eggs with minced garlic. Place the cornstarch and bread crumbs into separate shallow dishes.
2. Dredge the calamari rings in the cornstarch, then dip in the egg mixture, shaking off any excess, finally roll them in the bread crumbs to coat well. Let the calamari rings sit for 10 minutes in the refrigerator.
3. Spritz the perforated pan with cooking spray. Transfer the calamari rings to the pan.
4. Select Air Fry. Set temperature to 390°F (199°C) and set time to 12 minutes. Press Start to begin preheating.
5. Once preheated, place the pan into the oven. Stir the calamari rings once halfway through the cooking time.
6. When cooking is complete, remove the pan from the oven. Serve the calamari rings with the lemon slices sprinkled on top.

Basil Scallops with Broccoli

Prep time: 15 minutes | Cook time: 9 minutes | Serves 4

1 cup frozen peas
1 cup green beans
1 cup frozen chopped broccoli
2 teaspoons olive oil
½ teaspoon dried
oregano
½ teaspoon dried basil
12 ounces (340 g) sea scallops, rinsed and patted dry

1. Put the peas, green beans, and broccoli in a large bowl. Drizzle with the olive oil and toss to coat well. Transfer the vegetables to the perforated pan.
2. Select Air Fry. Set temperature to 400°F (205°C) and set time to 5 minutes. Press Start to begin preheating.
3. Once preheated, place the pan into the oven.
4. When cooking is complete, the vegetables should be fork-tender. Transfer the vegetables to a serving bowl. Scatter with the oregano and basil and set aside.
5. Place the scallops in the perforated pan.
6. Select Air Fry. Set temperature to 400°F (205°C) and set time to 4 minutes. Place the pan into the oven.
7. When cooking is complete, the scallops should be firm and just opaque in the center. Remove from the oven to the bowl of vegetables and toss well. Serve warm.

Fried Scallops with Thyme

Prep time: 5 minutes | Cook time: 4 minutes | Serves 2

12 medium sea scallops, rinsed and patted dry
1 teaspoon fine sea salt
¾ teaspoon ground black pepper, plus more for
garnish
Fresh thyme leaves, for garnish (optional)
Avocado oil spray

1. Coat the perforated pan with avocado oil spray.
2. Place the scallops in a medium bowl and spritz with avocado oil spray. Sprinkle the salt and pepper to season.
3. Transfer the seasoned scallops to the perforated pan, spacing them apart.
4. Select Air Fry. Set temperature to 390°F (199°C) and set time to 4 minutes. Press Start to begin preheating.
5. Once preheated, place the pan into the oven. Flip the scallops halfway through the cooking time.
6. When cooking is complete, the scallops should reach an internal temperature of just 145°F (63°C) on a meat thermometer. Remove the pan from the oven. Sprinkle the pepper and thyme leaves on top for garnish, if desired. Serve immediately.

Chapter 8 Poultry

Teriyaki Chicken Thighs
Prep time: 30 minutes | Cook time: 34 minutes | Serves 4

¼ cup chicken broth
½ teaspoon grated fresh ginger
⅛ teaspoon red pepper flakes
1½ tablespoons soy sauce
4 (5-ounce / 142-g) bone-in chicken thighs, trimmed
1 tablespoon mirin
½ teaspoon cornstarch
1 tablespoon sugar
6 ounces (170 g) snow peas, strings removed
⅛ teaspoon lemon zest
1 garlic clove, minced
¼ teaspoon salt
Ground black pepper, to taste
½ teaspoon lemon juice

1. Combine the broth, ginger, pepper flakes, and soy sauce in a large bowl. Stir to mix well.
2. Pierce 10 to 15 holes into the chicken skin. Put the chicken in the broth mixture and toss to coat well. Let sit for 10 minutes to marinate.
3. Transfer the marinated chicken on a plate and pat dry with paper towels.
4. Scoop 2 tablespoons of marinade in a microwave-safe bowl and combine with mirin, cornstarch and sugar. Stir to mix well. Microwave for 1 minute or until frothy and has a thick consistency. Set aside.
5. Arrange the chicken in the perforated pan, skin side up.
6. Select Air Fry. Set temperature to 400ºF (205ºC) and set time to 25 minutes. Press Start to begin preheating.
7. Once preheated, place the pan into the oven. Flip the chicken halfway through.
8. When cooking is complete, brush the chicken skin with marinade mixture. Air fry the chicken for 5 more minutes or until glazed.
9. Remove the chicken from the oven. Allow the chicken to cool for 10 minutes.
10. Meanwhile, combine the snow peas, lemon zest, garlic, salt, and ground black pepper in a small bowl. Toss to coat well.
11. Transfer the snow peas in the perforated pan.
12. Select Air Fry. Set temperature to 400ºF (205ºC) and set time to 3 minutes. Place the pan into the oven.
13. When cooking is complete, the peas should be soft.
14. Remove the peas from the oven and toss with lemon juice.
15. Serve the chicken with lemony snow peas.

Chicken Breast in Mango Sauce
Prep time: 10 minutes | Cook time: 40 minutes | Serves 2

2 skinless and boneless chicken breast halves
Mango Mixture:
1 cup mango pieces
1 teaspoon balsamic vinegar
½ teaspoon garlic powder
1 teaspoon fresh ginger, peeled and minced
1 tablespoon capers
1 tablespoon raisins
½ teaspoon soy sauce
½ teaspoon curry powder
1 tablespoon pimientos, minced
Salt and pepper, to taste

1. Process the mango mixture ingredients in a food processor or blender until smooth. Transfer to an oiled or nonstick square (cake) pan and add the capers, raisins, and pimientos, stirring well to blend. Add the chicken breasts and spoon the mixture over the breasts to coat well.
2. Select Bake. Set temperature to 375ºF (190ºC) and set time to 40 minutes. Select Start to begin preheating.
3. Once preheated, slide the pan into the oven.
4. When done, serve the breasts with the sauce.

Dijon-Rosemary Chicken Breasts
Prep time: 5 minutes | Cook time: 30 minutes | Serves 2

2 skinless, boneless chicken breast halves
Sauce:
3 tablespoons dry white wine
1 tablespoon Dijon mustard
2 tablespoons nonfat plain yogurt
Salt and freshly ground black pepper, to taste
2 rosemary sprigs

1. Place each breast on a 12 × 12-inch square of heavy-duty aluminum foil (or regular foil doubled) and turn up the edges of the foil.
2. Mix together the sauce ingredients and spoon over the chicken breasts. Lay a rosemary sprig on each breast. Bring up the edges of the foil and fold to form a sealed packet. Transfer to a baking pan.
3. Select Bake. Set temperature to 400ºF (205ºC) and set time to 25 minutes. Select Start to begin preheating.
4. Once preheated, slide the pan into the oven.
5. Bake for 25 minutes or until juices run clear when the meat is pierced with a fork. Remove the rosemary sprigs.
6. Broil for 5 minutes, or until lightly browned. Replace the sprigs and serve.

Quit slacking and make shit happen.

Teriyaki Roasted Chicken with Snow Peas

Prep time: 10 minutes | Cook time: 18 minutes | Serves 4

½ cup tamari or other gluten-free soy sauce
3 tablespoons honey
1 tablespoon rice vinegar
1 tablespoon rice wine or dry sherry
2 teaspoons minced fresh ginger
2 garlic cloves, minced
1½ pounds (680 g) boneless, skinless chicken thighs
2 teaspoons toasted sesame oil
8 to 12 ounces (227 to 340 g) snow peas

1. In a small bowl, whisk together the tamari, honey, vinegar, rice wine, ginger, and garlic until the honey is dissolved. Set aside 2 tablespoons of the marinade and pour the rest into a zip-top bag. Put the chicken thighs in the bag and seal, squeezing as much air out as possible. Squish the chicken around to coat it completely, then let the chicken marinate for 30 minutes, turning the bag every 10 minutes.
2. Put the snow peas on a sheet pan and toss with the reserved marinade and the oil. Move the peas to the outer edges of the pan.
3. Arrange the chicken in a single layer in the center of the pan.
4. Select Bake. Set temperature to 400ºF (205ºC) and set time to 18 minutes. Select Start to begin preheating.
5. Once preheated, slide the pan into the oven.
6. Bake the chicken and peas for 8 minutes. Remove from the oven. Turn the chicken over and stir the peas. Bake for another 10 minutes, or until the chicken is browning in spots and the peas are tender.

Oregano Stuffed Chicken with Feta

Prep time: 15 minutes | Cook time: 1¼ hours | Serves 6

4 pound (1.8 kg) whole chicken
½ cup crumbled Feta cheese
¼ pound (113 g) tomatoes, chopped
1 cup crusty sourdough bread, torn into small pieces
4 tablespoons extra-virgin olive oil, plus more to drizzle
2 garlic cloves, finely grated
3 teaspoons dried oregano
Sea salt flakes and freshly ground black pepper, to taste
½ teaspoon cayenne pepper
1¼ cups orzo
2 cups boiling chicken stock
1 tablespoon chopped flat-leaf parsley leaves, or chopped leaves from 4 oregano sprigs
Salad greens or roasted bell peppers, to serve

1. Put the chicken into a baking pan. Mix the Feta, tomatoes, bread, olive oil, garlic, half the dried oregano, and some seasoning in a bowl. Stuff this into the chicken cavity.
2. Rub the chicken with the cayenne, sprinkle with the rest of the dried oregano, then season the bird and drizzle it with olive oil.
3. Select Bake. Set temperature to 400ºF (205ºC) and set time to 70 minutes. Select Start to begin preheating.
4. Once preheated, slide the pan into the oven.
5. After 50 minutes, slide out the pan. Sprinkle the orzo around the chicken and pour on the boiling stock. Return to the oven for a final 20 minutes. Check during this time to make sure the orzo isn't becoming dry: there should be enough stock in it, but top it up with a little boiling water if you need to.
6. The chicken should be cooked: check by piercing it deeply between the leg and the body, the juices that run out should be clear, with no traces of pink. The orzo should be tender and the stock should have been absorbed.
7. Stir the fresh chopped herbs into the orzo and serve the chicken right from the dish. Salad greens or roasted red peppers is all you need on the side.

Chicken Pot Pie

Prep time: 10 minutes | Cook time: 45 minutes | Serves 4

4 tablespoons (½ stick) unsalted butter
½ cup chopped onion
¼ cup all-purpose flour
½ teaspoon kosher salt
¼ teaspoon freshly ground black pepper
1¾ cups low-sodium chicken broth
½ cup whole milk
2½ cups shredded cooked chicken
2 cups frozen mixed vegetables, thawed
1 (9-inch) refrigerated piecrust

1. In a large cast-iron skillet, melt the butter over medium heat. Add the onion and cook, stirring, until softened. Stir in the flour, salt, and pepper until well blended. Gradually stir in the broth and milk, and cook, stirring occasionally, until bubbly and thickened, about 5 minutes.
2. Stir in the chicken and mixed vegetables. Remove from the heat. Top with the crust, pressing the dough over the edges of the skillet to seal. Cut 3 or 4 slits into the crust.
3. Select Bake. Set temperature to 400ºF (205ºC) and set time to 40 minutes. Select Start to begin preheating.
4. Once preheated, put the skillet in the oven.
5. When done, the crust will be golden brown and the filling will be bubbling. Let stand for 5 minutes before serving.

Barbecue Drumsticks with Vegetable
Prep time: 10 minutes | Cook time: 30 minutes | Serves 4

8 chicken drumsticks
1 teaspoon kosher salt, divided
1 pound (454 g) sweet potatoes, peeled and cut into 1-inch chunks
3 tablespoons vegetable oil, divided
1 cup barbecue sauce, plus more if desired
8 ounces (227 g) green beans, trimmed

1. Season the drumsticks on all sides with ½ teaspoon of salt. Let sit for a few minutes, then blot dry with a paper towel.
2. Put the sweet potato chunks on a sheet pan and drizzle with 2 tablespoons of oil. Move them to one side of the pan.
3. Place the drumsticks on the other side of the pan. Brush all sides of the chicken with half the barbecue sauce.
4. Select Bake. Set temperature to 375ºF (190ºC) and set time to 30 minutes. Select Start to begin preheating.
5. Once preheated, slide the pan into the oven.
6. Bake for 15 minutes. Brush the drumsticks with the remaining barbecue sauce. Add the beans to the sweet potatoes and drizzle with the remaining 1 tablespoon of oil. Add the remaining ½ teaspoon of salt, and toss the beans and potatoes together. Bake for another 15 minutes, until the vegetables are sizzling and browned in spots and the chicken is cooked through.
7. If you like, brush the drumsticks with additional barbecue sauce, and serve with the beans and sweet potatoes on the side.

Simple Chicken Cordon Bleu
Prep time: 10 minutes | Cook time: 30 minutes | Serves 4

Nonstick cooking spray
2 (10- to 12-ounce / 283- to 340-g) boneless, skinless chicken breasts
½ teaspoon kosher salt
4 teaspoons Dijon mustard
4 thin slices prosciutto
4 thin slices Gruyère, Emmental, or other Swiss-style cheese
⅔ cup panko bread crumbs (gluten-free if necessary)
2 tablespoons unsalted butter, melted
¼ cup grated Parmesan cheese

1. Spray a baking pan with cooking spray.
2. Lay the chicken breasts flat on a cutting board. With your knife parallel to the board, slice each breast across, for a total of four flat pieces. Sprinkle the chicken with the salt. Lay a piece of plastic wrap over the chicken pieces, and use the heel of your hand to press the chicken into a more even thickness.
3. Transfer the chicken pieces to the prepared baking pan. Spread 1 teaspoon of mustard on each chicken piece. Layer one slice of ham and one slice of cheese evenly over each chicken piece.
4. In a small bowl, mix together the bread crumbs, melted butter, and Parmesan cheese. Sprinkle the mixture over the top of each piece.
5. Select Bake. Set temperature to 375ºF (190ºC) and set time to 30 minutes. Select Start to begin preheating.
6. Once preheated, slide the pan into the oven.
7. When done, the topping will be browned and the chicken will be done—slide a paring knife into one of the chicken pieces to be sure.

Balsamic Turkey with Carrots and Snap Peas
Prep time: 10 minutes | Cook time: 20 minutes | Serves 4

2 (12-ounce / 340-g) turkey tenderloins
1 teaspoon kosher salt, divided
3 tablespoons balsamic vinegar
2 tablespoons honey
1 tablespoon Dijon mustard
½ teaspoon dried thyme
6 large carrots, peeled and cut into ¼-inch-thick slices
8 ounces (227 g) snap peas
1 tablespoon extra-virgin olive oil

1. If your turkey tenderloins are not pre-brined, sprinkle them with ¾ teaspoon of salt. Place the turkey on a sheet pan.
2. In a small bowl, mix the balsamic vinegar, honey, mustard, and thyme.
3. Put the carrots and snap peas in a medium bowl and drizzle with the oil. Add 1 tablespoon of the balsamic mixture and the remaining ¼ teaspoon of salt, and toss to coat. Scatter the vegetables on the pan around the turkey tenderloins. Brush the tenderloins with about half of the remaining balsamic mixture.
4. Select Bake. Set temperature to 375ºF (190ºC) and set time to 20 minutes. Select Start to begin preheating.
5. Once preheated, slide the pan into the oven.
6. Bake the turkey and vegetables for 10 minutes, then remove the pan from the oven. Gently stir the vegetables. Flip the tenderloins and baste them with the remaining balsamic mixture. Cook for another 10 minutes, until the center of the tenderloins registers 155ºF (68ºC) on a meat thermometer.
7. Slice the turkey and serve with the vegetables.

Cheesy Chicken Tenders with Veggie
Prep time: 10 minutes | Cook time: 37 minutes | Serves 4

1½ pounds (680 g) chicken tenders
1 teaspoon kosher salt, divided
2 tablespoons unsalted butter
1 small onion, chopped
3 garlic cloves, minced
1 pound (454 g) baby spinach
1 (14-ounce / 397-g) can artichoke hearts, drained
½ cup heavy (whipping) cream
4 ounces (113 g) cream cheese, softened
¼ cup grated Parmesan cheese
1 cup shredded Mozzarella cheese

1. Sprinkle the chicken with ½ teaspoon of salt and set aside.
2. In a large cast-iron or other oven-safe skillet, melt the butter over medium heat. When the butter is foaming, add the onion, sprinkle with the remaining ½ teaspoon of salt, and cook, stirring, for 1 to 2 minutes, until the onion starts to soften. Add the garlic and stir for about 30 seconds. Add the spinach in large handfuls, stirring to wilt. Add the artichoke hearts, stirring them into the spinach. Add the heavy cream and cream cheese and cook until the cream cheese has melted into the vegetables. Stir in the Parmesan.
3. Pat the chicken dry and arrange the tenders in a single layer on top of the spinach mixture. Top with the Mozzarella cheese.
4. Select Bake. Set temperature to 350ºF (180ºC) and set time to 35 minutes. Select Start to begin preheating.
5. Once preheated, put the skillet in the oven.
6. When done, the cheese will be lightly browned on top and the mixture will be bubbling.
7. Let cool for 5 to 10 minutes, then serve.

Marinated Coconut Chicken with Pineapple
Prep time: 10 minutes | Cook time: 20 minutes | Serves 4

2 skinless, boneless chicken breasts, cut into 1 × 3-inch strips
2 tablespoons chopped onion
1 bell pepper, chopped
Marinade:
1 teaspoon finely chopped fresh ginger
2 garlic cloves, finely chopped
1 teaspoon toasted sesame oil
1 tablespoon brown sugar
2 tablespoons soy sauce
¾ cup dry white wine
1 (5-ounce / 142-g) can pineapple chunks, drained
2 tablespoons grated unsweetened coconut

1. Combine the marinade ingredients in a medium bowl and blend well. Add the chicken strips and spoon the mixture over them. Marinate in the refrigerator for at least 1 hour. Remove the strips from the marinade and place in an oiled or nonstick square (cake) pan. Add the onion and pepper and mix well.
2. Select Broil. Set temperature to 400ºF (205ºC) and set time to 20 minutes. Select Start to begin preheating.
3. Once preheated, slide the pan into the oven.
4. Broil for 8 minutes. Then remove from the oven and, using tongs, turn the chicken, pepper, and onion pieces. (Spoon the reserved marinade over the pieces, if desired.)
5. Broil again for 8 minutes, or until the chicken, pepper, and onion are cooked through and tender. Add the pineapple chunks and coconut and toss to mix well.
6. Broil for another 4 minutes, or until the coconut is lightly browned.

Chicken Thighs with Mirin
Prep time: 10 minutes | Cook time: 15 minutes | Serves 4

½ cup mirin
¼ cup dry white wine
½ cup soy sauce
1 tablespoon light brown sugar
1½ pounds (680 g) boneless, skinless chicken thighs, cut into 1½-inch pieces, fat trimmed
4 medium scallions, trimmed, cut into 1½-inch pieces
Cooking spray

Special Equipment:
4 (4-inch) bamboo skewers, soaked in water for at least 30 minutes

1. Combine the mirin, dry white wine, soy sauce, and brown sugar in a saucepan. Bring to a boil over medium heat. Keep stirring.
2. Boil for another 2 minutes or until it has a thick consistency. Turn off the heat.
3. Spritz the perforated pan with cooking spray.
4. Run the bamboo skewers through the chicken pieces and scallions alternatively.
5. Arrange the skewers in the perforated pan, then brush with mirin mixture on both sides. Spritz with cooking spray.
6. Select Air Fry. Set temperature to 400ºF (205ºC) and set time to 10 minutes. Press Start to begin preheating.
7. Once preheated, place the pan into the oven. Flip the skewers halfway through.
8. When cooking is complete, the chicken and scallions should be glossy.
9. Serve immediately.

Chicken and Pepper Baguette with Mayo

Prep time: 10 minutes | Cook time: 20 minutes | Serves 2

1¼ pounds (567 g) assorted small chicken parts, breasts cut into halves
¼ teaspoon salt
¼ teaspoon ground black pepper
2 teaspoons olive oil
½ pound (227 g) mini sweet peppers
¼ cup light mayonnaise
¼ teaspoon smoked paprika
½ clove garlic, crushed
Baguette, for serving
Cooking spray

1. Spritz the perforated pan with cooking spray.
2. Toss the chicken with salt, ground black pepper, and olive oil in a large bowl.
3. Arrange the sweet peppers and chicken in the perforated pan.
4. Select Air Fry. Set temperature to 375°F (190°C) and set time to 20 minutes. Press Start to begin preheating.
5. Once preheated, place the pan into the oven. Flip the chicken and transfer the peppers on a plate halfway through.
6. When cooking is complete, the chicken should be well browned.
7. Meanwhile, combine the mayo, paprika, and garlic in a small bowl. Stir to mix well.
8. Assemble the baguette with chicken and sweet pepper, then spread with mayo mixture and serve.

Dijon Turkey Breast with Sage

Prep time: 5 minutes | Cook time: 30 minutes | Serves 4

1 teaspoon chopped fresh sage
1 teaspoon chopped fresh tarragon
1 teaspoon chopped fresh thyme leaves
1 teaspoon chopped fresh rosemary leaves
1½ teaspoons sea salt
1 teaspoon ground black pepper
1 (2-pound / 907-g) turkey breast
3 tablespoons Dijon mustard
3 tablespoons butter, melted
Cooking spray

1. Spritz the perforated pan with cooking spray.
2. Combine the herbs, salt, and black pepper in a small bowl. Stir to mix well. Set aside.
3. Combine the Dijon mustard and butter in a separate bowl. Stir to mix well.
4. Rub the turkey with the herb mixture on a clean work surface, then brush the turkey with Dijon mixture.
5. Arrange the turkey in the perforated pan.
6. Select Air Fry. Set temperature to 390°F (199°C) and set time to 30 minutes. Press Start to begin preheating.
7. Once preheated, place the pan into the oven. Flip the turkey breast halfway through.
8. When cooking is complete, an instant-read thermometer inserted in the thickest part of the turkey breast should reach at least 165°F (74°C).
9. Transfer the cooked turkey breast on a large plate and slice to serve.

Turkey and Mushroom Meatballs

Prep time: 10 minutes | Cook time: 15 minutes | Serves 6

Sauce:
2 tablespoons tamari
2 tablespoons tomato sauce
1 tablespoon lime juice
¼ teaspoon peeled and grated fresh ginger
1 clove garlic, smashed to a paste
½ cup chicken broth
⅓ cup sugar
2 tablespoons toasted sesame oil
Cooking spray

Meatballs:
2 pounds (907 g) ground turkey
¾ cup finely chopped button mushrooms
2 large eggs, beaten
1½ teaspoons tamari
¼ cup finely chopped green onions, plus more for garnish
2 teaspoons peeled and grated fresh ginger
1 clove garlic, smashed
2 teaspoons toasted sesame oil
2 tablespoons sugar

For Serving:
Lettuce leaves, for serving
Sliced red chiles, for garnish (optional)
Toasted sesame seeds, for garnish (optional)

1. Spritz the perforated pan with cooking spray.
2. Combine the ingredients for the sauce in a small bowl. Stir to mix well. Set aside.
3. Combine the ingredients for the meatballs in a large bowl. Stir to mix well, then shape the mixture in twelve 1½-inch meatballs.
4. Arrange the meatballs in the perforated pan, then baste with the sauce.
5. Select Air Fry. Set temperature to 350°F (180°C) and set time to 15 minutes. Press Start to begin preheating.
6. Once preheated, place the pan into the oven. Flip the balls halfway through.
7. When cooking is complete, the meatballs should be golden brown.
8. Unfold the lettuce leaves on a large serving plate, then transfer the cooked meatballs on the leaves. Spread the red chiles and sesame seeds over the balls, then serve.

Quit slacking and make shit happen. -Chapter 8 Poultry

Perfect Upside-Down Chicken Nachos

Prep time: 10 minutes | Cook time: 34 minutes | Serves

1½ pounds (680 g) boneless, skinless chicken thighs
1 teaspoon kosher salt
1¼ cups tomato-based salsa
1 (14-ounce / 397-g) can pinto beans, rinsed and drained
8 ounces (227 g) Monterey Jack cheese, shredded
4 ounces (113 g) tortilla chips, or more as needed
1 medium jalapeño pepper, seeded and minced, or ¼ cup sliced pickled jalapeños (optional)

1. Season the chicken thighs on both sides with the salt, and place the thighs in a single layer in a baking pan. Pour about ⅔ cup of salsa over the chicken.
2. Select Bake. Set temperature to 350°F (180°C) and set time to 20 minutes. Select Start to begin preheating.
3. Once preheated, slide the pan into the oven.
4. The chicken will be nearly done.
5. Remove the chicken from the pan and chop or pull the meat into ½-inch pieces, discarding any gristle or fat.
6. Pour the beans into the pan and smash lightly with a potato masher or large fork so they are broken up but not smooth. Return the chicken to the pan, add the remaining salsa, and stir to combine.
7. Increase the oven temperature to 400°F (205°C) and place the pan in the oven. Bake the chicken and beans for 7 to 8 minutes, until bubbling.
8. Sprinkle about one-quarter of the cheese over the chicken mixture. Arrange the tortilla chips over the chicken in an even layer, covering the chicken mixture but not overlapping the chips too much. Sprinkle the remaining cheese over the chips, then top with the jalapeño (if using).
9. Return to the oven and bake for 5 to 7 minutes, until the cheese is melted and the chips are beginning to brown on the edges.
10. Serve immediately, scooping the chicken and beans out with the chips.

Orange-Glazed Whole Chicken

Prep time: 5 minutes | Cook time: 1 hours 40 minutes | Serves 6

1 (3-pound / 1.4-kg) whole chicken, rinsed and patted dry with paper towels
Brushing Mixture:
2 tablespoons orange juice concentrate
1 tablespoon soy sauce
1 tablespoon toasted sesame oil
1 teaspoon ground ginger
Salt and freshly ground black pepper, to taste

1. Place the chicken, breast side up, in an oiled or nonstick square (cake) pan and brush with the mixture, which has been combined in a small bowl, reserving the remaining mixture. Cover with aluminum foil.
2. Select Bake. Set temperature to 400°F (205°C) and set time to 1 hour and 40 minutes. Select Start to begin preheating.
3. Once preheated, slide the pan into the oven.
4. Bake for 1 hour 20 minutes. Uncover and brush the chicken with remaining mixture.
5. Bake, uncovered, for 20 minutes, or until the breast is tender when pierced with a fork and golden brown.

Satay Chicken Skewers

Prep time: 5 minutes | Cook time: 10 minutes | Serves 4

4 (6-ounce / 170-g) boneless, skinless chicken breasts, sliced into strips
Satay Sauce:
¼ cup creamy almond butter
½ teaspoon hot sauce
1½ tablespoons coconut vinegar
2 tablespoons chicken
For Serving:
¼ cup chopped cilantro leaves
Red pepper flakes, to taste
1 teaspoon sea salt
1 teaspoon paprika
Cooking spray

broth
1 teaspoon peeled and minced fresh ginger
1 clove garlic, minced
1 teaspoon sugar

Thinly sliced red, orange, or / and yellow bell peppers

Special Equipment:
16 wooden or bamboo skewers, soaked in water for 15 minutes

1. Spritz the perforated pan with cooking spray.
2. Run the bamboo skewers through the chicken strips, then arrange the chicken skewers in the perforated pan and sprinkle with salt and paprika.
3. Select Air Fry. Set temperature to 400°F (205°C) and set time to 10 minutes. Press Start to begin preheating.
4. Once preheated, place the pan into the oven. Flip the chicken skewers halfway during the cooking.
5. When cooking is complete, the chicken should be lightly browned.
6. Meanwhile, combine the ingredients for the sauce in a small bowl. Stir to mix well.
7. Transfer the cooked chicken skewers on a large plate, then top with cilantro, sliced bell peppers, red pepper flakes. Serve with the sauce or just baste the sauce over before serving.

Sweet-and-Sour Chicken Breasts

Prep time: 15 minutes | Cook time: 15 minutes | Serves 4

1 cup cornstarch
Chicken seasoning or rub, to taste
Salt and ground black pepper, to taste
2 eggs
2 (4-ounce/ 113-g) boneless, skinless chicken breasts, cut into 1-inch pieces
1½ cups sweet-and-sour sauce
Cooking spray

1. Spritz the perforated pan with cooking spray.
2. Combine the cornstarch, chicken seasoning, salt, and pepper in a large bowl. Stir to mix well. Whisk the eggs in a separate bowl.
3. Dredge the chicken pieces in the bowl of cornstarch mixture first, then in the bowl of whisked eggs, and then in the cornstarch mixture again.
4. Arrange the well-coated chicken pieces in the perforated pan. Spritz with cooking spray.
5. Select Air Fry. Set temperature to 360ºF (182ºC) and set time to 15 minutes. Press Start to begin preheating.
6. Once preheated, place the pan into the oven. Flip the chicken halfway through.
7. When cooking is complete, the chicken should be golden brown and crispy.
8. Transfer the chicken pieces on a large serving plate, then baste with sweet-and-sour sauce before serving.

Turkey Breast with Strawberries

Prep time: 15 minutes | Cook time: 37 minutes | Serves 2

2 pounds (907 g) turkey breast
1 tablespoon olive oil
Salt and ground black pepper, to taste
1 cup fresh strawberries

1. Rub the turkey bread with olive oil on a clean work surface, then sprinkle with salt and ground black pepper.
2. Transfer the turkey in the perforated pan and spritz with cooking spray.
3. Select Air Fry. Set temperature to 375ºF (190ºC) and set time to 30 minutes. Press Start to begin preheating.
4. Once preheated, place the pan into the oven. Flip the turkey breast halfway through.
5. Meanwhile, put the strawberries in a food processor and pulse until smooth.
6. When cooking is complete, spread the puréed strawberries over the turkey and cook for 7 more minutes.
7. Serve immediately.

Cheddar Turkey Burgers with Mayo

Prep time: 10 minutes | Cook time: 25 minutes | Serves 4

2 medium yellow onions
1 tablespoon olive oil
1½ teaspoons kosher salt, divided
1¼ pound (567 g) ground turkey
⅓ cup mayonnaise
1 tablespoon Dijon mustard
2 teaspoons Worcestershire sauce
4 slices sharp Cheddar cheese (about 4 ounces / 113 g in total)
4 hamburger buns, sliced

1. Trim the onions and cut them in half through the root. Cut one of the halves in half. Grate one quarter. Place the grated onion in a large bowl. Thinly slice the remaining onions and place in a medium bowl with the oil and ½ teaspoon of kosher salt. Toss to coat. Place the onions in a single layer on a baking pan.
2. Select Roast. Set temperature to 350ºF (180ºC) and set time to 10 minutes. Press Start to begin preheating.
3. Once preheated, place the pan into the oven.
4. While the onions are cooking, add the turkey to the grated onion. Add the remaining kosher salt, mayonnaise, mustard, and Worcestershire sauce. Mix just until combined, being careful not to overwork the turkey. Divide the mixture into 4 patties, each about ¾-inch thick.
5. When cooking is complete, remove the pan from the oven. Move the onions to one side of the pan and place the burgers on the pan. Poke your finger into the center of each burger to make a deep indentation.
6. Select Broil. Set temperature to 400ºF (205ºC), and set time to 12 minutes.
7. Place the pan into the oven. After 6 minutes, remove the pan. Turn the burgers and stir the onions. Return the pan to the oven and continue cooking. After about 4 minutes, remove the pan and place the cheese slices on the burgers. Return the pan to the oven and continue cooking for about 1 minute, or until the cheese is melted and the center of the burgers has reached at least 165ºF (74ºC) on a meat thermometer.
8. When cooking is complete, remove the pan from the oven. Loosely cover the burgers with foil.
9. Lay out the buns, cut-side up, on the oven rack. Select Broil. Set temperature to 400ºF (205ºC), and set time to 3 minutes. Place the pan into the oven. Check the buns after 2 minutes; they should be lightly browned.
10. Remove the buns from the oven. Assemble the burgers and serve.

Quit slacking and make shit happen. -Chapter 8 Poultry

Paprika Hens in Wine

Prep time: 2 hours 15 minutes | Cook time: 30 minutes | Serves 8

4 (1¼-pound / 567-g) Cornish hens, giblets removed, split lengthwise
2 cups white wine, divided
2 garlic cloves, minced
1 small onion, minced
½ teaspoon celery seeds
½ teaspoon poultry seasoning
½ teaspoon paprika
½ teaspoon dried oregano
¼ teaspoon freshly ground black pepper

1. Place the hens, cavity side up, on a rack in a baking pan. Pour 1½ cups of the wine over the hens; set aside.
2. In a shallow bowl, combine the garlic, onion, celery seeds, poultry seasoning, paprika, oregano, and pepper. Sprinkle half of the combined seasonings over the cavity of each split half. Cover and refrigerate. Allow the hens to marinate for 2 hours.
3. Transfer the hens in the perforated pan.
4. Select Bake. Set temperature to 350ºF (180ºC) and set time to 90 minutes. Press Start to begin preheating.
5. Once preheated, place the pan into the oven.
6. Remove the panpan from the oven halfway through the baking, turn breast side up, and remove the skin. Pour the remaining ½ cup of wine over the top, and sprinkle with the remaining seasonings.
7. When cooking is complete, the inner temperature of the hens should be at least 165ºF (74ºC). Transfer the hens to a serving platter and serve hot.

Chicken Thighs with Cabbage Slaw

Prep time: 10 minutes | Cook time: 27 minutes | Serves 4

4 bone-in, skin-on chicken thighs
1½ teaspoon kosher salt, divided
1 tablespoon smoked paprika
½ teaspoon granulated garlic
½ teaspoon dried oregano
¼ teaspoon freshly ground black pepper
3 cups shredded cabbage
½ small red onion, thinly sliced
4 large radishes, julienned
3 tablespoons red wine vinegar
2 tablespoons olive oil
Cooking spray

1. Salt the chicken thighs on both sides with 1 teaspoon of kosher salt. In a small bowl, combine the paprika, garlic, oregano, and black pepper. Sprinkle half this mixture over the skin sides of the thighs. Spritz a baking pan with cooking spray and place the thighs skin-side down on the pan. Sprinkle the remaining spice mixture over the other sides of the chicken pieces.
2. Select Roast. Set temperature to 375ºF (190ºC) and set time to 27 minutes. Press Start to begin preheating.
3. Once preheated, place the pan into the oven.
4. After 10 minutes, remove the pan from the oven and turn over the chicken thighs. Return the pan to the oven and continue cooking.
5. While the chicken cooks, place the cabbage, onion, and radishes in a large bowl. Sprinkle with the remaining kosher salt, vinegar, and olive oil. Toss to coat.
6. After another 9 to 10 minutes, remove the pan from the oven and place the chicken thighs on a cutting board. Place the cabbage mixture in the pan and toss with the chicken fat and spices.
7. Spread the cabbage in an even layer on the pan and place the chicken on it, skin-side up. place the pan into the oven and continue cooking. Roast for another 7 to 8 minutes.
8. When cooking is complete, the cabbage is just becoming tender. Remove the pan from the oven. Taste and adjust the seasoning if necessary. Serve.

Vinegary Chicken with Pineapple

Prep time: 10 minutes | Cook time: 10 minutes | Serves 6

1½ pounds (680 g) boneless, skinless chicken breasts, cut into 1-inch chunks
¾ cup soy sauce
2 tablespoons ketchup
2 tablespoons brown sugar
2 tablespoons rice vinegar
1 red bell pepper, cut into 1-inch chunks
1 green bell pepper, cut into 1-inch chunks
6 scallions, cut into 1-inch pieces
1 cup (¾-inch chunks) fresh pineapple, rinsed and drained
Cooking spray

1. Place the chicken in a large bowl. Add the soy sauce, ketchup, brown sugar, vinegar, red and green peppers, and scallions. Toss to coat.
2. Spritz a baking pan with cooking spray and place the chicken and vegetables on the pan.
3. Select Roast. Set temperature to 375ºF (190ºC) and set time to 10 minutes. Press Start to begin preheating.
4. Once preheated, place the pan into the oven.
5. After 6 minutes, remove the pan from the oven. Add the pineapple chunks to the pan and stir. Return the pan to the oven and continue cooking.
6. When cooking is complete, remove the pan from the oven. Serve with steamed rice, if desired.

Dijon Turkey with Carrots

Prep time: 10 minutes | Cook time: 25 minutes | Serves 4

2 (12-ounce / 340-g) turkey tenderloins
1 teaspoon kosher salt, divided
6 slices bacon
3 tablespoons balsamic vinegar
2 tablespoons honey
1 tablespoon Dijon mustard
½ teaspoon dried thyme
6 large carrots, peeled and cut into ¼-inch rounds
1 tablespoon olive oil

1. Sprinkle the turkey with ¾ teaspoon of the salt. Wrap each tenderloin with 3 strips of bacon, securing the bacon with toothpicks. Place the turkey in a baking pan.
2. In a small bowl, mix the balsamic vinegar, honey, mustard, and thyme.
3. Place the carrots in a medium bowl and drizzle with the oil. Add 1 tablespoon of the balsamic mixture and ¼ teaspoon of kosher salt and toss to coat. Place these on the pan around the turkey tenderloins. Baste the tenderloins with about one-half of the remaining balsamic mixture.
4. Select Roast. Set temperature to 375ºF (190ºC) and set time to 25 minutes. Press Start to begin preheating.
5. Once preheated, place the pan into the oven.
6. After 13 minutes, remove the pan from the oven. Gently stir the carrots. Flip the tenderloins and baste with the remaining balsamic mixture. Return the pan to the oven and continue cooking.
7. When cooking is complete, the carrots should tender and the center of the tenderloins should register 165ºF (74ºC) on a meat thermometer. Remove the pan from the oven. Slice the turkey and serve with the carrots.

Chicken and Veggies with 'Nduja

Prep time: 10 minutes | Cook time: 40 minutes | Serves 4

8 good-sized skin-on, bone-in chicken thighs, excess skin neatly trimmed
1 pound (454 g) head cauliflower, broken into florets
1 pound (454 g) baby waxy potatoes, scrubbed, then halved or quartered, depending on size
2¾ ounces (78 g) 'nduja, broken into nuggets
6 thyme sprigs
3 tablespoons olive oil
Sea salt flakes and freshly ground black pepper, to taste
Green salad, or bitter greens, to serve

1. Put all the ingredients in a baking pan, season, and toss around with your hands. The chicken should end up skin-side up. Make sure the nuggets of 'nduja aren't lying on top, or they'll burn.
2. Select Bake. Set temperature to 400ºF (205ºC) and set time to 40 minutes. Select Start to begin preheating.
3. Once preheated, slide the pan into the oven. Stir the mixture three times during cooking. The 'nduja partly melts and you need to ensure it gets well mixed in.
4. Towards the end of the cooking time, it's good to spoon the bits of 'nduja over the chicken, as it gives it a lovely color. The potatoes should be tender when pierced with a sharp knife and the chicken cooked through. Serve with a green salad or bitter greens.

Duck Breast with Potato

Prep time: 5 minutes | Cook time: 12 minutes | Serves 4

2 (1-pound / 454-g) boneless, skin-on duck breast halves
2 teaspoons kosher salt
1 pound (454 g) russet potatoes, peeled and cut into very thin sticks

1. With a very sharp knife, gently score the skin side of each duck breast, cutting through the skin and fat but not into the flesh. Space the scores ¼ to ½ inch apart. Turn the breast 90 degrees and score at right angles to the first series of scores. You'll have a diamond pattern of cuts over the skin. Sprinkle both sides with 1 teaspoon of salt.
2. Arrange the breasts on a baking pan, skin-side down.
3. Select Bake. Set temperature to 400ºF (205ºC) and set time to 4 minutes. Select Start to begin preheating.
4. Once preheated, slide the pan into the oven.
5. When done, the skin will be light brown and beginning to crisp and most of the fat has rendered
6. Remove the pan from the oven and arrange the potatoes around the breasts. Toss them to coat with the rendered duck fat and sprinkle with the remaining 1 teaspoon of salt. Bake for another 3 to 4 minutes, until the duck skin is dark golden brown.
7. Turn the breasts over and toss the potatoes. Continue to bake until the duck reaches an internal temperature of 150ºF (66ºC). This can take anywhere from 4 to 8 minutes, depending on the type of duck and the size of the breasts.
8. Remove the pan from the oven and let it rest for 5 minutes before slicing the duck. Serve with the fries.

Quit slacking and make shit happen. -Chapter 8 Poultry

Garlicky Oregano Chicken with Chipotle Allioli

Prep time: 15 minutes | Cook time: 1 hour | Serves 6

For the Chicken:
- 4 pound (1.8 kg) whole chicken
- 10 garlic cloves, finely grated
- ½ tablespoon sea salt flakes
- 1 red Fresno chili, halved, seeded, and finely chopped
- 1½ tablespoons dried oregano
- 2 tablespoons extra-virgin olive oil
- Juice of 1 lemon
- Roast sweet potato wedges, to serve (optional)

For the Chipotle Allioli:
- 1 egg yolk
- 1 teaspoon Dijon mustard
- 2 garlic cloves, finely grated
- ½ cup mixed peanut and extra-virgin olive oils
- 1 tablespoon chipotle paste
- Lemon juice, to taste
- Sea salt flakes and freshly ground black pepper, to taste

1. To spatchcock the chicken, set the bird on a work surface, breast side down, legs towards you. Using good kitchen scissors or poultry shears, cut through the flesh and bone along both sides of the backbone. Remove the backbone (you can keep it for stock). Open the chicken, turn it over, then flatten it by pressing hard on the breastbone with the heel of your hand. You'll feel it breaking and flattening under your hand. Remove any big globules of fat and neaten the ragged bits of skin. Now you have a spatchcocked bird.
2. Put the chicken into a dish that fits in your refrigerator. Mix all the other ingredients to make a marinade. Gently loosen the skin of the breast, pushing your fingers between the skin and flesh. Work your way under the skin down to the legs. Spoon some marinade in here, then spread it over the chicken on both sides. Cover and put into the refrigerator for a few hours if you can, turning it once. Bring the bird to room temperature. Transfer chicken to a baking pan.
3. Select Bake. Set temperature to 400ºF (205ºC) and set time to 1 hour. Select Start to begin preheating.
4. Once preheated, slide the pan into the oven. Baste the chicken a few times during the cooking.
5. Make the allioli while the chicken is cooking. Mix the egg yolk, mustard, and garlic in a bowl. Using electric beaters or a wooden spoon, gradually add the oils in little drops, making sure each is incorporated before you add the next. If it splits, start again with a new egg yolk and gradually add the curdled mixture. Add the chipotle paste, lemon juice to taste (start with about 1 tablespoon), and seasoning. If you're making this more than 1 hour ahead, cover and keep it in the fridge, stirring it when you take it out. (Don't serve it cold from the refrigerator.)
6. Check to see if the chicken is cooked properly. Cut into pieces and serve with the chipotle allioli. Roasted sweet potato wedges are brilliant with it.

Herb Buttery Turkey Breast

Prep time: 10 minutes | Cook time: 35 minutes | Serves 4

- 1 (4- to 5-pound / 1.8- to 2.3-kg) bone-in turkey breast, split at the breastbone
- 2½ teaspoons kosher salt, divided
- 6 tablespoons (¾ stick) unsalted butter, softened, divided
- ½ small onion, finely chopped
- 1 celery stalk, finely chopped
- ½ teaspoon freshly ground black pepper, divided
- 2 tablespoons finely chopped fresh sage, divided
- 2 teaspoons finely chopped fresh thyme, divided
- ¾ cup chicken broth
- 4 cups stale cornbread, crumbled into large pieces
- 1 large egg, beaten

1. Sprinkle the turkey breast halves with 1¼ teaspoons of salt. Let it rest while you make the dressing.
2. In a large, oven-safe skillet, melt 3 tablespoons of butter over medium-high heat. Add the onion, celery, remaining 1¼ teaspoons of salt, and ¼ teaspoon of pepper and sauté until the vegetables soften, 5 to 6 minutes. Stir in 1 tablespoon of sage, 1 teaspoon of thyme, and the chicken broth and simmer, uncovered, until the liquid is reduced by about a third, about 3 minutes. Add the cornbread and toss to mix. Stir in the egg.
3. In a small bowl, mix the remaining 3 tablespoons of butter with the remaining 1 tablespoon of sage, 1 teaspoon of thyme, and ¼ teaspoon of pepper. With your fingers, loosen the skin over the turkey breast meat. Scoop half the butter mixture under the skin on each breast half and spread it around with your hands as evenly as possible. Place the turkey breast halves on top of the dressing in the skillet.
4. Select Bake. Set temperature to 400ºF (205ºC) and set time to 35 minutes. Select Start to begin preheating.
5. Once preheated, put the skillet in the oven.
6. When done, a meat thermometer inserted into the turkey will reach 160ºF (71ºC).
7. Remove the skillet from the oven and let the turkey rest for 5 to 10 minutes before carving. Serve the turkey with the dressing.

Chicken Thighs with Peppers
Prep time: 10 minutes | Cook time: 27 minutes | Serves 4

4 bone-in, skin-on chicken thighs (about 1½ pounds / 680 g)
1½ teaspoon kosher salt, divided
1 link sweet Italian sausage (about 4 ounces / 113 g) whole
8 ounces (227 g) miniature bell peppers, halved and deseeded
1 small onion, thinly sliced
2 garlic cloves, minced
1 tablespoon olive oil
4 hot pickled cherry peppers, deseeded and quartered, along with 2 tablespoons pickling liquid from the jar
¼ cup chicken stock
Cooking spray

1. Salt the chicken thighs on both sides with 1 teaspoon of kosher salt. Spritz a baking pan with cooking spray and place the thighs skin-side down on the pan. Add the sausage.
2. Select Roast. Set temperature to 375ºF (190ºC) and set time to 27 minutes. Press Start to begin preheating.
3. Once preheated, place the pan into the oven.
4. While the chicken and sausage cook, place the bell peppers, onion, and garlic in a large bowl. Sprinkle with the remaining kosher salt and add the olive oil. Toss to coat.
5. After 10 minutes, remove the pan from the oven and flip the chicken thighs and sausage. Add the pepper mixture to the pan. Return the pan to the oven and continue cooking.
6. After another 10 minutes, remove the pan from the oven and add the pickled peppers, pickling liquid, and stock. Stir the pickled peppers into the peppers and onion. Return the pan to the oven and continue cooking.
7. When cooking is complete, the peppers and onion should be soft and the chicken should read 165ºF (74ºC) on a meat thermometer. Remove the pan from the oven. Slice the sausage into thin pieces and stir it into the pepper mixture. Spoon the peppers over four plates. Top with a chicken thigh.

Sesame Balsamic Chicken Breast
Prep time: 5 minutes | Cook time: 20 minutes | Serves 2

2 skinless, boneless chicken breast filets
Mixture:
2 tablespoons sesame oil
2 teaspoons soy sauce
3 tablespoons sesame seeds
2 teaspoons balsamic vinegar

1. Combine the mixture ingredients in a small bowl and brush the fillets liberally. Reserve the mixture. Place the fillets on a broiling rack with a pan underneath.
2. Select Broil. Set temperature to 400ºF (205ºC) and set time to 15 minutes. Select Start to begin preheating.
3. Once preheated, slide the pan into the oven.
4. When done, the meat will be tender and the juices will run clear when the meat is pierced. Remove from the oven and brush the fillets with the remaining mixture. Place the sesame seeds on a plate and press the chicken breast halves into the seeds, coating well.
5. Broil for 5 minutes, or until the sesame seeds are browned.

Garlic Chicken Wings
Prep time: 10 minutes | Cook time: 15 minutes | Serves 4

1 tablespoon olive oil
8 whole chicken wings
Chicken seasoning or rub, to taste
1 teaspoon garlic powder
Freshly ground black pepper, to taste

1. Grease the perforated pan with olive oil.
2. On a clean work surface, rub the chicken wings with chicken seasoning and rub, garlic powder, and ground black pepper.
3. Arrange the well-coated chicken wings in the perforated pan.
4. Select Air Fry. Set temperature to 400ºF (205ºC) and set time to 15 minutes. Press Start to begin preheating.
5. Once preheated, place the pan into the oven. Flip the chicken wings halfway through.
6. When cooking is complete, the internal temperature of the chicken wings should reach at least 165ºF (74ºC).
7. Remove the chicken wings from the oven. Serve immediately.

Barbecue Turkey Burgers
Prep time: 5 minutes | Cook time: 20 minutes | Serves 4

1 pound (454 g) lean ground turkey breast
2 tablespoons bread crumbs
2 tablespoons barbecue sauce
½ teaspoon garlic powder
½ teaspoon chili powder
Salt and freshly ground black pepper, to taste

1. Combine all ingredients in a bowl, mixing well. Divide into 4 portions and shape into patties. Transfer to a baking pan.
2. Select Broil. Set temperature to 400ºF (205ºC) and set time to 20 minutes. Select Start to begin preheating.
3. Once preheated, slide the pan into the oven.
4. When done, the meat will be browned and the juice will run clear when pierced with a fork.

Chicken, Vegetable and Rice Casserole

Prep time: 10 minutes | Cook time: 52 minutes | Serves 4

4 skinless, boneless chicken thighs, cut into 1-inch cubes
½ cup brown rice
4 scallions, chopped
1 plum tomato, chopped
1 cup frozen peas
1 cup frozen corn
1 cup peeled and chopped carrots
2 tablespoons chopped fresh parsley
1 teaspoon mustard seed
1 teaspoon dried dill weed
¼ teaspoon celery seed
Salt and freshly ground black pepper, to taste
½ cup finely chopped pecans

1. Combine all the ingredients, except the pecans, with 2½ cups water in an ovenproof baking dish. Adjust the seasonings to taste. Cover with aluminum foil.
2. Select Bake. Set temperature to 400ºF (205ºC) and set time to 45 minutes. Select Start to begin preheating.
3. Once preheated, slide the baking dish into the oven.
4. When done, the rice will be tender. Uncover and sprinkle the top with the pecans.
5. Broil for 7 minutes, or until the pecans are browned.

Whole Duck with Cherry Sauce

Prep time: 20 minutes | Cook time: 32 minutes | Serves 12

1 whole duck (about 5 pounds / 2.3 kg in total) split in half, back and rib bones removed, fat trimmed
1 teaspoon olive oil
Salt and freshly ground black pepper, to taste
Cherry Sauce:
1 tablespoon butter
1 shallot, minced
½ cup sherry
1 cup chicken stock
1 teaspoon white wine vinegar
¾ cup cherry preserves
1 teaspoon fresh thyme leaves
Salt and freshly ground black pepper, to taste

1. On a clean work surface, rub the duck with olive oil, then sprinkle with salt and ground black pepper to season.
2. Place the duck in the perforated pan, breast side up.
3. Select Air Fry. Set temperature to 400ºF (205ºC) and set time to 25 minutes. Press Start to begin preheating.
4. Once preheated, place the pan into the oven. Flip the ducks halfway through the cooking time.
5. Meanwhile, make the cherry sauce: Heat the butter in a skillet over medium-high heat or until melted.
6. Add the shallot and sauté for 5 minutes or until lightly browned.
7. Add the sherry and simmer for 6 minutes or until it reduces in half.
8. Add the chicken stick, white wine vinegar, and cherry preserves. Stir to combine well. Simmer for 6 more minutes or until thickened.
9. Fold in the thyme leaves and sprinkle with salt and ground black pepper. Stir to mix well.
10. When the cooking of the duck is complete, glaze the duck with a quarter of the cherry sauce, then air fry for another 4 minutes.
11. Flip the duck and glaze with another quarter of the cherry sauce. Air fry for an additional 3 minutes.
12. Transfer the duck on a large plate and serve with remaining cherry sauce.

Chili Chicken Fries

Prep time: 20 minutes | Cook time: 6 minutes | Serves 4 to 6

1 pound (454 g) chicken tenders, cut into about ½-inch-wide strips
Salt, to taste
¼ cup all-purpose flour
2 eggs
¾ cup panko bread crumbs
¾ cup crushed organic nacho cheese tortilla chips
Cooking spray
Seasonings:
½ teaspoon garlic powder
1 tablespoon chili powder
½ teaspoon onion powder
1 teaspoon ground cumin

1. Stir together all seasonings in a small bowl and set aside.
2. Sprinkle the chicken with salt. Place strips in a large bowl and sprinkle with 1 tablespoon of the seasoning mix. Stir well to distribute seasonings.
3. Add flour to chicken and stir well to coat all sides.
4. Beat eggs in a separate bowl.
5. In a shallow dish, combine the panko, crushed chips, and the remaining 2 teaspoons of seasoning mix.
6. Dip chicken strips in eggs, then roll in crumbs. Mist with oil or cooking spray. Arrange the chicken strips in a single layer in the perforated pan.
7. Select Air Fry. Set temperature to 400ºF (205ºC) and set time to 6 minutes. Press Start to begin preheating.
8. Once preheated, place the pan into the oven.
9. After 4 minutes, remove the pan from the oven. Flip the strips with tongs. Return the pan to the oven and continue cooking.
10. When cooking is complete, the chicken should be crispy and its juices should be run clear.
11. Allow to cool under room temperature before serving.

Garlic Duck Leg Quarters

Prep time: 5 minutes | Cook time: 45 minutes | Serves 4

4 (½-pound / 227-g) skin-on duck leg quarters
2 medium garlic cloves, minced
½ teaspoon salt
½ teaspoon ground black pepper

1. Spritz the perforated pan with cooking spray.
2. On a clean work surface, rub the duck leg quarters with garlic, salt, and black pepper.
3. Arrange the leg quarters in the perforated pan and spritz with cooking spray.
4. Select Air Fry. Set temperature to 300ºF (150ºC) and set time to 30 minutes. Press Start to begin preheating.
5. Once preheated, place the pan into the oven.
6. After 30 minutes, remove the pan from the oven. Flip the leg quarters. Increase temperature to 375ºF (190ºC) and set time to 15 minutes. Return the pan to the oven and continue cooking.
7. When cooking is complete, the leg quarters should be well browned and crispy.
8. Remove the duck leg quarters from the oven and allow to cool for 10 minutes before serving.

Balsamic Chicken Breast with Oregano

Prep time: 35 minutes | Cook time: 40 minutes | Serves 2

¼ cup balsamic vinegar
2 teaspoons dried oregano
2 garlic cloves, minced
1 tablespoon olive oil
⅛ teaspoon salt
½ teaspoon freshly ground black pepper
2 (4-ounce / 113-g) boneless, skinless, chicken-breast halves
Cooking spray

1. In a small bowl, add the vinegar, oregano, garlic, olive oil, salt, and pepper. Mix to combine.
2. Put the chicken in a resealable plastic bag. Pour the vinegar mixture in the bag with the chicken, seal the bag, and shake to coat the chicken. Refrigerate for 30 minutes to marinate.
3. Spritz a baking pan with cooking spray. Put the chicken in the prepared baking pan and pour the marinade over the chicken.
4. Select Bake. Set temperature to 400ºF (205ºC) and set time to 40 minutes. Press Start to begin preheating.
5. Once preheated, place the pan into the oven.
6. After 20 minutes, remove the pan from the oven. Flip the chicken. Return the pan to the oven and continue cooking.
7. When cooking is complete, the internal temperature of the chicken should registers at least 165ºF (74ºC).
8. Let sit for 5 minutes, then serve.

Five-Spice Turkey Thighs

Prep time: 10 minutes | Cook time: 25 minutes | Serves 6

2 pounds (907 g) turkey thighs
1 teaspoon Chinese five-spice powder
¼ teaspoon Sichuan pepper
1 teaspoon pink Himalayan salt
1 tablespoon Chinese rice vinegar
1 tablespoon mustard
1 tablespoon chili sauce
2 tablespoons soy sauce
Cooking spray

1. Spritz the perforated pan with cooking spray.
2. Rub the turkey thighs with five-spice powder, Sichuan pepper, and salt on a clean work surface.
3. Put the turkey thighs in the perforated pan and spritz with cooking spray.
4. Select Air Fry. Set temperature to 360ºF (182ºC) and set time to 22 minutes. Press Start to begin preheating.
5. Once preheated, place the pan into the oven. Flip the thighs at least three times during the cooking.
6. When cooking is complete, the thighs should be well browned.
7. Meanwhile, heat the remaining ingredients in a saucepan over medium-high heat. Cook for 3 minutes or until the sauce is thickened and reduces to two thirds.
8. Transfer the thighs onto a plate and baste with sauce before serving.

Balsamic Duck Breasts with Orange Marmalade

Prep time: 5 minutes | Cook time: 13 minutes | Serves 4

4 (6-ounce / 170-g) skin-on duck breasts
1 teaspoon salt
¼ cup orange marmalade
1 tablespoon white balsamic vinegar
¾ teaspoon ground black pepper

1. Cut 10 slits into the skin of the duck breasts, then sprinkle with salt on both sides.
2. Place the breasts in the perforated pan, skin side up.
3. Select Air Fry. Set temperature to 400ºF (205ºC) and set time to 10 minutes. Press Start to begin preheating.
4. Once preheated, place the pan into the oven.
5. Meanwhile, combine the remaining ingredients in a small bowl. Stir to mix well.
6. When cooking is complete, brush the duck skin with the marmalade mixture. Flip the breast and air fry for 3 more minutes or until the skin is crispy and the breast is well browned.
7. Serve immediately.

Quit slacking and make shit happen. -Chapter 8 Poultry

Garlicky Whole Chicken Bake

Prep time: 10 minutes | Cook time: 1 hour | Serves 2 to 4

½ cup melted butter
3 tablespoons garlic, minced
Salt, to taste
1 teaspoon ground black pepper
1 (1-pound / 454-g) whole chicken

1. Combine the butter with garlic, salt, and ground black pepper in a small bowl.
2. Brush the butter mixture over the whole chicken, then place the chicken in the perforated pan, skin side down.
3. Select Bake. Set temperature to 350°F (180°C) and set time to 60 minutes. Press Start to begin preheating.
4. Once preheated, place the pan into the oven. Flip the chicken halfway through.
5. When cooking is complete, an instant-read thermometer inserted in the thickest part of the chicken should register at least 165°F (74°C).
6. Remove the chicken from the oven and allow to cool for 15 minutes before serving.

Maple Turkey Breast with Rosemary

Prep time: 2 hours 20 minutes | Cook time: 30 minutes | Serves 6

½ teaspoon dried rosemary
2 minced garlic cloves
2 teaspoons salt
1 teaspoon ground black pepper
¼ cup olive oil
2½ pounds (1.1 kg) turkey breast
¼ cup pure maple syrup
1 tablespoon stone-ground brown mustard
1 tablespoon melted vegan butter

1. Combine the rosemary, garlic, salt, ground black pepper, and olive oil in a large bowl. Stir to mix well.
2. Dunk the turkey breast in the mixture and wrap the bowl in plastic. Refrigerate for 2 hours to marinate.
3. Remove the bowl from the refrigerator and let sit for half an hour before cooking.
4. Spritz the perforated pan with cooking spray.
5. Remove the turkey from the marinade and place in the perforated pan.
6. Select Air Fry. Set temperature to 400°F (205°C) and set time to 20 minutes. Press Start to begin preheating.
7. Once preheated, place the pan into the oven. Flip the breast halfway through.
8. When cooking is complete, the breast should be well browned.
9. Meanwhile, combine the remaining ingredients in a small bowl. Stir to mix well.
10. Pour half of the butter mixture over the turkey breast in the oven and air fry for 10 more minutes. Flip the breast and pour the remaining half of butter mixture over halfway through.
11. Transfer the turkey on a plate and slice to serve.

Mozzarella Chicken Breasts with Basil

Prep time: 30 minutes | Cook time: 1 hour | Serves 2

1 large egg
¼ cup almond meal
2 (6-ounce / 170-g) boneless, skinless chicken breast halves
1 (8-ounce / 227-g) jar marinara sauce, divided
4 tablespoons shredded Mozzarella cheese, divided
4 tablespoons grated Parmesan cheese, divided
4 tablespoons chopped fresh basil, divided
Salt and freshly ground black pepper, to taste
Cooking spray

1. Spritz the perforated pan with cooking spray.
2. In a shallow bowl, beat the egg.
3. In a separate shallow bowl, place the almond meal.
4. Dip 1 chicken breast half into the egg, then into the almond meal to coat. Place the coated chicken in the perforated pan. Repeat with the remaining 1 chicken breast half.
5. Select Bake. Set temperature to 350°F (180°C) and set time to 40 minutes. Press Start to begin preheating.
6. Once preheated, place the pan into the oven.
7. After 20 minutes, remove the pan from the oven and flip the chicken. Return the pan to oven and continue cooking.
8. When cooking is complete, the chicken should no longer pink and the juices run clear.
9. In a baking pan, pour half of marinara sauce.
10. Place the cooked chicken in the sauce. Cover with the remaining marinara.
11. Sprinkle 2 tablespoons of Mozzarella cheese and 2 tablespoons of soy Parmesan cheese on each chicken breast. Top each with 2 tablespoons of basil.
12. Place the baking pan back in the oven and set the baking time to 20 minutes. Flip the chicken halfway through the cooking time.
13. When cooking is complete, an instant-read thermometer inserted into the center of the chicken should read at least 165°F (74°C).
14. Remove the pan from oven and divide between 2 plates. Season with salt and pepper and serve.

Buttery Chicken with Corn
Prep time: 10 minutes | Cook time: 25 minutes | Serves 4

4 bone-in, skin-on chicken thighs
2 teaspoons kosher salt, divided
1 cup Bisquick baking mix
½ cup butter, melted, divided
1 pound (454 g) small red potatoes, quartered
3 ears corn, shucked and cut into rounds 1- to 1½-inches thick
⅓ cup heavy whipping cream
½ teaspoon freshly ground black pepper

1. Sprinkle the chicken on all sides with 1 teaspoon of kosher salt. Place the baking mix in a shallow dish. Brush the thighs on all sides with ¼ cup of butter, then dredge them in the baking mix, coating them all on sides. Place the chicken in the center of a baking pan.
2. Place the potatoes in a large bowl with 2 tablespoons of butter and toss to coat. Place them on one side of the chicken on the pan.
3. Place the corn in a medium bowl and drizzle with the remaining butter. Sprinkle with ¼ teaspoon of kosher salt and toss to coat. Place on the pan on the other side of the chicken.
4. Select Roast. Set temperature to 375°F (190°C) and set time to 25 minutes. Press Start to begin preheating.
5. Once preheated, place the pan into the oven.
6. After 20 minutes, remove the pan from the oven and transfer the potatoes back to the bowl. Return the pan to oven and continue cooking.
7. As the chicken continues cooking, add the cream, black pepper, and remaining kosher salt to the potatoes. Lightly mash the potatoes with a potato masher.
8. When cooking is complete, the corn should be tender and the chicken cooked through, reading 165°F (74°C) on a meat thermometer. Remove the pan from the oven and serve the chicken with the smashed potatoes and corn on the side.

Turkey and Cauliflower Meatloaf
Prep time: 15 minutes | Cook time: 50 minutes | Serves 6

2 pounds (907 g) lean ground turkey
1⅓ cups riced cauliflower
2 large eggs, lightly beaten
¼ cup almond flour
⅔ cup chopped yellow or white onion
1 teaspoon ground dried turmeric
1 teaspoon ground cumin
1 teaspoon ground coriander
1 tablespoon minced garlic
1 teaspoon salt
1 teaspoon ground black pepper
Cooking spray

1. Spritz a loaf pan with cooking spray.
2. Combine all the ingredients in a large bowl. Stir to mix well. Pour half of the mixture in the prepared loaf pan and press with a spatula to coat the bottom evenly. Spritz the mixture with cooking spray.
3. Select Bake. Set temperature to 350°F (180°C) and set time to 25 minutes. Press Start to begin preheating.
4. Once preheated, place the pan into the oven.
5. When cooking is complete, the meat should be well browned and the internal temperature should reach at least 165°F (74°C).
6. Remove the loaf pan from the oven and serve immediately.

Paprika Whole Chicken Roast
Prep time: 15 minutes | Cook time: 1 hour | Serves 6

1 teaspoon Italian seasoning
½ teaspoon garlic powder
½ teaspoon paprika
1 teaspoon salt
½ teaspoon freshly ground black pepper
½ teaspoon onion powder
2 tablespoons olive oil
1 (3-pound / 1.4-kg) whole chicken, giblets removed, pat dry
Cooking spray

1. Spritz the perforated pan with cooking spray.
2. In a small bowl, mix the Italian seasoning, garlic powder, paprika, salt, pepper, and onion powder.
3. Brush the chicken with the olive oil and rub it with the seasoning mixture.
4. Tie the chicken legs with butcher's twine. Place the chicken in the perforated pan, breast side down.
5. Select Air Fry. Set temperature to 350°F (180°C) and set time to an hour. Press Start to begin preheating.
6. Once preheated, place the pan into the oven.
7. After 30 minutes, remove the pan from the oven. Flip the chicken over and baste it with any drippings collected in the bottom drawer of the oven. Return the pan to the oven and continue cooking.
8. When cooking is complete, a thermometer inserted into the thickest part of the thigh should reach at least 165°F (74°C).
9. Let the chicken rest for 10 minutes before carving and serving.

Curried Chicken and Brussels Sprouts
Prep time: 10 minutes | Cook time: 20 minutes | Serves 4

1 pound (454 g) boneless, skinless chicken thighs
1 teaspoon kosher salt, divided
¼ cup unsalted butter, melted
1 tablespoon curry powder
2 medium sweet potatoes, peeled and cut in 1-inch cubes
12 ounces (340 g) Brussels sprouts, halved

1. Sprinkle the chicken thighs with ½ teaspoon of kosher salt. Place them in the single layer on a baking pan.
2. In a small bowl, stir together the butter and curry powder.
3. Place the sweet potatoes and Brussels sprouts in a large bowl. Drizzle half the curry butter over the vegetables and add the remaining kosher salt. Toss to coat. Transfer the vegetables to the baking pan and place in a single layer around the chicken. Brush half of the remaining curry butter over the chicken.
4. Select Roast. Set temperature to 400°F (205°C) and set time to 20 minutes. Press Start to begin preheating.
5. Once preheated, place the pan into the oven.
6. After 10 minutes, remove the pan from the oven and turn over the chicken thighs. Baste them with the remaining curry butter. Return the pan to the oven and continue cooking.
7. Cooking is complete when the sweet potatoes are tender and the chicken is cooked through and reads 165°F (74°C) on a meat thermometer.

Tasty Meat and Vegetable Loaf
Prep time: 10 minutes | Cook time: 35 minutes | Serves 4

1 to 1½ pounds (454- to 680-g) ground turkey or chicken breast
1 egg
1 tablespoon chopped fresh parsley
2 tablespoons chopped bell pepper
3 tablespoons chopped canned mushrooms
2 tablespoons chopped onion
2 garlic cloves, minced
½ cup multigrain bread crumbs
1 tablespoon Worcestershire sauce
1 tablespoon ketchup
Freshly ground black pepper, to taste

1. Combine all the ingredients in a large bowl and press into a loaf pan.
2. Select Bake. Set temperature to 400°F (205°C) and set time to 35 minutes. Select Start to begin preheating.
3. Once preheated, slide the pan into the oven.
4. When done, the loaf will be browned on top.

Peach Chicken with Dark Cherry
Prep time: 8 minutes | Cook time: 15 minutes | Serves 4

⅓ cup peach preserves
1 teaspoon ground rosemary
½ teaspoon black pepper
½ teaspoon salt
½ teaspoon marjoram
1 teaspoon light olive oil
1 pound (454 g) boneless chicken breasts, cut in 1½-inch chunks
1 (10-ounce / 284-g) package frozen dark cherries, thawed and drained
Cooking spray

1. In a medium bowl, mix peach preserves, rosemary, pepper, salt, marjoram, and olive oil.
2. Stir in chicken chunks and toss to coat well with the preserve mixture.
3. Spritz the perforated pan with cooking spray and lay chicken chunks in the perforated pan.
4. Select Bake. set temperature to 400°F (205°C) and set time to 15 minutes. Press Start to begin preheating.
5. Once preheated, place the pan into the oven.
6. After 7 minutes, remove the pan from the oven. Flip the chicken chunks. Return the pan to the oven and continue cooking.
7. When cooking is complete, the chicken should no longer pink and the juices should run clear.
8. Scatter the cherries over and cook for an additional minute to heat cherries.
9. Serve immediately.

Turkey Meatloaves with Onion
Prep time: 6 minutes | Cook time: 24 minutes | Serves 4

¼ cup grated carrot
2 garlic cloves, minced
2 tablespoons ground almonds
⅓ cup minced onion
2 teaspoons olive oil
1 teaspoon dried marjoram
1 egg white
¾ pound (340 g) ground turkey breast

1. In a medium bowl, stir together the carrot, garlic, almonds, onion, olive oil, marjoram, and egg white.
2. Add the ground turkey. Mix until combined.
3. Double 16 foil muffin cup liners to make 8 cups. Divide the turkey mixture evenly among the liners.
4. Select Bake. Set temperature to 400°F (205°C) and set time to 24 minutes. Press Start to begin preheating.
5. Once preheated, place the muffin cups into the oven.
6. When cooking is complete, the meatloaves should reach an internal temperature of 165°F (74°C) on a meat thermometer.
7. Serve immediately.

Chicken and Cheese Sandwiches

Prep time: 12 minutes | Cook time: 13 minutes | Serves 4

2 (8-ounce / 227-g) boneless, skinless chicken breasts
1 teaspoon kosher salt, divided
1 cup all-purpose flour
1 teaspoon Italian seasoning
2 large eggs
2 tablespoons plain yogurt
2 cups panko bread crumbs
1⅓ cups grated Parmesan cheese, divided
2 tablespoons olive oil
4 ciabatta rolls, split in half
½ cup marinara sauce
½ cup shredded Mozzarella cheese

1. Lay the chicken breasts on a cutting board and cut each one in half parallel to the board so you have 4 fairly even, flat fillets. Place a piece of plastic wrap over the chicken pieces and use a rolling pin to gently pound them to an even thickness, about ½-inch thick. Season the chicken on both sides with ½ teaspoon of kosher salt.
2. Place the flour on a plate and add the remaining kosher salt and the Italian seasoning. Mix with a fork to distribute evenly. In a wide bowl, whisk together the eggs with the yogurt. In a small bowl combine the panko, 1 cup of Parmesan cheese, and olive oil. Place this in a shallow bowl.
3. Lightly dredge both sides of the chicken pieces in the seasoned flour, and then dip them in the egg wash to coat completely, letting the excess drip off. Finally, dredge the chicken in the bread crumbs. Carefully place the breaded chicken pieces in the perforated pan.
4. Select Air Fry. Set temperature to 375ºF (190ºC) and set time to 10 minutes. Press Start to begin preheating.
5. Once preheated, place the perforated pan into the oven.
6. After 5 minutes, remove the perforated pan from the oven. Carefully turn the chicken over. Return the perforated pan to the oven and continue cooking. When cooking is complete, remove the perforated pan from the oven.
7. Unfold the rolls on the perforated pan and spread each half with 1 tablespoon of marinara sauce. Place a chicken breast piece on the bottoms of the buns and sprinkle the remaining Parmesan cheese over the chicken pieces. Divide the Mozzarella among the top halves of the buns.
8. Select Broil. Set temperature to 400ºF (205ºC), and set time to 3 minutes.
9. Place the pan into the oven. Check the sandwiches halfway through. When cooking is complete, the Mozzarella cheese should be melted and bubbly.
10. Remove the perforated pan from the oven. Close the sandwiches and serve.

Game Hens with Cucumber Salad

Prep time: 25 minutes | Cook time: 25 minutes | Serves 6

2 (1¼-pound / 567-g) Cornish game hens, giblets discarded
1 tablespoon fish sauce
6 tablespoons chopped fresh cilantro
2 teaspoons lime zest
1 teaspoon ground coriander
2 garlic cloves, minced
2 tablespoons packed light brown sugar
2 teaspoons vegetable oil
Salt and ground black pepper, to taste
1 English cucumber, halved lengthwise and sliced thin
1 Thai chile, stemmed, deseeded, and minced
2 tablespoons chopped dry-roasted peanuts
1 small shallot, sliced thinly
1 tablespoon lime juice
Lime wedges, for serving
Cooking spray

1. Arrange a game hen on a clean work surface, remove the backbone with kitchen shears, then pound the hen breast to flat. Cut the breast in half. Repeat with the remaining game hen.
2. Loose the breast and thigh skin with your fingers, then pat the game hens dry and pierce about 10 holes into the fat deposits of the hens. Tuck the wings under the hens.
3. Combine 2 teaspoons of fish sauce, ¼ cup of cilantro, lime zest, coriander, garlic, 4 teaspoons of sugar, 1 teaspoon of vegetable oil, ½ teaspoon of salt, and ⅛ teaspoon of ground black pepper in a small bowl. Stir to mix well.
4. Rub the fish sauce mixture under the breast and thigh skin of the game hens, then let sit for 10 minutes to marinate.
5. Spritz the perforated pan with cooking spray.
6. Arrange the marinated game hens in the pan, skin side down.
7. Select Air Fry. Set temperature to 400ºF (205ºC) and set time to 25 minutes. Press Start to begin preheating.
8. Once preheated, place the pan into the oven. Flip the game hens halfway through the cooking time.
9. When cooking is complete, the hen skin should be golden brown and the internal temperature of the hens should read at least 165ºF (74ºC).
10. Meanwhile, combine all the remaining ingredients, except for the lime wedges, in a large bowl and sprinkle with salt and black pepper. Toss to mix well.
11. Transfer the fried hens on a large plate, then sit the salad aside and squeeze the lime wedges over before serving.

Chicken Thighs with Cherry Tomatoes
Prep time: 10 minutes | Cook time: 18 minutes | Serves 4

1½ pounds (680 g) boneless, skinless chicken thighs	(about 1 medium lemon)
1¼ teaspoon kosher salt, divided	4 garlic cloves, minced, divided
2 tablespoons plus 1 teaspoon olive oil, divided	1 tablespoon Shawarma Seasoning
⅔ cup plus 2 tablespoons plain Greek yogurt, divided	4 pita breads, cut in half
	2 cups cherry tomatoes
2 tablespoons freshly squeezed lemon juice	½ small cucumber, peeled, deseeded, and chopped
	1 tablespoon chopped fresh parsley

1. Sprinkle the chicken thighs on both sides with 1 teaspoon of kosher salt. Place in a resealable plastic bag and set aside while you make the marinade.
2. In a small bowl, mix 2 tablespoons of olive oil, 2 tablespoons of yogurt, the lemon juice, 3 garlic cloves, and Shawarma Seasoning until thoroughly combined. Pour the marinade over the chicken. Seal the bag, squeezing out as much air as possible. And massage the chicken to coat it with the sauce. Set aside.
3. Wrap 2 pita breads each in two pieces of aluminum foil and place on a baking pan.
4. Select Bake. Set temperature to 300ºF (150ºC) and set time to 6 minutes. Press Start to begin preheating.
5. Once the oven has preheated, place the pan into the oven. After 3 minutes, remove the pan from the oven and turn over the foil packets. Return the pan to the oven and continue cooking. When cooking is complete, remove the pan from the oven and place the foil-wrapped pitas on the top of the oven to keep warm.
6. Remove the chicken from the marinade, letting the excess drip off into the bag. Place them on the baking pan. Arrange the tomatoes around the sides of the chicken. Discard the marinade.
7. Select Broil. Set temperature to 400ºF (205ºC), and set time to 12 minutes.
8. Place the pan into the oven.
9. After 6 minutes, remove the pan from the oven and turn over the chicken. Return the pan to the oven and continue cooking.
10. Wrap the cucumber in a paper towel to remove as much moisture as possible. Place them in a small bowl. Add the remaining yogurt, kosher salt, olive oil, garlic clove, and parsley. Whisk until combined.
11. When cooking is complete, the chicken should be browned, crisp along its edges, and sizzling. Remove the pan from the oven and place the chicken on a cutting board. Cut each thigh into several pieces. Unwrap the pitas. Spread a tablespoon of sauce into a pita half. Add some chicken and add 2 roasted tomatoes. Serve.

Chicken Kebabs with Corn Salad
Prep time: 17 minutes | Cook time: 10 minutes | Serves 4

1 pound (454 g) boneless, skinless chicken breast, cut into 1½-inch chunks	3 tablespoons vegetable oil, divided
1 green bell pepper, deseeded and cut into 1-inch pieces	2 teaspoons kosher salt, divided
	2 cups corn, drained
1 red bell pepper, deseeded and cut into 1-inch pieces	¼ teaspoon granulated garlic
	1 teaspoon freshly squeezed lime juice
1 large onion, cut into large chunks	1 tablespoon mayonnaise
2 tablespoons fajita seasoning	3 tablespoons grated Parmesan cheese

Special Equipment:
12 wooden skewers, soaked in water for at least 30 minutes

1. Place the chicken, bell peppers, and onion in a large bowl. Add the fajita seasoning, 2 tablespoons of vegetable oil, and 1½ teaspoons of kosher salt. Toss to coat evenly.
2. Alternate the chicken and vegetables on the skewers, making about 12 skewers.
3. Place the corn in a medium bowl and add the remaining vegetable oil. Add the remaining kosher salt and the garlic, and toss to coat. Place the corn in an even layer on a baking pan and place the skewers on top.
4. Select Roast. Set temperature to 375ºF (190ºC) and set time to 10 minutes. Press Start to begin preheating.
5. Once preheated, place the pan into the oven.
6. After about 5 minutes, remove the pan from the oven and turn the skewers. Return the pan to the oven and continue cooking.
7. When cooking is complete, remove the pan from the oven. Place the skewers on a platter. Put the corn back to the bowl and combine with the lime juice, mayonnaise, and Parmesan cheese. Stir to mix well. Serve the skewers with the corn.

Turkey Scotch Eggs with Rosemary

Prep time: 15 minutes | Cook time: 12 minutes | Serves 4

1 egg
1 cup panko bread crumbs
½ teaspoon rosemary
1 pound (454 g) ground turkey
4 hard-boiled eggs, peeled
Salt and ground black pepper, to taste
Cooking spray

1. Spritz the perforated pan with cooking spray.
2. Whisk the egg with salt in a bowl. Combine the bread crumbs with rosemary in a shallow dish.
3. Stir the ground turkey with salt and ground black pepper in a separate large bowl, then divide the ground turkey into four portions.
4. Wrap each hard-boiled egg with a portion of ground turkey. Dredge in the whisked egg, then roll over the bread crumb mixture.
5. Place the wrapped eggs in the perforated pan and spritz with cooking spray.
6. Select Air Fry. Set temperature to 400°F (205°C) and set time to 12 minutes. Press Start to begin preheating.
7. Once preheated, place the pan into the oven. Flip the eggs halfway through.
8. When cooking is complete, the scotch eggs should be golden brown and crunchy.
9. Serve immediately.

Turkey-Stuffed Peppers with Cheddar

Prep time: 20 minutes | Cook time: 15 minutes | Serves 4

½ pound (227 g) lean ground turkey
4 medium bell peppers
1 (15-ounce / 425-g) can black beans, drained and rinsed
1 cup shredded Cheddar cheese
1 cup cooked long-grain brown rice
1 cup mild salsa
1¼ teaspoons chili powder
1 teaspoon salt
½ teaspoon ground cumin
½ teaspoon freshly ground black pepper
Chopped fresh cilantro, for garnish
Cooking spray

1. In a large skillet over medium-high heat, cook the turkey, breaking it up with a spoon, until browned, about 5 minutes. Drain off any excess fat.
2. Cut about ½ inch off the tops of the peppers and then cut in half lengthwise. Remove and discard the seeds and set the peppers aside.
3. In a large bowl, combine the browned turkey, black beans, Cheddar cheese, rice, salsa, chili powder, salt, cumin, and black pepper. Spoon the mixture into the bell peppers.
4. Lightly spray the perforated pan with cooking spray. Arrange the bell peppers in the pan.
5. Select Air Fry. Set temperature to 350°F (180°C) and set time to 15 minutes. Press Start to begin preheating.
6. Once preheated, place the pan into the oven.
7. When cooking is complete, the stuffed peppers should be lightly charred and wilted.
8. Allow to cool for a few minutes and garnish with cilantro before serving.

Chicken Gnocchi with Spinach

Prep time: 10 minutes | Cook time: 16 minutes | Serves 4

1 (1-pound / 454-g) package shelf-stable gnocchi
1¼ cups chicken stock
½ teaspoon kosher salt
1 pound (454 g) chicken breast, cut into 1-inch chunks
1 cup heavy whipping cream
2 tablespoons sun-dried tomato purée
1 garlic clove, minced
1 cup frozen spinach, thawed and drained
1 cup grated Parmesan cheese

1. Place the gnocchi in an even layer on a baking pan. Pour the chicken stock over the gnocchi.
2. Select Bake. Set temperature to 400°F (205°C) and set time to 10 minutes. Press Start to begin preheating.
3. Once preheated, place the pan into the oven.
4. While the gnocchi are cooking, sprinkle the salt over the chicken pieces. In a small bowl, mix the cream, tomato purée, and garlic.
5. When cooking is complete, blot off any remaining stock, or drain the gnocchi and return it to the pan. Top the gnocchi with the spinach and chicken. Pour the cream mixture over the ingredients in the pan.
6. Select Roast. Set temperature to 400°F (205°C) and set time to 6 minutes. Place the pan into the oven.
7. After 4 minutes, remove the pan from the oven and gently stir the ingredients. Return the pan to the oven and continue cooking.
8. When cooking is complete, the gnocchi should be tender and the chicken should be cooked through. Remove the pan from the oven. Stir in the Parmesan cheese until it's melted and serve.

Paprika Hens with Creole Seasoning

Prep time: 10 minutes | Cook time: 40 minutes | Serves 4

½ tablespoon Creole seasoning
½ tablespoon garlic powder
½ tablespoon onion powder
½ tablespoon freshly ground black pepper
½ tablespoon paprika
2 tablespoons olive oil
2 Cornish hens
Cooking spray

1. Spritz the perforated pan with cooking spray.
2. In a small bowl, mix the Creole seasoning, garlic powder, onion powder, pepper, and paprika.
3. Pat the Cornish hens dry and brush each hen all over with the olive oil. Rub each hen with the seasoning mixture. Place the Cornish hens in the perforated pan.
4. Select Air Fry. Set temperature to 375°F (190°C) and set time to 30 minutes. Press Start to begin preheating.
5. Once preheated, place the pan into the oven.
6. After 15 minutes, remove the pan from the oven. Flip the hens over and baste it with any drippings collected in the bottom drawer of the oven. Return the pan to the oven and continue cooking.
7. When cooking is complete, a thermometer inserted into the thickest part of the hens should reach at least 165°F (74°C).
8. Let the hens rest for 10 minutes before carving.

Chicken Drumsticks with Green Beans

Prep time: 5 minutes | Cook time: 25 minutes | Serves 4

8 skin-on chicken drumsticks
1 teaspoon kosher salt, divided
1 pound (454 g) green beans, trimmed
2 garlic cloves, minced
2 tablespoons vegetable oil
⅓ cup Thai sweet chili sauce

1. Salt the drumsticks on all sides with ½ teaspoon of kosher salt. Let sit for a few minutes, then blot dry with a paper towel. Place on a baking pan.
2. Select Roast. Set temperature to 375°F (190°C) and set time to 25 minutes. Press Start to begin preheating.
3. Once preheated, place the pan into the oven.
4. While the chicken cooks, place the green beans in a large bowl. Add the remaining kosher salt, the garlic, and oil. Toss to coat.
5. After 15 minutes, remove the pan from the oven. Brush the drumsticks with the sweet chili sauce. Place the green beans in the pan. Return the pan to the oven and continue cooking.
6. When cooking is complete, the green beans should be sizzling and browned in spots and the chicken cooked through, reading 165°F (74°C) on a meat thermometer. Serve the chicken with the green beans on the side.

Lemon Chicken with Oregano

Prep time: 5 minutes | Cook time: 35 minutes | Serves 6

3 (8-ounce / 227-g) boneless, skinless chicken breasts, halved, rinsed
1 cup dried bread crumbs
¼ cup olive oil
¼ cup chicken broth
Zest of 1 lemon
3 medium garlic cloves, minced
½ cup fresh lemon juice
½ cup water
¼ cup minced fresh oregano
1 medium lemon, cut into wedges
¼ cup minced fresh parsley, divided
Cooking spray

1. Pour the bread crumbs in a shadow dish, then roll the chicken breasts in the bread crumbs to coat.
2. Spritz a skillet with cooking spray, and brown the coated chicken breasts over medium heat about 3 minutes on each side. Transfer the browned chicken to a baking pan.
3. In a small bowl, combine the remaining ingredients, except the lemon and parsley. Pour the sauce over the chicken.
4. Select Bake. Set temperature to 325°F (163°C) and set time to 30 minutes. Press Start to begin preheating.
5. Once preheated, place the pan into the oven.
6. After 15 minutes, remove the pan from the oven. Flip the breasts. Return the pan to the oven and continue cooking.
7. When cooking is complete, the chicken should no longer pink.
8. Transfer to a serving platter, and spoon the sauce over the chicken. Garnish with the lemon and parsley.

Chapter 9 Pizza

Simple Pizza Dough

Prep time: 15 minutes | Cook time: 0 minutes | Makes 2 (12- to 14-inch) pizzas

1 package active dry yeast
1½ cups warm water (about 110o F)
2 tablespoons extra-virgin olive oil
4 cups all-purpose flour, plus more for dusting
1½ teaspoons salt

1. In a medium bowl, add the yeast to the warm water and let bloom for about 10 minutes. Add the olive oil.
2. In a food processor or standing mixer fitted with a paddle attachment, pulse to blend the flour and salt. With the machine running, add the yeast mixture in a slow, steady stream, mixing just until the dough comes together. Turn the dough out onto a well-floured board, and with lightly floured hands, knead the dough using the heels of your hands, pushing the dough and then folding it over. Shape it into a ball, then cut it into 2 or 4 equal pieces.
3. Place the balls of dough on a lightly floured baking sheet and cover with a clean dishtowel. Let them rise in a warm, draft-free spot until they are doubled in size, about 45 minutes.
4. Proceed with the desired recipe.

Escarole and Radicchio Pizza with Walnuts

Prep time: 10 minutes | Cook time: 25 minutes | Makes 1 pan pizza

1 head escarole, cored, center ribs removed, leaves chopped
½ head radicchio, sliced
1 small red onion, sliced thin
1 tablespoon extra-virgin olive oil
¼ teaspoon fine sea salt
Pinch red pepper flakes
No-Knead Pan Pizza Dough
6 slices provolone cheese
½ cup grated pecorino romano cheese
¼ cup walnuts, toasted

1. Toss the escarole, radicchio, and red onion slices in a bowl with the olive oil. Season with the salt and red pepper flakes. Cover the dough with the slices of provolone. Top the pizza with the escarole mixture, spreading it into a thin, even layer. Sprinkle with the pecorino.
2. Slide the baking sheet into the air fryer oven. Press the Power Button. Cook at 400ºF (205ºC) for 25 minutes, until the crust is golden.
3. Remove the pizza from the air fryer oven and use a spatula to transfer it to a cutting board. Let it sit for 5 minutes. Top the pizza with a drizzle of olive oil and the toasted walnuts. Slice and serve.

Chicken and Butternut Squash Pizza

Prep time: 10 minutes | Cook time: 40 minutes | Makes 2 (12- to 14-inch) pizzas

3 tablespoons extra-virgin olive oil, divided, plus more for brushing and drizzling
2 cups diced butternut squash
1 fresh rosemary sprig, stemmed and chopped
Salt
Freshly ground black pepper
3 cups stemmed, roughly chopped kale
1½ cups shredded cooked chicken
Simple Pizza Dough
1½ cups grated Gruyère cheese
3 tablespoons grated Asiago cheese
2 tablespoons toasted walnuts, roughly chopped

1. Brush two baking sheets with olive oil.
2. In a medium skillet over medium-high heat, heat 1 tablespoon of olive oil. When it shimmers, add the butternut squash and rosemary. Season with salt and pepper. Cook the squash until tender and browned, about 20 minutes, stirring frequently.
3. In a large bowl, use your hands to toss the kale and shredded chicken with the remaining 2 tablespoons of olive oil, and season with salt and pepper.
4. Roll out one of the dough balls to the desired size, and place it on the prepared baking sheet.
5. Sprinkle half of the Gruyère over the dough and top with half of the kale and chicken, followed by half of the caramelized butternut squash and Asiago.
6. Slide the baking sheet into the air fryer oven. Press the Power Button. Cook at 400ºF (205ºC) for 10 minutes, until the crust is golden and the cheese has melted.
7. Remove the pizza from the air fryer oven and transfer it to a cutting board. Let it rest for 5 minutes, then drizzle it with a little olive oil, season with salt and pepper, and sprinkle on half of the walnuts. Slice and serve.
8. Repeat with the remaining dough ball and toppings.

No-Knead Pan Pizza Dough

Prep time: 5 minutes | Cook time: 0 minutes | Makes 2 (13-by-18-inch) pizzas

3½ cups bread flour, plus more for dusting
¼ teaspoon active dry yeast
1 teaspoon kosher salt
¾ teaspoon sugar
1⅓ cups warm water
Extra-virgin olive oil, for drizzling

1. In the bowl of a standing mixer fitted with the paddle attachment, combine the flour, yeast, salt, and sugar. With the mixer on low, add the water and mix just until combined, about 3 minutes.
2. Cover the bowl with a towel and let the mixture rise at room temperature for 8 to 18 hours, or until it is doubled in volume.
3. Turn the dough onto a well-floured board and divide in half. Lightly drizzle two large (13-by-18-inch) sheet pans with olive oil, and spread to cover with a thin, even coating.
4. Stretch one piece of dough to the length of the pan, then place it in the center of one pan. Gently pull and stretch the dough to fit the width. If it resists, refrigerate the dough for 10 minutes. When the dough fits the pan, cover the pan with a damp kitchen towel and let it rest for 30 minutes at room temperature. Repeat with the second piece of dough and the second sheet pan.
5. Proceed with the desired recipe.

Chorizo Pizza with Piquillo Peppers

Prep time: 15 minutes | Cook time: 30 minutes | Makes 2 (12- to 14-inch) pizzas

2 tablespoons extra-virgin olive oil, plus extra for brushing
3 fresh chorizo sausage links
Simple Pizza Dough
1 cup Garlic Tomato Pizza Sauce
1 cup grated Mozzarella cheese
4 smoked piquillo peppers, drained and sliced lengthwise
4 slices prosciutto, torn into small pieces
¼ cup halved black olives
¼ cup chopped fresh flat-leaf parsley
½ cup grated manchego cheese
⅛ teaspoon freshly ground black pepper

1. Brush two baking sheets with olive oil.
2. In a medium skillet over medium heat, heat the oil until hot but not smoking. Add the sausages and cook for 7 to 10 minutes, turning occasionally, until they are browned on all sides. Remove the skillet from the heat and set it aside to cool. When the chorizo is cool enough to handle, cut it into thin slices.
3. Roll out one of the dough balls to the desired size, and place it on the prepared baking sheet.
4. Leaving a 1-inch border, spoon the sauce evenly onto the pizza. Top with half of the Mozzarella cheese, followed by half of the piquillo peppers. Scatter half of the chorizo and prosciutto over the pizza, followed by half of the olives and parsley.
5. Slide the baking sheet into the air fryer oven. Press the Power Button. Cook at 400ºF (205ºC) for 10 minutes, until the crust is golden and the cheese has melted.
6. Remove the pizza from the air fryer oven, transfer it to a cutting board, and let it rest for 5 minutes. Top with half of the manchego and pepper, slice, and serve.
7. Repeat with the remaining dough ball and toppings.

Pro Dough

Prep time: 40 minutes | Cook time: 0 minutes | Makes 2 (12- to 14-inch) pizzas

¼ teaspoon active dry yeast
1½ cups warm water
4 cups "00" flour or all-purpose flour, plus more
for dusting
2 teaspoons salt
Extra-virgin olive oil, for greasing

1. In a medium bowl, add the yeast to the warm water and let it stand for 10 minutes. While the yeast is blooming, rinse the bowl of a standing mixer with hot water and dry thoroughly. It should be warm to the touch. In the warm mixing bowl, combine the flour and salt. Add the yeast mixture and mix on low speed with a dough hook for 2 minutes. Raise the speed to medium-low and continue to mix for about 10 minutes, until the dough is cohesive and smooth and has pulled away from the sides of the bowl.
2. Knead again on medium-low speed for an additional 10 minutes, or until the dough is soft and warm to the touch.
3. Transfer the dough to a large, lightly oiled bowl, rolling the dough to coat it on all sides. Cover with plastic wrap and refrigerate overnight.
4. The next day, transfer the dough to a lightly floured board and punch it down. Cut it into 2 or 4 equal pieces and shape into smooth balls. Lightly flour the balls, place them on a baking tray, and cover with a damp kitchen towel. Let the dough rise again in the refrigerator for at least 4 hours or overnight.
5. Remove the dough from the refrigerator, place on a lightly floured baking sheet, and cover with a damp kitchen towel. Let it rise for 1½ to 2 hours, until it is doubled in size.
6. Proceed with the desired recipe.

Garlic Tomato Pizza Sauce

Prep time: 10 minutes | **Cook time:** 25 minutes | **Makes** 1 quart

2 tablespoons extra-virgin olive oil	Marzano tomatoes, undrained
1 small yellow onion, chopped (½ cup)	1 teaspoon fine sea salt
3 garlic cloves, smashed	⅛ teaspoon freshly ground black pepper
1 (28-ounce / 794-g) can whole peeled San	1 to 2 tablespoons sugar

1. In a large saucepan over medium-high heat, heat the olive oil until it shimmers. Reduce the heat to medium and add the chopped onion. Cook, stirring occasionally, for 5 minutes. Add the garlic and continue to cook for 2 to 3 minutes more, until the onion is translucent and the garlic is aromatic.
2. Add the tomatoes and their juice, and bring to a simmer, stirring occasionally with a wooden spoon to break them apart. Simmer for 10 to 15 minutes, until the sauce has thickened.
3. Using an immersion blender or food processor, pulse until the sauce is smooth. Season with the salt, pepper, and sugar.

Pepperoni Pizza with Mozzarella

Prep time: 5 minutes | **Cook time:** 20 minutes | **Makes** 2 (12-inch) pizzas

Extra-virgin olive oil, for brushing	1 cup grated Mozzarella cheese
Simple Pizza Dough	6 ounces (170 g) pepperoni, sliced thin
1 cup Garlic Tomato Pizza Sauce	¼ teaspoon salt

1. Brush two baking sheets with olive oil.
2. Roll out one of the dough balls and place it on the prepared baking sheet.
3. Leaving a 1-inch border, spread half of the sauce evenly over the dough. Top with half the Mozzarella and then half the pepperoni. Sprinkle with half the salt.
4. Slide the baking sheet into the air fryer oven. Press the Power Button. Cook at 400ºF (205ºC) for 10 minutes, until the crust is golden and the cheese has melted,.
5. Remove the pizza from the air fryer oven and transfer it to a cutting board. Let it rest for 5 minutes, then slice and serve.
6. Repeat with the remaining dough ball and toppings.

Mozzarella Meatball Pizza

Prep time: 10 minutes | **Cook time:** 25 minutes | **Makes** 2 (12- to 14-inch) pizzas

All-purpose flour, for coating	¼ teaspoon salt, plus more for sprinkling
½ pound (227 g) ground pork	⅛ teaspoon freshly ground black pepper, plus more for sprinkling
½ pound (227 g) ground veal	2½ cups Garlic Tomato Pizza Sauce , divided
1 cup ricotta cheese	2 tablespoons olive oil, plus more for brushing
¼ cup grated Parmesan cheese plus 2 tablespoons, divided	Simple Pizza Dough
2 tablespoons finely chopped fresh flat-leaf parsley	2 cups grated Mozzarella cheese

1. Lightly flour a baking sheet.
2. In a large mixing bowl, use your hands to combine the ground pork and veal, ricotta, ¼ cup of Parmesan, and the parsley. Season with the salt and pepper, and mix again.
3. Form each meatball by rolling 1 heaping tablespoon of the meat mixture between your palms. Place the meatballs on the prepared baking sheet, lightly rolling each one in flour.
4. In a medium saucepan over medium heat, heat 1½ cups of sauce; let it come to a gentle simmer.
5. Meanwhile, in a large skillet over medium-high heat, heat the olive oil. When it shimmers, add the meatballs, cooking on all sides for about 3 minutes, until browned. As they brown, transfer the meatballs to the simmering sauce to finish cooking, about 5 minutes total.
6. Brush two baking sheets with olive oil.
7. Roll out one of the dough balls to the desired size and place it on the prepared baking sheet.
8. Leaving a 1-inch border, spread ½ cup of the remaining sauce evenly onto the dough. Top the sauce with half of the Mozzarella and half of the meatballs. Spoon a little extra sauce from the pan onto the pizza, and finish with 1 tablespoon of the remaining Parmesan cheese and a sprinkling of salt and pepper.
9. Slide the baking sheet into the air fryer oven. Press the Power Button. Cook at 400ºF (205ºC) for 10 minutes, until the crust is golden and the cheese has melted.
10. Remove the pizza from the air fryer oven and transfer it to a cutting board. Let it rest for 5 minutes, then slice and serve.
11. Repeat with the remaining dough ball and toppings.

You will never win if you never begin.

Ham and Pineapple Pizza

Prep time: 10 minutes | Cook time: 25 minutes | Makes 2 (12- to 14-inch) pizzas

Extra-virgin olive oil, for brushing
4 slices center-cut bacon
Simple Pizza Dough or Pro Dough
1 cup Garlic Tomato Pizza Sauce
1 cup grated Mozzarella cheese
¼ pound (113 g) smoked ham, cut into ½-inch dice
1 cup diced fresh pineapple
2 tablespoons grated Parmesan cheese

1. Brush two baking sheets with olive oil.
2. In a medium skillet over medium heat, cook the bacon until crisp, 2 to 3 minutes per side. Transfer to a paper towel–lined plate to cool. Cut into bits.
3. Roll out one of the dough balls to the desired size and place it on the prepared baking sheet.
4. Leaving a 1-inch border, spread half of the sauce evenly onto the dough. Sprinkle on half of the Mozzarella, followed by half of the ham, chopped bacon, pineapple, and grated Parmesan cheese.
5. Slide the baking sheet into the air fryer oven. Press the Power Button. Cook at 400ºF (205ºC) for 10 minutes, until the crust is golden and the cheese has melted.
6. Remove the pizza from the air fryer oven and transfer it to a cutting board. Let it rest for 5 minutes, then slice and serve.
7. Repeat with the remaining dough ball and toppings.

Zucchini and Summer Squash Pizza

Prep time: 15 minutes | Cook time: 50 minutes | Makes 1 pan pizza

2 red bell peppers, cut into strips
1 zucchini, trimmed and cut into ¼-inch rounds
1 yellow summer squash, trimmed and cut into ¼-inch rounds
1 medium red onion, sliced
10 ounces (284 g) fingerling or red bliss potatoes, scrubbed and cut into ¼-inch slices
3 tablespoons extra-virgin olive oil
5 fresh thyme sprigs, stemmed
½ teaspoon fine sea salt
¼ teaspoon freshly ground black pepper
1 cup Garlic Tomato Pizza Sauce
No-Knead Pan Pizza Dough
1¼ cups grated fontina cheese
1½ cups arugula

1. On a foil-lined baking sheet, spread the bell peppers, zucchini, summer squash, onion, and potatoes. Drizzle with the olive oil, sprinkle on the thyme, and season with the salt and pepper. Toss well, then transfer the baking sheet to the air fryer oven and Press the Power Button. Cook at 400ºF (205ºC) for about 30 minutes, stirring twice during cooking. The potatoes should be fork tender.
2. Remove the vegetables from the air fryer oven and set aside. At this point, they can be used immediately or cooled to room temperature and refrigerated overnight in an airtight container.
3. Roll out the dough ball to the desired size, and place it on a greased baking pan.
4. Leaving a 1-inch border, spoon the sauce onto the dough, spreading it evenly. Scatter the fontina cheese over the dough, followed by the cooked vegetables.
5. Slide the baking sheet into the air fryer oven. Press the Power Button. Cook at 400ºF (205ºC) for 10 minutes, until the cheese has melted and the crust is golden. Remove it from the air fryer oven and let it cool for 5 minutes, then top it with the fresh arugula. Slice and serve.

Cheese Tomato Pizza with Basil

Prep time: 15 minutes | Cook time: 20 minutes | Makes 2 (12- to 14-inch) pizzas

Extra-virgin olive oil, for brushing
Simple Pizza Dough
1 cup Garlic Tomato Pizza Sauce
¾ cup grated Mozzarella
¾ cup grated fontina cheese
2 plum tomatoes, sliced thin
⅓ cup crumbled goat cheese
½ cup Parmesan cheese
8 fresh basil leaves, torn or roughly chopped
1 tablespoon chopped fresh parsley
¼ teaspoon salt
⅛ teaspoon freshly ground black pepper

1. Brush two baking sheets with olive oil.
2. Roll out one of the dough balls to the desired size, and place it on the prepared baking sheet.
3. Leaving a 1-inch border, spread half of the sauce evenly over the dough. Sprinkle on half of the Mozzarella and fontina. Arrange half of the tomato slices on top, and finish with half of the goat cheese and Parmesan.
4. Slide the baking sheet into the air fryer oven. Press the Power Button. Cook at 400ºF (205ºC) for 10 minutes, until the crust is golden and the cheese has melted.
5. Remove the pizza from the air fryer oven and transfer it to a cutting board. Let it rest for 5 minutes, then top with half of the basil and parsley and season with half of the salt and pepper. Slice and serve.
6. Repeat with the remaining dough ball and toppings.

Arugula and Prosciutto Pizza

Prep time: 10 minutes | Cook time: 20 minutes | Makes 2 (12- to 14-inch) pizzas

2 tablespoons extra-virgin olive oil, plus more for brushing
Simple Pizza Dough or Pro Dough
1 cup Garlic Tomato Pizza Sauce
8 slices prosciutto
6 ounces (170 g) fresh Mozzarella cheese, sliced or shredded
3 cups arugula
¼ teaspoon salt
⅛ teaspoon freshly ground black pepper
3 ounces (85 g) Parmesan cheese, shaved with a vegetable peeler

1. Brush two baking sheets with olive oil.
2. Roll out one of the dough balls to the desired size, and place it on the prepared baking sheet.
3. Leaving a 1-inch border, spread half of the sauce evenly onto the dough. Lay half of the prosciutto slices on top, then finish with half of the Mozzarella.
4. Slide the baking sheet into the air fryer oven. Press the Power Button. Cook at 400ºF (205ºC) for 10 minutes, until the crust is golden and the cheese has melted.
5. Remove the pizza from the air fryer oven and transfer it to a cutting board. Let it rest for 5 minutes, then top with half of the arugula, olive oil, salt, pepper, and Parmesan. Slice and serve.
6. Repeat with the remaining dough ball and toppings.

Prosciutto and Fig Pizza

Prep time: 10 minutes | Cook time: 20 minutes | Makes 2 (12- to 14-inch) pizzas

2 tablespoons extra-virgin olive oil, plus more for brushing
Simple Pizza Dough or Pro Dough
¼ cup fig jam
½ cup shredded Mozzarella cheese
½ cup crumbled goat cheese
8 slices prosciutto
8 figs, stemmed and quartered
4 fresh thyme sprigs, stemmed
¼ teaspoon fine sea salt
⅛ teaspoon freshly ground black pepper

1. Brush two baking sheets with olive oil.
2. Roll out one of the dough balls to the desired size, and place it on the prepared baking sheet.
3. Leaving a 1-inch border, spoon half of the fig jam evenly onto the dough. Top with half of the Mozzarella, goat cheese, and prosciutto. Arrange half of the figs on the pizza, sprinkle on half of the thyme, and season with half of the salt and pepper.
4. Slide the baking sheet into the air fryer oven. Press the Power Button. Cook at 400ºF (205ºC) for 10 minutes, until the crust is golden and the cheese has melted.
5. Remove the pizza from the air fryer oven and transfer it to a cutting board. Let it rest for 5 minutes, then drizzle with half of the olive oil. Slice and serve.
6. Repeat with the remaining dough ball and toppings.

Butternut Squash and Arugula Pizza

Prep time: 10 minutes | Cook time: 1 hour | Makes 2 (12- to 14-inch) pizzas

1 small (1-pound / 454-g) butternut squash, peeled, seeded, and cut into small dice
3 tablespoons extra-virgin olive oil, plus more for brushing
¼ teaspoon salt, plus more for finishing
⅛ teaspoon freshly ground black pepper, plus more for finishing
3 fresh thyme sprigs, stemmed
4 slices center-cut bacon
Simple Pizza Dough
½ cup grated fontina cheese
¼ cup crumbled blue cheese
4 cups arugula

1. Spread the butternut squash on a foil-lined baking pan and drizzle with the olive oil. Season with the salt, pepper, and thyme, and toss well. Press the Power Button. Cook at 400ºF (205ºC) for about 35 minutes, until the squash is fork tender and golden, stirring and rotating the pan halfway through. Remove from the air fryer oven and cool briefly.
2. Meanwhile, in a sauté pan over medium heat, brown the bacon until crisp, 2 to 3 minutes per side. Transfer to a paper towel–lined plate and, when cool, roughly chop.
3. Brush two baking sheets with olive oil.
4. Roll out one of the dough balls to the desired size, and place it on the prepared baking sheet.
5. Spread half of the fontina and blue cheeses evenly over the dough. Top with half of the cooked butternut squash and half of the bacon.
6. Slide the baking sheet into the air fryer oven. Press the Power Button. Cook at 400ºF (205ºC) for 10 minutes, until the crust is golden and the cheese is bubbly.
7. Remove the pizza from the air fryer oven and transfer it to a cutting board. Let it rest for 5 minutes, then top with half of the arugula. Slice and serve.
8. Repeat with the remaining dough ball and toppings.

Ricotta Margherita with Basil

Prep time: 10 minutes | Cook time: 20 minutes | Makes 2 (12- to 14-inch) pizzas

1 tablespoon extra-virgin olive oil, plus more for brushing
Simple Pizza Dough or Pro Dough
1 cup Garlic Tomato Pizza Sauce
1 teaspoon dried oregano
½ cup fresh ricotta cheese
6 ounces (170 g) fresh Mozzarella cheese, sliced thin
¼ teaspoon fine sea salt
⅛ teaspoon freshly ground black pepper
8 fresh basil leaves, torn

1. Brush two baking sheets with olive oil.
2. Roll out one of the dough balls to the desired size, and place it on the prepared baking sheet.
3. Leaving a 1-inch border, spoon half of the sauce onto the dough, spreading it evenly. Sprinkle on half of the oregano.
4. Spoon half of the ricotta cheese in small dollops all over the pizza, then arrange half of the Mozzarella slices on top. Season with half of the salt and pepper, and scatter on half of the torn basil leaves.
5. Slide the baking sheet into the air fryer oven. Press the Power Button. Cook at 400ºF (205ºC) for 10 minutes, until the crust is golden and the cheese has melted.
6. Remove the pizza from the air fryer oven and transfer it to a cutting board. Let it rest for 5 minutes. Slice and serve.
7. Repeat with the remaining dough ball and toppings.

Double-Cheese Clam Pizza

Prep time: 15 minutes | Cook time: 15 minutes | Serves 4

¼ cup extra-virgin olive oil, plus a little extra for forming the crust
2 large garlic cloves, chopped
¼ teaspoon red pepper flakes
1 pound (454 g) store-bought pizza dough
½ cup shredded Mozzarella cheese (4 ounces / 113 g)
2 (6.5-ounce / 184-g) cans chopped clams, drained
¼ cup grated Parmesan cheese
½ cup coarsely chopped fresh parsley
2 teaspoons chopped fresh oregano (optional)

1. In a small bowl, whisk together the olive oil with the garlic and red pepper flakes. Let it sit while you work on the dough.
2. Punch down the pizza dough to release as much air as possible. Place the dough in the baking pan and press it out toward the edges. The dough will likely spring back and shrink. Be patient and keep working at it, leaving it to relax for a few minutes from time to time. As it stretches, I find it helpful to coat my fingers with some olive oil and then poke the dough lightly with my fingertips to keep it from shrinking as much. Don't worry if you can't get it all the way to the edges of the pan.
3. Brush half of the garlic oil over the dough. Evenly distribute the Mozzarella cheese over the dough.
4. Slide the baking pan into the air fryer oven. Press the Power Button. Cook at 400ºF (205ºC) for 15 minutes.
5. After about 8 minutes, remove the pan from the air fryer oven. Scatter the clams over the pizza and sprinkle the Parmesan cheese on top. Return the pan to the air fryer oven and continue cooking for another 7 minutes.
6. When cooking is complete, the cheese on top is lightly browned and bubbling and the crust is deep golden brown. Remove the pan from the air fryer oven. Place the pizza on a wire rack to cool for a few minutes (a rack will keep the crust from getting soggy as it cools). Sprinkle the parsley and oregano (if using) over the pizza and drizzle with the remaining garlic oil. Slice and serve.

Pear Pizza with Basil

Prep time: 15 minutes | Cook time: 25 minutes | Makes 1 (12- to 14-inch) pizza

½ recipe Simple Pizza Dough
4 Bosc pears
½ lemon
Zest of 1 orange
1 tablespoon chopped fresh basil leaves
1 teaspoon chopped fresh rosemary leaves
2 tablespoons sugar
⅛ teaspoon freshly ground black pepper
2 tablespoons extra-virgin olive oil

1. On a baking sheet, roll out the pizza dough to form a 12- to 14-inch disc.
2. Peel, halve, and cut away the core of the pears. Slice each pear half into thin wedges. Squeeze lemon juice over the pears.
3. Arrange the pears, starting at the outer edge of the crust (leaving no border), in a spiral toward the center. Sprinkle the orange zest, basil, rosemary, sugar, and pepper over the pears. Drizzle with the olive oil.
4. Slide the baking sheet into the air fryer oven. Press the Power Button. Cook at 400ºF (205ºC) for 25 minutes, until the pizza appears golden and crisp.
5. Remove the pizza from the air fryer oven and let sit for 5 minutes. Slice and serve warm or at room temperature.

Zucchini Pizza with Pistachios
Prep time: 15 minutes | Cook time: 30 minutes | Makes 2 (12- to 14-inch) pizzas

2 tablespoons extra-virgin olive oil, plus more for brushing
1 medium green zucchini, halved lengthwise and cut thinly into half-moons
1 medium yellow summer squash, halved lengthwise and cut thinly into half-moons
¼ teaspoon salt
Simple Pizza Dough
1 medium red onion, sliced thin
1 teaspoon fresh thyme leaves
¼ teaspoon red pepper flakes
1 teaspoon freshly squeezed lemon juice
¼ cup shelled pistachios, toasted

1. Brush two baking sheets with olive oil.
2. In a large strainer set over a large bowl, toss the zucchini and summer squash well with the salt, and let it sit for about 5 minutes. Use a kitchen towel to press and squeeze the liquid from the squash mixture, removing as much moisture as possible.
3. Roll out one of the dough balls to the desired size, and place it on the prepared baking sheet.
4. In a large mixing bowl, toss together the drained squash mixture, onion, thyme, red pepper flakes, olive oil, and lemon juice. Arrange half of the vegetables on the dough.
5. Slide the baking sheet into the air fryer oven. Press the Power Button. Cook at 400ºF (205ºC) for 10 minutes, until the crust is golden and the cheese has melted.
6. Remove the pizza from the air fryer oven and transfer it to a cutting board. Let it rest for 5 minutes, then garnish with half of the toasted pistachios. Slice and serve.
7. Repeat with the remaining dough ball and toppings.

Spring Pea Pizza with Ramps
Prep time: 10 minutes | Cook time: 25 minutes | Makes 2 (12- to 14-inch) pizzas

2 tablespoons extra-virgin olive oil, plus more for brushing
½ cup shelled fresh English peas (or frozen and thawed peas)
10 ramps
¼ teaspoon fine sea salt
Simple Pizza Dough or Pro Dough
¾ cup ricotta cheese
2 tablespoons chopped fresh mint

1. Brush two baking sheets with olive oil.
2. If using fresh peas, bring a large pot of salted water to a boil. Fill a large bowl with ice water. Blanch the peas for 1 minute then, using a slotted spoon, transfer them to the ice water. Drain and set aside.
3. Spread the ramps on a baking sheet, drizzle with the olive oil, and sprinkle with the salt. Press the Power Button. Cook at 400ºF (205ºC) for 5 minutes to wilt. Transfer to a cutting board and cut into thirds.
4. Roll out one of the dough balls to the desired size, and place it on the prepared baking sheet.
5. Spoon half of the ricotta in dollops all over the dough. Scatter on half of the peas, ramps, and mint.
6. Slide the baking sheet into the air fryer oven. Press the Power Button. Cook at 400ºF (205ºC) for 10 minutes, until the crust is golden.
7. Remove the pizza from the air fryer oven, transfer it to a cutting board, and let it sit for 5 minutes. Slice and serve.
8. Repeat with the remaining dough ball and toppings.

Strawberry Pizza
Prep time: 10 minutes | Cook time: 10 minutes | Serves 4

2 tablespoons all-purpose flour, plus more as needed
½ store-bought pizza dough (about 8 ounces / 227 g)
1 tablespoon canola oil
1 cup sliced fresh strawberries
1 tablespoon sugar
½ cup chocolate-hazelnut spread

1. Dust a clean work surface with the flour. Place the dough on the floured surface, and roll it out to a 9-inch round of even thickness. Dust your rolling pin and work surface with additional flour, as needed, to ensure the dough does not stick.
2. Brush the surface of the rolled-out dough evenly with half the oil. Flip the dough over, and brush with the remaining oil. Poke the dough with a fork 5 or 6 times across its surface to prevent air pockets from forming during cooking.
3. Place the dough on a greased baking sheet. Slide the baking sheet into the air fryer oven. Press the Power Button. Cook at 400ºF (205ºC) for 10 minutes.
4. After 5 minutes, flip the dough. Continue cooking for the remaining 5 minutes.
5. Meanwhile, in a medium mixing bowl, combine the strawberries and sugar.
6. Transfer the pizza to a cutting board and let cool. Top with the chocolate-hazelnut spread and strawberries. Cut into pieces and serve.

Prosciutto and Bacon Pizza

Prep time: 15 minutes | Cook time: 35 minutes | Makes 2 (12- to 14-inch) pizzas

Extra-virgin olive oil, for brushing and drizzling
4 slices center-cut bacon
4 slices prosciutto, cut into strips
½ pound (227 g) sweet or hot Italian sausage, casings removed
Simple Pizza Dough or Pro Dough
1 cup Garlic Tomato Pizza Sauce
1½ cups grated Mozzarella cheese
¼ cup thinly sliced pepperoni or soppressata
2 tablespoons chopped fresh flat-leaf parsley
½ teaspoon fine sea salt
¼ teaspoon freshly ground black pepper

1. Brush two baking sheets with olive oil.
2. In a medium skillet over medium heat, cook the bacon until crisp, 2 to 3 minutes per side. Transfer to a paper towel–lined plate and set aside to cool.
3. Add the prosciutto to the skillet and cook over medium heat for about 3 minutes, stirring constantly, until crisp. Transfer the prosciutto to the plate with the bacon. Chop the bacon and prosciutto into bite-size pieces.
4. If there's not enough bacon fat in the skillet to prevent sticking, add a drizzle of olive oil and return the skillet to medium heat. Add the sausage to the skillet and cook for about 5 minutes, stirring constantly and breaking it up with a wooden spoon, until no pink color remains. Use a slotted spoon to transfer the sausage to another paper towel-lined plate.
5. Roll out one of the dough balls to the desired size, and place it on the prepared baking sheet.
6. Leaving a 1-inch border, spread half of the sauce evenly onto the dough. Sprinkle on half of the Mozzarella, then half of the sausage, bacon, and prosciutto. Finish with half of the pepperoni so that the meat forms a single, even layer.
7. Slide the baking sheet into the air fryer oven. Press the Power Button. Cook at 400ºF (205ºC) for 10 minutes, until the crust is golden and the pepperoni is sizzling.
8. Remove the pizza from the air fryer oven and transfer it to a cutting board. Let it rest for 5 minutes, then top with half of the chopped parsley, salt, and pepper. Slice and serve.
9. Repeat with the remaining dough ball and toppings.

Italian Sausage and Bell Pepper Pizza

Prep time: 10 minutes | Cook time: 40 minutes | Makes 2 (12-inch) pizzas

3 tablespoons extra-virgin olive oil, plus more for brushing
¾ pound (340 g) sweet Italian sausage (3 sausages)
1 medium yellow onion, sliced
1 red bell pepper, cut into ½-inch strips
1 green bell pepper, cut into ½-inch strips
2 garlic cloves, minced
¼ teaspoon red pepper flakes
Simple Pizza Dough or Pro Dough
Garlic Tomato Pizza Sauce
1⅓ cups grated Mozzarella cheese
1 teaspoon fine sea salt
⅛ teaspoon freshly ground black pepper
½ teaspoon dried oregano

1. Brush two baking sheets with olive oil.
2. In a large skillet over medium heat, heat the olive oil until it shimmers. Add the sausages and cook until they are browned on all sides and register 160ºF (70ºC) on an instant-read thermometer, about 8 minutes total. Transfer to a cutting board.
3. Add the onion to the hot pan (adding more oil if necessary), and sauté over medium heat until translucent, about 4 minutes. Add the red and green bell peppers. Sauté the mixture until the onions turn golden, about 4 minutes more, and then add the garlic and red pepper flakes. Cook, stirring, for about 2 additional minutes to infuse the mixture with the garlic. Using a slotted spoon, transfer the mixture to a small bowl.
4. Cut the sausages into ¼-inch-thick slices.
5. Roll out one of the dough balls to the desired size, and place it on the prepared baking sheet.
6. Leaving a 1-inch border, spread half of the sauce evenly over the dough. Sprinkle half of the grated Mozzarella over the pizza and then arrange half of the sausage slices on top. Spread half of the peppers and onions evenly over all.
7. Slide the baking sheet into the air fryer oven. Press the Power Button. Cook at 400ºF (205ºC) for 10 minutes, until the cheese has melted and the crust has browned.
8. Transfer the pizza to a cutting board and season with the salt, pepper, and dried oregano. Let it rest for 5 minutes, then slice and serve.
9. Repeat with the remaining dough ball and toppings.

Mushroom and Spinach Pizza

Prep time: 10 minutes | Cook time: 30 minutes | Makes 2 (12- to 14-inch) pizzas

4 tablespoons extra-virgin olive oil, divided, plus more for brushing
2 cups sliced cremini mushrooms
¼ teaspoon fine sea salt
⅛ teaspoon freshly ground black pepper
1 garlic clove
Pinch red pepper flakes, plus more for seasoning
4 cups baby spinach, stems removed
Simple Pizza Dough or Pro Dough
1 cup Garlic Tomato Pizza Sauce
1 cup grated Mozzarella cheese

1. Brush two baking sheets with olive oil.
2. In a large skillet over medium-high heat, heat 3 tablespoons of olive oil until it shimmers. Add the mushrooms and the salt, and let the mushrooms sit undisturbed for 2 minutes. Give the pan a shake and continue to cook for 3 minutes more, stirring occasionally, until the mushrooms have darkened in color but are still firm and vibrant. Season with the pepper and transfer to a medium bowl.
3. Reduce the heat to medium and add the remaining 1 tablespoon of olive oil, the garlic, and the red pepper flakes. Swirl the garlic and red pepper flakes to flavor the oil, then add the spinach. Use tongs to turn the spinach, watching it decrease in volume. Cook the spinach for 2 to 3 minutes, until it's wilted but still has structure. Remove the skillet from the heat.
4. Roll out one of the dough balls to the desired size and place it on the prepared baking sheet.
5. Leaving a 1-inch border, spoon half of the sauce evenly over the dough, then sprinkle on half of the Mozzarella. Scatter half of the spinach over the pizza, followed by half of the mushrooms. The toppings should intermingle. Season with freshly ground black pepper or more red pepper flakes as desired.
6. Slide the baking sheet into the air fryer oven. Press the Power Button. Cook at 400°F (205°C) for 10 minutes, until the crust is golden and the cheese has melted.
7. Remove the pizza from the air fryer oven and transfer it to a cutting board. Let it rest for 5 minutes, then slice and serve.
8. Repeat with the remaining dough ball and toppings.

Chapter 10 Casseroles, Frittatas, and Quiches

Cheddar Chicken Sausage Casserole
Prep time: 10 minutes | Cook time: 20 minutes | Serves 8

10 eggs
1 cup Cheddar cheese, shredded and divided
¾ cup heavy whipping cream
1 (12-ounce / 340-g) package cooked chicken sausage
1 cup broccoli, chopped
2 cloves garlic, minced
½ tablespoon salt
¼ tablespoon ground black pepper
Cooking spray

1. Spritz a baking pan with cooking spray.
2. Whisk the eggs with Cheddar and cream in a large bowl to mix well.
3. Combine the cooked sausage, broccoli, garlic, salt, and ground black pepper in a separate bowl. Stir to mix well.
4. Pour the sausage mixture into the baking pan, then spread the egg mixture over to cover.
5. Select Bake. Set temperature to 400ºF (205ºC) and set time to 20 minutes. Press Start to begin preheating.
6. Once preheated, place the pan into the oven.
7. When cooking is complete, the egg should be set and a toothpick inserted in the center should come out clean.
8. Serve immediately.

Spinach and Shrimp Frittata
Prep time: 6 minutes | Cook time: 14 minutes | Serves 4

4 whole eggs
1 teaspoon dried basil
½ cup shrimp, cooked and chopped
½ cup baby spinach
½ cup rice, cooked
½ cup Monterey Jack cheese, grated
Salt, to taste
Cooking spray

1. Spritz a baking pan with cooking spray.
2. Whisk the eggs with basil and salt in a large bowl until bubbly, then mix in the shrimp, spinach, rice, and cheese.
3. Pour the mixture into the baking pan.
4. Select Bake. Set temperature to 360ºF (182ºC) and set time to 14 minutes. Press Start to begin preheating.
5. Once preheated, place the pan into the oven. Stir the mixture halfway through.
6. When cooking is complete, the eggs should be set and the frittata should be golden brown.
7. Slice to serve.

Cauliflower and Okra Casserole
Prep time: 8 minutes | Cook time: 12 minutes | Serves 4

1 head cauliflower, cut into florets
1 cup okra, chopped
1 yellow bell pepper, chopped
2 eggs, beaten
½ cup chopped onion
1 tablespoon soy sauce
2 tablespoons olive oil
Salt and ground black pepper, to taste

1. Spritz a baking pan with cooking spray.
2. Put the cauliflower in a food processor and pulse to rice the cauliflower.
3. Pour the cauliflower rice in the baking pan and add the remaining ingredients. Stir to mix well.
4. Select Bake. Set temperature to 380ºF (193ºC) and set time to 12 minutes. Press Start to begin preheating.
5. Once preheated, place the pan into the oven.
6. When cooking is complete, the eggs should be set.
7. Remove the baking pan from the oven and serve immediately.

Corn Casserole with Bell Pepper
Prep time: 10 minutes | Cook time: 20 minutes | Serves 4

1 cup corn kernels
¼ cup bell pepper, finely chopped
½ cup low-fat milk
1 large egg, beaten
½ cup yellow cornmeal
½ cup all-purpose flour
½ teaspoon baking powder
2 tablespoons melted unsalted butter
1 tablespoon granulated sugar
Pinch of cayenne pepper
¼ teaspoon kosher salt
Cooking spray

1. Spritz a baking pan with cooking spray.
2. Combine all the ingredients in a large bowl. Stir to mix well. Pour the mixture into the baking pan.
3. Select Bake. Set temperature to 330ºF (166ºC) and set time to 20 minutes. Press Start to begin preheating.
4. Once preheated, place the pan into the oven.
5. When cooking is complete, the casserole should be lightly browned and set.
6. Remove the baking pan from the oven and serve immediately.

Asparagus Casserole with Grits

Prep time: 5 minutes | Cook time: 30 minutes | Serves 4

10 fresh asparagus spears, cut into 1-inch pieces
2 cups cooked grits, cooled to room temperature
2 teaspoons Worcestershire sauce
1 egg, beaten
½ teaspoon garlic powder
¼ teaspoon salt
2 slices provolone cheese, crushed
Cooking spray

1. Spritz a baking pan with cooking spray.
2. Set the asparagus in the perforated pan. Spritz the asparagus with cooking spray.
3. Select Air Fry. Set temperature to 390°F (199°C) and set time to 5 minutes. Press Start to begin preheating.
4. Once preheated, place the pan into the oven. Flip the asparagus halfway through.
5. When cooking is complete, the asparagus should be lightly browned and crispy.
6. Meanwhile, combine the grits, Worcestershire sauce, egg, garlic powder, and salt in a bowl. Stir to mix well.
7. Pour half of the grits mixture in the prepared baking pan, then spread with fried asparagus.
8. Spread the cheese over the asparagus and pour the remaining grits over.
9. Select Bake. Set time to 25 minutes. Place the pan into the oven.
10. When cooking is complete, the egg should be set.
11. Serve immediately.

Parmesan Green Bean Casserole

Prep time: 4 minutes | Cook time: 6 minutes | Serves 4

1 tablespoon melted butter
1 cup green beans
6 ounces (170 g) Cheddar cheese, shredded
7 ounces (198 g) Parmesan cheese, shredded
¼ cup heavy cream
Sea salt, to taste

1. Grease a baking pan with the melted butter.
2. Add the green beans, Cheddar, salt, and black pepper to the prepared baking pan. Stir to mix well, then spread the Parmesan and cream on top.
3. Select Bake. Set temperature to 400°F (205°C) and set time to 6 minutes. Press Start to begin preheating.
4. Once preheated, place the pan into the oven.
5. When cooking is complete, the beans should be tender and the cheese should be melted.
6. Serve immediately.

Kale and Egg Frittata with Feta

Prep time: 5 minutes | Cook time: 10 minutes | Serves 2

1 cup kale, chopped
1 teaspoon olive oil
4 large eggs, beaten
Kosher salt, to taste
2 tablespoons water
3 tablespoons crumbled feta
Cooking spray

1.
2. Spritz a baking pan with cooking spray.
3. Add the kale to the baking pan and drizzle with olive oil.
4. Select Broil. Set temperature to 400°F (205°C) and set time to 2 minutes. Press Start to begin preheating.
5. Once preheated, place the pan into the oven. Stir the kale halfway through.
6. When cooking is complete, the kale should be wilted.
7. Meanwhile, combine the eggs with salt and water in a large bowl. Stir to mix well.
8. Make the frittata: When broiling is complete, pour the eggs into the baking pan and spread with feta cheese.
9. Select Bake. Set temperature to 300°F (150°C) and set time to 8 minutes. Place the pan into the oven.
10. When cooking is complete, the eggs should be set and the cheese should be melted.
11. Remove the baking pan from the oven and serve the frittata immediately.

Swiss Chicken and Ham Casserole

Prep time: 15 minutes | Cook time: 15 minutes | Serves 4 to 6

2 cups diced cooked chicken
1 cup diced ham
¼ teaspoon ground nutmeg
½ cup half-and-half
½ teaspoon ground black pepper
6 slices Swiss cheese
Cooking spray

1. Spritz a baking pan with cooking spray.
2. Combine the chicken, ham, nutmeg, half-and-half, and ground black pepper in a large bowl. Stir to mix well.
3. Pour half of the mixture into the baking pan, then top the mixture with 3 slices of Swiss cheese, then pour in the remaining mixture and top with remaining cheese slices.
4. Select Bake. Set temperature to 350°F (180°C) and set time to 15 minutes. Press Start to begin preheating.
5. Once preheated, place the pan into the oven.
6. When cooking is complete, the egg should be set and the cheese should be melted.
7. Serve immediately.

Cheddar Pastrami Casserole
Prep time: 10 minutes | Cook time: 8 minutes | Serves 2

1 cup pastrami, sliced
1 bell pepper, chopped
¼ cup Greek yogurt
2 spring onions, chopped
½ cup Cheddar cheese, grated
4 eggs
¼ teaspoon ground black pepper
Sea salt, to taste
Cooking spray

1. Spritz a baking pan with cooking spray.
2. Whisk together all the ingredients in a large bowl. Stir to mix well. Pour the mixture into the baking pan.
3. Select Bake. Set temperature to 330ºF (166ºC) and set time to 8 minutes. Press Start to begin preheating.
4. Once preheated, place the pan into the oven.
5. When cooking is complete, the eggs should be set and the casserole edges should be lightly browned.
6. Remove the baking pan from the oven and allow to cool for 10 minutes before serving.

Beef and Bean Casserole
Prep time: 15 minutes | Cook time: 31 minutes | Serves 4

1 tablespoon olive oil
½ cup finely chopped bell pepper
½ cup chopped celery
1 onion, chopped
2 garlic cloves, minced
1 pound (454 g) ground beef
1 can diced tomatoes
½ teaspoon parsley
½ tablespoon chili powder
1 teaspoon chopped cilantro
1½ cups vegetable broth
1 (8-ounce / 227-g) can cannellini beans
Salt and ground black pepper, to taste

1. Heat the olive oil in a nonstick skillet over medium heat until shimmering.
2. Add the bell pepper, celery, onion, and garlic to the skillet and sauté for 5 minutes or until the onion is translucent.
3. Add the ground beef and sauté for an additional 6 minutes or until lightly browned.
4. Mix in the tomatoes, parsley, chili powder, cilantro and vegetable broth, then cook for 10 more minutes. Stir constantly.
5. Pour them in a baking pan, then mix in the beans and sprinkle with salt and ground black pepper.
6. Select Bake. Set temperature to 350ºF (180ºC) and set time to 10 minutes. Press Start to begin preheating.
7. Once preheated, place the pan into the oven.
8. When cooking is complete, the vegetables should be tender and the beef should be well browned.
9. Remove the baking pan from the oven and serve immediately.

Mushroom and Beef Casserole
Prep time: 10 minutes | Cook time: 25 minutes | Serves 4

1½ pounds (680 g) beef steak
1 ounce (28 g) dry onion soup mix
2 cups sliced mushrooms
1 (14.5-ounce / 411-g) can cream of mushroom soup
½ cup beef broth
¼ cup red wine
3 garlic cloves, minced
1 whole onion, chopped

1. Put the beef steak in a large bowl, then sprinkle with dry onion soup mix. Toss to coat well.
2. Combine the mushrooms with mushroom soup, beef broth, red wine, garlic, and onion in a large bowl. Stir to mix well.
3. Transfer the beef steak in a baking pan, then pour in the mushroom mixture.
4. Select Bake. Set temperature to 360ºF (182ºC) and set time to 25 minutes. Press Start to begin preheating.
5. Once preheated, place the pan into the oven.
6. When cooking is complete, the mushrooms should be soft and the beef should be well browned.
7. Remove the baking pan from the oven and serve immediately.

Spinach and Mushroom Frittata
Prep time: 7 minutes | Cook time: 8 minutes | Serves 2

1 cup chopped mushrooms
2 cups spinach, chopped
4 eggs, lightly beaten
3 ounces (85 g) feta cheese, crumbled
2 tablespoons heavy cream
A handful of fresh parsley, chopped
Salt and ground black pepper, to taste
Cooking spray

1. Spritz a baking pan with cooking spray.
2. Whisk together all the ingredients in a large bowl. Stir to mix well.
3. Pour the mixture in the prepared baking pan.
4. Select Bake. Set temperature to 350ºF (180ºC) and set time to 8 minutes. Press Start to begin preheating.
5. Once preheated, place the pan into the oven. Stir the mixture halfway through.
6. When cooking is complete, the eggs should be set.
7. Serve immediately.

Tomato and Olive Quiche

Prep time: 10 minutes | Cook time: 30 minutes | Serves 4

4 eggs
¼ cup chopped Kalamata olives
½ cup chopped tomatoes
¼ cup chopped onion
½ cup milk
1 cup crumbled feta cheese
½ tablespoon chopped oregano
½ tablespoon chopped basil
Salt and ground black pepper, to taste
Cooking spray

1. Spritz a baking pan with cooking spray.
2. Whisk the eggs with remaining ingredients in a large bowl. Stir to mix well.
3. Pour the mixture into the prepared baking pan.
4. Select Bake. Set temperature to 340°F (171°C) and set time to 30 minutes. Press Start to begin preheating.
5. Once preheated, place the pan into the oven.
6. When cooking is complete, the eggs should be set and a toothpick inserted in the center should come out clean.
7. Serve immediately.

Potato and Chorizo Frittata

Prep time: 8 minutes | Cook time: 12 minutes | Serves 4

2 tablespoons olive oil
1 chorizo, sliced
4 eggs
½ cup corn
1 large potato, boiled and cubed
1 tablespoon chopped parsley
½ cup feta cheese, crumbled
Salt and ground black pepper, to taste

1. Heat the olive oil in a nonstick skillet over medium heat until shimmering.
2. Add the chorizo and cook for 4 minutes or until golden brown.
3. Whisk the eggs in a bowl, then sprinkle with salt and ground black pepper.
4. Mix the remaining ingredients in the egg mixture, then pour the chorizo and its fat into a baking pan. Pour in the egg mixture.
5. Select Bake. Set temperature to 330°F (166°C) and set time to 8 minutes. Press Start to begin preheating.
6. Once preheated, place the pan into the oven. Stir the mixture halfway through.
7. When cooking is complete, the eggs should be set.
8. Serve immediately.

Mexican Beef and Chile Casserole

Prep time: 10 minutes | Cook time: 15 minutes | Serves 4

1 pound (454 g) 85% lean ground beef
1 tablespoon taco seasoning
1 (7-ounce / 198-g) can diced mild green chiles
½ cup milk
2 large eggs
1 cup shredded Mexican cheese blend
2 tablespoons all-purpose flour
½ teaspoon kosher salt
Cooking spray

1. Spritz a baking pan with cooking spray.
2. Toss the ground beef with taco seasoning in a large bowl to mix well. Pour the seasoned ground beef in the prepared baking pan.
3. Combing the remaining ingredients in a medium bowl. Whisk to mix well, then pour the mixture over the ground beef.
4. Select Bake. Set temperature to 350°F (180°C) and set time to 15 minutes. Press Start to begin preheating.
5. Once preheated, place the pan into the oven.
6. When cooking is complete, a toothpick inserted in the center should come out clean.
7. Remove the casserole from the oven and allow to cool for 5 minutes, then slice to serve.

Chickpea and Spinach Casserole

Prep time: 10 minutes | Cook time: 21 to 22 minutes | Serves 4

2 tablespoons olive oil
2 garlic cloves, minced
1 tablespoon ginger, minced
1 onion, chopped
1 chili pepper, minced
Salt and ground black pepper, to taste
1 pound (454 g) spinach
1 can coconut milk
½ cup dried tomatoes, chopped
1 (14-ounce / 397-g) can chickpeas, drained

1. Heat the olive oil in a saucepan over medium heat. Sauté the garlic and ginger in the olive oil for 1 minute, or until fragrant.
2. Add the onion, chili pepper, salt and pepper to the saucepan. Sauté for 3 minutes.
3. Mix in the spinach and sauté for 3 to 4 minutes or until the vegetables become soft. Remove from heat.
4. Pour the vegetable mixture into a baking pan. Stir in coconut milk, dried tomatoes and chickpeas until well blended.
5. Select Bake. Set temperature to 370°F (188°C) and set time to 15 minutes. Press Start to begin preheating.
6. Once preheated, place the pan into the oven.
7. When cooking is complete, transfer the casserole to a serving dish. Let cool for 5 minutes before serving.

Turkey Casserole with Almond Mayo
Prep time: 5 minutes | Cook time: 32 minutes | Serves 4

1 pound (454 g) turkey breasts
1 tablespoon olive oil
2 boiled eggs, chopped
2 tablespoons chopped pimentos
¼ cup slivered almonds, chopped
¼ cup mayonnaise
½ cup diced celery
2 tablespoons chopped green onion
¼ cup cream of chicken soup
¼ cup bread crumbs
Salt and ground black pepper, to taste

1. Put the turkey breasts in a large bowl. Sprinkle with salt and ground black pepper and drizzle with olive oil. Toss to coat well.
2. Transfer the turkey in the perforated pan.
3. Select Air Fry. Set temperature to 390ºF (199ºC) and set time to 12 minutes. Press Start to begin preheating.
4. Once preheated, place the pan into the oven. Flip the turkey halfway through.
5. When cooking is complete, the turkey should be well browned.
6. Remove the turkey breasts from the oven and cut into cubes, then combine the chicken cubes with eggs, pimentos, almonds, mayo, celery, green onions, and chicken soup in a large bowl. Stir to mix.
7. Pour the mixture into a baking pan, then spread with bread crumbs.
8. Select Bake. Set time to 20 minutes. Place the pan into the oven.
9. When cooking is complete, the eggs should be set.
10. Remove the baking pan from the oven and serve immediately.

Cauliflower Casserole with Pecan Butter
Prep time: 15 minutes | Cook time: 50 minutes | Serves 6

1 cup chicken broth
2 cups cauliflower florets
1 cup canned pumpkin purée
¼ cup heavy cream
1 teaspoon vanilla extract
2 large eggs, beaten
Topping:
½ cup blanched almond flour
1 cup chopped pecans
⅓ cup unsalted butter, melted, plus more for greasing the pan
¼ cup sugar
1 teaspoon fine sea salt
Chopped fresh parsley leaves, for garnish
⅓ cup unsalted butter, melted
½ cup sugar

1. Pour the chicken broth in a baking pan, then add the cauliflower.
2. Select Bake. Set temperature to 350ºF (180ºC) and set time to 20 minutes. Press Start to begin preheating.
3. Once preheated, place the pan into the oven.
4. When cooking is complete, the cauliflower should be soft.
5. Meanwhile, combine the ingredients for the topping in a large bowl. Stir to mix well.
6. Pat the cauliflower dry with paper towels, then place in a food processor and pulse with pumpkin purée, heavy cream, vanilla extract, eggs, butter, sugar, and salt until smooth.
7. Clean the baking pan and grease with more butter, then pour the purée mixture in the pan. Spread the topping over the mixture.
8. Place the baking pan back to the oven. Select Bake and set time to 30 minutes.
9. When baking is complete, the topping of the casserole should be lightly browned.
10. Remove the casserole from the oven and serve with fresh parsley on top.

Chicken and Broccoli Casserole
Prep time: 15 minutes | Cook time: 15 minutes | Serves 4

4 boneless and skinless chicken breasts, cut into cubes
2 carrots, sliced
1 yellow bell pepper, cut into strips
1 red bell pepper, cut into strips
15 ounces (425 g) broccoli florets
1 cup snow peas
1 scallion, sliced
Cooking spray
Sauce:
1 teaspoon Sriracha
3 tablespoons soy sauce
2 tablespoons oyster sauce
1 tablespoon rice wine vinegar
1 teaspoon cornstarch
1 tablespoon grated ginger
2 garlic cloves, minced
1 teaspoon sesame oil
1 tablespoon brown sugar

1. Spritz a baking pan with cooking spray.
2. Combine the chicken, carrot, and bell peppers in a large bowl. Stir to mix well.
3. Combine the ingredients for the sauce in a separate bowl. Stir to mix well.
4. Pour the chicken mixture into the baking pan, then pour the sauce over. Stir to coat well.
5. Select Bake. Set temperature to 370ºF (188ºC) and set time to 13 minutes. Press Start to begin preheating.
6. Once preheated, place the pan into the oven. Add the broccoli and snow peas to the pan halfway through.
7. When cooking is complete, the vegetables should be tender.
8. Remove the pan from the oven and sprinkle with sliced scallion before serving.

Tilapia and Rockfish Casserole

Prep time: 8 minutes | Cook time: 22 minutes | Serves 2

1 tablespoon olive oil
1 small yellow onion, chopped
2 garlic cloves, minced
4 ounces (113 g) tilapia pieces
4 ounces (113 g) rockfish pieces
½ teaspoon dried basil
Salt and ground white pepper, to taste
4 eggs, lightly beaten
1 tablespoon dry sherry
4 tablespoons cheese, shredded

1. Heat the olive oil in a nonstick skillet over medium-high heat until shimmering.
2. Add the onion and garlic and sauté for 2 minutes or until fragrant.
3. Add the tilapia, rockfish, basil, salt, and white pepper to the skillet. Sauté to combine well and transfer them on a baking pan.
4. Combine the eggs, sherry and cheese in a large bowl. Stir to mix well. Pour the mixture in the baking pan over the fish mixture.
5. Select Bake. Set temperature to 360°F (182°C) and set time to 20 minutes. Press Start to begin preheating.
6. Once preheated, place the pan into the oven.
7. When cooking is complete, the eggs should be set and the casserole edges should be lightly browned.
8. Serve immediately.

Cheddar and Egg Frittata with Parsley

Prep time: 10 minutes | Cook time: 20 minutes | Serves 4

½ cup shredded Cheddar cheese
½ cup half-and-half
4 large eggs
2 tablespoons chopped scallion greens
2 tablespoons chopped fresh parsley
½ teaspoon kosher salt
½ teaspoon ground black pepper
Cooking spray

1. Spritz a baking pan with cooking spray.
2. Whisk together all the ingredients in a large bowl, then pour the mixture into the prepared baking pan.
3. Select Bake. Set temperature to 300°F (150°C) and set time to 20 minutes. Press Start to begin preheating.
4. Once preheated, place the pan into the oven. Stir the mixture halfway through.
5. When cooking is complete, the eggs should be set.
6. Serve immediately.

Zucchini and Spinach Frittata

Prep time: 15 minutes | Cook time: 20 minutes | Serves 2

4 eggs
⅓ cup milk
2 teaspoons olive oil
1 large zucchini, sliced
2 asparagus, sliced thinly
⅓ cup sliced mushrooms
1 cup baby spinach
1 small red onion, sliced
⅓ cup crumbled feta cheese
⅓ cup grated Cheddar cheese
¼ cup chopped chives
Salt and ground black pepper, to taste

1. Line a baking pan with parchment paper.
2. Whisk together the eggs, milk, salt, and ground black pepper in a large bowl. Set aside.
3. Heat the olive oil in a nonstick skillet over medium heat until shimmering.
4. Add the zucchini, asparagus, mushrooms, spinach, and onion to the skillet and sauté for 5 minutes or until tender.
5. Pour the sautéed vegetables into the prepared baking pan, then spread the egg mixture over and scatter with cheeses.
6. Select Bake. Set temperature to 380°F (193°C) and set time to 15 minutes. Press Start to begin preheating.
7. Once preheated, place the pan into the oven. Stir the mixture halfway through.
8. When cooking is complete, the egg should be set and the edges should be lightly browned.
9. Remove the frittata from the oven and sprinkle with chives before serving.

Cheddar Broccoli Casserole

Prep time: 5 minutes | Cook time: 30 minutes | Serves 6

4 cups broccoli florets
¼ cup heavy whipping cream
½ cup sharp Cheddar cheese, shredded
¼ cup ranch dressing
Kosher salt and ground black pepper, to taste

1. Combine all the ingredients in a large bowl. Toss to coat well broccoli well.
2. Pour the mixture into a baking pan.
3. Select Bake. Set temperature to 375°F (190°C) and set time to 30 minutes. Press Start to begin preheating.
4. Once preheated, place the pan into the oven.
5. When cooking is complete, the broccoli should be tender.
6. Remove the baking pan from the oven and serve immediately.

You are your only limit. -Chapter 10 Casseroles, Frittatas, and Quiches

Peppery Sausage Casserole with Cheddar

Prep time: 15 minutes | Cook time: 25 minutes | Serves 6

1 pound (454 g) minced breakfast sausage
1 yellow pepper, diced
1 red pepper, diced
1 green pepper, diced
1 sweet onion, diced
2 cups Cheddar cheese, shredded
6 eggs
Salt and freshly ground black pepper, to taste
Fresh parsley, for garnish

1. Cook the sausage in a nonstick skillet over medium heat for 10 minutes or until well browned. Stir constantly.
2. When the cooking is finished, transfer the cooked sausage to a baking pan and add the peppers and onion. Scatter with Cheddar cheese.
3. Whisk the eggs with salt and ground black pepper in a large bowl, then pour the mixture into the baking pan.
4. Select Bake. Set temperature to 360ºF (182ºC) and set time to 15 minutes. Press Start to begin preheating.
5. Once preheated, place the pan into the oven.
6. When cooking is complete, the egg should be set and the edges of the casserole should be lightly browned.
7. Remove the baking pan from the oven and top with fresh parsley before serving.

Cheddar Chicken and Broccoli Divan

Prep time: 5 minutes | Cook time: 24 minutes | Serves 4

4 chicken breasts
Salt and ground black pepper, to taste
1 head broccoli, cut into florets
½ cup cream of mushroom soup
1 cup shredded Cheddar cheese
½ cup croutons
Cooking spray

1. Spritz the perforated pan with cooking spray.
2. Put the chicken breasts in the perforated pan and sprinkle with salt and ground black pepper.
3. Select Air Fry. Set temperature to 390ºF (199ºC) and set time to 14 minutes. Press Start to begin preheating.
4. Once preheated, place the pan into the oven. Flip the breasts halfway through the cooking time.
5. When cooking is complete, the breasts should be well browned and tender.
6. Remove the breasts from the oven and allow to cool for a few minutes on a plate, then cut the breasts into bite-size pieces.
7. Combine the chicken, broccoli, mushroom soup, and Cheddar cheese in a large bowl. Stir to mix well.
8. Spritz a baking pan with cooking spray. Pour the chicken mixture into the pan. Spread the croutons over the mixture.
9. Select Bake. Set time to 10 minutes. Place the pan into the oven.
10. When cooking is complete, the croutons should be lightly browned and the mixture should be set.
11. Remove the baking pan from the oven and serve immediately.

Cheese and Egg Quiche

Prep time: 20 minutes | Cook time: 1 hour | Serves 8

Crust:
1¼ cups blanched almond flour
1 large egg, beaten
1¼ cups grated Parmesan cheese
¼ teaspoon fine sea salt

Filling:
4 ounces (113 g) cream cheese
1 cup shredded Swiss cheese
⅓ cup minced leeks
4 large eggs, beaten
½ cup chicken broth
⅛ teaspoon cayenne pepper
¾ teaspoon fine sea salt
1 tablespoon unsalted butter, melted
Chopped green onions, for garnish
Cooking spray

1. Spritz a pie pan with cooking spray.
2. Combine the flour, egg, Parmesan, and salt in a large bowl. Stir to mix until a satiny and firm dough forms.
3. Arrange the dough between two grease parchment papers, then roll the dough into a 1/16-inch thick circle.
4. Make the crust: Transfer the dough into the prepared pie pan and press to coat the bottom.
5. Select Bake. Set temperature to 325ºF (163ºC) and set time to 12 minutes. Press Start to begin preheating.
6. Once preheated, place the pan into the oven.
7. When cooking is complete, the edges of the crust should be lightly browned.
8. Meanwhile, combine the ingredient for the filling, except for the green onions in a large bowl.
9. Pour the filling over the cooked crust and cover the edges of the crust with aluminum foil.
10. Select Bake. Set time to 15 minutes. Place the pan into the oven.
11. When cooking is complete, reduce the heat to 300ºF (150ºC) and set time to 30 minutes.
12. When cooking is complete, a toothpick inserted in the center should come out clean.
13. Remove the pie pan from the oven and allow to cool for 10 minutes before serving.

Cheddar Broccoli and Carrot Quiche

Prep time: 6 minutes | Cook time: 14 minutes | Serves 4

4 eggs
1 teaspoon dried thyme
1 cup whole milk
1 steamed carrots, diced
2 cups steamed broccoli florets
2 medium tomatoes, diced
¼ cup crumbled feta cheese
1 cup grated Cheddar cheese
1 teaspoon chopped parsley
Salt and ground black pepper, to taste
Cooking spray

1. Spritz a baking pan with cooking spray.
2. Whisk together the eggs, thyme, salt, and ground black pepper in a bowl and fold in the milk while mixing.
3. Put the carrots, broccoli, and tomatoes in the prepared baking pan, then spread with feta cheese and ½ cup Cheddar cheese. Pour the egg mixture over, then scatter with remaining Cheddar on top.
4. Select Bake. Set temperature to 350°F (180°C) and set time to 14 minutes. Press Start to begin preheating.
5. Once preheated, place the pan into the oven.
6. When cooking is complete, the egg should be set and the quiche should be puffed.
7. Remove the quiche from the oven and top with chopped parsley, then slice to serve.

Ricotta Pork Gratin with Mustard

Prep time: 15 minutes | Cook time: 21 minutes | Serves 4

2 tablespoons olive oil
2 pounds (907 g) pork tenderloin, cut into serving-size pieces
1 teaspoon dried marjoram
¼ teaspoon chili powder
1 teaspoon coarse sea salt
½ teaspoon freshly ground black pepper
1 cup Ricotta cheese
1½ cups chicken broth
1 tablespoon mustard
Cooking spray

1. Spritz a baking pan with cooking spray.
2. Heat the olive oil in a nonstick skillet over medium-high heat until shimmering.
3. Add the pork and sauté for 6 minutes or until lightly browned.
4. Transfer the pork to the prepared baking pan and sprinkle with marjoram, chili powder, salt, and ground black pepper.
5. Combine the remaining ingredients in a large bowl. Stir to mix well. Pour the mixture over the pork in the pan.
6. Select Bake. Set temperature to 350°F (180°C) and set time to 15 minutes. Press Start to begin preheating.
7. Once preheated, place the pan into the oven. Stir the mixture halfway through.
8. When cooking is complete, the mixture should be frothy and the cheese should be melted.
9. Serve immediately.

Asparagus Frittata with Goat Cheese

Prep time: 5 minutes | Cook time: 25 minutes | Serves 2 to 4

1 cup asparagus spears, cut into 1-inch pieces
1 teaspoon vegetable oil
1 tablespoon milk
6 eggs, beaten
2 ounces (57 g) goat cheese, crumbled
1 tablespoon minced chives, optional
Kosher salt and pepper, to taste

1. Add the asparagus spears to a small bowl and drizzle with the vegetable oil. Toss until well coated and transfer to the perforated pan.
2. Select Air Fry. Set temperature to 400°F (205°C) and set time to 5 minutes. Press Start to begin preheating.
3. Once preheated, place the pan into the oven. Flip the asparagus halfway through.
4. When cooking is complete, the asparagus should be tender and slightly wilted.
5. Remove the asparagus from the oven to a baking pan.
6. Stir together the milk and eggs in a medium bowl. Pour the mixture over the asparagus in the pan. Sprinkle with the goat cheese and the chives (if using) over the eggs. Season with salt and pepper.
7. Select Bake. Set temperature to 320°F (160°C) and set time to 20 minutes. Place the pan into the oven
8. When cooking is complete, the top should be golden and the eggs should be set.
9. Transfer to a serving dish. Slice and serve.

Chapter 11 Wraps and Sandwiches

Gochujang Beef and Onion Tacos

Prep time: 1 hour 15 minutes | Cook time: 12 minutes | Serves 6

2 tablespoons gochujang
1 tablespoon soy sauce
2 tablespoons sesame seeds
2 teaspoons minced fresh ginger
2 cloves garlic, minced
2 tablespoons toasted sesame oil
2 teaspoons sugar
½ teaspoon kosher salt
1½ pounds (680 g) thinly sliced beef chuck
1 medium red onion, sliced
6 corn tortillas, warmed
¼ cup chopped fresh cilantro
½ cup kimchi
½ cup chopped green onions

1. Combine the gochujang, soy sauce, sesame seeds, ginger, garlic, sesame oil, sugar, and salt in a large bowl. Stir to mix well.
2. Dunk the beef chunk in the large bowl. Press to submerge, then wrap the bowl in plastic and refrigerate to marinate for at least 1 hour.
3. Remove the beef chunk from the marinade and transfer to the perforated pan. Add the onion to the pan.
4. Select Air Fry. Set temperature to 400ºF (205ºC) and set time to 12 minutes. Press Start to begin preheating.
5. Once preheated, place the pan into the oven. Stir the mixture halfway through the cooking time.
6. When cooked, the beef will be well browned.
7. Unfold the tortillas on a clean work surface, then divide the fried beef and onion on the tortillas. Spread the cilantro, kimchi, and green onions on top.
8. Serve immediately.

Chicken and Cabbage Wraps

Prep time: 10 minutes | Cook time: 23 to 24 minutes | Serves 4

1 pound (454 g) ground chicken
2 teaspoons olive oil
2 garlic cloves, minced
1 teaspoon grated fresh ginger
2 cups white cabbage, shredded
1 onion, chopped
¼ cup soy sauce
8 egg roll wrappers
1 egg, beaten
Cooking spray

1. Spritz the perforated pan with cooking spray.
2. Heat olive oil in a saucepan over medium heat. Sauté the garlic and ginger in the olive oil for 1 minute, or until fragrant. Add the ground chicken to the saucepan. Sauté for 5 minutes, or until the chicken is cooked through. Add the cabbage, onion and soy sauce and sauté for 5 to 6 minutes, or until the vegetables become soft. Remove the saucepan from the heat.
3. Unfold the egg roll wrappers on a clean work surface. Divide the chicken mixture among the wrappers and brush the edges of the wrappers with the beaten egg. Tightly roll up the egg rolls, enclosing the filling. Arrange the rolls in the pan.
4. Select Air Fry. Set temperature to 370ºF (188ºC) and set time to 12 minutes. Press Start to begin preheating.
5. Once the oven has preheated, place the pan into the oven. Flip the rolls halfway through the cooking time.
6. When cooked, the rolls will be crispy and golden brown.
7. Transfer to a platter and let cool for 5 minutes before serving.

Curried Shrimp and Zucchini Potstickers

Prep time: 35 minutes | Cook time: 5 minutes | Serves 10

½ pound (227 g) peeled and deveined shrimp, finely chopped
1 medium zucchini, coarsely grated
1 tablespoon fish sauce
1 tablespoon green curry paste
2 scallions, thinly sliced
¼ cup basil, chopped
30 round dumpling wrappers
Cooking spray

1. Combine the chopped shrimp, zucchini, fish sauce, curry paste, scallions, and basil in a large bowl. Stir to mix well.
2. Unfold the dumpling wrappers on a clean work surface, dab a little water around the edges of each wrapper, then scoop up 1 teaspoon of filling in the middle of each wrapper.
3. Make the potstickers: Fold the wrappers in half and press the edges to seal.
4. Spritz the perforated pan with cooking spray.
5. Transfer the potstickers to the pan and spritz with cooking spray.
6. Select Air Fry. Set temperature to 350ºF (180ºC) and set time to 5 minutes. Press Start to begin preheating.
7. Once preheated, place the pan into the oven. Flip the potstickers halfway through the cooking time.
8. When cooking is complete, the potstickers should be crunchy and lightly browned.
9. Serve immediately.

Cod Fish Tacos with Mango Salsa

Prep time: 15 minutes | Cook time: 17 minutes | Makes 6 tacos

1 egg
5 ounces (142 g) Mexican beer
¾ cup all-purpose flour
¾ cup cornstarch
¼ teaspoon chili powder
½ teaspoon ground cumin
½ pound (227 g) cod, cut into large pieces
6 corn tortillas
Cooking spray

Salsa:
1 mango, peeled and diced
¼ red bell pepper, diced
½ small jalapeño, diced
¼ red onion, minced
Juice of half a lime
Pinch chopped fresh cilantro
¼ teaspoon salt
¼ teaspoon ground black pepper

1. Spritz the perforated pan with cooking spray.
2. Whisk the egg with beer in a bowl. Combine the flour, cornstarch, chili powder, and cumin in a separate bowl.
3. Dredge the cod in the egg mixture first, then in the flour mixture to coat well. Shake the excess off.
4. Arrange the cod in the perforated pan and spritz with cooking spray.
5. Select Air Fry. Set temperature to 380°F (193°C) and set time to 17 minutes. Press Start to begin preheating.
6. Once preheated, place the pan into the oven. Flip the cod halfway through the cooking time.
7. When cooked, the cod should be golden brown and crunchy.
8. Meanwhile, combine the ingredients for the salsa in a small bowl. Stir to mix well.
9. Unfold the tortillas on a clean work surface, then divide the fish on the tortillas and spread the salsa on top. Fold to serve.

Avocado and Tomato Wraps

Prep time: 10 minutes | Cook time: 5 minutes | Serves 5

10 egg roll wrappers
3 avocados, peeled and pitted
1 tomato, diced
Salt and ground black pepper, to taste
Cooking spray

1. Spritz the perforated pan with cooking spray.
2. Put the tomato and avocados in a food processor. Sprinkle with salt and ground black pepper. Pulse to mix and coarsely mash until smooth.
3. Unfold the wrappers on a clean work surface, then divide the mixture in the center of each wrapper. Roll the wrapper up and press to seal.
4. Transfer the rolls to the pan and spritz with cooking spray.
5. Select Air Fry. Set temperature to 350°F (180°C) and set time to 5 minutes. Press Start to begin preheating.
6. Once the oven has preheated, place the pan into the oven. Flip the rolls halfway through the cooking time.
7. When cooked, the rolls should be golden brown.
8. Serve immediately.

Sweet Potato and Spinach Burritos

Prep time: 15 minutes | Cook time: 30 minutes | Makes 6 burritos

2 sweet potatoes, peeled and cut into a small dice
1 tablespoon vegetable oil
Kosher salt and ground black pepper, to taste
6 large flour tortillas
1 (16-ounce / 454-g) can refried black beans, divided
1½ cups baby spinach, divided
6 eggs, scrambled
¾ cup grated Cheddar cheese, divided
¼ cup salsa
¼ cup sour cream
Cooking spray

1. Put the sweet potatoes in a large bowl, then drizzle with vegetable oil and sprinkle with salt and black pepper. Toss to coat well.
2. Place the potatoes in the perforated pan.
3. Select Air Fry. Set temperature to 400°F (205°C) and set time to 10 minutes. Press Start to begin preheating.
4. Once preheated, place the pan into the oven. Flip the potatoes halfway through the cooking time.
5. When done, the potatoes should be lightly browned. Remove the potatoes from the oven.
6. Unfold the tortillas on a clean work surface. Divide the black beans, spinach, air fried sweet potatoes, scrambled eggs, and cheese on top of the tortillas.
7. Fold the long side of the tortillas over the filling, then fold in the shorter side to wrap the filling to make the burritos.
8. Wrap the burritos in the aluminum foil and put in the pan.
9. Select Air Fry. Set temperature to 350°F (180°C) and set time to 20 minutes. Place the pan into the oven. Flip the burritos halfway through the cooking time.
10. Remove the burritos from the oven and spread with sour cream and salsa. Serve immediately.

Carrot and Mushroom Spring Rolls

Prep time: 10 minutes | Cook time: 18 minutes | Serves 4

4 spring roll wrappers
½ cup cooked vermicelli noodles
1 teaspoon sesame oil
1 tablespoon freshly minced ginger
1 tablespoon soy sauce
1 clove garlic, minced
½ red bell pepper, deseeded and chopped
½ cup chopped carrot
½ cup chopped mushrooms
¼ cup chopped scallions
Cooking spray

1. Spritz the perforated pan with cooking spray and set aside.
2. Heat the sesame oil in a saucepan on medium heat. Sauté the ginger and garlic in the sesame oil for 1 minute, or until fragrant. Add soy sauce, red bell pepper, carrot, mushrooms and scallions. Sauté for 5 minutes or until the vegetables become tender. Mix in vermicelli noodles. Turn off the heat and remove them from the saucepan. Allow to cool for 10 minutes.
3. Lay out one spring roll wrapper with a corner pointed toward you. Scoop the noodle mixture on spring roll wrapper and fold corner up over the mixture. Fold left and right corners toward the center and continue to roll to make firmly sealed rolls.
4. Arrange the spring rolls in the pan and spritz with cooking spray.
5. Select Air Fry. Set temperature to 340ºF (171ºC) and set time to 12 minutes. Press Start to begin preheating.
6. Once the oven has preheated, place the pan into the oven. Flip the spring rolls halfway through the cooking time.
7. When done, the spring rolls will be golden brown and crispy.
8. Serve warm.

Chicken Wraps with Ricotta Cheese

Prep time: 30 minutes | Cook time: 5 minutes | Serves 12

2 large-sized chicken breasts, cooked and shredded
2 spring onions, chopped
10 ounces (284 g) Ricotta cheese
1 tablespoon rice vinegar
1 tablespoon molasses
1 teaspoon grated fresh ginger
¼ cup soy sauce
⅓ teaspoon sea salt
¼ teaspoon ground black pepper, or more to taste
48 wonton wrappers
Cooking spray

1. Spritz the perforated pan with cooking spray.
2. Combine all the ingredients, except for the wrappers in a large bowl. Toss to mix well.
3. Unfold the wrappers on a clean work surface, then divide and spoon the mixture in the middle of the wrappers.
4. Dab a little water on the edges of the wrappers, then fold the edge close to you over the filling. Tuck the edge under the filling and roll up to seal.
5. Arrange the wraps in the pan.
6. Select Air Fry. Set temperature to 375ºF (190ºC) and set time to 5 minutes. Press Start to begin preheating.
7. Once preheated, place the pan into the oven. Flip the wraps halfway through the cooking time.
8. When cooking is complete, the wraps should be lightly browned.
9. Serve immediately.

Ricotta Spinach and Basil Pockets

Prep time: 20 minutes | Cook time: 10 minutes | Makes 8 pockets

2 large eggs, divided
1 tablespoon water
1 cup baby spinach, roughly chopped
¼ cup sun-dried tomatoes, finely chopped
1 cup ricotta cheese
1 cup basil, chopped
¼ teaspoon red pepper flakes
¼ teaspoon kosher salt
2 refrigerated rolled pie crusts
2 tablespoons sesame seeds

1. Spritz the perforated pan with cooking spray.
2. Whisk an egg with water in a small bowl.
3. Combine the spinach, tomatoes, the other egg, ricotta cheese, basil, red pepper flakes, and salt in a large bowl. Whisk to mix well.
4. Unfold the pie crusts on a clean work surface and slice each crust into 4 wedges. Scoop up 3 tablespoons of the spinach mixture on each crust and leave ½ inch space from edges.
5. Fold the crust wedges in half to wrap the filling and press the edges with a fork to seal.
6. Arrange the wraps in the pan and spritz with cooking spray. Sprinkle with sesame seeds.
7. Select Air Fry. Set temperature to 380ºF (193ºC) and set time to 10 minutes. Press Start to begin preheating.
8. Once the oven has preheated, place the pan into the oven. Flip the wraps halfway through the cooking time.
9. When cooked, the wraps will be crispy and golden.
10. Serve immediately.

Cream Cheese and Crab Wontons

Prep time: 10 minutes | Cook time: 10 minutes | Serves 6 to 8

24 wonton wrappers, thawed if frozen
Cooking spray
Filling:
5 ounces (142 g) lump crabmeat, drained and patted dry
4 ounces (113 g) cream cheese, at room temperature
2 scallions, sliced
1½ teaspoons toasted sesame oil
1 teaspoon Worcestershire sauce
Kosher salt and ground black pepper, to taste

1. Spritz the perforated pan with cooking spray.
2. In a medium-size bowl, place all the ingredients for the filling and stir until well mixed. Prepare a small bowl of water alongside.
3. On a clean work surface, lay the wonton wrappers. Scoop 1 teaspoon of the filling in the center of each wrapper. Wet the edges with a touch of water. Fold each wonton wrapper diagonally in half over the filling to form a triangle.
4. Arrange the wontons in the pan. Spritz the wontons with cooking spray.
5. Select Air Fry. Set temperature to 350ºF (180ºC) and set time to 10 minutes. Press Start to begin preheating.
6. Once preheated, place the pan into the oven. Flip the wontons halfway through the cooking time.
7. When cooking is complete, the wontons will be crispy and golden brown.
8. Serve immediately.

Cabbage and Prawn Wraps

Prep time: 20 minutes | Cook time: 18 minutes | Serves 4

2 tablespoons olive oil
1 carrot, cut into strips
1-inch piece fresh ginger, grated
1 tablespoon minced garlic
2 tablespoons soy sauce
¼ cup chicken broth
1 tablespoon sugar
1 cup shredded Napa cabbage
1 tablespoon sesame oil
8 cooked prawns, minced
8 egg roll wrappers
1 egg, beaten
Cooking spray

1. Spritz the perforated pan with cooking spray. Set aside.
2. Heat the olive oil in a nonstick skillet over medium heat until shimmering.
3. Add the carrot, ginger, and garlic and sauté for 2 minutes or until fragrant.
4. Pour in the soy sauce, broth, and sugar. Bring to a boil. Keep stirring.
5. Add the cabbage and simmer for 4 minutes or until the cabbage is tender.
6. Turn off the heat and mix in the sesame oil. Let sit for 15 minutes.
7. Use a strainer to remove the vegetables from the liquid, then combine with the minced prawns.
8. Unfold the egg roll wrappers on a clean work surface, then divide the prawn mixture in the center of wrappers.
9. Dab the edges of a wrapper with the beaten egg, then fold a corner over the filling and tuck the corner under the filling. Fold the left and right corner into the center. Roll the wrapper up and press to seal. Repeat with remaining wrappers.
10. Arrange the wrappers in the pan and spritz with cooking spray.
11. Select Air Fry. Set temperature to 370ºF (188ºC) and set time to 12 minutes. Press Start to begin preheating.
12. Once the oven has preheated, place the pan into the oven. Flip the wrappers halfway through the cooking time.
13. When cooking is complete, the wrappers should be golden.
14. Serve immediately.

Parmesan Eggplant Hoagies

Prep time: 15 minutes | Cook time: 12 minutes | Makes 3 hoagies

6 peeled eggplant slices (about ½ inch thick and 3 inches in diameter)
¼ cup jarred pizza sauce
6 tablespoons grated Parmesan cheese
3 Italian sub rolls, split open lengthwise, warmed
Cooking spray

1. Spritz the perforated pan with cooking spray.
2. Arrange the eggplant slices in the pan and spritz with cooking spray.
3. Select Air Fry. Set temperature to 350ºF (180ºC) and set time to 10 minutes. Press Start to begin preheating.
4. Once the oven has preheated, place the pan into the oven. Flip the slices halfway through the cooking time.
5. When cooked, the eggplant slices should be lightly wilted and tender.
6. Divide and spread the pizza sauce and cheese on top of the eggplant slice
7. Select Air Fry. Set temperature to 375ºF (190ºC) and set time to 2 minutes. place the pan into the oven. When cooked, the cheese will be melted.
8. Assemble each sub roll with two slices of eggplant and serve immediately.

It is never too late. -Chapter 11 Wraps and Sandwiches|121

Bacon and Egg Wraps with Salsa

Prep time: 15 minutes | Cook time: 10 minutes | Serves 3

3 corn tortillas
3 slices bacon, cut into strips
2 scrambled eggs
3 tablespoons salsa
1 cup grated Pepper Jack cheese
3 tablespoons cream cheese, divided
Cooking spray

1. Spritz the perforated pan with cooking spray.
2. Unfold the tortillas on a clean work surface, divide the bacon and eggs in the middle of the tortillas, then spread with salsa and scatter with cheeses. Fold the tortillas over.
3. Arrange the tortillas in the pan.
4. Select Air Fry. Set temperature to 390ºF (199ºC) and set time to 10 minutes. Press Start to begin preheating.
5. Once the oven has preheated, place the pan into the oven. Flip the tortillas halfway through the cooking time.
6. When cooking is complete, the cheeses will be melted and the tortillas will be lightly browned.
7. Serve immediately.

Cajun Beef and Bell Pepper Fajitas

Prep time: 15 minutes | Cook time: 10 minutes | Serves 4

1 pound (454 g) beef sirloin steak, cut into strips
2 shallots, sliced
1 orange bell pepper, sliced
1 red bell pepper, sliced
2 garlic cloves, minced
2 tablespoons Cajun seasoning
1 tablespoon paprika
Salt and ground black pepper, to taste
4 corn tortillas
½ cup shredded Cheddar cheese
Cooking spray

1. Spritz the perforated pan with cooking spray.
2. Combine all the ingredients, except for the tortillas and cheese, in a large bowl. Toss to coat well.
3. Pour the beef and vegetables in the pan and spritz with cooking spray.
4. Select Air Fry. Set temperature to 360ºF (182ºC) and set time to 10 minutes. Press Start to begin preheating.
5. Once preheated, place the pan into the oven. Stir the beef and vegetables halfway through the cooking time.
6. When cooking is complete, the meat will be browned and the vegetables will be soft and lightly wilted.
7. Unfold the tortillas on a clean work surface and spread the cooked beef and vegetables on top. Scatter with cheese and fold to serve.

Mozzarella Chicken Taquitos

Prep time: 15 minutes | Cook time: 12 minutes | Serves 4

1 cup cooked chicken, shredded
¼ cup Greek yogurt
¼ cup salsa
1 cup shredded Mozzarella cheese
Salt and ground black pepper, to taste
4 flour tortillas
Cooking spray

1. Spritz the perforated pan with cooking spray.
2. Combine all the ingredients, except for the tortillas, in a large bowl. Stir to mix well.
3. Make the taquitos: Unfold the tortillas on a clean work surface, then scoop up 2 tablespoons of the chicken mixture in the middle of each tortilla. Roll the tortillas up to wrap the filling.
4. Arrange the taquitos in the pan and spritz with cooking spray.
5. Select Air Fry. Set temperature to 380ºF (193ºC) and set time to 12 minutes. Press Start to begin preheating.
6. Once preheated, place the pan into the oven. Flip the taquitos halfway through the cooking time.
7. When cooked, the taquitos should be golden brown and the cheese should be melted.
8. Serve immediately.

Turkey and Pepper Hamburger

Prep time: 10 minutes | Cook time: 20 minutes | Serves 4

1 cup leftover turkey, cut into bite-sized chunks
1 leek, sliced
1 Serrano pepper, seeded and chopped
2 bell peppers, seeded and chopped
2 tablespoons Tabasco sauce
½ cup sour cream
1 heaping tablespoon fresh cilantro, chopped
1 teaspoon hot paprika
¾ teaspoon kosher salt
½ teaspoon ground black pepper
4 hamburger buns
Cooking spray

1. Spritz a baking pan with cooking spray.
2. Mix all the ingredients, except for the buns, in a large bowl. Toss to combine well.
3. Pour the mixture in the baking pan.
4. Select Bake. Set temperature to 385ºF (196ºC) and set time to 20 minutes. Press Start to begin preheating.
5. Once preheated, place the pan into the oven.
6. When done, the turkey will be well browned and the leek will be tender.
7. Assemble the hamburger buns with the turkey mixture and serve immediately.

Lamb Hamburgers with Feta Cheese

Prep time: 15 minutes | Cook time: 16 minutes | Makes 4 burgers

1½ pounds (680 g) ground lamb	1 teaspoon ground coriander
¼ cup crumbled feta	¼ teaspoon salt
1½ teaspoons tomato paste	¼ teaspoon cayenne pepper
1½ teaspoons minced garlic	4 kaiser rolls or hamburger buns, split open lengthwise, warmed
1 teaspoon ground dried ginger	Cooking spray

1. Spritz the perforated pan with cooking spray.
2. Combine all the ingredients, except for the buns, in a large bowl. Coarsely stir to mix well.
3. Shape the mixture into four balls, then pound the balls into four 5-inch diameter patties.
4. Arrange the patties in the pan and spritz with cooking spray.
5. Select Air Fry. Set temperature to 375ºF (190ºC) and set time to 16 minutes. Press Start to begin preheating.
6. Once preheated, place the pan into the oven. Flip the patties halfway through the cooking time.
7. When cooking is complete, the patties should be well browned.
8. Assemble the buns with patties to make the burgers and serve immediately.

Beef Steak and Bell Pepper Rolls

Prep time: 20 minutes | Cook time: 20 minutes | Serves 2

12 ounces (340 g) boneless rib-eye steak, sliced thinly	½ small onion, halved and thinly sliced
½ teaspoon Worcestershire sauce	1 tablespoon vegetable oil
½ teaspoon soy sauce	2 soft hoagie rolls, split three-fourths of the way through
Kosher salt and ground black pepper, to taste	1 tablespoon butter, softened
½ green bell pepper, stemmed, deseeded, and thinly sliced	2 slices provolone cheese, halved

1. Combine the steak, Worcestershire sauce, soy sauce, salt, and ground black pepper in a large bowl. Toss to coat well. Set aside.
2. Combine the bell pepper, onion, salt, ground black pepper, and vegetable oil in a separate bowl. Toss to coat the vegetables well.
3. Pour the steak and vegetables in the perforated pan.
4. Select Air Fry. Set temperature to 400ºF (205ºC) and set time to 15 minutes. Press Start to begin preheating.
5. Once preheated, place the pan into the oven.
6. When cooked, the steak will be browned and vegetables will be tender. Transfer them on a plate. Set aside.
7. Brush the hoagie rolls with butter and place in the pan.
8. Select Toast and set time to 3 minutes. Place the pan into the oven. When done, the rolls should be lightly browned.
9. Transfer the rolls to a clean work surface and divide the steak and vegetable mix in between the rolls. Spread with cheese. Place the stuffed rolls back in the pan.
10. Select Air Fry and set time to 2 minutes. Place the pan into the oven. When done, the cheese should be melted.
11. Serve immediately.

Chickpea and Mushroom Wraps

Prep time: 15 minutes | Cook time: 9 minutes | Serves 4

8 ounces (227 g) green beans	3 tablespoons lemon juice
2 portobello mushroom caps, sliced	¼ teaspoon ground black pepper
1 large red pepper, sliced	4 (6-inch) whole-grain wraps
2 tablespoons olive oil, divided	4 ounces (113 g) fresh herb or garlic goat cheese, crumbled
¼ teaspoon salt	1 lemon, cut into wedges
1 (15-ounce / 425-g) can chickpeas, drained	

1. Add the green beans, mushrooms, red pepper to a large bowl. Drizzle with 1 tablespoon olive oil and season with salt. Toss until well coated.
2. Transfer the vegetable mixture to a baking pan.
3. Select Air Fry. Set temperature to 400ºF (205ºC) and set time to 9 minutes. Press Start to begin preheating.
4. Once preheated, slide the pan into the oven. Stir the vegetable mixture three times during cooking.
5. When cooked, the vegetables should be tender.
6. Meanwhile, mash the chickpeas with lemon juice, pepper and the remaining 1 tablespoon oil until well blended
7. Unfold the wraps on a clean work surface. Spoon the chickpea mash on the wraps and spread all over.
8. Divide the cooked veggies among wraps. Sprinkle 1 ounce crumbled goat cheese on top of each wrap. Fold to wrap. Squeeze the lemon wedges on top and serve.

Potato Taquitos with Mexican Cheese

Prep time: 5 minutes | Cook time: 6 minutes | Makes 12 taquitos

2 cups mashed potatoes
½ cup shredded Mexican cheese
12 corn tortillas
Cooking spray

1. Line a baking pan with parchment paper.
2. In a bowl, combine the potatoes and cheese until well mixed. Microwave the tortillas on high heat for 30 seconds, or until softened. Add some water to another bowl and set alongside.
3. On a clean work surface, lay the tortillas. Scoop 3 tablespoons of the potato mixture in the center of each tortilla. Roll up tightly and secure with toothpicks if necessary.
4. Arrange the filled tortillas, seam side down, in the prepared baking pan. Spritz the tortillas with cooking spray.
5. Select Air Fry. Set temperature to 400ºF (205ºC) and set time to 6 minutes. Press Start to begin preheating.
6. Once preheated, place the pan into the oven. Flip the tortillas halfway through the cooking time.
7. When cooked, the tortillas should be crispy and golden brown.
8. Serve hot.

Curried Pork Sliders

Prep time: 10 minutes | Cook time: 14 minutes | Makes 6 sliders

1 pound (454 g) ground pork
1 tablespoon Thai curry paste
1½ tablespoons fish sauce
¼ cup thinly sliced scallions, white and green parts
2 tablespoons minced peeled fresh ginger
1 tablespoon light brown sugar
1 teaspoon ground black pepper
6 slider buns, split open lengthwise, warmed
Cooking spray

1. Spritz the perforated pan with cooking spray.
2. Combine all the ingredients, except for the buns in a large bowl. Stir to mix well.
3. Divide and shape the mixture into six balls, then bash the balls into six 3-inch-diameter patties.
4. Arrange the patties in the pan and spritz with cooking spray.
5. Select Air Fry. Set temperature to 375ºF (190ºC) and set time to 14 minutes. Press Start to begin preheating.
6. Once the oven has preheated, place the pan into the oven. Flip the patties halfway through the cooking time.
7. When cooked, the patties should be well browned.
8. Assemble the buns with patties to make the sliders and serve immediately.

Smoked Paprika Chicken Burgers

Prep time: 15 minutes | Cook time: 20 minutes | Serves 6 to 8

4 skinless and boneless chicken breasts
1 small head of cauliflower, sliced into florets
1 jalapeño pepper
3 tablespoons smoked paprika
1 tablespoon thyme
1 tablespoon oregano
1 tablespoon mustard powder
1 teaspoon cayenne pepper
1 egg
Salt and ground black pepper, to taste
2 tomatoes, sliced
2 lettuce leaves, chopped
6 to 8 brioche buns, sliced lengthwise
¾ cup taco sauce
Cooking spray

1. Spritz the perforated pan with cooking spray. Set aside.
2. In a blender, add the cauliflower florets, jalapeño pepper, paprika, thyme, oregano, mustard powder and cayenne pepper and blend until the mixture has a texture similar to bread crumbs.
3. Transfer ¾ of the cauliflower mixture to a medium bowl and set aside. Beat the egg in a different bowl and set aside.
4. Add the chicken breasts to the blender with remaining cauliflower mixture. Sprinkle with salt and pepper. Blend until finely chopped and well mixed.
5. Remove the mixture from the blender and form into 6 to 8 patties. One by one, dredge each patty in the reserved cauliflower mixture, then into the egg. Dip them in the cauliflower mixture again for additional coating.
6. Place the coated patties into the pan and spritz with cooking spray.
7. Select Air Fry. Set temperature to 350ºF (180ºC) and set time to 20 minutes. Press Start to begin preheating.
8. Once preheated, place the pan into the oven. Flip the patties halfway through the cooking time.
9. When cooking is complete, the patties should be golden and crispy.
10. Transfer the patties to a clean work surface and assemble with the buns, tomato slices, chopped lettuce leaves and taco sauce to make burgers. Serve and enjoy.

Pork Momos with Carrot

Prep time: 20 minutes | Cook time: 20 minutes | Serves 4

2 tablespoons olive oil
1 pound (454 g) ground pork
1 shredded carrot
1 onion, chopped
1 teaspoon soy sauce
16 wonton wrappers
Salt and ground black pepper, to taste
Cooking spray

1. Heat the olive oil in a nonstick skillet over medium heat until shimmering.
2. Add the ground pork, carrot, onion, soy sauce, salt, and ground black pepper and sauté for 10 minutes or until the pork is well browned and carrots are tender.
3. Unfold the wrappers on a clean work surface, then divide the cooked pork and vegetables on the wrappers. Fold the edges around the filling to form momos. Nip the top to seal the momos.
4. Arrange the momos in the perforated pan and spritz with cooking spray.
5. Select Air Fry. Set temperature to 320ºF (160ºC) and set time to 10 minutes. Press Start to begin preheating.
6. Once the oven has preheated, place the pan into the oven.
7. When cooking is complete, the wrappers will be lightly browned.
8. Serve immediately.

Cheddar Chicken Empanadas

Prep time: 25 minutes | Cook time: 12 minutes | Makes 12 empanadas

1 cup boneless, skinless rotisserie chicken breast meat, chopped finely
¼ cup salsa verde
⅔ cup shredded Cheddar cheese
1 teaspoon ground cumin
1 teaspoon ground black pepper
2 purchased refrigerated pie crusts, from a minimum 14.1-ounce (400 g) box
1 large egg
2 tablespoons water
Cooking spray

1. Spritz the perforated pan with cooking spray. Set aside.
2. Combine the chicken meat, salsa verde, Cheddar, cumin, and black pepper in a large bowl. Stir to mix well. Set aside.
3. Unfold the pie crusts on a clean work surface, then use a large cookie cutter to cut out 3½-inch circles as much as possible.
4. Roll the remaining crusts to a ball and flatten into a circle which has the same thickness of the original crust. Cut out more 3½-inch circles until you have 12 circles in total.
5. Make the empanadas: Divide the chicken mixture in the middle of each circle, about 1½ tablespoons each. Dab the edges of the circle with water. Fold the circle in half over the filling to shape like a half-moon and press to seal, or you can press with a fork.
6. Whisk the egg with water in a small bowl.
7. Arrange the empanadas in the pan and spritz with cooking spray. Brush with whisked egg.
8. Select Air Fry. Set temperature to 350ºF (180ºC) and set time to 12 minutes. Press Start to begin preheating.
9. Once preheated, place the pan into the oven. Flip the empanadas halfway through the cooking time.
10. When cooking is complete, the empanadas will be golden and crispy.
11. Serve immediately.

Beef Burgers with Seeds

Prep time: 15 minutes | Cook time: 10 minutes | Serves 4

1 teaspoon cumin seeds
1 teaspoon mustard seeds
1 teaspoon coriander seeds
1 teaspoon dried minced garlic
1 teaspoon dried red pepper flakes
1 teaspoon kosher salt
2 teaspoons ground black pepper
1 pound (454 g) 85% lean ground beef
2 tablespoons Worcestershire sauce
4 hamburger buns
Mayonnaise, for serving
Cooking spray

1. Spritz the perforated pan with cooking spray.
2. Put the seeds, garlic, red pepper flakes, salt, and ground black pepper in a food processor. Pulse to coarsely ground the mixture.
3. Put the ground beef in a large bowl. Pour in the seed mixture and drizzle with Worcestershire sauce. Stir to mix well.
4. Divide the mixture into four parts and shape each part into a ball, then bash each ball into a patty. Arrange the patties in the pan.
5. Select Air Fry. Set temperature to 350ºF (180ºC) and set time to 10 minutes. Press Start to begin preheating.
6. Once the oven has preheated, place the pan into the oven. Flip the patties with tongs halfway through the cooking time.
7. When cooked, the patties will be well browned.
8. Assemble the buns with the patties, then drizzle the mayo over the patties to make the burgers. Serve immediately.

Jalapeño Turkey Sliders with Chive Mayo

Prep time: 10 minutes | Cook time: 15 minutes | Serves 6

12 burger buns
Turkey Sliders:
¾ pound (340 g) turkey, minced
1 tablespoon oyster sauce
¼ cup pickled jalapeño, chopped
2 tablespoons chopped scallions
1 tablespoon chopped fresh cilantro
1 to 2 cloves garlic, minced
Sea salt and ground black pepper, to taste
Chive Mayo:
1 tablespoon chives
1 cup mayonnaise
Zest of 1 lime
1 teaspoon salt
Cooking spray

1. Spritz the perforated pan with cooking spray.
2. Combine the ingredients for the turkey sliders in a large bowl. Stir to mix well. Shape the mixture into 6 balls, then bash the balls into patties.
3. Arrange the patties in the pan and spritz with cooking spray.
4. Select Air Fry. Set temperature to 365°F (185°C) and set time to 15 minutes. Press Start to begin preheating.
5. Once preheated, place the pan into the oven. Flip the patties halfway through the cooking time.
6. Meanwhile, combine the ingredients for the chive mayo in a small bowl. Stir to mix well.
7. When cooked, the patties will be well browned.
8. Smear the patties with chive mayo, then assemble the patties between two buns to make the sliders. Serve immediately.

Beef Burgers with Korean Mayo

Prep time: 15 minutes | Cook time: 10 minutes | Serves 4

Burgers:
1 pound (454 g) 85% lean ground beef
2 tablespoons gochujang
¼ cup chopped scallions
2 teaspoons minced garlic
2 teaspoons minced fresh ginger
1 tablespoon soy sauce
1 tablespoon toasted sesame oil
2 teaspoons sugar
½ teaspoon kosher salt
4 hamburger buns
Cooking spray
Korean Mayo:
1 tablespoon gochujang
¼ cup mayonnaise
2 teaspoons sesame seeds
¼ cup chopped scallions
1 tablespoon toasted sesame oil

1. Combine the ingredients for the burgers, except for the buns, in a large bowl. Stir to mix well, then wrap the bowl in plastic and refrigerate to marinate for at least an hour.
2. Spritz the perforated pan with cooking spray.
3. Divide the meat mixture into four portions and form into four balls. Bash the balls into patties.
4. Arrange the patties in the pan and spritz with cooking spray.
5. Select Air Fry. Set temperature to 350°F (180°C) and set time to 10 minutes. Press Start to begin preheating.
6. Once the oven has preheated, place the pan into the oven. Flip the patties halfway through the cooking time.
7. Meanwhile, combine the ingredients for the Korean mayo in a small bowl. Stir to mix well.
8. When cooking is complete, the patties should be golden brown.
9. Remove the patties from the oven and assemble with the buns, then spread the Korean mayo over the patties to make the burgers. Serve immediately.

Pork and Cabbage Gyoza

Prep time: 10 minutes | Cook time: 10 minutes | Makes 48 gyozas

1 pound (454 g) ground pork
1 head Napa cabbage (about 1 pound / 454 g) sliced thinly and minced
½ cup minced scallions
1 teaspoon minced fresh chives
1 teaspoon soy sauce
1 teaspoon minced fresh ginger
1 tablespoon minced garlic
1 teaspoon granulated sugar
2 teaspoons kosher salt
48 to 50 wonton or dumpling wrappers
Cooking spray

1. Spritz the perforated pan with cooking spray. Set aside.
2. Make the filling: Combine all the ingredients, except for the wrappers in a large bowl. Stir to mix well.
3. Unfold a wrapper on a clean work surface, then dab the edges with a little water. Scoop up 2 teaspoons of the filling mixture in the center.
4. Make the gyoza: Fold the wrapper over to filling and press the edges to seal. Pleat the edges if desired. Repeat with remaining wrappers and fillings.
5. Arrange the gyozas in the pan and spritz with cooking spray.
6. Select Air Fry. Set temperature to 360°F (182°C) and set time to 10 minutes. Press Start to begin preheating.
7. Once preheated, place the pan into the oven. Flip the gyozas halfway through the cooking time.
8. When cooked, the gyozas will be golden brown.
9. Serve immediately.

Potato Samosas with Mint Chutney

Prep time: 30 minutes | Cook time: 22 minutes | Makes 16 samosas

Dough:
4 cups all-purpose flour, plus more for flouring the work surface
¼ cup plain yogurt
½ cup cold unsalted butter, cut into cubes
2 teaspoons kosher salt
1 cup ice water

Filling:
2 tablespoons vegetable oil
1 onion, diced
1½ teaspoons coriander
1½ teaspoons cumin
1 clove garlic, minced
1 teaspoon turmeric
1 teaspoon kosher salt
½ cup peas, thawed if frozen
2 cups mashed potatoes
2 tablespoons yogurt
Cooking spray

Chutney:
1 cup mint leaves, lightly packed
2 cups cilantro leaves, lightly packed
1 green chile pepper, deseeded and minced
½ cup minced onion
Juice of 1 lime
1 teaspoon granulated sugar
1 teaspoon kosher salt
2 tablespoons vegetable oil

1. Put the flour, yogurt, butter, and salt in a food processor. Pulse to combine until grainy. Pour in the water and pulse until a smooth and firm dough forms.
2. Transfer the dough on a clean and lightly floured working surface. Knead the dough and shape it into a ball. Cut in half and flatten the halves into 2 discs. Wrap them in plastic and let sit in refrigerator until ready to use.
3. Meanwhile, make the filling: Heat the vegetable oil in a saucepan over medium heat.
4. Add the onion and sauté for 5 minutes or until lightly browned.
5. Add the coriander, cumin, garlic, turmeric, and salt and sauté for 2 minutes or until fragrant.
6. Add the peas, potatoes, and yogurt and stir to combine well. Turn off the heat and allow to cool.
7. Meanwhile, combine the ingredients for the chutney in a food processor. Pulse to mix well until glossy. Pour the chutney in a bowl and refrigerate until ready to use.
8. Make the samosas: Remove the dough discs from the refrigerator and cut each disc into 8 parts. Shape each part into a ball, then roll the ball into a 6-inch circle. Cut the circle in half and roll each half into a cone.
9. Scoop up 2 tablespoons of the filling into the cone, press the edges of the cone to seal and form into a triangle. Repeat with remaining dough and filling.
10. Spritz the perforated pan with cooking spray. Arrange the samosas in the pan and spritz with cooking spray.
11. Select Air Fry. Set temperature to 360ºF (182ºC) and set time to 15 minutes. Press Start to begin preheating.
12. Once the oven has preheated, place the pan into the oven. Flip the samosas halfway through the cooking time.
13. When cooked, the samosas will be golden brown and crispy.
14. Serve the samosas with the chutney.

Crispy Cream Cheese Wontons

Prep time: 5 minutes | Cook time: 6 minutes | Serves 4

2 ounces (57 g) cream cheese, softened
1 tablespoon sugar
16 square wonton wrappers
Cooking spray

1. Spritz the perforated pan with cooking spray.
2. In a mixing bowl, stir together the cream cheese and sugar until well mixed. Prepare a small bowl of water alongside.
3. On a clean work surface, lay the wonton wrappers. Scoop ¼ teaspoon of cream cheese in the center of each wonton wrapper. Dab the water over the wrapper edges. Fold each wonton wrapper diagonally in half over the filling to form a triangle.
4. Arrange the wontons in the pan. Spritz the wontons with cooking spray.
5. Select Air Fry. Set temperature to 350ºF (180ºC) and set time to 6 minutes. Press Start to begin preheating.
6. Once preheated, place the pan into the oven. Flip the wontons halfway through the cooking time.
7. When cooking is complete, the wontons will be golden brown and crispy.
8. Divide the wontons among four plates. Let rest for 5 minutes before serving.

Chapter 12 Holiday Specials

Vanilla Banana Cake
Prep time: 25 minutes | Cook time: 20 minutes | Serves 8

1 cup plus 1 tablespoon all-purpose flour
¼ teaspoon baking soda
¾ teaspoon baking powder
¼ teaspoon salt
9½ tablespoons granulated white sugar
5 tablespoons butter, at room temperature
2½ small ripe bananas, peeled
2 large eggs
5 tablespoons buttermilk
1 teaspoon vanilla extract
Cooking spray

1. Spritz a baking pan with cooking spray.
2. Combine the flour, baking soda, baking powder, and salt in a large bowl. Stir to mix well.
3. Beat the sugar and butter in a separate bowl with a hand mixer on medium speed for 3 minutes.
4. Beat in the bananas, eggs, buttermilk, and vanilla extract into the sugar and butter mix with a hand mixer.
5. Pour in the flour mixture and whip with hand mixer until sanity and smooth.
6. Scrape the batter into the pan and level the batter with a spatula.
7. Select Bake. Set temperature to 325ºF (163ºC) and set time to 20 minutes. Press Start to begin preheating.
8. Once the oven has preheated, place the pan into the oven.
9. After 15 minutes, remove the pan from the oven. Check the doneness. Return the pan to the oven and continue cooking.
10. When done, a toothpick inserted in the center should come out clean.
11. Invert the cake on a cooling rack and allow to cool for 15 minutes before slicing to serve.

Buttermilk Chocolate Cake
Prep time: 20 minutes | Cook time: 20 minutes | Serves 8

1 cup all-purpose flour
⅔ cup granulated white sugar
¼ cup unsweetened cocoa powder
¾ teaspoon baking soda
¼ teaspoon salt
⅔ cup buttermilk
2 tablespoons plus 2 teaspoons vegetable oil
1 teaspoon vanilla extract
Cooking spray

1. Spritz a baking pan with cooking spray.
2. Combine the flour, cocoa powder, baking soda, sugar, and salt in a large bowl. Stir to mix well.
3. Mix in the buttermilk, vanilla, and vegetable oil. Keep stirring until it forms a grainy and thick dough.
4. Scrape the chocolate batter from the bowl and transfer to the pan, level the batter in an even layer with a spatula.
5. Select Bake. Set temperature to 325ºF (163ºC) and set time to 20 minutes. Press Start to begin preheating.
6. Once preheated, place the pan into the oven.
7. After 15 minutes, remove the pan from the oven. Check the doneness. Return the pan to the oven and continue cooking.
8. When done, a toothpick inserted in the center should come out clean.
9. Invert the cake on a cooling rack and allow to cool for 15 minutes before slicing to serve.

Mozzarella Rice Arancini
Prep time: 5 minutes | Cook time: 30 minutes | Makes 10 arancini

⅔ cup raw white Arborio rice
2 teaspoons butter
½ teaspoon salt
1⅓ cups water
2 large eggs, well beaten
1¼ cups seasoned Italian-style dried bread crumbs
10 ¾-inch semi-firm Mozzarella cubes
Cooking spray

1. Pour the rice, butter, salt, and water in a pot. Stir to mix well and bring a boil over medium-high heat. Keep stirring.
2. Reduce the heat to low and cover the pot. Simmer for 20 minutes or until the rice is tender.
3. Turn off the heat and let sit, covered, for 10 minutes, then open the lid and fluffy the rice with a fork. Allow to cool for 10 more minutes.
4. Pour the beaten eggs in a bowl, then pour the bread crumbs in a separate bowl.
5. Scoop 2 tablespoons of the cooked rice up and form it into a ball, then press the Mozzarella into the ball and wrap.
6. Dredge the ball in the eggs first, then shake the excess off the dunk the ball in the bread crumbs. Roll to coat evenly. Repeat to make 10 balls in total with remaining rice.
7. Transfer the balls in the perforated pan and spritz with cooking spray.
8. Select Air Fry. Set temperature to 375ºF (190ºC) and set time to 10 minutes. Press Start to begin preheating.
9. Once preheated, place the pan into the oven.
10. When cooking is complete, the balls should be lightly browned and crispy.
11. Remove the balls from the oven and allow to cool before serving.

Chocolate-Glazed Donut Holes

Prep time: 1 hour 50 minutes | Cook time: 4 minutes | Makes 24 donut holes

Dough:
1½ cups bread flour
2 egg yolks
1 teaspoon active dry yeast
½ cup warm milk
½ teaspoon pure vanilla extract
2 tablespoons butter, melted
1 tablespoon sugar
¼ teaspoon salt
Cooking spray

Custard Filling:
1 (3.4-ounce / 96-g) box French vanilla instant pudding mix
¼ cup heavy cream
¾ cup whole milk

Chocolate Glaze:
⅓ cup heavy cream
1 cup chocolate chips

Special Equipment:
A pastry bag with a long tip

1. Combine the ingredients for the dough in a food processor, then pulse until a satiny dough ball forms.
2. Transfer the dough on a lightly floured work surface, then knead for 2 minutes by hand and shape the dough back to a ball.
3. Spritz a large bowl with cooking spray, then transfer the dough ball into the bowl. Wrap the bowl in plastic and let it rise for 1½ hours or until it doubled in size.
4. Transfer the risen dough on a floured work surface, then shape it into a 24-inch long log. Cut the log into 24 parts and shape each part into a ball.
5. Transfer the balls on two baking sheets and let sit to rise for 30 more minutes.
6. Spritz the balls with cooking spray.
7. Select Bake. Set temperature to 400ºF (205ºC) and set time to 4 minutes. Press Start to begin preheating.
8. Once preheated, place the baking sheets into the oven. Flip the balls halfway through the cooking time.
9. When cooked, the balls should be golden brown.
10. Meanwhile, combine the ingredients for the filling in a large bowl and whisk for 2 minutes with a hand mixer until well combined.
11. Pour the heavy cream in a saucepan, then bring to a boil. Put the chocolate chips in a small bowl and pour in the boiled heavy cream immediately. Mix until the chocolate chips are melted and the mixture is smooth.
12. Transfer the baked donut holes to a large plate, then pierce a hole into each donut hole and lightly hollow them.
13. Pour the filling in a pastry bag with a long tip and gently squeeze the filling into the donut holes. Then top the donut holes with chocolate glaze.
14. Allow to sit for 10 minutes, then serve.

Maple Pecan Tart

Prep time: 2 hours 25 minutes | Cook time: 26 minutes | Serves 8

Tart Crust:
¼ cup firmly packed brown sugar
⅓ cup butter, softened
1 cup all-purpose flour
¼ teaspoon kosher salt

Filling:
¼ cup whole milk
4 tablespoons butter, diced
½ cup packed brown sugar
¼ cup pure maple syrup
1½ cups finely chopped pecans
¼ teaspoon pure vanilla extract
¼ teaspoon sea salt

1. Line a baking pan with aluminum foil, then spritz the pan with cooking spray.
2. Stir the brown sugar and butter in a bowl with a hand mixer until puffed, then add the flour and salt and stir until crumbled.
3. Pour the mixture in the prepared baking pan and tilt the pan to coat the bottom evenly.
4. Select Bake. Set temperature to 350ºF (180ºC) and set time to 13 minutes. Press Start to begin preheating.
5. Once the oven has preheated, place the pan into the oven.
6. When done, the crust will be golden brown.
7. Meanwhile, pour the milk, butter, sugar, and maple syrup in a saucepan. Stir to mix well. Bring to a simmer, then cook for 1 more minute. Stir constantly.
8. Turn off the heat and mix the pecans and vanilla into the filling mixture.
9. Pour the filling mixture over the golden crust and spread with a spatula to coat the crust evenly.
10. Select Bake and set time to 12 minutes. Place the pan into the oven. When cooked, the filling mixture should be set and frothy.
11. Remove the baking pan from the oven and sprinkle with salt. Allow to sit for 10 minutes or until cooled.
12. Transfer the pan to the refrigerator to chill for at least 2 hours, then remove the aluminum foil and slice to serve.

Leap, and the net will appear. -Chapter 12 Holiday Specials

Pork Egg Rolls with Vinegar Dipping

Prep time: 40 minutes | Cook time: 33 minutes | Makes 25 egg rolls

Egg Rolls:
1 tablespoon mirin
3 tablespoons soy sauce, divided
1 pound (454 g) ground pork
3 tablespoons vegetable oil, plus more for brushing
5 ounces (142 g) shiitake mushrooms, minced
4 cups shredded Napa cabbage
¼ cup sliced scallions
1 teaspoon grated fresh ginger
1 clove garlic, minced
¼ teaspoon cornstarch
1 (1-pound / 454-g) package frozen egg roll wrappers, thawed

Dipping Sauce:
1 scallion, white and light green parts only, sliced
¼ cup rice vinegar
¼ cup soy sauce
Pinch sesame seeds
Pinch red pepper flakes
1 teaspoon granulated sugar

1. Line the perforated pan with parchment paper. Set aside.
2. Combine the mirin and 1 tablespoon of soy sauce in a large bowl. Stir to mix well.
3. Dunk the ground pork in the mixture and stir to mix well. Wrap the bowl in plastic and marinate in the refrigerator for at least 10 minutes.
4. Heat the vegetable oil in a nonstick skillet over medium-high heat until shimmering. Add the mushrooms, cabbage, and scallions and sauté for 5 minutes or until tender.
5. Add the marinated meat, ginger, garlic, and remaining 2 tablespoons of soy sauce. Sauté for 3 minutes or until the pork is lightly browned. Turn off the heat and allow to cool until ready to use.
6. Put the cornstarch in a small bowl and pour in enough water to dissolve the cornstarch. Put the bowl alongside a clean work surface.
7. Put the egg roll wrappers in the perforated pan.
8. Select Air Fry. Set temperature to 400ºF (205ºC) and set time to 15 minutes. Press Start to begin preheating.
9. Once preheated, place the pan into the oven. Flip the wrappers halfway through the cooking time.
10. When cooked, the wrappers will be golden brown. Remove the egg roll wrappers from the oven and allow to cool for 10 minutes or until you can handle them with your hands.
11. Lay out one egg roll wrapper on the work surface with a corner pointed toward you. Place 2 tablespoons of the pork mixture on the egg roll wrapper and fold corner up over the mixture. Fold left and right corners toward the center and continue to roll. Brush a bit of the dissolved cornstarch on the last corner to help seal the egg wrapper. Repeat with remaining wrappers to make 25 egg rolls in total.
12. Arrange the rolls in the pan and brush the rolls with more vegetable oil.
13. Select Air Fry and set time to 10 minutes. Place the pan into the oven When done, the rolls should be well browned and crispy.
14. Meanwhile, combine the ingredients for the dipping sauce in a small bowl. Stir to mix well.
15. Serve the rolls with the dipping sauce immediately.

Dill Pickles with Buttermilk Dressing

Prep time: 45 minutes | Cook time: 8 minutes | Serves 6 to 8

Buttermilk Dressing:
¼ cup buttermilk
¼ cup chopped scallions
¾ cup mayonnaise
½ cup sour cream
½ teaspoon cayenne pepper
½ teaspoon onion powder
½ teaspoon garlic powder
1 tablespoon chopped chives
2 tablespoons chopped fresh dill
Kosher salt and ground black pepper, to taste

Fried Dill Pickles:
¾ cup all-purpose flour
1 (2-pound / 907-g) jar kosher dill pickles, cut into 4 spears, drained
2½ cups panko bread crumbs
2 eggs, beaten with 2 tablespoons water
Kosher salt and ground black pepper, to taste
Cooking spray

1. Combine the ingredients for the dressing in a bowl. Stir to mix well.
2. Wrap the bowl in plastic and refrigerate for 30 minutes or until ready to serve.
3. Pour the flour in a bowl and sprinkle with salt and ground black pepper. Stir to mix well. Put the bread crumbs in a separate bowl. Pour the beaten eggs in a third bowl.
4. Dredge the pickle spears in the flour, then into the eggs, and then into the panko to coat well. Shake the excess off.
5. Arrange the pickle spears in a single layer in the perforated pan and spritz with cooking spray.
6. Select Air Fry. Set temperature to 400ºF (205ºC) and set time to 8 minutes. Press Start to begin preheating.
7. Once the oven has preheated, place the pan into the oven. Flip the pickle spears halfway through the cooking time.
8. When cooking is complete, remove the pan from the oven.
9. Serve the pickle spears with buttermilk dressing.

Chocolate Macaroons with Coconut

Prep time: 10 minutes | Cook time: 8 minutes | Makes 24 macaroons

3 large egg whites, at room temperature	4½ tablespoons unsweetened cocoa powder
¼ teaspoon salt	
¾ cup granulated white sugar	2¼ cups unsweetened shredded coconut

1. Line the perforated pan with parchment paper.
2. Whisk the egg whites with salt in a large bowl with a hand mixer on high speed until stiff peaks form.
3. Whisk in the sugar with the hand mixer on high speed until the mixture is thick. Mix in the cocoa powder and coconut.
4. Scoop 2 tablespoons of the mixture and shape the mixture in a ball. Repeat with remaining mixture to make 24 balls in total.
5. Arrange the balls in a single layer in the perforated pan and leave a little space between each two balls.
6. Select Air Fry. Set temperature to 375°F (190°C) and set time to 8 minutes. Press Start to begin preheating.
7. Once the oven has preheated, place the pan into the oven.
8. When cooking is complete, the balls should be golden brown.
9. Serve immediately.

Olive and Basil Stromboli with Garlic

Prep time: 25 minutes | Cook time: 25 minutes | Serves 8

4 large cloves garlic, unpeeled	pepper
3 tablespoons grated Parmesan cheese	½ pound (227 g) pizza dough, at room temperature
½ cup packed fresh basil leaves	4 ounces (113 g) sliced provolone cheese (about 8 slices)
½ cup marinated, pitted green and black olives	Cooking spray
¼ teaspoon crushed red	

1. Spritz the perforated pan with cooking spray. Put the unpeeled garlic in the perforated pan.
2. Select Air Fry. Set temperature to 370°F (188°C) and set time to 10 minutes. Press Start to begin preheating.
3. Once preheated, place the pan into the oven.
4. When cooked, the garlic will be softened completely. Remove from the oven and allow to cool until you can handle.
5. Peel the garlic and place into a food processor with 2 tablespoons of Parmesan, basil, olives, and crushed red pepper. Pulse to mix well. Set aside.
6. Arrange the pizza dough on a clean work surface, then roll it out with a rolling pin into a rectangle. Cut the rectangle in half.
7. Sprinkle half of the garlic mixture over each rectangle half, and leave ½-inch edges uncover. Top them with the provolone cheese.
8. Brush one long side of each rectangle half with water, then roll them up. Spritz the perforated pan with cooking spray. Transfer the rolls to the perforated pan. Spritz with cooking spray and scatter with remaining Parmesan.
9. Select Air Fry and set time to 15 minutes. Place the pan into the oven. Flip the rolls halfway through the cooking time. When done, the rolls should be golden brown.
10. Remove the rolls from the oven and allow to cool for a few minutes before serving.

Pigs in a Blanket with Sesame Seeds

Prep time: 10 minutes | Cook time: 8 minutes | Makes 16 rolls

1 can refrigerated crescent roll dough	2 tablespoons melted butter
1 small package mini smoked sausages, patted dry	2 teaspoons sesame seeds
	1 teaspoon onion powder

1. Place the crescent roll dough on a clean work surface and separate into 8 pieces. Cut each piece in half and you will have 16 triangles.
2. Make the pigs in the blanket: Arrange each sausage on each dough triangle, then roll the sausages up.
3. Brush the pigs with melted butter and place of the pigs in the blanket in the perforated pan. Sprinkle with sesame seeds and onion powder.
4. Select Bake. Set temperature to 330°F (166°C) and set time to 8 minutes. Press Start to begin preheating.
5. Once the oven has preheated, place the pan into the oven. Flip the pigs halfway through the cooking time.
6. When cooking is complete, the pigs should be fluffy and golden brown.
7. Serve immediately.

Leap, and the net will appear. -Chapter 12 Holiday Specials

Risotto Croquettes with Tomato Sauce

Prep time: 1 hour 40 minutes | Cook time: 54 minutes | Serves 6

Risotto Croquettes:
- 4 tablespoons unsalted butter
- 1 small yellow onion, minced
- 1 cup Arborio rice
- 3½ cups chicken stock
- ½ cup dry white wine
- 3 eggs
- Zest of 1 lemon
- ½ cup grated Parmesan cheese
- 2 ounces (57 g) fresh Mozzarella cheese
- ¼ cup peas
- 2 tablespoons water
- ½ cup all-purpose flour
- 1½ cups panko bread crumbs
- Kosher salt and ground black pepper, to taste
- Cooking spray

Tomato Sauce:
- 2 tablespoons extra-virgin olive oil
- 4 cloves garlic, minced
- ¼ teaspoon red pepper flakes
- 1 (28-ounce / 794-g) can crushed tomatoes
- 2 teaspoons granulated sugar
- Kosher salt and ground black pepper, to taste

1. Melt the butter in a pot over medium heat, then add the onion and salt to taste. Sauté for 5 minutes or until the onion in translucent.
2. Add the rice and stir to coat well. Cook for 3 minutes or until the rice is lightly browned. Pour in the chicken stock and wine.
3. Bring to a boil. Then cook for 20 minutes or until the rice is tender and liquid is almost absorbed.
4. Make the risotto: When the rice is cooked, break the egg into the pot. Add the lemon zest and Parmesan cheese. Sprinkle with salt and ground black pepper. Stir to mix well.
5. Pour the risotto in a baking sheet, then level with a spatula to spread the risotto evenly. Wrap the baking sheet in plastic and refrigerate for 1 hour.
6. Meanwhile, heat the olive oil in a saucepan over medium heat until shimmering.
7. Add the garlic and sprinkle with red pepper flakes. Sauté for a minute or until fragrant.
8. Add the crushed tomatoes and sprinkle with sugar. Stir to mix well. Bring to a boil. Reduce the heat to low and simmer for 15 minutes or until lightly thickened. Sprinkle with salt and pepper to taste. Set aside until ready to serve.
9. Remove the risotto from the refrigerator. Scoop the risotto into twelve 2-inch balls, then flatten the balls with your hands.
10. Arrange a about ½-inch piece of Mozzarella and 5 peas in the center of each flattened ball, then wrap them back into balls.
11. Transfer the balls to a baking sheet lined with parchment paper, then refrigerate for 15 minutes or until firm.
12. Whisk the remaining 2 eggs with 2 tablespoons of water in a bowl. Pour the flour in a second bowl and pour the panko in a third bowl.
13. Dredge the risotto balls in the bowl of flour first, then into the eggs, and then into the panko. Shake the excess off.
14. Transfer the balls to the perforated pan and spritz with cooking spray.
15. Select Bake. Set temperature to 400°F (205°C) and set time to 10 minutes. Press Start to begin preheating.
16. Once the oven has preheated, place the pan into the oven. Flip the balls halfway through the cooking time.
17. When cooking is complete, the balls should be until golden brown.
18. Serve the risotto balls with the tomato sauce.

Garlic Nuggets

Prep time: 15 minutes | Cook time: 4 minutes | Makes 20 nuggets

- 1 cup all-purpose flour, plus more for dusting
- 1 teaspoon baking powder
- ½ teaspoon butter, at room temperature, plus more for brushing
- ¼ teaspoon salt
- ¼ cup water
- ⅛ teaspoon onion powder
- ¼ teaspoon garlic powder
- ⅛ teaspoon seasoning salt
- Cooking spray

1. Line the perforated pan with parchment paper.
2. Mix the flour, baking powder, butter, and salt in a large bowl. Stir to mix well. Gradually whisk in the water until a sanity dough forms.
3. Put the dough on a lightly floured work surface, then roll it out into a ½-inch thick rectangle with a rolling pin.
4. Cut the dough into about twenty 1- or 2-inch squares, then arrange the squares in a single layer in the perforated pan. Spritz with cooking spray.
5. Combine onion powder, garlic powder, and seasoning salt in a small bowl. Stir to mix well, then sprinkle the squares with the powder mixture.
6. Select Air Fry. Set temperature to 370°F (188°C) and set time to 4 minutes. Press Start to begin preheating.
7. Once the oven has preheated, place the pan into the oven. Flip the squares halfway through the cooking time.
8. When cooked, the dough squares should be golden brown.
9. Remove the golden nuggets from the oven and brush with more butter immediately. Serve warm.

Vanilla Cheese Blintzes

Prep time: 5 minutes | Cook time: 10 minutes | Makes 8 blintzes

2 (7½-ounce / 213-g) packages farmer cheese, mashed
¼ cup cream cheese
¼ teaspoon vanilla extract
¼ cup granulated white sugar
8 egg roll wrappers
4 tablespoons butter, melted

1. Combine the farmer cheese, cream cheese, vanilla extract, and sugar in a bowl. Stir to mix well.
2. Unfold the egg roll wrappers on a clean work surface, spread ¼ cup of the filling at the edge of each wrapper and leave a ½-inch edge uncovering.
3. Wet the edges of the wrappers with water and fold the uncovered edge over the filling. Fold the left and right sides in the center, then tuck the edge under the filling and fold to wrap the filling.
4. Brush the wrappers with melted butter, then arrange the wrappers in a single layer in the perforated pan, seam side down. Leave a little space between each two wrappers.
5. Select Air Fry. Set temperature to 375°F (190°C) and set time to 10 minutes. Press Start to begin preheating.
6. Once preheated, place the pan into the oven.
7. When cooking is complete, the wrappers will be golden brown.
8. Serve immediately.

Cream-Glazed Cinnamon Rolls

Prep time: 2 hours 15 minutes | Cook time: 5 minutes | Serves 8

1 pound (454 g) frozen bread dough, thawed
2 tablespoons melted butter
Cream Glaze:
4 ounces (113 g) softened cream cheese
½ teaspoon vanilla extract
2 tablespoons melted
1½ tablespoons cinnamon
¾ cup brown sugar
Cooking spray

butter
1¼ cups powdered erythritol

1. Place the bread dough on a clean work surface, then roll the dough out into a rectangle with a rolling pin.
2. Brush the top of the dough with melted butter and leave 1-inch edges uncovered.
3. Combine the cinnamon and sugar in a small bowl, then sprinkle the dough with the cinnamon mixture.
4. Roll the dough over tightly, then cut the dough log into 8 portions. Wrap the portions in plastic, better separately, and let sit to rise for 1 or 2 hours.
5. Meanwhile, combine the ingredients for the glaze in a separate small bowl. Stir to mix well.
6. Spritz the perforated pan with cooking spray. Transfer the risen rolls to the perforated pan.
7. Select Air Fry. Set temperature to 350°F (180°C) and set time to 5 minutes. Press Start to begin preheating.
8. Once the oven has preheated, place the pan into the oven. Flip the rolls halfway through the cooking time.
9. When cooking is complete, the rolls will be golden brown.
10. Serve the rolls with the glaze.

Teriyaki-Marinated Shrimp Skewers

Prep time: 10 minutes | Cook time: 6 minutes | Makes 12 skewered shrimp

1½ tablespoons mirin
1½ teaspoons ginger juice
1½ tablespoons soy sauce
12 large shrimp (about
20 shrimps per pound) peeled and deveined
1 large egg
¾ cup panko bread crumbs
Cooking spray

1. Combine the mirin, ginger juice, and soy sauce in a large bowl. Stir to mix well.
2. Dunk the shrimp in the bowl of mirin mixture, then wrap the bowl in plastic and refrigerate for 1 hour to marinate.
3. Spritz the perforated pan with cooking spray.
4. Run twelve 4-inch skewers through each shrimp.
5. Whisk the egg in the bowl of marinade to combine well. Pour the bread crumbs on a plate.
6. Dredge the shrimp skewers in the egg mixture, then shake the excess off and roll over the bread crumbs to coat well.
7. Arrange the shrimp skewers in the perforated pan and spritz with cooking spray.
8. Select Air Fry. Set temperature to 400°F (205°C) and set time to 6 minutes. Press Start to begin preheating.
9. Once preheated, place the pan into the oven. Flip the shrimp skewers halfway through the cooking time.
10. When done, the shrimp will be opaque and firm.
11. Serve immediately.

Leap, and the net will appear. -Chapter 12 Holiday Specials

Asiago Balls

Prep time: 37 minutes | Cook time: 12 minutes | Makes 12 balls

2 tablespoons butter, plus more for greasing
½ cup milk
1½ cups tapioca flour
½ teaspoon salt
1 large egg
⅔ cup finely grated aged Asiago cheese

1. Put the butter in a saucepan and pour in the milk, heat over medium heat until the liquid boils. Keep stirring.
2. Turn off the heat and mix in the tapioca flour and salt to form a soft dough. Transfer the dough in a large bowl, then wrap the bowl in plastic and let sit for 15 minutes.
3. Break the egg in the bowl of dough and whisk with a hand mixer for 2 minutes or until a sanity dough forms. Fold the cheese in the dough. Cover the bowl in plastic again and let sit for 10 more minutes.
4. Grease a baking pan with butter.
5. Scoop 2 tablespoons of the dough into the baking pan. Repeat with the remaining dough to make dough 12 balls. Keep a little distance between each two balls.
6. Select Bake. Set temperature to 375ºF (190ºC) and set time to 12 minutes. Press Start to begin preheating.
7. Once preheated, place the pan into the oven. Flip the balls halfway through the cooking time.
8. When cooking is complete, the balls should be golden brown and fluffy.
9. Remove the balls from the oven and allow to cool for 5 minutes before serving.

Cinnamon Churros

Prep time: 35 minutes | Cook time: 10 minutes | Makes 12 churros

4 tablespoons butter
¼ teaspoon salt
½ cup water
½ cup all-purpose flour
2 large eggs
2 teaspoons ground cinnamon
¼ cup granulated white sugar
Cooking spray

1. Put the butter, salt, and water in a saucepan. Bring to a boil until the butter is melted on high heat. Keep stirring.
2. Reduce the heat to medium and fold in the flour to form a dough. Keep cooking and stirring until the dough is dried out and coat the pan with a crust.
3. Turn off the heat and scrape the dough in a large bowl. Allow to cool for 15 minutes.
4. Break and whisk the eggs into the dough with a hand mixer until the dough is sanity and firm enough to shape.
5. Scoop up 1 tablespoon of the dough and roll it into a ½-inch-diameter and 2-inch-long cylinder. Repeat with remaining dough to make 12 cylinders in total.
6. Combine the cinnamon and sugar in a large bowl and dunk the cylinders into the cinnamon mix to coat.
7. Arrange the cylinders on a plate and refrigerate for 20 minutes.
8. Spritz the perforated pan with cooking spray. Place the cylinders in the perforated pan and spritz with cooking spray.
9. Select Air Fry. Set temperature to 375ºF (190ºC) and set time to 10 minutes. Press Start to begin preheating.
10. Once preheated, place the pan into the oven. Flip the cylinders halfway through the cooking time.
11. When cooked, the cylinders should be golden brown and fluffy.
12. Serve immediately.

Balsamic Cherry Tomatoes

Prep time: 5 minutes | Cook time: 10 minutes | Serves 4 to 6

2 pounds (907 g) cherry tomatoes
2 tablespoons olive oil
2 teaspoons balsamic vinegar
½ teaspoon salt
½ teaspoon ground black pepper

1. Toss the cherry tomatoes with olive oil in a large bowl to coat well. Pour the tomatoes in a baking pan.
2. Select Air Fry. Set temperature to 400ºF (205ºC) and set time to 10 minutes. Press Start to begin preheating.
3. Once preheated, slide the pan into the oven. Stir the tomatoes halfway through the cooking time.
4. When cooking is complete, the tomatoes will be blistered and lightly wilted.
5. Transfer the blistered tomatoes to a large bowl and toss with balsamic vinegar, salt, and black pepper before serving.

Sriracha Shrimp with Mayo

Prep time: 15 minutes | Cook time: 10 minutes | Serves 4

1 tablespoon Sriracha sauce
1 teaspoon Worcestershire sauce
2 tablespoons sweet chili sauce
¾ cup mayonnaise
1 egg, beaten
1 cup panko bread crumbs
1 pound (454 g) raw shrimp, shelled and deveined, rinsed and drained
Lime wedges, for serving
Cooking spray

1. Spritz the perforated pan with cooking spray.
2. Combine the Sriracha sauce, Worcestershire sauce, chili sauce, and mayo in a bowl. Stir to mix well. Reserve ⅓ cup of the mixture as the dipping sauce.
3. Combine the remaining sauce mixture with the beaten egg. Stir to mix well. Put the panko in a separate bowl.
4. Dredge the shrimp in the sauce mixture first, then into the panko. Roll the shrimp to coat well. Shake the excess off.
5. Place the shrimp in the perforated pan, then spritz with cooking spray.
6. Select Air Fry. Set temperature to 360°F (182°C) and set time to 10 minutes. Press Start to begin preheating.
7. Once preheated, place the pan into the oven. Flip the shrimp halfway through the cooking time.
8. When cooking is complete, the shrimp should be opaque.
9. Remove the shrimp from the oven and serve with reserve sauce mixture and squeeze the lime wedges over.

Vanilla Butter Cake

Prep time: 25 minutes | Cook time: 20 minutes | Serves 8

1 cup all-purpose flour
1¼ teaspoons baking powder
¼ teaspoon salt
½ cup plus 1½ tablespoons granulated white sugar
9½ tablespoons butter, at room temperature
2 large eggs
1 large egg yolk
2½ tablespoons milk
1 teaspoon vanilla extract
Cooking spray

1. Spritz a baking pan with cooking spray.
2. Combine the flour, baking powder, and salt in a large bowl. Stir to mix well.
3. Whip the sugar and butter in a separate bowl with a hand mixer on medium speed for 3 minutes.
4. Whip the eggs, egg yolk, milk, and vanilla extract into the sugar and butter mix with a hand mixer.
5. Pour in the flour mixture and whip with hand mixer until sanity and smooth.
6. Scrape the batter into the baking pan and level the batter with a spatula.
7. Select Bake. Set temperature to 325°F (163°C) and set time to 20 minutes. Press Start to begin preheating.
8. Once the oven has preheated, place the pan into the oven.
9. After 15 minutes, remove the pan from the oven. Check the doneness. Return the pan to the oven and continue cooking.
10. When done, a toothpick inserted in the center should come out clean.
11. Invert the cake on a cooling rack and allow to cool for 15 minutes before slicing to serve.

Leap, and the net will appear. -Chapter 12 Holiday Specials

Chapter 13 Rotisserie Recipes

Porchetta with Lemony Sage Rub

Prep time: 15 minutes | Cook time: 3½ hours | Serves 6

1 slab pork belly, skin on, 5 to 6 pounds (2.3 to 2.7 kg)
1 boneless pork loin roast, about 3 pounds (1.4 kg)
Rub:
2 tablespoons fennel seeds
1 tablespoon finely chopped fresh sage
Zest of 1 lemon
4 or 5 cloves garlic
2 teaspoons coarse salt
2 teaspoons freshly ground black pepper
1 teaspoon chopped fresh rosemary
1 teaspoon red pepper flakes
1½ teaspoons coarse salt
1 teaspoon freshly ground black pepper

1. Lay the pork belly, skin-side down, on a large cutting board. Place the pork loin on top and roll the pork belly together so that the ends meet. Trim any excess pork belly and loin so that it is a uniform cylinder. Do not tie yet.
2. To make the rub: Using a mortar and pestle or spice grinder, crush the fennel seeds to a medium grind. Combine with the remaining rub ingredients in a small bowl and apply all over the pork loin.
3. Roll the pork loin inside the pork belly and tie with kitchen twine every inch into a secure, round bundle. Season the outside of the pork belly with the coarse salt and pepper. Set onto a baking sheet and place in the refrigerator, uncovered, for 24 hours.
4. Run a long sword skewer through the center of the roast lengthwise to create a pilot hole. Run the rotisserie spit through the hole and secure with the forks. Balance as necessary.
5. Select Roast, set temperature to 400ºF (205ºC), Rotate, and set time to 3½ hours. Select Start to begin preheating.
6. Once preheated, place the prepared porchetta with rotisserie spit into the oven. Set a drip tray underneath. Watch for burning or excessive browning and adjust the heat as necessary. Once the porchetta has reached an internal temperature of 145ºF (63ºC), the roast is done.
7. When cooking is complete, remove the porchetta using the rotisserie lift. Carefully remove the rotisserie forks and slide the spit out, and then set the meat on a large cutting board. Tent the roast with aluminum foil and let the meat rest for 15 minutes. Slice the meat ½ inch thick and serve.

Dried Fruit Stuffed Pork Loin

Prep time: 10 minutes | Cook time: 1 hour | Serves 4

2 (2-pound / 907-g) boneless pork loin roasts
Apple Cider Brine:
Dried Fruit Stuffing:
2 cups mixed dried fruit, chopped (apples, apricots, cranberries and raisins)
2 quarts apple cider
1 quart water
½ cup table salt
1 teaspoon fresh ground black pepper
½ teaspoon dried ginger

1. Combine the brine ingredients in a large container and stir until the salt and sugar dissolve. Roll cut the pork roasts to open them up like a book. Set a roast with the fat cap facing down. Make a cut the length of the roast, one third of the way from the bottom, which goes almost all the way to the other side of the roast but not through. Open the roast up like a book along that cut, then make another cut halfway up the opened part of the roast, almost all the way to the other side, and open up the roast again. Submerge the pork roasts in the brine. Store in the refrigerator for one to four hours.
2. One hour before cooking, remove the pork from the brine and pat dry with paper towels. Open up the pork with the cut side facing up, and sprinkle evenly with the chopped fruit, ginger, and pepper. Carefully roll the pork back into a cylinder, then truss each roast at the edges to hold the cylinder shape. Truss the roasts together with the fat caps facing out, then skewer on the rotisserie spit, running the spit between the roasts and securing them with the rotisserie forks. Let the pork rest at room temperature.
3. Select Roast, set temperature to 400ºF (205ºC), Rotate, and set time to 1 hour. Select Start to begin preheating.
4. Once preheated, place the prepared pork with rotisserie spit into the oven. Set a drip tray underneath. Roast until it reaches 135ºF (57ºC) in its thickest part.
5. When cooking is complete, remove the pork using the rotisserie lift. Remove the pork from the rotisserie spit and remove the twine trussing the roast. Be careful - the spit and forks are blazing hot. Let the pork rest for 15 minutes, then slice into ½ inch thick rounds and serve.

Spareribs with Paprika Rub

Prep time: 15 minutes | Cook time: 3½ hours | Serves 4 to 6

2 racks spareribs
Sauce:
1 tablespoon olive oil
2 cloves garlic, minced
1 cup ketchup
¾ cup water
⅓ cup packed brown sugar
Rub:
⅓ cup packed brown sugar
2 tablespoons paprika
2 teaspoons salt
2 teaspoons mild chili powder
1 tablespoon paprika
2 teaspoons mild chili powder
¼ teaspoon cayenne powder
1 teaspoon onion powder
½ teaspoon garlic powder
¼ teaspoon cayenne

1. To make the sauce: Heat the oil in a medium-size saucepan over medium heat and sauté the garlic for 15 seconds, until aromatic. Add the remaining sauce ingredients and simmer for 5 minutes, stirring often. Remove from the heat and let cool to room temperature before using.
2. To make the rub: Combine the rub ingredients in a small bowl and set aside.
3. Place the ribs on a cutting board and pat dry with paper towels. Cut away any excess fat from the ribs. Remove the membrane from the back of the ribs by using a blunt knife to work the membrane away from the bone in one corner. Grab hold of the membrane with a paper towel for a good grip and gently peel away. With a little practice, this becomes an easy process.
4. Lay the rib racks meat-side down. Apply a small portion of the rub, just enough to season, to the bone side of the racks. Lay one rack on top of the other, bone side to bone side, to form an even shape. Tie the two racks together with kitchen twine between every other bone. The ribs should be held tightly together. Run the rotisserie spit between the racks and secure with the forks. The fork tines should run through the meat as best as possible. The ribs will move a little as the rotisserie turns. They should not flop around, however. Secure to prevent this. Apply the remaining rub evenly over the outer surface of the ribs. A general rule with rubs is that what sticks is the amount needed.
5. Select Roast, set temperature to 375ºF (190ºC), Rotate, and set time to 3½ hours. Select Start to begin preheating.
6. Once preheated, place the prepared ribs with rotisserie spit into the oven. Set a drip tray underneath. Roast until the ribs reach an internal temperature of 185ºF (85ºC). Test the temperature in several locations. Baste the ribs several times with the sauce during the last hour of cooking to build up a sticky surface.
7. When cooking is complete, remove the ribs using the rotisserie lift. Carefully remove the rotisserie forks and slide the spit out, and then set the ribs on a large cutting board. Tent the ribs with aluminum foil and let the meat rest for 5 to 10 minutes. Cut away the twine and cut the racks into individual ribs. Serve.

Paprika Pulled Pork Butt

Prep time: 10 minutes | Cook time: 6 hours | Serves 10

1 pork butt, 5 to 6 pounds (2.3 to 2.7 kg)
Rub:
2 tablespoons paprika
2 tablespoons packed brown sugar
1 tablespoon kosher salt
1 tablespoon mild chili powder
1 teaspoon freshly ground black pepper
1 teaspoon celery salt
½ teaspoon cayenne
½ teaspoon garlic powder

1. Run a long sword skewer through the center of the roast lengthwise to create a pilot hole. Run the rotisserie spit through the hole and secure with the forks. Balance as necessary.
2. To make the rub: Combine the rub ingredients in a small bowl and apply evenly all over the roast. Let sit at room temperature for 15 minutes. By this time the air fryer oven should be ready.
3. Select Roast, set temperature to 350ºF (180ºC), Rotate, and set time to 6 hours. Select Start to begin preheating.
4. Once preheated, place the prepared roast with rotisserie spit into the oven. Set a drip tray underneath. Roast until the internal temperature reaches 185ºF (85ºC). The roast will shrink during cooking, so adjust the forks when appropriate.
5. When cooking is complete, remove the roast using the rotisserie lift. Carefully remove the rotisserie forks and slide the spit out, and then set the pork on a large cutting board. Tent the roast with aluminum foil and let the meat rest for 20 minutes. Remove the foil and let stand for an additional 10 minutes.
6. Using two forks, check to see how easily the meat shreds. Some parts will do this more easily than others. Be sure to use heat-resistant gloves to break the roast apart. Begin shredding each large chunk one at a time. Add pieces to a large bowl and either add the barbecue sauce directly to the shredded meat or serve on the side. Keep the bowl covered as you're working on each section. This will help keep the meat warm. Serve by itself or with your favorite sides or in sandwiches.

Leap, and the net will appear. -Chapter 13 Rotisserie Recipes

Chicken Roast with Mustard Paste
Prep time: 5 minutes | Cook time: 1 hour | Serves 4

1 (4-pound / 1.8-kg) chicken
Mustard Paste:
¼ cup Dijon mustard
1 tablespoon kosher salt
1 tablespoon Herbes de Provence
1 teaspoon freshly ground black pepper

1. Mix the mustard paste ingredients in a small bowl. Rub the chicken with the mustard paste, inside and out. Gently work your fingers under the skin on the breast, then rub some of the paste directly onto the breast meat. Refrigerate for at least two hours, preferably overnight.
2. One hour before cooking, remove the chicken from the refrigerator. Fold the wingtips under the wings and truss the chicken. Skewer the chicken on the rotisserie spit, securing it with the rotisserie forks. Let the chicken rest at room temperature.
3. Select Roast, set temperature to 400ºF (205ºC), Rotate, and set time to 1 hour. Select Start to begin preheating.
4. Once preheated, place the prepared chicken with rotisserie spit into the oven. Set a drip tray underneath. Roast until the chicken reaches 160ºF (70ºC) in the thickest part of the breast.
5. When cooking is complete, remove the chicken using the rotisserie lift. Remove the chicken from the rotisserie spit and remove the twine trussing the chicken. Be careful - the spit and forks are blazing hot. Let the chicken rest for 15 minutes, then carve and serve.

Mustard Lamb Shoulder
Prep time: 5 minutes | Cook time: 2 hours | Serves 4

1 (4-pound / 1.8-kg) boneless lamb shoulder roast
Mustard Herb Paste:
¼ cup whole grain mustard
1 tablespoon kosher salt
1 tablespoon minced fresh thyme
1 teaspoon minced fresh oregano
1 teaspoon minced fresh rosemary
1 teaspoon fresh ground black pepper

1. Mix the paste ingredients in a small bowl. Open up the lamb like a book, then rub all over with the paste, working it into any natural seams in the meat. Refrigerate for at least two hours, preferably overnight.
2. One hour before cooking, remove the lamb from the refrigerator. Fold the lamb into its original shape, truss the lamb, and skewer it on the rotisserie spit, securing it with the rotisserie forks. Let the lamb rest at room temperature until the air fryer oven is ready.
3. Select Roast, set temperature to 375ºF (190ºC), Rotate, and set time to 2 hours. Select Start to begin preheating.
4. Once preheated, place the prepared lamb with rotisserie spit into the oven. Set a drip tray underneath. Roast the lamb until it reaches 190ºF (88ºC) in its thickest part.
5. When cooking is complete, remove the lamb shoulder using the rotisserie lift. Remove the lamb shoulder from the rotisserie spit and remove the twine trussing the roast. Be careful - the spit and forks are blazing hot. Let the lamb rest for 15 minutes, then carve and serve.

Pork Loin Roast with Brown Sugar Brine
Prep time: 10 minutes | Cook time: 1 hour | Serves 4

1 (4-pound / 1.8-kg) bone-in pork loin roast
Brine:
3 quarts water
½ cup table salt (or 1 cup kosher salt)
¼ cup brown sugar
Spice Rub:
4 cloves garlic, minced or pressed through a garlic press
1 teaspoon minced rosemary
1 teaspoon fresh ground black pepper
½ teaspoon hot red pepper flakes

1. Combine the brine ingredients in a large container and stir until the salt and sugar dissolve. Submerge the pork in the brine. Store in the refrigerator for four to eight hours.
2. One hour before cooking, remove the pork from the brine and pat dry with paper towels. Mix the rub ingredients in a small bowl, then rub over the pork shoulder, working the rub into any natural seams in the meat. Truss the pork roast, skewer it on the rotisserie spit, and secure it with the rotisserie forks. Let the pork rest at room temperature.
3. Select Roast, set temperature to 400ºF (205ºC), Rotate, and set time to 1 hour. Select Start to begin preheating.
4. Once preheated, place the prepared pork roast with rotisserie spit into the oven. Set a drip tray underneath. Roast until it reaches 135ºF (57ºC) in its thickest part.
5. When cooking is complete, remove the pork using the rotisserie lift. Remove the pork from the rotisserie spit and remove the twine trussing the roast. Be careful - the spit and forks are blazing hot. Let the pork rest for 15 minutes, then slice and serve.

Sirloin Roast with Porcini-Wine Baste

Prep time: 20 minutes | Cook time: 2 hours | Serves 8

1 top sirloin roast, 4 to 4½ pounds (1.8 to 2.0 kg)

Wet Rub:
- ½ cup dried porcini mushrooms
- ¼ cup olive oil
- 4 teaspoons salt
- 1 tablespoon chopped fresh thyme
- 2 cloves garlic, minced
- 1 teaspoon onion powder
- 1 teaspoon chili powder
- 1 teaspoon coarsely ground black pepper

Baste:
- ½ cup dried porcini mushrooms
- 1 or 2 cups boiling water
- ½ cup red wine (Cabernet Sauvignon recommended)
- 1 tablespoon wet rub mixture
- 1 teaspoon Worcestershire sauce

1. For the wet rub: Chop the mushrooms into small pieces. Place in a clean spice or coffee grinder and grind to a fine powder. Transfer to a bowl and add the remaining rub ingredients. Remove 1 tablespoon (6 g) of the mixture and set aside.
2. If the sirloin roast is loose or uneven, tie it with kitchen twine to hold it to a consistent and even shape. Run a long sword skewer through the center of the roast lengthwise to create a pilot hole. Run the rotisserie spit through the hole and secure with the forks. Balance as necessary. Apply the wet rub evenly to the meat.
3. Select Roast, set temperature to 400°F (205°C), Rotate, and set time to 2 hours. Select Start to begin preheating.
4. Once preheated, place the prepared roast with rotisserie spit into the oven. Set a drip tray underneath, and add 1 to 2 cups hot water to the tray. Roast until it reaches the desired doneness: 125°F (52°C) for rare, 135°F (57°C) for medium rare, 145°F (63°C) for medium, 155°F (68°C) for medium well, or 165°F (74°C) for well done. Adjust the forks when appropriate.
5. While the roast cooks, make the baste: Add the dried porcini mushrooms to 1 cup boiling water, or 2 cups boiling water if you would like to use the porcini broth for the gravy. Steep the mushrooms for 30 minutes, covered. Strain the broth and reserve the porcinis (for the gravy) and broth separately. Divide the broth into two equal portions, one for the baste and one for the gravy. Combine 1 cup broth with remaining baste ingredients. Let sit for 15 to 30 minutes to come to room temperature before using. Begin basting the roast during the last half of the cooking time and repeat every 10 to 12 minutes until the roast is ready.
6. When cooking is complete, remove the roast using the rotisserie lift. Carefully remove the rotisserie forks and slide the spit out. Tent the roast with aluminum foil and let the meat rest for 20 minutes. Cut into ¼-inch slices and serve.

Smoked Paprika Lamb Leg

Prep time: 10 minutes | Cook time: 1 hour 20 minutes | Serves 6 to 8

1 boneless leg of lamb (partial bone-in is fine), 4 to 5 pounds (1.8 to 2.3 kg)

Rub:
- ¼ cup packed brown sugar
- 1 tablespoon coarse salt
- 2 teaspoons smoked paprika
- 1½ to 2 teaspoons spicy chili powder or cayenne
- 2 teaspoons onion powder
- 1 teaspoon garlic powder
- 1 teaspoon freshly ground black pepper
- ½ teaspoon ground cloves
- ⅛ teaspoon ground cinnamon

1. Trim off the excess fat and any loose hanging pieces from the lamb. With kitchen twine, tie the roast into a uniform and solid roast. It will take four to five ties to hold it together properly. Run a long sword skewer through the center of the roast lengthwise to create a pilot hole. Run the rotisserie spit through the hole and secure with the forks. Balance as necessary.
2. To make the rub: Combine the rub ingredients in a small bowl and apply evenly to the lamb. Make sure you get as much of the rub on the meat as possible.
3. Select Roast, set temperature to 375°F (190°C), Rotate, and set time to 80 minutes. Select Start to begin preheating.
4. Once preheated, place the prepared lamb with rotisserie spit into the oven. Set a drip tray underneath. Roast until the lamb reaches an internal temperature of 140°F (60°C) for medium or 150°F (66°C) for medium well. The lamb will shrink during cooking, so adjust the forks when appropriate.
5. When cooking is complete, remove the lamb using the rotisserie lift. Carefully remove the rotisserie forks and slide the spit out, and then set the lamb on a large cutting board. Tent the roast with aluminum foil and let the meat rest for 10 to 12 minutes. Cut off the twine and carve. Serve.

Leap, and the net will appear. -Chapter 13 Rotisserie Recipes

Whiskey-Basted Prime Rib Roast

Prep time: 10 minutes | Cook time: 2 hours | Serves 8 to 10

1 4-bone prime rib roast (8 to 10 pounds / 3.6 to 4.5 kg)

Rub:
- ¼ cup coarse salt
- 1 small shallot, finely chopped
- 2 cloves garlic, minced
- 2 tablespoons olive oil
- 1 tablespoon coarsely ground black pepper
- Zest of 1 large lemon
- 1 teaspoon paprika
- 1 teaspoon sugar

Baste:
- ⅓ cup whiskey
- ¼ cup water
- Juice of 1 lemon
- ⅛ teaspoon salt

1. Trim off any straggling pieces of meat or fat from the roast. If the fat cap is too thick, cut it down to between ¼ to ½ inch in thickness depending on how you like your prime rib.
2. Run a long sword skewer through the center of the roast lengthwise to create a pilot hole. Run the rotisserie spit through the hole and secure with the forks. Balance as necessary.
3. To make the rub: Combine the rub ingredients in a small bowl to form an even paste. Use additional olive oil if necessary to get it to a thick but workable consistency. Apply evenly to the roast, focusing on the outer shell of the roast.
4. To make the baste: Combine the baste ingredients in a small bowl and set aside for 15 to 30 minutes to come to room temperature.
5. Select Roast, set temperature to 400°F (205°C), Rotate, and set time to 2 hours. Select Start to begin preheating.
6. Once preheated, place the prepared roast with rotisserie spit into the oven. Set a drip tray underneath, and add 1 to 2 cups hot water to the tray. If you intend to make a gravy from the drippings, monitor the drip tray to make sure it does not run dry. Add extra water if needed.
7. During the last hour of cooking time, begin basting. Apply the baste gently so as not to wash away the seasonings on the outside of the roast. Do this 6 to 8 times, until the roast is well coated with the baste. Roast until it is near the desired doneness: 125°F (52°C) for rare, 135°F (57°C) for medium rare, 145°F (63°C) for medium, 155°F (68°C) for medium well, or 165°F (74°C) for well done. The roast will shrink during cooking, so adjust the forks when appropriate.
8. When cooking is complete, remove the roast using the rotisserie lift. Carefully remove the rotisserie forks and slide the spit out, and then set the roast on a large cutting board. Tent the roast with aluminum foil and let the meat rest for 15 to 20 minutes. Cut away the bones first by passing a knife against the bones and cutting through (save the bones for later). Cut the meat into thin slices.

BBQ Chicken with Mustard Rub

Prep time: 15 minutes | Cook time: 1 hour 10 minutes | Serves 4 to 6

- 1 whole chicken, 3 to 4 pounds (1.4 to 1.8 kg)
- 1 medium-size onion, peeled but whole (for cavity)

Barbecue Sauce:
- ¾ cup ketchup
- ⅔ cup cherry cola
- ¼ cup apple cider vinegar
- 2 tablespoons packed brown sugar
- 1 tablespoon molasses
- ¼ teaspoon salt
- ¼ teaspoon freshly ground black pepper

Rub:
- 2 teaspoons salt
- 2 teaspoons onion powder
- 1 teaspoon mustard powder
- ½ teaspoon freshly ground black pepper
- ½ teaspoon garlic powder

1. To make the barbecue sauce: Combine all the ingredients in a medium-size saucepan over medium heat and simmer for 5 to 6 minutes, until the mixture is smooth and well blended. Stir often and watch for burning. Remove from the heat and let the sauce cool at least 10 minutes before using.
2. To make the rub: Combine all the rub ingredients in a small bowl.
3. Pat the chicken dry inside and out with paper towels. Apply the rub all over the bird, under the breast skin, and inside the body cavity.
4. Truss the chicken with kitchen twine. Run the rotisserie spit through the onion and insert it into the chicken cavity. Use a paring knife to cut a pilot hole in the onion to make this easier. Continue to run the spit through the chicken and secure with the rotisserie forks.
5. Select Roast, set temperature to 400°F (205°C), Rotate, and set time to 70 minutes. Select Start to begin preheating.
6. Once preheated, place the prepared chicken with rotisserie spit into the oven. Set a drip tray underneath. Roast until the meat in the thighs and legs reaches 175°F (79°C). The breasts should be 165°F (74°C). Baste the chicken with the barbecue sauce during the last half of the cooking time. Do so every 7 to 10 minutes, until the bird is nearly done and well coated with the sauce.
7. When cooking is complete, remove the chicken using the rotisserie lift. Carefully remove the rotisserie forks and slide the spit out, and then set the chicken on a large cutting board. Tent the chicken with aluminum foil and let it rest for 10 to 15 minutes before cutting off the twine and carving.

Orange Honey Glazed Ham

Prep time: 10 minutes | Cook time: 45 minutes | Serves 12 to 14

1 ham, bone in and unsliced, 7 to 8 pounds (3.2 to 3.6 kg)
1 cup packed brown sugar
Glaze:
1½ cups orange juice
½ cup honey
2 tablespoons packed brown sugar
¼ teaspoon ground cinnamon
⅛ teaspoon ground nutmeg
⅛ teaspoon ground allspice
⅛ teaspoon ground cloves
⅛ teaspoon white pepper
2 tablespoons unsalted butter

1. To make the glaze: Combine the orange juice, honey, brown sugar, and spices in a saucepan and bring almost to a boil over medium-high heat. Decrease the heat to medium and simmer for 10 minutes, stirring often. The mixture should be a little runnier than real maple syrup. Remove from the heat and add the butter, stirring until melted. Let the mixture cool.
2. Run a long sword skewer through the center of the ham lengthwise to create a pilot hole. There is a bone in the middle of this ham, but generally it is just to one side. The skewer should easily go through, but feel for the bone before you start so you will know how to navigate around it. Run the rotisserie spit through the hole and secure with the forks. Balance the ham on the spit as well as possible.
3. Select Roast, set temperature to 375°F (190°C), Rotate, and set time to 45 minutes. Select Start to begin preheating.
4. Once preheated, place the prepared ham with rotisserie spit into the oven. Set a drip tray underneath. The ham should not take too long to heat up. Look for an internal temperature around 130°F (54°C). The surface should be hot.
5. Baste the ham with the glaze after 20 minutes on the air fryer oven. Repeat the process every 5 minutes and about 3 more times.
6. During the last 5 to 10 minutes of cooking time, the ham should be hot as well as sticky from the glaze. Increase the temperature to 400°F (205°C) and sprinkle the brown sugar evenly on the surface of the ham in small amounts until it is completely coated. Continue to cook until the sugar starts to bubble. Move quickly, as sugar tends to burn.
7. Once the sugar is bubbling rapidly, remove the ham using the rotisserie lift and place on a large cutting board. Remove the rotisserie forks and slide the spit out, loosely cover the ham with aluminum foil, and let it rest for 5 minutes. Carve into thin slices and serve warm.

Bacon-Wrapped Sirloin Roast

Prep time: 5 minutes | Cook time: 1 hour | Serves 4

1 (4-pound / 1.8-kg) sirloin roast
1 tablespoon kosher salt
4 slices bacon

1. Season the sirloin roast with the salt, then refrigerate for at least two hours, preferably overnight.
2. One hour before cooking, remove the sirloin roast from the refrigerator. Cut the butcher's twine and lay the strings on a platter, spaced where you want to tie the sirloin roast. Put two slices of bacon on top of the string, with a gap between them. Put the sirloin roast on top of the bacon, then lay the last two pieces of bacon on top of the sirloin roast. Tie the twine to truss the sirloin roast and the bacon. Trim off any loose ends of bacon so they don't burn in the air fryer oven. Skewer the sirloin roast on the rotisserie spit, securing it with the rotisserie forks. Let the beef rest at room temperature until the air fryer oven is ready.
3. Select Roast, set temperature to 400°F (205°C), Rotate, and set time to 1 hour. Select Start to begin preheating.
4. Once preheated, place the prepared sirloin roast with rotisserie spit into the oven. Set a drip tray underneath. Roast until it reaches 120°F (49°C) in its thickest part for medium-rare. (Cook to 115°F (46°C) for rare, 130°F (54°C) for medium.)
5. When cooking is complete, remove the sirloin roast using the rotisserie lift. Remove the sirloin roast from the rotisserie spit and remove the twine trussing the roast, leaving as much bacon behind as possible. Be careful - the spit and forks are blazing hot. Let the beef rest for 15 minutes, then carve into thin slices and serve.

Balsamic Chuck Roast

Prep time: 15 minutes | Cook time: 1 hour | Serves 8

1 chuck roast, 4 to 4½ pounds (1.8 to 2.0 kg)
1¼ teaspoons salt
½ teaspoon freshly ground black pepper

Marinade:

1 tablespoon olive oil	1 teaspoon Worcestershire sauce
1 shallot, finely chopped	1 teaspoon chopped fresh thyme
2 or 3 cloves garlic, minced	¼ teaspoon salt
1½ cups tawny port	¼ teaspoon freshly ground black pepper
¼ cup beef broth	
1½ tablespoons balsamic vinegar	

1. To make the marinade: Heat the olive oil in a saucepan over medium-low heat and cook the shallot for 3 minutes until translucent. Add the garlic and cook for 30 seconds. Increase the heat to medium-high and add the port. Stir thoroughly and cook for 1 minute. Add the remaining ingredients and simmer the sauce for 5 minutes, stirring occasionally. Remove from the heat and let cool for 10 to 15 minutes. Divide the mixture into two even portions, reserving one half for the baste and one for the marinade. Store in the refrigerator until ready to cook, then bring to room temperature before using.
2. Trim away excess fat from the outer edges of the chuck roast. Place the roast in a resealable plastic bag. Add half of the port mixture to the bag, making sure that all of the meat is well covered. Seal the bag and place in the refrigerator for 6 to 8 hours.
3. Remove the roast from the bag, discarding the marinade, and place on a large cutting board or platter. With kitchen twine, tie the roast into a round and uniform shape, pulling tightly. Start in the center and work toward the ends until it is tied into a solid round roast. This will take four or five ties. Run a long sword skewer through the center of the roast lengthwise to create a pilot hole. Run the rotisserie spit through the hole and secure with the forks. Balance as necessary. Season the roast with the salt and pepper.
4. Select Roast, set temperature to 400ºF (205ºC), Rotate, and set time to 1 hour. Select Start to begin preheating.
5. Once preheated, place the prepared roast with rotisserie spit into the oven. Set a drip tray underneath. Roast until it reaches the desired doneness: 125ºF (52ºC) for rare, 135ºF (57ºC) for medium rare, 145ºF (63ºC) for medium, 155ºF (68ºC) for medium well, or 165ºF (74ºC) for well done. Baste halfway through the cooking time, and repeat the process at least 3 times until the roast is done.
6. When cooking is complete, remove the roast using the rotisserie lift. Carefully remove the rotisserie forks and slide the spit out, and then set the roast on a large cutting board. Tent the roast with aluminum foil and let the meat rest for 15 to 20 minutes. Cut off the twine. Slice into ¼-inch slices and serve.

Ham with Dijon Bourbon Baste

Prep time: 5 minutes | Cook time: 50 minutes | Serves 10 to 12

1 ham, unsliced, 5 to 6 pounds (2.3 to 2.7 kg)

Baste:

⅓ cup apple butter	mustard
¼ cup packed brown sugar	¼ teaspoon ground ginger
2 tablespoons bourbon	¼ teaspoon white pepper
1½ teaspoons Dijon	

1. Run a long sword skewer through the center of the ham lengthwise to create a pilot hole. Run the rotisserie spit through the hole and secure with the forks. Balance as necessary and secure tightly. Place the ham on the preheated air fryer oven and cook for 50 to 60 minutes. If there is room, set a drip tray underneath.
2. To make the baste: Combine all the baste ingredients in a small saucepan and simmer over medium heat for 2 minutes, stirring often. Remove from the heat and let sit for 5 to 10 minutes before using.
3. Select Roast, set temperature to 400ºF (205ºC), Rotate, and set time to 45 minutes. Select Start to begin preheating.
4. Once preheated, place the prepared ham with rotisserie spit into the oven. Set a drip tray underneath. During the last 20 minutes of the cooking time, begin basting the ham with the apple butter-bourbon mixture. Make at least 4 or 5 passes with the baste to coat evenly. Focus the coating on the outside of the ham and not on the cut side. The ham should not take too long to heat up. Look for an internal temperature around 130ºF (54ºC). The surface should be hot.
5. When cooking is complete, remove the ham using the rotisserie lift. Carefully remove the rotisserie forks and slide the spit out, and then set the ham on a large cutting board. Tent the ham with aluminum foil and let the meat rest for 10 minutes. Carve and serve immediately.

Baby Back Ribs with Paprika Rub

Prep time: 15 minutes | Cook time: 2½ hours | Serves 4 to 6

2 racks baby back ribs
Sauce:
1 tablespoon vegetable oil
1 cup finely chopped sweet onion
2 cloves garlic, minced
1½ cups ketchup
¼ cup red wine vinegar
¼ cup packed brown sugar
2 tablespoons yellow mustard
⅛ teaspoon salt
Rub:
1 tablespoon paprika
2 teaspoons salt
2 teaspoons freshly ground black pepper
½ teaspoon cayenne

1. To make the sauce: Heat the oil in a medium-size saucepan over medium heat. Add the onions and sauté for 5 minutes. Add the garlic and sauté for 15 seconds. Add the remaining sauce ingredients and simmer for 4 to 5 minutes, stirring often. Remove from the heat and let cool for 15 to 30 minutes before using.
2. To make the rub: Combine the rub ingredients in a small bowl and set aside.
3. Place the ribs on a cutting board and pat dry with paper towels. Cut away any excess fat from the ribs. Remove the membrane from the back of the ribs by using a blunt knife to work the membrane away from the bone in one corner. Grab hold of the membrane with a paper towel for a good grip and gently peel away. With a little practice, this becomes an easy process. Apply the rub all over the ribs' surface, focusing more on the meat side than the bone side.
4. Place one rack of ribs bone-side up on a large cutting board. Place the other rack of ribs bone-side down on top. Position to match up the racks of ribs as evenly as possible. With kitchen twine, tie the racks together between ever other bone, end to end. The whole bundle should be secure and tight. Run the rotisserie spit between the racks and secure tightly with the rotisserie forks. There will be a little movement in the middle, which is fine. As the ribs cook it may be necessary to tighten the forks to keep them secure. Make sure the forks pass through the meat of each rack on each end.
5. Select Roast, set temperature to 375°F (190°C), Rotate, and set time to 2½ hours. Select Start to begin preheating.
6. Once preheated, place the prepared ribs with rotisserie spit into the oven. Set a drip tray underneath. Roast until the internal temperature reaches 185°F (85°C). Test the temperature in several locations. Baste the ribs evenly with barbecue sauce during the last 45 minutes of cooking time.
7. When cooking is complete, remove the ribs using the rotisserie lift. Carefully remove the rotisserie forks and slide the spit out, and then set the ribs on a large cutting board. Tent the ribs with aluminum foil and let the meat rest for 5 to 10 minutes.
8. Cut away the twine and cut the racks into individual ribs. Serve.

Teriyaki Chicken

Prep time: 5 minutes | Cook time: 1 hour 10 minutes | Serves 4

1 (4-pound / 1.8-kg) chicken
1 tablespoon kosher salt
Teriyaki Sauce:
¼ cup soy sauce
¼ cup mirin
¼ cup honey (or sugar)
¼ inch slice of ginger, smashed

1. Season the chicken with the salt, inside and out. Gently work your fingers under the skin on the breast, then rub some of the salt directly onto the breast meat. Fold the wingtips under the wings and truss the chicken. Skewer the chicken on the rotisserie spit, securing it with the rotisserie forks. Let the chicken rest at room temperature.
2. Select Roast, set temperature to 400°F (205°C), Rotate, and set time to 1 hour. Select Start to begin preheating.
3. While the air fryer oven is preheating, combine the soy sauce, mirin, honey, and ginger in a saucepan. Bring to a boil over medium-high heat, stirring often, then decrease the heat to low and simmer for 10 minutes, until the liquid is reduced by half.
4. Once preheated, place the prepared chicken with rotisserie spit into the oven. Set a drip tray underneath. Roast until the chicken reaches 160°F (70°C) in the thickest part of the breast. During the last 15 minutes of cooking, brush the chicken with the teriyaki sauce every five minutes.
5. When cooking is complete, remove the chicken using the rotisserie lift. Remove the chicken from the rotisserie spit and transfer to a platter. Be careful - the spit and forks are blazing hot. Remove the trussing twine, then brush the chicken one last time with the teriyaki sauce. Let the chicken rest for 15 minutes, then carve and serve, passing any remaining teriyaki sauce at the table.

Leap, and the net will appear. -Chapter 13 Rotisserie Recipes

Chicken with Brown Sugar Brine

Prep time: 5 minutes | Cook time: 1 hour | Serves 4

1 (4-pound / 1.8-kg) chicken
Brine:
2 quarts cold water
½ cup table salt (or 1 cup kosher salt)
¼ cup brown sugar
½ head of garlic (6 to 8 cloves), skin on, crushed
3 bay leaves, crumbled
1 tablespoon peppercorns, crushed or coarsely ground

1. Combine the brine ingredients in large container, and stir until the salt and sugar dissolve. Submerge the chicken in the brine. Store in the refrigerator for at least one hour, preferably four hours, no longer than eight hours.
2. Remove the chicken from the brine and pat dry with paper towels, picking off any pieces of bay leaves or garlic that stick to the chicken. Fold the wingtips underneath the wings, then truss the chicken. Skewer the chicken on the rotisserie spit, securing it with the rotisserie forks. Let the chicken rest at room temperature.
3. Select Roast, set temperature to 400ºF (205ºC), Rotate, and set time to 1 hour. Select Start to begin preheating.
4. Once preheated, place the prepared chicken with rotisserie spit into the oven. Set a drip tray underneath. Roast until the chicken reaches 160ºF (70ºC) in the thickest part of the breast.
5. When cooking is complete, remove the chicken using the rotisserie lift. Remove the chicken from the rotisserie spit and remove the twine trussing the chicken. Be careful - the spit and forks are blazing hot. Let the chicken rest for 15 minutes, then carve and serve.

Turkey with Thyme-Sage Brine

Prep time: 5 minutes | Cook time: 2½ hours | Serves 12 to 14

1 (12- to 14-pound / 5.4- to 6.3-kg) turkey
Dry Brine:
¼ cup kosher salt
1 tablespoon minced fresh sage
1 tablespoon minced fresh thyme
1 teaspoon fresh ground black pepper
Fist sized chunk of smoking wood (or 1 cup wood chips)

1. Mix the dry brine ingredients in a small bowl. Sprinkle the turkey with the dry brine, inside and out. Gently work your fingers under the skin on the breast, then rub some of the dry brine directly onto the breast meat. Refrigerate at least overnight, preferably two to three days. If dry brining more than a day in advance, cover the turkey with plastic wrap until the night before cooking, then remove the plastic wrap to let the skin dry out overnight.
2. Two hours before cooking, remove the turkey from the refrigerator. Fold the wingtips underneath the wings, then truss the turkey. Skewer the turkey on the rotisserie spit, securing it with the rotisserie forks. Let the turkey rest at room temperature. Submerge the smoking wood in water and let it soak until the air fryer oven is ready.
3. Select Roast, set temperature to 375ºF (190ºC), Rotate, and set time to 2½ hours. Select Start to begin preheating.
4. Once preheated, place the prepared turkey with rotisserie spit into the oven. Set a drip tray underneath. Roast until the turkey reaches 155ºF (68ºC) in the thickest part of the breast.
5. When cooking is complete, remove the turkey using the rotisserie lift. Remove the turkey from the rotisserie spit and remove the twine trussing the turkey. Be very careful - the spit and forks are blazing hot. Let the turkey rest for 15 to 30 minutes, then carve and serve.

Chapter 14 Appetizers and Snacks

Sausage and Onion Rolls with Mustard
Prep time: 15 minutes | Cook time: 15 minutes | Serves 12

1 pound (454 g) bulk breakfast sausage
½ cup finely chopped onion
½ cup fresh bread crumbs
½ teaspoon dried mustard
½ teaspoon dried sage
¼ teaspoon cayenne pepper
1 large egg, beaten
1 garlic clove, minced
2 sheets (1 package) frozen puff pastry, thawed
All-purpose flour, for dusting

1. In a medium bowl, break up the sausage. Stir in the onion, bread crumbs, mustard, sage, cayenne pepper, egg and garlic. Divide the sausage mixture in half and tightly wrap each half in plastic wrap. Refrigerate for 5 to 10 minutes.
2. Lay the pastry sheets on a lightly floured work surface. Using a rolling pin, lightly roll out the pastry to smooth out the dough. Take out one of the sausage packages and form the sausage into a long roll. Remove the plastic wrap and place the sausage on top of the puff pastry about 1 inch from one of the long edges. Roll the pastry around the sausage and pinch the edges of the dough together to seal. Repeat with the other pastry sheet and sausage.
3. Slice the logs into lengths about 1½ inches long. Place the sausage rolls on the sheet pan, cut-side down.
4. Select Roast. Set temperature to 350ºF (180ºC) and set time to 15 minutes. Press Start to begin preheating.
5. Once the unit has preheated, place the pan into the oven.
6. After 7 or 8 minutes, rotate the pan and continue cooking.
7. When cooking is complete, the rolls will be golden brown and sizzling. Remove the pan from the oven and let cool for 5 minutes.

Parmesan Cauliflower with Turmeric
Prep time: 15 minutes | Cook time: 15 minutes | Makes 5 cups

8 cups small cauliflower florets (about 1¼ pounds / 567 g)
3 tablespoons olive oil
1 teaspoon garlic powder
½ teaspoon salt
½ teaspoon turmeric
¼ cup shredded Parmesan cheese

1. In a bowl, combine the cauliflower florets, olive oil, garlic powder, salt, and turmeric and toss to coat. Transfer to the perforated pan.
2. Select Air Fry. Set temperature to 390ºF (199ºC) and set time to 15 minutes. Press Start to begin preheating.
3. Once preheated, place the pan into the oven.
4. After 5 minutes, remove from the oven and stir the cauliflower florets. Return the pan to the oven and continue cooking.
5. After 6 minutes, remove from the oven and stir the cauliflower. Return the pan to the oven and continue cooking for 4 minutes. The cauliflower florets should be crisp-tender.
6. When cooking is complete, remove from the oven to a plate. Sprinkle with the shredded Parmesan cheese and toss well. Serve warm.

Pepperoni Pizza Bites with Marinara
Prep time: 5 minutes | Cook time: 12 minutes | Serves 8

1 cup finely shredded Mozzarella cheese
½ cup chopped pepperoni
¼ cup Marinara sauce
1 (8-ounce / 227-g) can crescent roll dough
All-purpose flour, for dusting

1. In a small bowl, stir together the cheese, pepperoni and Marinara sauce.
2. Lay the dough on a lightly floured work surface. Separate it into 4 rectangles. Firmly pinch the perforations together and pat the dough pieces flat.
3. Divide the cheese mixture evenly between the rectangles and spread it out over the dough, leaving a ¼-inch border. Roll a rectangle up tightly, starting with the short end. Pinch the edge down to seal the roll. Repeat with the remaining rolls.
4. Slice the rolls into 4 or 5 even slices. Place the slices on the sheet pan, leaving a few inches between each slice.
5. Select Roast. Set temperature to 350ºF (180ºC) and set time to 12 minutes. Press Start to begin preheating.
6. Once the unit has preheated, place the pan into the oven.
7. After 6 minutes, rotate the pan and continue cooking.
8. When cooking is complete, the rolls will be golden brown with crisp edges. Remove the pan from the oven. Serve hot.

Cheddar Mushrooms with Pimientos
Prep time: 10 minutes | Cook time: 18 minutes | Serves 12

24 medium raw white button mushrooms, rinsed and drained
4 ounces (113 g) shredded extra-sharp Cheddar cheese
2 ounces (57 g) cream cheese, at room temperature
1 ounce (28 g) chopped jarred pimientos
2 tablespoons grated onion
⅛ teaspoon smoked paprika
⅛ teaspoon hot sauce
2 tablespoons butter, melted, divided
⅓ cup panko bread crumbs
2 tablespoons grated Parmesan cheese

1. Gently pull out the stems of the mushrooms and discard. Set aside.
2. In a medium bowl, stir together the Cheddar cheese, cream cheese, pimientos, onion, paprika and hot sauce.
3. Brush the sheet pan with 1 tablespoon of the melted butter. Arrange the mushrooms evenly on the pan, hollow-side up.
4. Place the cheese mixture into a large heavy plastic bag and cut off the end. Fill the mushrooms with the cheese mixture.
5. In a small bowl, whisk together the remaining 1 tablespoon of the melted butter, bread crumbs and Parmesan cheese. Sprinkle the panko mixture over each mushroom.
6. Select Roast. Set temperature to 350ºF (180ºC) and set time to 18 minutes. Press Start to begin preheating.
7. When the unit has preheated, place the pan into the oven.
8. After about 9 minutes, rotate the pan and continue cooking.
9. When cooking is complete, let the stuffed mushrooms rest for 2 minutes before serving.

Roasted Mushrooms with Garlic
Prep time: 5 minutes | Cook time: 27 minutes | Serves 4

16 garlic cloves, peeled
2 teaspoons olive oil, divided
16 button mushrooms
½ teaspoon dried marjoram
⅛ teaspoon freshly ground black pepper
1 tablespoon white wine

1. Place the garlic cloves on the sheet pan and drizzle with 1 teaspoon of the olive oil. Toss to coat well.
2. Select Roast. Set temperature to 350ºF (180ºC) and set time to 12 minutes. Press Start to begin preheating.
3. Once the unit has preheated, place the pan into the oven.
4. When cooking is complete, remove the pan from the oven. Stir in the mushrooms, marjoram and pepper. Drizzle with the remaining 1 teaspoon of the olive oil and the white wine. Toss to coat well. Return the pan to the oven.
5. Select Roast. Set temperature to 350ºF (180ºC) and set time to 15 minutes. place the pan into the oven.
6. Once done, the mushrooms and garlic cloves will be softened. Remove the pan from the oven.
7. Serve warm.

Cheddar Baked Potatoes with Chives
Prep time: 5 minutes | Cook time: 20 minutes | Serves 6

12 small red potatoes
1 teaspoon kosher salt, divided
1 tablespoon extra-virgin olive oil
¼ cup grated sharp Cheddar cheese
¼ cup sour cream
2 tablespoons chopped chives
2 tablespoons grated Parmesan cheese

1. Add the potatoes to a large bowl. Sprinkle with the ½ teaspoon of the salt and drizzle with the olive oil. Toss to coat. Place the potatoes in the sheet pan.
2. Select Roast. Set temperature to 375ºF (190ºC) and set time to 15 minutes. Press Start to begin preheating.
3. When the unit has preheated, place the pan into the oven.
4. After 10 minutes, rotate the pan and continue cooking.
5. When cooking is complete, remove the pan and let the potatoes rest for 5 minutes. Halve the potatoes lengthwise. Using a spoon, scoop the flesh into a bowl, leaving a thin shell of skin. Arrange the potato halves on the sheet pan.
6. Mash the potato flesh until smooth. Stir in the remaining ½ teaspoon of the salt, Cheddar cheese, sour cream and chives. Transfer the filling into a pastry bag with one corner snipped off. Pipe the filling into the potato shells, mounding up slightly. Sprinkle with the Parmesan cheese.
7. Select Roast. Set temperature to 375ºF (190ºC) and set time to 5 minutes. Place the pan into the oven.
8. When cooking is complete, the tops should be browning slightly. Remove the pan from the oven and let the potatoes cool slightly before serving.

Jalapeño Poppers with Cheddar
Prep time: 10 minutes | Cook time: 15 minutes | Serves 8

6 ounces (170 g) cream cheese, at room temperature
4 ounces (113 g) shredded Cheddar cheese
1 teaspoon chili powder
12 large jalapeño peppers, deseeded and sliced in half lengthwise
2 slices cooked bacon, chopped
¼ cup panko bread crumbs
1 tablespoon butter, melted

1. In a medium bowl, whisk together the cream cheese, Cheddar cheese and chili powder. Spoon the cheese mixture into the jalapeño halves and arrange them on the sheet pan.
2. In a small bowl, stir together the bacon, bread crumbs and butter. Sprinkle the mixture over the jalapeño halves.
3. Select Roast. Set temperature to 375ºF (190ºC) and set time to 15 minutes. Press Start to begin preheating.
4. When the unit has preheated, place the pan into the oven.
5. After 7 or 8 minutes, rotate the pan and continue cooking until the peppers are softened, the filling is bubbling and the bread crumbs are browned.
6. When cooking is complete, remove the pan from the oven. Let the poppers cool for 5 minutes before serving.

Green Chiles and Cheese Nachos
Prep time: 10 minutes | Cook time: 10 minutes | Serves 6

8 ounces (227 g) tortilla chips
3 cups shredded Monterey Jack cheese, divided
2 (7-ounce / 198-g) cans chopped green chiles, drained
1 (8-ounce / 227-g) can tomato sauce
¼ teaspoon dried oregano
¼ teaspoon granulated garlic
¼ teaspoon freshly ground black pepper
Pinch cinnamon
Pinch cayenne pepper

1. Arrange the tortilla chips close together in a single layer on the sheet pan. Sprinkle 1½ cups of the cheese over the chips. Arrange the green chiles over the cheese as evenly as possible. Top with the remaining 1½ cups of the cheese.
2. Select Roast. Set temperature to 375ºF (190ºC) and set time to 10 minutes. Press Start to begin preheating.
3. When the unit has preheated, place the pan into the oven.
4. After 5 minutes, rotate the pan and continue cooking.
5. Meanwhile, stir together the remaining ingredients in a bowl.
6. When cooking is complete, the cheese will be melted and starting to crisp around the edges of the pan. Remove the pan from the oven. Drizzle the sauce over the nachos and serve warm.

Honey Roasted Grapes with Basil
Prep time: 5 minutes | Cook time: 10 minutes | Serves 6

2 cups seedless red grapes, rinsed and patted dry
1 tablespoon apple cider vinegar
1 tablespoon honey
1 cup low-fat Greek yogurt
2 tablespoons 2 percent milk
2 tablespoons minced fresh basil

1. Spread the red grapes in the perforated pan and drizzle with the cider vinegar and honey. Lightly toss to coat.
2. Select Roast. Set temperature to 380ºF (193ºC) and set time to 10 minutes. Press Start to begin preheating.
3. Once the unit has preheated, place the pan into the oven.
4. When cooking is complete, the grapes will be wilted but still soft. Remove the pan from the oven.
5. In a medium bowl, whisk together the yogurt and milk. Gently fold in the grapes and basil.
6. Serve immediately.

Lemon-Pepper Chicken Wings
Prep time: 5 minutes | Cook time: 24 minutes | Serves 10

2 pounds (907 g) chicken wings
4½ teaspoons salt-free lemon pepper seasoning
1½ teaspoons baking powder
1½ teaspoons kosher salt

1. In a large bowl, toss together all the ingredients until well coated. Place the wings on the sheet pan, making sure they don't crowd each other too much.
2. Select Air Fry. Set temperature to 375ºF (190ºC) and set time to 24 minutes. Press Start to begin preheating.
3. Once preheated, slide the pan into the oven.
4. After 12 minutes, remove the pan from the oven. Use tongs to turn the wings over. Rotate the pan and return the pan to the oven to continue cooking.
5. When cooking is complete, the wings should be dark golden brown and a bit charred in places. Remove the pan from the oven and let rest for 5 minutes before serving.

Cheddar Sausage Balls
Prep time: 10 minutes | Cook time: 10 minutes | Serves 8

12 ounces (340 g) mild ground sausage
1½ cups baking mix
1 cup shredded mild Cheddar cheese
3 ounces (85 g) cream cheese, at room temperature
1 to 2 tablespoons olive oil

1. Line the perforated pan with parchment paper. Set aside.
2. Mix together the ground sausage, baking mix, Cheddar cheese, and cream cheese in a large bowl and stir to incorporate.
3. Divide the sausage mixture into 16 equal portions and roll them into 1-inch balls with your hands. Arrange the sausage balls on the parchment, leaving space between each ball. Brush the sausage balls with the olive oil.
4. Select Air Fry. Set temperature to 325ºF (163ºC) and set time to 10 minutes. Press Start to begin preheating.
5. Once preheated, place the pan into the oven. Flip the balls halfway through the cooking time.
6. When cooking is complete, the balls should be firm and lightly browned on both sides. Remove from the oven to a plate and serve warm.

Sugar Roasted Walnuts
Prep time: 5 minutes | Cook time: 15 minutes | Makes 4 cups

1 pound (454 g) walnut halves and pieces
½ cup granulated sugar
3 tablespoons vegetable oil
1 teaspoon cayenne pepper
½ teaspoon fine salt

1. Soak the walnuts in a large bowl with boiling water for a minute or two. Drain the walnuts. Stir in the sugar, oil and cayenne pepper to coat well. Spread the walnuts in a single layer on the sheet pan.
2. Select Roast. Set temperature to 325ºF (163ºC) and set time to 15 minutes. Press Start to begin preheating.
3. When the unit has preheated, place the pan into the oven.
4. After 7 or 8 minutes, remove the pan from the oven. Stir the nuts. Return the pan to the oven and continue cooking, check frequently.
5. When cooking is complete, the walnuts should be dark golden brown. Remove the pan from the oven. Sprinkle the nuts with the salt and let cool. Serve.

Balsamic Prosciutto-Wrapped Pears
Prep time: 12 minutes | Cook time: 6 minutes | Serves 8

2 large, ripe Anjou pears
4 thin slices Parma prosciutto
2 teaspoons aged balsamic vinegar

1. Peel the pears. Slice into 8 wedges and cut out the core from each wedge.
2. Cut the prosciutto into 8 long strips. Wrap each pear wedge with a strip of prosciutto. Place the wrapped pears in the sheet pan.
3. Select Broil. Set temperature to 400ºF (205ºC) and set time to 6 minutes. Press Start to begin preheating.
4. When the unit has preheated, place the pan into the oven.
5. After 2 or 3 minutes, check the pears. The pears should be turned over if the prosciutto is beginning to crisp up and brown. Return the pan to the oven and continue cooking.
6. When cooking is complete, remove the pan from the oven. Drizzle the pears with the balsamic vinegar and serve warm.

Breaded Zucchini Tots
Prep time: 15 minutes | Cook time: 6 minutes | Serves 8

2 medium zucchini (about 12 ounces / 340 g) shredded
1 large egg, whisked
½ cup grated pecorino romano cheese
½ cup panko bread crumbs
¼ teaspoon black pepper
1 clove garlic, minced
Cooking spray

1. Using your hands, squeeze out as much liquid from the zucchini as possible. In a large bowl, mix the zucchini with the remaining ingredients except the oil until well incorporated.
2. Make the zucchini tots: Use a spoon or cookie scoop to place tablespoonfuls of the zucchini mixture onto a lightly floured cutting board and form into 1-inch logs.
3. Spritz the perforated pan with cooking spray. Place the zucchini tots in the pan.
4. Select Air Fry. Set temperature to 375ºF (190ºC) and set time to 6 minutes. Press Start to begin preheating.
5. Once preheated, place the pan into the oven.
6. When cooking is complete, the tots should be golden brown. Remove from the oven to a serving plate and serve warm.

Ginger Shrimp with Sesame Seeds

Prep time: 15 minutes | Cook time: 8 minutes | Serves 4 to 6

½ pound (227 g) raw shrimp, peeled and deveined
1 egg, beaten
2 scallions, chopped, plus more for garnish
2 tablespoons chopped fresh cilantro
2 teaspoons grated fresh ginger
1 to 2 teaspoons sriracha sauce
1 teaspoon soy sauce
½ teaspoon toasted sesame oil
6 slices thinly sliced white sandwich bread
½ cup sesame seeds
Cooking spray
Thai chili sauce, for serving

1. In a food processor, add the shrimp, egg, scallions, cilantro, ginger, sriracha sauce, soy sauce and sesame oil, and pulse until chopped finely. You'll need to stop the food processor occasionally to scrape down the sides. Transfer the shrimp mixture to a bowl.
2. On a clean work surface, cut the crusts off the sandwich bread. Using a brush, generously brush one side of each slice of bread with shrimp mixture.
3. Place the sesame seeds on a plate. Press bread slices, shrimp-side down, into sesame seeds to coat evenly. Cut each slice diagonally into quarters.
4. Spritz the perforated pan with cooking spray. Spread the coated slices in a single layer in the perforated pan.
5. Select Air Fry. Set temperature to 400°F (205°C) and set time to 8 minutes. Press Start to begin preheating.
6. Once preheated, place the pan into the oven. Flip the bread slices halfway through.
7. When cooking is complete, they should be golden and crispy. Remove from the oven to a plate and let cool for 5 minutes. Top with the chopped scallions and serve warm with Thai chili sauce.

Tuna Melts with Mayo

Prep time: 10 minutes | Cook time: 6 minutes | Serves 6

2 (5- to 6-ounce / 142- to 170-g) cans oil-packed tuna, drained
1 large scallion, chopped
1 small stalk celery, chopped
⅓ cup mayonnaise
1 tablespoon chopped fresh dill
1 tablespoon capers, drained
¼ teaspoon celery salt
12 slices cocktail rye bread
2 tablespoons butter, melted
6 slices sharp Cheddar cheese

1. In a medium bowl, stir together the tuna, scallion, celery, mayonnaise, dill, capers and celery salt.
2. Brush one side of the bread slices with the butter. Arrange the bread slices on the sheet pan, buttered-side down. Scoop a heaping tablespoon of the tuna mixture on each slice of bread, spreading it out evenly to the edges.
3. Cut the cheese slices to fit the dimensions of the bread and place a cheese slice on each piece.
4. Select Roast. Set temperature to 375°F (190°C) and set time to 6 minutes. Press Start to begin preheating.
5. Once the unit has preheated, place the pan into the oven.
6. After 4 minutes, remove the pan from the oven and check the tuna melts. The tuna melts are done when the cheese has melted and the tuna is heated through. If needed, continue cooking.
7. When cooking is complete, remove the pan from the oven. Use a spatula to transfer the tuna melts to a clean work surface and slice each one in half diagonally. Serve warm.

Paprika Polenta Fries with Chili-Lime Mayo

Prep time: 10 minutes | Cook time: 28 minutes | Serves 4

Polenta Fries:
2 teaspoons vegetable or olive oil
¼ teaspoon paprika
1 pound (454 g) prepared polenta, cut into 3-inch × ½-inch strips
Salt and freshly ground black pepper, to taste

Chili-Lime Mayo:
½ cup mayonnaise
1 teaspoon chili powder
1 teaspoon chopped fresh cilantro
¼ teaspoon ground cumin
Juice of ½ lime
Salt and freshly ground black pepper, to taste

1. Mix the oil and paprika in a bowl. Add the polenta strips and toss until evenly coated. Transfer the polenta strips to the perforated pan.
2. Select Air Fry. Set temperature to 400°F (205°C) and set time to 28 minutes. Press Start to begin preheating.
3. Once preheated, place the pan into the oven. Stir the polenta strips halfway through the cooking time.
4. Meanwhile, whisk together all the ingredients for the chili-lime mayo in a small bowl.
5. When cooking is complete, remove the polenta fries from the oven to a plate. Season as desired with salt and pepper. Serve alongside the chili-lime mayo as a dipping sauce.

Lemon Ricotta with Capers

Prep time: 10 minutes | Cook time: 8 minutes | Serves 4 to 6

1½ cups whole milk ricotta cheese
2 tablespoons extra-virgin olive oil
2 tablespoons capers, rinsed
Zest of 1 lemon, plus more for garnish
1 teaspoon finely chopped fresh rosemary
Pinch crushed red pepper flakes
Salt and freshly ground black pepper, to taste
1 tablespoon grated Parmesan cheese

1. In a mixing bowl, stir together the ricotta cheese, olive oil, capers, lemon zest, rosemary, red pepper flakes, salt, and pepper until well combined.
2. Spread the mixture evenly in a baking dish.
3. Select Air Fry. Set temperature to 380ºF (193ºC) and set time to 8 minutes. Press Start to begin preheating.
4. Once preheated, place the baking dish in the oven.
5. When cooking is complete, the top should be nicely browned. Remove from the oven and top with a sprinkle of grated Parmesan cheese. Garnish with the lemon zest and serve warm.

Fried Pickle Spears with Chili

Prep time: 5 minutes | Cook time: 15 minutes | Serves 6

2 jars sweet and sour pickle spears, patted dry
2 medium-sized eggs
⅓ cup milk
1 teaspoon garlic powder
1 teaspoon sea salt
½ teaspoon shallot powder
⅓ teaspoon chili powder
⅓ cup all-purpose flour
Cooking spray

1. Spritz the perforated pan with cooking spray.
2. In a bowl, beat together the eggs with milk. In another bowl, combine garlic powder, sea salt, shallot powder, chili powder and all-purpose flour until well blended.
3. One by one, roll the pickle spears in the powder mixture, then dredge them in the egg mixture. Dip them in the powder mixture a second time for additional coating.
4. Place the coated pickles in the perforated pan.
5. Select Air Fry. Set temperature to 385ºF (196ºC) and set time to 15 minutes. Press Start to begin preheating.
6. Once preheated, place the pan into the oven. Stir the pickles halfway through the cooking time.
7. When cooking is complete, they should be golden and crispy. Transfer to a plate and let cool for 5 minutes before serving.

Honey Snack Mix

Prep time: 5 minutes | Cook time: 10 minutes | Makes about 10 cups

3 tablespoons butter, melted
½ cup honey
1 teaspoon salt
2 cups granola
2 cups sesame sticks
2 cups crispy corn puff cereal
2 cups mini pretzel crisps
1 cup cashews
1 cup pepitas
1 cup dried cherries

1. In a small mixing bowl, mix together the butter, honey, and salt until well incorporated.
2. In a large bowl, combine the granola, sesame sticks, corn puff cereal and pretzel crisps, cashews, and pepitas. Drizzle with the butter mixture and toss until evenly coated. Transfer the snack mix to a sheet pan.
3. Select Air Fry. Set temperature to 370ºF (188ºC) and set time to 10 minutes. Press Start to begin preheating.
4. Once preheated, slide the pan into the oven. Stir the snack mix halfway through the cooking time.
5. When cooking is complete, they should be lightly toasted. Remove from the oven and allow to cool completely. Scatter with the dried cherries and mix well. Serve immediately.

Cumin Tortilla Chips

Prep time: 5 minutes | Cook time: 5 minutes | Serves 4

½ teaspoon ground cumin
½ teaspoon paprika
½ teaspoon chili powder
½ teaspoon salt
Pinch cayenne pepper
8 (6-inch) corn tortillas, each cut into 6 wedges
Cooking spray

1. Lightly spritz the perforated pan with cooking spray.
2. Stir together the cumin, paprika, chili powder, salt, and pepper in a small bowl.
3. Place the tortilla wedges in the perforated pan in a single layer. Lightly mist them with cooking spray. Sprinkle the seasoning mixture on top of the tortilla wedges.
4. Select Air Fry. Set temperature to 375ºF (190ºC) and set time to 5 minutes. Press Start to begin preheating.
5. Once preheated, place the pan into the oven. Stir the tortilla wedges halfway through the cooking time.
6. When cooking is complete, the chips should be lightly browned and crunchy. Remove the pan from the oven. Let the tortilla chips cool for 5 minutes and serve.

Parmesan Snack Mix

Prep time: 5 minutes | Cook time: 6 minutes | Makes 6 cups

2 cups oyster crackers
2 cups Chex rice
1 cup sesame sticks
⅔ cup finely grated Parmesan cheese
8 tablespoons unsalted butter, melted
1½ teaspoons granulated garlic
½ teaspoon kosher salt

1. Toss together all the ingredients in a large bowl until well coated. Spread the mixture on the sheet pan in an even layer.
2. Select Roast. Set temperature to 350°F (180°C) and set time to 6 minutes. Press Start to begin preheating.
3. When the unit has preheated, place the pan into the oven.
4. After 3 minutes, remove the pan and stir the mixture. Return the pan to the oven and continue cooking.
5. When cooking is complete, the mixture should be lightly browned and fragrant. Let cool before serving.

Paprika Potato Chips

Prep time: 5 minutes | Cook time: 22 minutes | Serves 3

2 medium potatoes, preferably Yukon Gold, scrubbed
Cooking spray
2 teaspoons olive oil
½ teaspoon garlic granules
¼ teaspoon paprika
¼ teaspoon plus ⅛ teaspoon sea salt
¼ teaspoon freshly ground black pepper
Ketchup or hot sauce, for serving

1. Spritz the perforated pan with cooking spray.
2. On a flat work surface, cut the potatoes into ¼-inch-thick slices. Transfer the potato slices to a medium bowl, along with the olive oil, garlic granules, paprika, salt, and pepper and toss to coat well. Transfer the potato slices to the perforated pan.
3. Select Air Fry. Set temperature to 392°F (200°C) and set time to 22 minutes. Press Start to begin preheating.
4. Once preheated, place the pan into the oven. Stir the potato slices twice during the cooking process.
5. When cooking is complete, the potato chips should be tender and nicely browned. Remove from the oven and serve alongside the ketchup for dipping.

Cinnamon Apple Chips

Prep time: 10 minutes | Cook time: 10 minutes | Serves 4

2 apples, cored and cut into thin slices
2 heaped teaspoons ground cinnamon
Cooking spray

1. Spritz the perforated pan with cooking spray.
2. In a medium bowl, sprinkle the apple slices with the cinnamon. Toss until evenly coated. Spread the coated apple slices on the pan in a single layer.
3. Select Air Fry. Set temperature to 350°F (180°C) and set time to 10 minutes. Press Start to begin preheating.
4. Once preheated, place the pan into the oven.
5. After 5 minutes, remove the pan from the oven. Stir the apple slices and return the pan to the oven to continue cooking.
6. When cooking is complete, the slices should be until crispy Remove the pan from the oven and let rest for 5 minutes before serving.

Parmesan Crab Toasts

Prep time: 10 minutes | Cook time: 5 minutes | Makes 15 to 18 toasts

1 (6-ounce / 170-g) can flaked crab meat, well drained
3 tablespoons light mayonnaise
¼ cup shredded Parmesan cheese
¼ cup shredded Cheddar cheese
1 teaspoon Worcestershire sauce
½ teaspoon lemon juice
1 loaf artisan bread, French bread, or baguette, cut into ⅜-inch-thick slices

1. In a large bowl, stir together all the ingredients except the bread slices.
2. On a clean work surface, lay the bread slices. Spread ½ tablespoon of crab mixture onto each slice of bread.
3. Arrange the bread slices in the perforated pan in a single layer.
4. Select Bake. Set temperature to 360°F (182°C) and set time to 5 minutes. Press Start to begin preheating.
5. Once preheated, place the pan into the oven.
6. When cooking is complete, the tops should be lightly browned. Remove the pan from the oven. Serve warm.

Hush Puppies with Jalapeño
Prep time: 45 minutes | Cook time: 10 minutes | Serves 12

1 cup self-rising yellow cornmeal
½ cup all-purpose flour
1 teaspoon sugar
1 teaspoon salt
1 teaspoon freshly ground black pepper
1 large egg
⅓ cup canned creamed corn
1 cup minced onion
2 teaspoons minced jalapeño pepper
2 tablespoons olive oil, divided

1. Thoroughly combine the cornmeal, flour, sugar, salt, and pepper in a large bowl.
2. Whisk together the egg and corn in a small bowl. Pour the egg mixture into the bowl of cornmeal mixture and stir to combine. Stir in the minced onion and jalapeño. Cover the bowl with plastic wrap and place in the refrigerator for 30 minutes.
3. Line the perforated pan with parchment paper and lightly brush it with 1 tablespoon of olive oil.
4. Scoop out the cornmeal mixture and form into 24 balls, about 1 inch.
5. Arrange the balls on the parchment, leaving space between each ball.
6. Select Air Fry. Set temperature to 375ºF (190ºC) and set time to 10 minutes. Press Start to begin preheating.
7. Once preheated, place the pan into the oven.
8. After 5 minutes, remove the pan from the oven. Flip the balls and brush them with the remaining 1 tablespoon of olive oil. Return to the oven and continue cooking for 5 minutes until golden brown.
9. When cooking is complete, remove the balls (hush puppies) from the oven and serve on a plate.

Turkey-Wrapped Dates and Almonds
Prep time: 10 minutes | Cook time: 6 minutes | Makes 16 appetizers

16 whole dates, pitted
16 whole almonds
6 to 8 strips turkey bacon, cut in half

Special Equipment:
16 toothpicks, soaked in water for at least 30 minutes

1. On a flat work surface, stuff each pitted date with a whole almond.
2. Wrap half slice of bacon around each date and secure it with a toothpick.
3. Place the bacon-wrapped dates in the perforated pan.
4. Select Air Fry. Set temperature to 390ºF (199ºC) and set time to 6 minutes. Press Start to begin preheating.
5. Once preheated, place the pan into the oven.
6. When cooking is complete, transfer the dates to a paper towel-lined plate to drain. Serve hot.

Ginger Apple Wedges
Prep time: 10 minutes | Cook time: 12 minutes | Serves 4

2 medium apples, cored and sliced into ¼-inch wedges
1 teaspoon canola oil
2 teaspoons peeled and grated fresh ginger
½ teaspoon ground cinnamon
½ cup low-fat Greek vanilla yogurt, for serving

1. In a large bowl, toss the apple wedges with the canola oil, ginger, and cinnamon until evenly coated. Put the apple wedges in the perforated pan.
2. Select Air Fry. Set temperature to 360ºF (182ºC) and set time to 12 minutes. Press Start to begin preheating.
3. Once preheated, place the pan into the oven.
4. When cooking is complete, the apple wedges should be crisp-tender. Remove the apple wedges from the oven and serve drizzled with the yogurt.

Avocado Chips with Lime
Prep time: 15 minutes | Cook time: 10 minutes | Serves 4

1 egg
1 tablespoon lime juice
⅛ teaspoon hot sauce
2 tablespoons flour
¾ cup panko bread crumbs
¼ cup cornmeal
¼ teaspoon salt
1 large avocado, pitted, peeled, and cut into ½-inch slices
Cooking spray

1. Whisk together the egg, lime juice, and hot sauce in a small bowl.
2. On a sheet of wax paper, place the flour. In a separate sheet of wax paper, combine the bread crumbs, cornmeal, and salt.
3. Dredge the avocado slices one at a time in the flour, then in the egg mixture, finally roll them in the bread crumb mixture to coat well.
4. Place the breaded avocado slices in the perforated pan and mist them with cooking spray.
5. Select Air Fry. Set temperature to 390ºF (199ºC) and set time to 10 minutes. Press Start to begin preheating.
6. Once preheated, place the pan into the oven.
7. When cooking is complete, the slices should be nicely browned and crispy. Transfer the avocado slices to a plate and serve.

Carrot Chips

Prep time: 15 minutes | Cook time: 10 minutes | Serves 4

4 to 5 medium carrots, trimmed and thinly sliced
1 tablespoon olive oil, plus more for greasing
1 teaspoon seasoned salt

1. Toss the carrot slices with 1 tablespoon of olive oil and salt in a medium bowl until thoroughly coated.
2. Grease the perforated pan with the olive oil. Place the carrot slices in the greased pan.
3. Select Air Fry. Set temperature to 390°F (199°C) and set time to 10 minutes. Press Start to begin preheating.
4. Once preheated, place the pan into the oven. Stir the carrot slices halfway through the cooking time.
5. When cooking is complete, the chips should be crisp-tender. Remove the pan from the oven and allow to cool for 5 minutes before serving.

Mushroom and Sausage Empanadas

Prep time: 5 minutes | Cook time: 12 minutes | Serves 4

½ pound (227 g) Kielbasa smoked sausage, chopped
4 chopped canned mushrooms
2 tablespoons chopped onion
½ teaspoon ground cumin
¼ teaspoon paprika
Salt and black pepper, to taste
½ package puff pastry dough, at room temperature
1 egg, beaten
Cooking spray

1. Combine the sausage, mushrooms, onion, cumin, paprika, salt, and pepper in a bowl and stir to mix well.
2. Make the empanadas: Place the puff pastry dough on a lightly floured surface. Cut circles into the dough with a glass. Place 1 tablespoon of the sausage mixture into the center of each pastry circle. Fold each in half and pinch the edges to seal. Using a fork, crimp the edges. Brush them with the beaten egg and mist with cooking spray.
3. Spritz the perforated pan with cooking spray. Place the empanadas in the perforated pan.
4. Select Air Fry. Set temperature to 360°F (182°C) and set time to 12 minutes. Press Start to begin preheating.
5. Once preheated, place the pan into the oven. Flip the empanadas halfway through the cooking time.
6. When cooking is complete, the empanadas should be golden brown. Remove the pan from the oven. Allow them to cool for 5 minutes and serve hot.

Old Bay Fried Chicken Wings

Prep time: 10 minutes | Cook time: 13 minutes | Serves 4

2 tablespoons Old Bay seasoning
2 teaspoons baking powder
2 teaspoons salt
2 pounds (907 g) chicken wings, patted dry
Cooking spray

1. Combine the Old Bay seasoning, baking powder, and salt in a large zip-top plastic bag. Add the chicken wings, seal, and shake until the wings are thoroughly coated in the seasoning mixture.
2. Lightly spray the perforated pan with cooking spray. Lay the chicken wings in the perforated pan in a single layer and lightly mist them with cooking spray.
3. Select Air Fry. Set temperature to 400°F (205°C) and set time to 13 minutes. Press Start to begin preheating.
4. Once preheated, place the pan into the oven. Flip the wings halfway through the cooking time.
5. When cooking is complete, the wings should reach an internal temperature of 165°F (74°C) on a meat thermometer. Remove from the oven to a plate and serve hot.

Deviled Eggs with Mayo

Prep time: 20 minutes | Cook time: 16 minutes | Serves 12

3 cups ice
12 large eggs
½ cup mayonnaise
10 hamburger dill pickle chips, diced
¼ cup diced onion
2 teaspoons salt
2 teaspoons yellow mustard
1 teaspoon freshly ground black pepper
½ teaspoon paprika

1. Put the ice in a large bowl and set aside. Carefully place the eggs in the perforated pan.
2. Select Bake. Set temperature to 250°F (121°C) and set time to 16 minutes. Press Start to begin preheating.
3. Once preheated, place the pan into the oven.
4. When cooking is complete, transfer the eggs to the large bowl of ice to cool.
5. When cool enough to handle, peel the eggs. Slice them in half lengthwise and scoop out yolks into a small bowl. Stir in the mayonnaise, pickles, onion, salt, mustard, and pepper. Mash the mixture with a fork until well combined.
6. Fill each egg white half with 1 to 2 teaspoons of the egg yolk mixture.
7. Sprinkle the paprika on top and serve immediately.

Cumin Fried Chickpeas

Prep time: 5 minutes | Cook time: 18 minutes | Serves 4

½ teaspoon chili powder
½ teaspoon ground cumin
¼ teaspoon cayenne pepper
¼ teaspoon salt
1 (19-ounce / 539-g) can chickpeas, drained and rinsed
Cooking spray

1. Lina the perforated pan with parchment paper and lightly spritz with cooking spray.
2. Mix the chili powder, cumin, cayenne pepper, and salt in a small bowl.
3. Place the chickpeas in a medium bowl and lightly mist with cooking spray.
4. Add the spice mixture to the chickpeas and toss until evenly coated. Transfer the chickpeas to the parchment.
5. Select Air Fry. Set temperature to 390ºF (199ºC) and set time to 18 minutes. Press Start to begin preheating.
6. Once preheated, place the pan into the oven. Stir the chickpeas twice during cooking.
7. When cooking is complete, the chickpeas should be crunchy. Remove the pan from the oven. Let the chickpeas cool for 5 minutes before serving.

Paprika Nut Mix

Prep time: 5 minutes | Cook time: 20 minutes | Serves 6

2 cups mixed nuts (walnuts, pecans, and almonds)
2 tablespoons egg white
2 tablespoons sugar
1 teaspoon paprika
1 teaspoon ground cinnamon
Cooking spray

1. Line the perforated pan with parchment paper and spray with cooking spray.
2. Stir together the mixed nuts, egg white, sugar, paprika, and cinnamon in a small bowl until the nuts are fully coated. Place the nuts in the perforated pan.
3. Select Roast. Set temperature to 300ºF (150ºC) and set time to 20 minutes. Press Start to begin preheating.
4. Once preheated, place the pan into the oven. Stir the nuts halfway through the cooking time.
5. When cooking is complete, remove the pan from the oven. Transfer the nuts to a bowl and serve warm.

Garlic Fried Edamame

Prep time: 5 minutes | Cook time: 9 minutes | Serves 4

1 (16-ounce / 454-g) bag frozen edamame in pods
2 tablespoon olive oil, divided
½ teaspoon garlic salt
½ teaspoon salt
¼ teaspoon freshly ground black pepper
½ teaspoon red pepper flakes (optional)

1. Place the edamame in a medium bowl and drizzle with 1 tablespoon of olive oil. Toss to coat well.
2. Stir together the garlic salt, salt, pepper, and red pepper flakes (if desired) in a small bowl. Pour the mixture into the bowl of edamame and toss until the edamame is fully coated.
3. Grease the perforated pan with the remaining 1 tablespoon of olive oil.
4. Place the edamame in the greased pan.
5. Select Air Fry. Set temperature to 375ºF (190ºC) and set time to 9 minutes. Press Start to begin preheating.
6. Once preheated, place the pan into the oven. Stir the edamame once halfway through the cooking time.
7. When cooking is complete, the edamame should be crisp. Remove from the oven to a plate and serve warm.

Nutmeg Apple Chips

Prep time: 10 minutes | Cook time: 10 minutes | Serves 4

4 medium apples (any type will work) cored and thinly sliced
¼ teaspoon nutmeg
¼ teaspoon cinnamon
Cooking spray

1. Place the apple slices in a large bowl and sprinkle the spices on top. Toss to coat.
2. Put the apple slices in the perforated pan in a single layer and spray them with cooking spray.
3. Select Air Fry. Set temperature to 360ºF (182ºC) and set time to 10 minutes. Press Start to begin preheating.
4. Once preheated, place the pan into the oven. Stir the apple slices halfway through.
5. When cooking is complete, the apple chips should be crispy. Transfer the apple chips to a paper towel-lined plate and rest for 5 minutes before serving.

Brie Pear Sandwiches

Prep time: 10 minutes | Cook time: 6 minutes | Serves 4 to 8

8 ounces (227 g) Brie
8 slices oat nut bread
1 large ripe pear, cored and cut into ½-inch-thick slices
2 tablespoons butter, melted

1. Make the sandwiches: Spread each of 4 slices of bread with ¼ of the Brie. Top the Brie with the pear slices and remaining 4 bread slices.
2. Brush the melted butter lightly on both sides of each sandwich.
3. Arrange the sandwiches in the perforated pan.
4. Select Bake. Set temperature to 360°F (182°C) and set time to 6 minutes. Press Start to begin preheating.
5. Once preheated, place the pan into the oven.
6. When cooking is complete, the cheese should be melted. Remove the pan from the oven and serve warm.

Parmesan Bruschetta with Tomato

Prep time: 5 minutes | Cook time: 3 minutes | Serves 6

4 tomatoes, diced
⅓ cup shredded fresh basil
¼ cup shredded Parmesan cheese
1 tablespoon balsamic vinegar
1 tablespoon minced garlic
1 teaspoon olive oil
1 teaspoon salt
1 teaspoon freshly ground black pepper
1 loaf French bread, cut into 1-inch-thick slices
Cooking spray

1. Mix together the tomatoes and basil in a medium bowl. Add the cheese, vinegar, garlic, olive oil, salt, and pepper and stir until well incorporated. Set aside.
2. Spritz the perforated pan with cooking spray and lay the bread slices in the pan in a single layer. Spray the slices with cooking spray.
3. Select Bake. Set temperature to 250°F (121°C) and set time to 3 minutes. Press Start to begin preheating.
4. Once preheated, place the pan into the oven.
5. When cooking is complete, remove from the oven to a plate. Top each slice with a generous spoonful of the tomato mixture and serve.

Sesame Kale Chips

Prep time: 15 minutes | Cook time: 8 minutes | Serves 5

8 cups deribbed kale leaves, torn into 2-inch pieces
1½ tablespoons olive oil
¾ teaspoon chili powder
¼ teaspoon garlic powder
½ teaspoon paprika
2 teaspoons sesame seeds

1. In a large bowl, toss the kale with the olive oil, chili powder, garlic powder, paprika, and sesame seeds until well coated.
2. Transfer the kale to the perforated pan.
3. Select Air Fry. Set temperature to 350°F (180°C) and set time to 8 minutes. Press Start to begin preheating.
4. Once preheated, place the pan into the oven. Flip the kale twice during cooking.
5. When cooking is complete, the kale should be crispy. Remove from the oven and serve warm.

Pork and Turkey Sandwiches

Prep time: 20 minutes | Cook time: 8 minutes | Makes 4 sandwiches

8 slices ciabatta bread, about ¼-inch thick
Cooking spray
Toppings:
6 to 8 ounces (170 to 227 g) thinly sliced leftover roast pork
4 ounces (113 g) thinly sliced deli turkey
1 tablespoon brown mustard
⅓ cup bread and butter pickle slices
2 to 3 ounces (57 to 85 g) Pepper Jack cheese slices

1. On a clean work surface, spray one side of each slice of bread with cooking spray. Spread the other side of each slice of bread evenly with brown mustard.
2. Top 4 of the bread slices with the roast pork, turkey, pickle slices, cheese, and finish with remaining bread slices. Transfer to the perforated pan.
3. Select Air Fry. Set temperature to 390°F (199°C) and set time to 8 minutes. Press Start to begin preheating.
4. Once preheated, place the pan into the oven.
5. When cooking is complete, remove the pan from the oven. Cool for 5 minutes and serve warm.

Italian Rice Balls with Olives

Prep time: 20 minutes | Cook time: 10 minutes | Makes 8 rice balls

1½ cups cooked sticky rice
½ teaspoon Italian seasoning blend
¾ teaspoon salt, divided
8 black olives, pitted
1 ounce (28 g) Mozzarella cheese, cut into tiny pieces (small enough to stuff into olives)
2 eggs
⅓ cup Italian bread crumbs
¾ cup panko bread crumbs
Cooking spray

1. Stuff each black olive with a piece of Mozzarella cheese.
2. In a bowl, combine the cooked sticky rice, Italian seasoning blend, and ½ teaspoon of salt and stir to mix well. Form the rice mixture into a log with your hands and divide it into 8 equal portions. Mold each portion around a black olive and roll into a ball.
3. Transfer to the freezer to chill for 10 to 15 minutes until firm.
4. In a shallow dish, place the Italian bread crumbs. In a separate shallow dish, whisk the eggs. In a third shallow dish, combine the panko bread crumbs and remaining salt.
5. One by one, roll the rice balls in the Italian bread crumbs, then dip in the whisked eggs, finally coat them with the panko bread crumbs.
6. Arrange the rice balls in the perforated pan and spritz both sides with cooking spray.
7. Select Air Fry. Set temperature to 390ºF (199ºC) and set time to 10 minutes. Press Start to begin preheating.
8. Once preheated, place the pan into the oven. Flip the balls halfway through the cooking time.
9. When cooking is complete, the rice balls should be golden brown. Remove from the oven and serve warm.

Buttermilk-Marinated Chicken Wings

Prep time: 20 minutes | Cook time: 18 minutes | Serves 4

2 pounds (907 g) chicken wings
Cooking spray
Marinade:
1 cup buttermilk
½ teaspoon salt
½ teaspoon black pepper
Coating:
1 cup flour
1 cup panko bread crumbs
2 tablespoons poultry seasoning
2 teaspoons salt

1. Whisk together all the ingredients for the marinade in a large bowl.
2. Add the chicken wings to the marinade and toss well. Transfer to the refrigerator to marinate for at least an hour.
3. Spritz the perforated pan with cooking spray. Set aside.
4. Thoroughly combine all the ingredients for the coating in a shallow bowl.
5. Remove the chicken wings from the marinade and shake off any excess. Roll them in the coating mixture.
6. Place the chicken wings in the perforated pan in a single layer. Mist the wings with cooking spray.
7. Select Air Fry. Set temperature to 360ºF (182ºC) and set time to 18 minutes. Press Start to begin preheating.
8. Once preheated, place the pan into the oven. Flip the wings halfway through the cooking time.
9. When cooking is complete, the wings should be crisp and golden brown on the outside. Remove from the oven to a plate and serve hot.

Breaded Artichoke Bites

Prep time: 10 minutes | Cook time: 8 minutes | Serves 4

14 whole artichoke hearts packed in water
½ cup all-purpose flour
1 egg
⅓ cup panko bread crumbs
1 teaspoon Italian seasoning
Cooking spray

1. Drain the artichoke hearts and dry thoroughly with paper towels.
2. Place the flour on a plate. Beat the egg in a shallow bowl until frothy. Thoroughly combine the bread crumbs and Italian seasoning in a separate shallow bowl.
3. Dredge the artichoke hearts in the flour, then in the beaten egg, and finally roll in the bread crumb mixture until evenly coated.
4. Place the artichoke hearts in the perforated pan and mist them with cooking spray.
5. Select Air Fry. Set temperature to 375ºF (190ºC) and set time to 8 minutes. Press Start to begin preheating.
6. Once preheated, place the pan into the oven. Flip the artichoke hearts halfway through the cooking time.
7. When cooking is complete, the artichoke hearts should start to brown and the edges should be crispy. Remove the pan from the oven. Let the artichoke hearts sit for 5 minutes before serving.

Cinnamon Peach Wedges

Prep time: 10 minutes | Cook time: 10 to 13 minutes | Serves 4

2 tablespoons sugar
¼ teaspoon ground cinnamon
4 peaches, cut into wedges
Cooking spray

1. Toss the peaches with the sugar and cinnamon in a medium bowl until evenly coated.
2. Lightly spray the perforated pan with cooking spray. Place the peaches in the perforated pan in a single layer. Lightly mist the peaches with cooking spray.
3. Select Air Fry. Set temperature to 350ºF (180ºC) and set time to 10 minutes. Press Start to begin preheating.
4. Once preheated, place the pan into the oven.
5. After 5 minutes, remove from the oven and flip the peaches. Return to the oven and continue cooking for 5 minutes.
6. When cooking is complete, the peaches should be caramelized. If necessary, continue cooking for 3 minutes. Remove the pan from the oven. Let the peaches cool for 5 minutes and serve warm.

Horseradish Green Tomatoes

Prep time: 18 minutes | Cook time: 13 minutes | Serves 4

2 eggs
¼ cup buttermilk
½ cup bread crumbs
½ cup cornmeal
¼ teaspoon salt
1½ pounds (680 g) firm green tomatoes, cut into ¼-inch slices
Cooking spray
Horseradish Sauce:
¼ cup sour cream
¼ cup mayonnaise
2 teaspoons prepared horseradish
½ teaspoon lemon juice
½ teaspoon Worcestershire sauce
⅛ teaspoon black pepper

1. Spritz the perforated pan with cooking spray. Set aside.
2. In a small bowl, whisk together all the ingredients for the horseradish sauce until smooth. Set aside.
3. In a shallow dish, beat the eggs and buttermilk.
4. In a separate shallow dish, thoroughly combine the bread crumbs, cornmeal, and salt.
5. Dredge the tomato slices, one at a time, in the egg mixture, then roll in the bread crumb mixture until evenly coated.
6. Place the tomato slices in the perforated pan in a single layer. Spray them with cooking spray.
7. Select Air Fry. Set temperature to 390ºF (199ºC) and set time to 13 minutes. Press Start to begin preheating.
8. Once preheated, place the pan into the oven. Flip the tomato slices halfway through the cooking time.
9. When cooking is complete, the tomato slices should be nicely browned and crisp. Remove from the oven to a platter and serve drizzled with the prepared horseradish sauce.

BBQ Cheese Chicken Pizza

Prep time: 5 minutes | Cook time: 8 minutes | Serves 1

1 piece naan bread
¼ cup Barbecue sauce
¼ cup shredded Monterrey Jack cheese
¼ cup shredded Mozzarella cheese
½ chicken herby sausage, sliced
2 tablespoons red onion, thinly sliced
Chopped cilantro or parsley, for garnish
Cooking spray

1. Spritz the bottom of naan bread with cooking spray, then transfer to the perforated pan.
2. Brush with the Barbecue sauce. Top with the cheeses, sausage, and finish with the red onion.
3. Select Air Fry. Set temperature to 400ºF (205ºC) and set time to 8 minutes. Press Start to begin preheating.
4. Once preheated, place the pan into the oven.
5. When cooking is complete, the cheese should be melted. Remove the pan from the oven. Garnish with the chopped cilantro or parsley before slicing to serve.

Cheddar Black Bean and Corn Salsa

Prep time: 10 minutes | Cook time: 10 minutes | Serves 4

½ (15-ounce / 425-g) can corn, drained and rinsed
½ (15-ounce / 425-g) can black beans, drained and rinsed
¼ cup chunky salsa
2 ounces (57 g) reduced-fat cream cheese, softened
¼ cup shredded reduced-fat Cheddar cheese
½ teaspoon paprika
½ teaspoon ground cumin
Salt and freshly ground black pepper, to taste

1. Combine the corn, black beans, salsa, cream cheese, Cheddar cheese, paprika, and cumin in a medium bowl. Sprinkle with salt and pepper and stir until well blended.
2. Pour the mixture into a baking dish.
3. Select Air Fry. Set temperature to 325ºF (163ºC) and set time to 10 minutes. Press Start to begin preheating.
4. Once preheated, place the baking dish in the oven.
5. When cooking is complete, the mixture should be heated through. Rest for 5 minutes and serve warm.

Spinach Calzones with Mushrooms

Prep time: 15 minutes | Cook time: 26 to 27 minutes | Serves 4

2 tablespoons olive oil
1 onion, chopped
2 garlic cloves, minced
¼ cup chopped mushrooms
1 pound (454 g) spinach, chopped
1 tablespoon Italian seasoning
½ teaspoon oregano
Salt and black pepper, to taste
1½ cups marinara sauce
1 cup ricotta cheese, crumbled
1 (13-ounce / 369-g) pizza crust
Cooking spray

Make the Filling:
1. Heat the olive oil in a pan over medium heat until shimmering.
2. Add the onion, garlic, and mushrooms and sauté for 4 minutes, or until softened.
3. Stir in the spinach and sauté for 2 to 3 minutes, or until the spinach is wilted. Sprinkle with the Italian seasoning, oregano, salt, and pepper and mix well.
4. Add the marinara sauce and cook for about 5 minutes, stirring occasionally, or until the sauce is thickened.
5. Remove the pan from the heat and stir in the ricotta cheese. Set aside.

Make the Calzones:
6. Spritz the perforated pan with cooking spray. Set aside.
7. Roll the pizza crust out with a rolling pin on a lightly floured work surface, then cut it into 4 rectangles.
8. Spoon ¼ of the filling into each rectangle and fold in half. Crimp the edges with a fork to seal. Mist them with cooking spray. Transfer the calzones to the perforated pan.
9. Select Air Fry. Set temperature to 375ºF (190ºC) and set time to 15 minutes. Press Start to begin preheating.
10. Once preheated, place the pan into the oven. Flip the calzones halfway through the cooking time.
11. When cooking is complete, the calzones should be golden brown and crisp. Transfer the calzones to a paper towel-lined plate and serve.

Muffuletta Sliders with Olive Mix

Prep time: 10 minutes | Cook time: 6 minutes | Makes 8 sliders

¼ pound (113 g) thinly sliced deli ham
¼ pound (113 g) thinly sliced pastrami
4 ounces (113 g) low-fat Mozzarella cheese, grated
8 slider buns, split in half
Cooking spray
1 tablespoon sesame seeds

Olive Mix:
½ cup sliced green olives with pimentos
¼ cup sliced black olives
¼ cup chopped kalamata olives
1 teaspoon red wine vinegar
¼ teaspoon basil
⅛ teaspoon garlic powder

1. Combine all the ingredients for the olive mix in a small bowl and stir well.
2. Stir together the ham, pastrami, and cheese in a medium bowl and divide the mixture into 8 equal portions.
3. Assemble the sliders: Top each bottom bun with 1 portion of meat and cheese, 2 tablespoons of olive mix, finished by the remaining buns. Lightly spritz the tops with cooking spray. Scatter the sesame seeds on top.
4. Arrange the sliders in the perforated pan.
5. Select Bake. Set temperature to 360ºF (182ºC) and set time to 6 minutes. Press Start to begin preheating.
6. Once preheated, place the pan into the oven.
7. When cooking is complete, the cheese should be melted. Remove the pan from the oven and serve.

Chapter 15 Desserts

Rhubarb with Sloe Gin and Rosemary
Prep time: 10 minutes | Cook time: 30 minutes | Serves 44

1½ pounds (680 g) hothouse or main crop rhubarb stalks, all about the same thickness
½ cup granulated sugar
Finely grated zest of ½ orange
7 tablespoons sloe gin
3 tablespoons orange juice
2 rosemary sprigs, bruised
Whipped cream or heavy cream, to serve

1. Remove any leaves from the rhubarb and trim the bottoms. Cut into 1¼in lengths and put them into a large ovenproof baking dish. Scatter the sugar and zest on top and turn it all over with your hands, then pour in the sloe gin, orange juice, and 2 tablespoons of water, and finally tuck the rosemary sprigs under the rhubarb. Cover tightly with foil.
2. Select Bake. Set temperature to 350ºF (180ºC) and set time to 30 minutes. Select Start to begin preheating.
3. Once preheated, slide the baking dish into the oven.
4. When done, the rhubarb should be tender, but holding its shape and not collapsing.
5. Remove from the oven and leave to cool a bit in the dish. Eat warm, at room temperature, or chilled, with whipped cream or heavy cream.

Apricot Brioche with Croûtes Fraîche
Prep time: 10 minutes | Cook time: 25 minutes | Serves 6

6 thick slices of brioche
2 tablespoons superfine sugar, plus 4 teaspoons
¼ cup amaretto or Marsala
5 tablespoons very soft unsalted butter
3¾ ounces (106 g) good-quality marzipan, broken into small chunks
12 small ripe apricots, or 6 plums, pitted and quartered
Juice of ½ lemon
Generous ¼ cup sliced almonds
Confectioners' sugar, to dust (optional)
Crème fraîche, to serve

1. Put the brioche slices on a sheet pan or in a baking pan in a single layer.
2. Spoon the 2 tablespoons sugar into a small heatproof bowl and pour in ¼ cup of boiling water. Stir until dissolved, then leave this simple syrup to cool. Stir in the amaretto or Marsala.
3. Spoon the cooled syrup over the brioche slices, covering both sides.
4. Carefully, because the brioche will be very soft now, butter each slice on both sides.
5. Arrange chunks of marzipan on top, then add the apricot quarters. Squeeze on the lemon juice and sprinkle with the 4 teaspoons of superfine sugar.
6. Select Bake. Set temperature to 400ºF (205ºC) and set time to 25 minutes. Select Start to begin preheating.
7. Once preheated, slide the pan into the oven.
8. After 15 minutes, sprinkle with the almonds and continue baking for 10 minutes.
9. When done, the apricots should be tender and the bread and marzipan both golden.
10. Leave to cool a little (the slices will be very hot), then sift over some confectioners' sugar, if you want. Serve with crème fraîche.

Easy Nutmeg Butter Cookies
Prep time: 10 minutes | Cook time: 11 minutes | Makes 4 dozen

½ cup (1 stick) unsalted butter, melted
1 cup sugar
1 teaspoon vanilla extract
¼ teaspoon kosher salt
1 large egg
1 cup all-purpose flour
1½ teaspoons freshly grated nutmeg

1. Line two sheet pans with silicone baking mats (or use one sheet pan and bake in batches).
2. In a large bowl, mix together the butter and sugar. Stir in the vanilla and salt. Add the egg and beat until the mixture is smooth.
3. In a small bowl, whisk together the flour and nutmeg. Stir the flour mixture into the sugar and butter mixture just until blended.
4. Drop the batter by level teaspoons onto the prepared pans, leaving about 2 inches around the dough balls.
5. Select Bake. Set temperature to 350ºF (180ºC) and set time to 11 minutes. Select Start to begin preheating.
6. Once preheated, slide the pans into the oven.
7. When done, the cookies will spread, the edges will be golden brown, and the tops will start to collapse. Let cool on the pans for a few minutes, then transfer to a rack to cool completely.

Rice Pudding with Quince Jelly and Blackberry

Prep time: 10 minutes | Cook time: 40 minutes | Serves 4 to 6

For the Rice Pudding:
3½ tablespoons unsalted butter, plus more for the dish
3 tablespoons superfine sugar
Scant ½ cup short-grain rice (not risotto rice)
1 quart whole milk
⅔ cup heavy cream
Pinch of salt
Lots of freshly grated nutmeg
Finely grated zest of ½ unwaxed lemon
¼ teaspoon vanilla extract

To Serve:
Quince jelly (blackcurrant jelly is a good substitute)
⅓ pound (151 g) blackberries

1. Butter a baking dish.
2. Put the butter, sugar, rice, milk, and cream into a saucepan and bring gently to a boil, stirring to help the sugar dissolve. Add the salt, nutmeg, lemon zest, and vanilla extract and return to a simmer.
3. Simmer for about 4 minutes, stirring all the time, until you can feel that the rice grains have become slightly (only slightly) swollen. Pour the mixture into the prepared dish.
4. Select Bake. Set temperature to 325ºF (163ºC) and set time to 2 hours. Select Start to begin preheating.
5. Once preheated, slide the pan into the oven.
6. When done, the rice should be creamy and cooked, but shouldn't be dry or overly sticky.
7. As the pudding looks beautiful baked—it develops a lovely golden skin on top—take it to the table in the baking dish, and put the quince jelly and the blackberries in separate serving bowls so people can help themselves.

Rum-Plums with Brown Sugar Cream

Prep time: 10 minutes | Cook time: 20 minutes | Serves 6

For the Cream:
¾ cup plus 2 tablespoons heavy cream
⅔ cup Greek yogurt
3 to 4 heaping tablespoons dark brown sugar

For the Plums:
1¾ pounds (793 g) plums (preferably crimson-fleshed), halved and pitted
2 slices of crystallized ginger, very finely chopped
½ cup light brown sugar
½ teaspoon ground ginger
3 broad strips of lime zest, plus juice of 1 lime
⅔ cup dark rum, plus 3 tablespoons

1. Make the cream about 12 hours before you want to serve it. Lightly whip the heavy cream, then fold in the yogurt. Put this in a bowl and sprinkle evenly with the sugar. Cover with plastic wrap and refrigerate. The sugar will become soft and molasses-like.
2. Put the plums into a baking pan in a single layer. Arrange the fruits so they are cut sides up. Scatter the crystallized ginger around the plums. Mix the sugar with the ground ginger and sprinkle it over the top. Squeeze the lime juice over and tuck the pieces of lime zest under the fruits, then pour the ⅔ cup rum around them.
3. Select Bake. Set temperature to 375ºF (190ºC) and set time to 20 minutes. Select Start to begin preheating.
4. Once preheated, slide the pan into the oven.
5. When done, the fruit should be tender when pierced with a sharp knife, but not collapsing. Leave to cool completely; the juices should thicken as they cool. If they aren't thick enough, drain off the juices and boil them in a saucepan until they become more syrupy. Add the remaining 3 tablespoons of rum. Serve the plums, at room temperature, with the brown sugar cream.

Pumpkin Pudding with Vanilla Wafers

Prep time: 10 minutes | Cook time: 15 minutes | Serves 4

1 cup canned no-salt-added pumpkin purée (not pumpkin pie filling)
¼ cup packed brown sugar
3 tablespoons all-purpose flour
1 egg, whisked
2 tablespoons milk
1 tablespoon unsalted butter, melted
1 teaspoon pure vanilla extract
4 low-fat vanilla wafers, crumbled
Cooking spray

1. Coat a baking pan with cooking spray. Set aside.
2. Mix the pumpkin purée, brown sugar, flour, whisked egg, milk, melted butter, and vanilla in a medium bowl and whisk to combine. Transfer the mixture to the baking pan.
3. Select Bake. Set temperature to 350ºF (180ºC) and set time to 15 minutes. Press Start to begin preheating.
4. Once the oven has preheated, place the pan into the oven.
5. When cooking is complete, the pudding should be set.
6. Remove the pudding from the oven to a wire rack to cool.
7. Divide the pudding into four bowls and serve with the vanilla wafers sprinkled on top.

Glazed Sweet Bundt Cake
Prep time: 10 minutes | Cook time: 55 minutes | Serves 8

For the Cake:
1½ cups unsalted butter, at room temperature, plus more for preparing the pan
2 cups light brown sugar
1 cup sugar
5 large eggs
3 cups all-purpose flour,
plus more for preparing the pan
1 teaspoon table salt
1 cup sour cream, at room temperature
1 tablespoon vanilla extract

For the Glaze:
1 cup confectioners' sugar
2 tablespoons milk

Make the Cake
1. Butter and flour a 10-cup Bundt pan.
2. In a large bowl, using a wooden spoon or an electric mixer, cream together the butter, brown sugar, and sugar until the mixture is pale yellow and fluffy.
3. Add the eggs, one at a time, mixing after each addition until incorporated.
4. Add the flour, salt, sour cream, and vanilla and beat until just combined. Transfer the batter to the prepared pan.
5. Select Bake. Set temperature to 300°F (150°C) and set time to 55 minutes. Select Start to begin preheating.
6. Once preheated, slide the pan into the oven.
7. Remove the cake from the oven and set on a wire rack to cool for 10 minutes before inverting it onto a cake platter and letting it cool completely.

Make the Glaze
1. In a small bowl, whisk the confectioners' sugar and milk until smooth. Drizzle the glaze over the completely cooled cake.

Mexican Brownie Squares
Prep time: 10 minutes | Cook time: 25 minutes | Serves 8

½ cup unsalted butter, plus more for greasing
8 ounces (227 g) dark chocolate (60 to 72 percent cocoa)
1 cup sugar
2 teaspoons vanilla extract
Pinch salt
2 large eggs, at room temperature
1 teaspoon ground cinnamon
¼ teaspoon cayenne
¾ cup all-purpose flour

1. Line a square baking pan with aluminum foil, with the ends extending over the edges of the pan on two sides. Butter the foil and pan.
2. In a small saucepan, gently melt the butter and chocolate together over low heat, stirring, just until melted. Remove from the heat and let cool slightly. Pour into a large bowl.
3. Stir in the sugar, vanilla, and salt. Add the eggs, one at a time, and stir until completely blended.
4. Mix the cinnamon and cayenne into the flour until evenly dispersed. Add the flour to the chocolate mixture and beat until incorporated, about a minute. The batter may be a bit grainy looking.
5. Pour the batter into the prepared pan.
6. Select Bake. Set temperature to 350°F (180°C) and set time to 25 minutes. Select Start to begin preheating.
7. Once preheated, slide the pan into the oven.
8. When done, a toothpick inserted into the center should come out with crumbs but no raw batter sticking to it. Let cool for about 10 minutes. Pick up the edges of the foil and carefully lift the brownies out of the pan. Peel off the foil and let cool for another 5 minutes. Cut into squares.

Honey-Glazed Peach and Plum Kebabs
Prep time: 10 minutes | Cook time: 4 minutes | Serves 4

2 peaches, peeled, pitted, and thickly sliced
3 plums, halved and pitted
3 nectarines, halved and pitted
1 tablespoon honey
½ teaspoon ground cinnamon
¼ teaspoon ground allspice
Pinch cayenne pepper

Special Equipment:
8 metal skewers

1. Thread, alternating peaches, plums, and nectarines onto the metal skewers that fit into the oven.
2. Thoroughly combine the honey, cinnamon, allspice, and cayenne in a small bowl. Brush generously the glaze over the fruit skewers.
3. Transfer the fruit skewers to the perforated pan.
4. Select Air Fry. Set temperature to 400°F (205°C) and set time to 4 minutes. Press Start to begin preheating.
5. Once the oven has preheated, place the pan into the oven.
6. When cooking is complete, the fruit should be caramelized.
7. Remove the fruit skewers from the oven and let rest for 5 minutes before serving.

Blueberry and Peach Crisp
Prep time: 15 minutes | Cook time: 30 minutes | Serves 4

For the Filling:
Nonstick cooking spray
5 ripe yellow peaches
1 cup fresh or frozen blueberries
⅓ cup granulated sugar
1 tablespoon all-purpose flour
1 teaspoon grated lemon zest

For the Topping:
½ cup quick-cooking oatmeal
⅓ cup brown sugar
⅓ cup all-purpose flour
¼ cup blanched slivered almonds
1 teaspoon ground cinnamon
½ teaspoon ground cardamom
Pinch salt
4 tablespoons unsalted butter or vegan margarine

1. Spray a square baking pan with cooking spray.
2. Peel and pit the peaches. Slice them about ½-inch thick, then cut the slices in half. You should have about 4 cups of slices. Put them in a medium bowl and add the blueberries, sugar, flour, and lemon zest. Toss gently. Pour into the prepared baking pan.
3. For the topping, mix together the oatmeal, brown sugar, flour, almonds, cinnamon, cardamom, and salt. With a pastry cutter or a large fork, cut in the butter until the mixture is crumbly.
4. Sprinkle the topping over the fruit.
5. Select Bake. Set temperature to 350ºF (180ºC) and set time to 30 minutes. Select Start to begin preheating.
6. Once preheated, slide the pan into the oven.
7. When done, the top is lightly browned and the peaches are bubbling. Let cool for about 15 minutes before cutting. Serve warm.

Vanilla Coconut Cookies with Pecans
Prep time: 10 minutes | Cook time: 25 minutes | Serves 10

1½ cups coconut flour
1½ cups extra-fine almond flour
½ teaspoon baking powder
⅓ teaspoon baking soda
3 eggs plus an egg yolk, beaten
¾ cup coconut oil, at room temperature
1 cup unsalted pecan nuts, roughly chopped
¾ cup monk fruit
¼ teaspoon freshly grated nutmeg
⅓ teaspoon ground cloves
½ teaspoon pure vanilla extract
½ teaspoon pure coconut extract
⅛ teaspoon fine sea salt

1. Line the perforated pan with parchment paper.
2. Mix the coconut flour, almond flour, baking powder, and baking soda in a large mixing bowl.
3. In another mixing bowl, stir together the eggs and coconut oil. Add the wet mixture to the dry mixture.
4. Mix in the remaining ingredients and stir until a soft dough forms.
5. Drop about 2 tablespoons of dough on the parchment paper for each cookie and flatten each biscuit until it's 1 inch thick.
6. Select Bake. Set temperature to 370ºF (188ºC) and set time to 25 minutes. Press Start to begin preheating.
7. Once the oven has preheated, place the pan into the oven.
8. When cooking is complete, the cookies should be golden and firm to the touch.
9. Remove from the oven to a plate. Let the cookies cool to room temperature and serve.

Chocolate Blueberry Cupcakes
Prep time: 5 minutes | Cook time: 15 minutes | Serves 6

¾ cup granulated erythritol
1¼ cups almond flour
1 teaspoon unsweetened baking powder
3 teaspoons cocoa powder
½ teaspoon baking soda
½ teaspoon ground cinnamon
¼ teaspoon grated nutmeg
⅛ teaspoon salt
½ cup milk
1 stick butter, at room temperature
3 eggs, whisked
1 teaspoon pure rum extract
½ cup blueberries
Cooking spray

1. Spray a 6-cup muffin tin with cooking spray.
2. In a mixing bowl, combine the erythritol, almond flour, baking powder, cocoa powder, baking soda, cinnamon, nutmeg, and salt and stir until well blended.
3. In another mixing bowl, mix together the milk, butter, egg, and rum extract until thoroughly combined. Slowly and carefully pour this mixture into the bowl of dry mixture. Stir in the blueberries.
4. Spoon the batter into the greased muffin cups, filling each about three-quarters full.
5. Select Bake. Set temperature to 345ºF (174ºC) and set time to 15 minutes. Press Start to begin preheating.
6. Once the oven has preheated, place the muffin tin into the oven.
7. When done, the center should be springy and a toothpick inserted in the middle should come out clean.
8. Remove from the oven and place on a wire rack to cool. Serve immediately.

Mixed Berry Bake with Almond Topping

Prep time: 5 minutes | Cook time: 17 minutes | Serves 3

½ cup mixed berries
Topping:
1 egg, beaten
3 tablespoons almonds, slivered
3 tablespoons chopped pecans
2 tablespoons chopped walnuts
Cooking spray
3 tablespoons granulated Swerve
2 tablespoons cold salted butter, cut into pieces
½ teaspoon ground cinnamon

1. Lightly spray a baking dish with cooking spray.
2. Make the topping: In a medium bowl, stir together the beaten egg, nuts, Swerve, butter, and cinnamon until well blended.
3. Put the mixed berries in the bottom of the baking dish and spread the topping over the top.
4. Select Bake. Set temperature to 340ºF (171ºC) and set time to 17 minutes. Press Start to begin preheating.
5. Once the oven has preheated, place the baking dish into the oven.
6. When cooking is complete, the fruit should be bubbly and topping should be golden brown.
7. Allow to cool for 5 to 10 minutes before serving.

Peach and Blueberry Galette

Prep time: 10 minutes | Cook time: 20 minutes | Serves 6

1 pint blueberries, rinsed and picked through (about 2 cups)
2 large peaches or nectarines, peeled and cut into ½-inch slices (about 2 cups)
⅓ cup plus 2 tablespoons granulated sugar, divided
2 tablespoons unbleached all-purpose flour
½ teaspoon grated lemon zest (optional)
¼ teaspoon ground allspice or cinnamon
Pinch kosher or fine salt
1 (9-inch) refrigerated piecrust (or use homemade)
2 teaspoons unsalted butter, cut into pea-size pieces
1 large egg, beaten

1. Mix together the blueberries, peaches, ⅓ cup of sugar, flour, lemon zest (if desired) allspice, and salt in a medium bowl.
2. Unroll the crust on the sheet pan, patching any tears if needed. Place the fruit in the center of the crust, leaving about 1½ inches of space around the edges. Scatter the butter pieces over the fruit. Fold the outside edge of the crust over the outer circle of the fruit, making pleats as needed.
3. Brush the egg over the crust. Sprinkle the crust and fruit with the remaining 2 tablespoons of sugar.
4. Select Bake. Set temperature to 350ºF (180ºC) and set time to 20 minutes. Press Start to begin preheating.
5. Once the unit has preheated, place the pan into the oven.
6. After about 15 minutes, check the galette, rotating the pan if the crust is not browning evenly. Continue cooking until the crust is deep golden brown and the fruit is bubbling.
7. When cooking is complete, remove the pan from the oven and allow to cool for 10 minutes before slicing and serving.

Cinnamon Apple Fritters

Prep time: 30 minutes | Cook time: 7 minutes | Serves 6

1 cup chopped, peeled Granny Smith apple
½ cup granulated sugar
1 teaspoon ground cinnamon
1 cup all-purpose flour
1 teaspoon baking powder
1 teaspoon salt
2 tablespoons milk
2 tablespoons butter, melted
1 large egg, beaten
Cooking spray
¼ cup confectioners' sugar (optional)

1. Mix together the apple, granulated sugar, and cinnamon in a small bowl. Allow to sit for 30 minutes.
2. Combine the flour, baking powder, and salt in a medium bowl. Add the milk, butter, and egg and stir to incorporate.
3. Pour the apple mixture into the bowl of flour mixture and stir with a spatula until a dough forms.
4. Make the fritters: On a clean work surface, divide the dough into 12 equal portions and shape into 1-inch balls. Flatten them into patties with your hands.
5. Line the perforated pan with parchment paper and spray it with cooking spray.
6. Transfer the apple fritters onto the parchment paper, evenly spaced but not too close together. Spray the fritters with cooking spray.
7. Select Bake. Set temperature to 350ºF (180ºC) and set time to 7 minutes. Press Start to begin preheating.
8. Once the oven has preheated, place the pan into the oven. Flip the fritters halfway through the cooking time.
9. When cooking is complete, the fritters should be lightly browned.
10. Remove from the oven to a plate and serve with the confectioners' sugar sprinkled on top, if desired.

Don't stop until you're proud. -Chapter 15 Desserts |163

Glazed Chocolate Cake

Prep time: 15 minutes | Cook time: 40 minutes | Serves 10

For the Cake:
7 ounces (198 g) unsalted butter, at room temperature, plus more for the pan
5½ ounces (156 g) 70% cocoa solids dark chocolate, broken into pieces
1½ cups dark brown sugar
4 extra-large eggs, at room temperature, lightly beaten
3 tablespoons cocoa powder
1¾ cups all-purpose flour
1 teaspoon baking powder
Pinch of fine sea salt
½ cup full-bodied red wine (Merlot is perfect here)
Finely grated zest of 1 orange

For the Glaze:
4½ ounces (128 g) 70% cocoa solids dark chocolate, broken into pieces
½ cup heavy cream
2 tablespoons port
3 tablespoons confectioners' sugar, sifted

1. Butter a spring form cake pan and line the bottom with parchment paper.
2. Put the chocolate in a heatproof bowl set over a pan of gently simmering water (the bottom of the bowl shouldn't touch the water). Melt the chocolate, stirring a little to help it along. Remove the bowl and leave it to cool a little.
3. Cream the butter and sugar with electric beaters until lighter in color and fluffy. Gradually add the eggs, beating well after each addition.
4. In a bowl, sift together the cocoa, flour, baking powder, and salt, then fold the mixture into the batter. Stir in the red wine and the orange zest, then the melted chocolate. Scrape into the prepared pan.
5. Select Bake. Set temperature to 350°F (180°C) and set time to 40 minutes. Select Start to begin preheating.
6. Once preheated, slide the pan into the oven.
7. When done, a skewer inserted into the middle should come out clean. Allow the cake to cool in the pan, then turn it out onto a wire rack to cool completely.
8. For the glaze, put the chocolate into a heatproof bowl and melt as before. Stir in the cream with the port until the mixture is smooth, then whisk in the confectioners' sugar. Leave this to cool a little (though don't leave it until it has set), then pour it over the cake. Let the glaze set a bit before serving.

Peach and Apple Crisp with Oatmeal

Prep time: 10 minutes | Cook time: 10 to 12 minutes | Serves 4

2 peaches, peeled, pitted, and chopped
1 apple, peeled and chopped
2 tablespoons honey
3 tablespoons packed brown sugar
2 tablespoons unsalted butter, at room temperature
½ cup quick-cooking oatmeal
⅓ cup whole-wheat pastry flour
½ teaspoon ground cinnamon

1. Place the peaches, apple, and honey in a baking pan and toss until thoroughly combined.
2. Mix together the brown sugar, butter, oatmeal, pastry flour, and cinnamon in a medium bowl and stir until crumbly. Sprinkle this mixture generously on top of the peaches and apples.
3. Select Bake. Set temperature to 380°F (193°C) and set time to 10 minutes. Press Start to begin preheating.
4. Once the unit has preheated, place the pan into the oven.
5. Bake until the fruit is bubbling and the topping is golden brown.
6. Once cooking is complete, remove the pan from the oven and allow to cool for 5 minutes before serving.

Vanilla Walnuts Tart with Cloves

Prep time: 5 minutes | Cook time: 13 minutes | Serves 6

1 cup coconut milk
½ cup walnuts, ground
½ cup Swerve
½ cup almond flour
½ stick butter, at room temperature
2 eggs
1 teaspoon vanilla essence
¼ teaspoon ground cardamom
¼ teaspoon ground cloves
Cooking spray

1. Coat a baking pan with cooking spray.
2. Combine all the ingredients except the oil in a large bowl and stir until well blended. Spoon the batter mixture into the baking pan.
3. Select Bake. Set temperature to 360°F (182°C) and set time to 13 minutes. Press Start to begin preheating.
4. Once the oven has preheated, place the pan into the oven.
5. When cooking is complete, a toothpick inserted into the center of the tart should come out clean.
6. Remove from the oven and place on a wire rack to cool. Serve immediately.

Vanilla Chocolate Chip Cookies

Prep time: 10 minutes | Cook time: 20 minutes | Makes 4 dozen (1-by-1½-inch) cookies

1 cup unsalted butter, at room temperature
1 cup dark brown sugar
½ cup granulated sugar
2 large eggs
1 tablespoon vanilla extract
Pinch salt
2 cups old-fashioned rolled oats
1½ cups all-purpose flour
1 teaspoon baking powder
1 teaspoon baking soda
2 cups chocolate chips

1. Stir together the butter, brown sugar, and granulated sugar in a large mixing bowl until smooth and light in color.
2. Crack the eggs into the bowl, one at a time, mixing after each addition. Stir in the vanilla and salt.
3. Mix together the oats, flour, baking powder, and baking soda in a separate bowl. Add the mixture to the butter mixture and stir until mixed. Stir in the chocolate chips.
4. Spread the dough onto the sheet pan in an even layer.
5. Select Bake. Set temperature to 350ºF (180ºC) and set time to 20 minutes. Press Start to begin preheating.
6. Once the unit has preheated, place the pan into the oven.
7. After 15 minutes, check the cookie, rotating the pan if the crust is not browning evenly. Continue cooking for a total of 18 to 20 minutes or until golden brown.
8. When cooking is complete, remove the pan from the oven and allow to cool completely before slicing and serving.

Pineapple Sticks with Coconut

Prep time: 10 minutes | Cook time: 10 minutes | Serves 4

½ fresh pineapple, cut into sticks
¼ cup desiccated coconut

1. Place the desiccated coconut on a plate and roll the pineapple sticks in the coconut until well coated.
2. Lay the pineapple sticks in the perforated pan.
3. Select Air Fry. Set temperature to 400ºF (205ºC) and set time to 10 minutes. Press Start to begin preheating.
4. Once the oven has preheated, place the pan into the oven.
5. When cooking is complete, the pineapple sticks should be crisp-tender.
6. Serve warm.

Vanilla Pound Cake

Prep time: 5 minutes | Cook time: 30 minutes | Serves 8

1 stick butter, at room temperature
1 cup Swerve
4 eggs
1½ cups coconut flour
½ cup buttermilk
½ teaspoon baking soda
½ teaspoon baking powder
¼ teaspoon salt
1 teaspoon vanilla essence
A pinch of ground star anise
A pinch of freshly grated nutmeg
Cooking spray

1. Spray a baking pan with cooking spray.
2. With an electric mixer or hand mixer, beat the butter and Swerve until creamy. One at a time, mix in the eggs and whisk until fluffy. Add the remaining ingredients and stir to combine.
3. Transfer the batter to the prepared baking pan.
4. Select Bake. Set temperature to 320ºF (160ºC) and set time to 30 minutes. Press Start to begin preheating.
5. Once the oven has preheated, place the pan into the oven. Rotate the pan halfway through the cooking time.
6. When cooking is complete, the center of the cake should be springy.
7. Allow the cake to cool in the pan for 10 minutes before removing and serving.

Honey Apple-Peach Crumble

Prep time: 10 minutes | Cook time: 11 minutes | Serves 4

1 apple, peeled and chopped
2 peaches, peeled, pitted, and chopped
2 tablespoons honey
½ cup quick-cooking oatmeal
⅓ cup whole-wheat pastry flour
2 tablespoons unsalted butter, at room temperature
3 tablespoons packed brown sugar
½ teaspoon ground cinnamon

1. Mix together the apple, peaches, and honey in a baking pan until well incorporated.
2. In a bowl, combine the oatmeal, pastry flour, butter, brown sugar, and cinnamon and stir to mix well. Spread this mixture evenly over the fruit.
3. Select Bake. Set temperature to 380ºF (193ºC) and set time to 11 minutes. Press Start to begin preheating.
4. Once the oven has preheated, place the pan into the oven.
5. When cooking is complete, the fruit should be bubbling around the edges and the topping should be golden brown.
6. Remove from the oven and serve warm.

Peanut Butter Bread Pudding

Prep time: 10 minutes | Cook time: 10 minutes | Serves 8

1 egg
1 egg yolk
¾ cup chocolate milk
3 tablespoons brown sugar
3 tablespoons peanut butter
2 tablespoons cocoa powder
1 teaspoon vanilla
5 slices firm white bread, cubed
Nonstick cooking spray

1. Spritz a baking pan with nonstick cooking spray.
2. Whisk together the egg, egg yolk, chocolate milk, brown sugar, peanut butter, cocoa powder, and vanilla until well combined.
3. Fold in the bread cubes and stir to mix well. Allow the bread soak for 10 minutes.
4. When ready, transfer the egg mixture to the prepared baking pan.
5. Select Bake. Set temperature to 330ºF (166ºC) and set time to 10 minutes. Press Start to begin preheating.
6. Once the oven has preheated, place the pan into the oven.
7. When done, the pudding should be just firm to the touch.
8. Serve at room temperature.

Chocolate Cake with Blackberries

Prep time: 10 minutes | Cook time: 22 minutes | Serves 8

½ cup butter, at room temperature
2 ounces (57 g) Swerve
4 eggs
1 cup almond flour
1 teaspoon baking soda
⅓ teaspoon baking powder
½ cup cocoa powder
1 teaspoon orange zest
⅓ cup fresh blackberries

1. With an electric mixer or hand mixer, beat the butter and Swerve until creamy.
2. One at a time, mix in the eggs and beat again until fluffy.
3. Add the almond flour, baking soda, baking powder, cocoa powder, orange zest and mix well. Add the butter mixture to the almond flour mixture and stir until well blended. Fold in the blackberries.
4. Scrape the batter into a baking pan.
5. Select Bake. Set temperature to 335ºF (168ºC) and set time to 22 minutes. Press Start to begin preheating.
6. Once the oven has preheated, place the pan into the oven.
7. When cooking is complete, a toothpick inserted into the center of the cake should come out clean.
8. Allow the cake cool on a wire rack to room temperature. Serve immediately.

Sour Cherry Brioche Pudding

Prep time: 10 minutes | Cook time: 45 minutes | Serves 8

1 cup dried sour cherries
Scant ½ cup unsweetened pomegranate juice
1¼ cups heavy cream
1¼ cups whole milk
Pinch of sea salt
Seeds from 2 cardamom pods, ground
3 extra-large eggs, plus 1 extra-large egg yolk
generous ½ cup superfine sugar
9 ounces (255 g) brioche loaf
2½ tablespoons unsalted butter, softened
1 teaspoon rose water, or to taste
Squeeze of lemon or lime juice
Confectioners' sugar, to dust

1. Put the dried cherries in a small saucepan and add enough pomegranate juice to just cover. Bring to a boil, then take off the heat and leave the cherries to sit and plump up (they need at least 30 minutes, but longer is fine).
2. Bring the cream, milk, and salt to a boil in a heavy-bottomed saucepan with the cardamom, then leave for 15 minutes off the heat. Beat the eggs, egg yolk, and sugar together. Pour the warm milk mixture onto this, stirring constantly.
3. Slice the brioche, butter it, and layer it in a 2 quart ovenproof dish, scattering the soaked cherries and any leftover pomegranate juice on as you layer the bread (try to get most of the cherries under the bread, or they might burn). Add some rose water to the egg and cream mixture—not too much—and a squeeze of lemon or lime juice, then taste it. You should be able to detect the rose water, but it shouldn't be too strong. Brands differ in strength, so you have to taste and decide if you need a little more.
4. Pour the egg and milk mixture evenly over the layers of bread. Leave the pudding to sit for 30 minutes; this will make it lighter.
5. Put the dish into a baking pan and carefully pour enough boiling water into the pan to come about one-third of the way up the sides of the dish.
6. Select Bake. Set temperature to 375ºF (190ºC) and set time to 45 minutes. Select Start to begin preheating.
7. Once preheated, slide the pan into the oven.
8. When done, the pudding will be puffy, golden, and just set on the top.
9. Remove the dish from the oven and leave to cool slightly—the pudding will continue to cook in the residual heat for a while—then dust with confectioners' sugar before serving.

Vanilla Ricotta Cake with Lemon
Prep time: 5 minutes | Cook time: 25 minutes | Serves 6

17.5 ounces (496 g) ricotta cheese
5.4 ounces (153 g) sugar
3 eggs, beaten
3 tablespoons flour
1 lemon, juiced and zested
2 teaspoons vanilla extract

1. In a large mixing bowl, stir together all the ingredients until the mixture reaches a creamy consistency.
2. Pour the mixture into a baking pan and place in the oven.
3. Select Bake. Set temperature to 320ºF (160ºC) and set time to 25 minutes. Press Start to begin preheating.
4. Once the oven has preheated, place the pan into the oven.
5. When cooking is complete, a toothpick inserted in the center should come out clean.
6. Allow to cool for 10 minutes on a wire rack before serving.

Cinnamon Pineapple Rings
Prep time: 5 minutes | Cook time: 7 minutes | Serves 6

1 cup rice milk
⅔ cup flour
½ cup water
¼ cup unsweetened flaked coconut
4 tablespoons sugar
½ teaspoon baking soda
½ teaspoon baking powder
½ teaspoon vanilla essence
½ teaspoon ground cinnamon
¼ teaspoon ground anise star
Pinch of kosher salt
1 medium pineapple, peeled and sliced

1. In a large bowl, stir together all the ingredients except the pineapple.
2. Dip each pineapple slice into the batter until evenly coated.
3. Arrange the pineapple slices in the perforated pan.
4. Select Air Fry. Set temperature to 380ºF (193ºC) and set time to 7 minutes. Press Start to begin preheating.
5. Once the oven has preheated, place the pan into the oven.
6. When cooking is complete, the pineapple rings should be golden brown.
7. Remove from the oven to a plate and cool for 5 minutes before serving.

Vanilla Fudge Pie
Prep time: 15 minutes | Cook time: 26 minutes | Serves 8

1½ cups sugar
½ cup self-rising flour
⅓ cup unsweetened cocoa powder
3 large eggs, beaten
12 tablespoons (1½ sticks) butter, melted
1½ teaspoons vanilla extract
1 (9-inch) unbaked pie crust
¼ cup confectioners' sugar (optional)

1. Thoroughly combine the sugar, flour, and cocoa powder in a medium bowl. Add the beaten eggs and butter and whisk to combine. Stir in the vanilla.
2. Pour the prepared filling into the pie crust and transfer to the perforated pan.
3. Select Bake. Set temperature to 350ºF (180ºC) and set time to 26 minutes. Press Start to begin preheating.
4. Once the oven has preheated, place the pan into the oven.
5. When cooking is complete, the pie should be set.
6. Allow the pie to cool for 5 minutes. Sprinkle with the confectioners' sugar, if desired. Serve warm.

Blackberry Cobbler
Prep time: 15 minutes | Cook time: 20 to 25 minutes | Serves 6

3 cups fresh or frozen blackberries
1¾ cups sugar, divided
1 teaspoon vanilla extract
8 tablespoons (1 stick) butter, melted
1 cup self-rising flour
Cooking spray

1. Spritz a baking pan with cooking spray.
2. Mix the blackberries, 1 cup of sugar, and vanilla in a medium bowl and stir to combine.
3. Stir together the melted butter, remaining sugar, and flour in a separate medium bowl.
4. Spread the blackberry mixture evenly in the prepared pan and top with the butter mixture.
5. Select Bake. Set temperature to 350ºF (180ºC) and set time to 25 minutes. Press Start to begin preheating.
6. Once the oven has preheated, place the pan into the oven.
7. After about 20 minutes, check if the cobbler has a golden crust and you can't see any batter bubbling while it cooks. If needed, bake for another 5 minutes.
8. Remove from the oven and place on a wire rack to cool to room temperature. Serve immediately.

Don't stop until you're proud. -Chapter 15 Desserts

Vanilla Baked Peaches and Blueberries
Prep time: 10 minutes | Cook time: 10 minutes | Serves 6

3 peaches, peeled, halved, and pitted
2 tablespoons packed brown sugar
1 cup plain Greek yogurt
¼ teaspoon ground cinnamon
1 teaspoon pure vanilla extract
1 cup fresh blueberries

1. Arrange the peaches in the perforated pan, cut-side up. Top with a generous sprinkle of brown sugar.
2. Select Bake. Set temperature to 380ºF (193ºC) and set time to 10 minutes. Press Start to begin preheating.
3. Once the oven has preheated, place the pan into the oven.
4. Meanwhile, whisk together the yogurt, cinnamon, and vanilla in a small bowl until smooth.
5. When cooking is complete, the peaches should be lightly browned and caramelized.
6. Remove the peaches from the oven to a plate. Serve topped with the yogurt mixture and fresh blueberries.

Chocolate Chip Brownies
Prep time: 10 minutes | Cook time: 20 minutes | Makes 1 dozen brownies

1 egg
¼ cup brown sugar
2 tablespoons white sugar
2 tablespoons safflower oil
1 teaspoon vanilla
⅓ cup all-purpose flour
¼ cup cocoa powder
¼ cup white chocolate chips
Nonstick cooking spray

1. Spritz a baking pan with nonstick cooking spray.
2. Whisk together the egg, brown sugar, and white sugar in a medium bowl. Mix in the safflower oil and vanilla and stir to combine.
3. Add the flour and cocoa powder and stir just until incorporated. Fold in the white chocolate chips.
4. Scrape the batter into the prepared baking pan.
5. Select Bake. Set temperature to 340ºF (171ºC) and set time to 20 minutes. Press Start to begin preheating.
6. Once the oven has preheated, place the pan into the oven.
7. When done, the brownie should spring back when touched lightly with your fingers.
8. Transfer to a wire rack and let cool for 30 minutes before slicing to serve.

White Chocolate Cookies with Nutmeg
Prep time: 5 minutes | Cook time: 11 minutes | Serves 10

8 ounces (227 g) unsweetened white chocolate
2 eggs, well beaten
¾ cup butter, at room temperature
1⅔ cups almond flour
½ cup coconut flour
¾ cup granulated Swerve
2 tablespoons coconut oil
⅓ teaspoon grated nutmeg
⅓ teaspoon ground allspice
⅓ teaspoon ground anise star
¼ teaspoon fine sea salt

1. Line a baking sheet with parchment paper.
2. Combine all the ingredients in a mixing bowl and knead for about 3 to 4 minutes, or until a soft dough forms. Transfer to the refrigerator to chill for 20 minutes.
3. Make the cookies: Roll the dough into 1-inch balls and transfer to the parchment-lined baking sheet, spacing 2 inches apart. Flatten each with the back of a spoon.
4. Select Bake. Set temperature to 350ºF (180ºC) and set time to 11 minutes. Press Start to begin preheating.
5. Once the oven has preheated, place the baking sheet into the oven.
6. When cooking is complete, the cookies should be golden and firm to the touch.
7. Transfer to a wire rack and let the cookies cool completely. Serve immediately.

Mixed Berry Crisp with Cloves
Prep time: 5 minutes | Cook time: 20 minutes | Serves 6

1 tablespoon butter, melted
12 ounces (340 g) mixed berries
⅓ cup granulated Swerve
1 teaspoon pure vanilla extract
½ teaspoon ground cinnamon
¼ teaspoon ground cloves
¼ teaspoon grated nutmeg
½ cup coconut chips, for garnish

1. Coat a baking pan with melted butter.
2. Put the remaining ingredients except the coconut chips in the prepared baking pan.
3. Select Bake. Set temperature to 330ºF (166ºC) and set time to 20 minutes. Press Start to begin preheating.
4. Once the oven has preheated, place the pan into the oven.
5. When cooking is complete, remove from the oven. Serve garnished with the coconut chips.

Chocolate S'mores

Prep time: 5 minutes | Cook time: 3 minutes | Makes 12 s'mores

12 whole cinnamon graham crackers, halved
2 (1.55-ounce / 44-g) chocolate bars, cut into 12 pieces
12 marshmallows

1. Arrange 12 graham cracker squares in the perforated pan in a single layer.
2. Top each square with a piece of chocolate.
3. Select Bake. Set temperature to 350ºF (180ºC) and set time to 3 minutes. Press Start to begin preheating.
4. Once the oven has preheated, place the pan into the oven.
5. After 2 minutes, remove the pan and place a marshmallow on each piece of melted chocolate. Return the pan to the oven and continue to cook for another 1 minute.
6. Remove from the oven to a serving plate.
7. Serve topped with the remaining graham cracker squares

Pecan Pie with Chocolate Chips

Prep time: 20 minutes | Cook time: 25 minutes | Serves 8

1 (9-inch) unbaked pie crust
Filling:
2 large eggs
⅓ cup butter, melted
1 cup sugar
½ cup all-purpose flour
1 cup milk chocolate chips
1½ cups coarsely chopped pecans
2 tablespoons bourbon

1. Whisk the eggs and melted butter in a large bowl until creamy.
2. Add the sugar and flour and stir to incorporate. Mix in the milk chocolate chips, pecans, and bourbon and stir until well combined.
3. Use a fork to prick holes in the bottom and sides of the pie crust. Pour the prepared filling into the pie crust. Place the pie crust in the perforated pan.
4. Select Bake. Set temperature to 350ºF (180ºC) and set time to 25 minutes. Press Start to begin preheating.
5. Once the oven has preheated, place the pan into the oven.
6. When cooking is complete, a toothpick inserted in the center should come out clean.
7. Allow the pie cool for 10 minutes in the pan before serving.

Apple Bake with Cinnamon

Prep time: 15 minutes | Cook time: 12 minutes | Serves 4

1 cup packed light brown sugar
2 teaspoons ground cinnamon
2 medium Granny Smith apples, peeled and diced

1. Thoroughly combine the brown sugar and cinnamon in a medium bowl.
2. Add the apples to the bowl and stir until well coated. Transfer the apples to a baking pan.
3. Select Bake. Set temperature to 350ºF (180ºC) and set time to 12 minutes. Press Start to begin preheating.
4. Once the oven has preheated, place the pan into the oven.
5. After about 9 minutes, stir the apples and bake for an additional 3 minutes. When cooking is complete, the apples should be softened.
6. Serve warm.

Spice Cake with Creamy Frosting

Prep time: 20 minutes | Cook time: 25 minutes | Serves 6

1 cup applesauce
¼ cup skim milk or low-fat soy milk
1 tablespoon vegetable oil
½ cup brown sugar
1 egg
1½ cups unbleached flour
1 teaspoon baking powder
½ teaspoon baking soda
¼ teaspoon grated nutmeg
½ teaspoon ground cinnamon
½ teaspoon grated orange zest
Salt, to taste
For the Creamy Frosting:
1½ cups confectioners' sugar, sifted
3 tablespoons margarine
1 tablespoon fat-free half-and-half or skim milk
½ teaspoon vanilla extract
Salt, to taste
½ cup sweetened flaked coconut
1 (5-ounce / 142-g) can mandarin oranges, drained well

1. Stir together the applesauce, milk, oil, sugar, and egg in a small bowl. Set aside.
2. Combine the flour, baking powder, nutmeg, cinnamon, orange zest, and salt in a medium bowl. Add the applesauce mixture and stir to mix well. Pour the batter into an oiled or nonstick square baking (cake) pan.
3. Select Bake. Set temperature to 350ºF (180ºC) and set time to 25 minutes. Select Start to begin preheating.
4. Once preheated, slide the pan into the oven.
5. When done, a toothpick inserted in the center should come out clean. Frost with creamy frosting.

Don't stop until you're proud. -Chapter 15 Desserts

Vanilla Chocolate Cake

Prep time: 5 minutes | Cook time: 15 minutes | Serves 6

½ cup unsweetened chocolate, chopped
½ stick butter, at room temperature
1 tablespoon liquid stevia
1½ cups coconut flour
2 eggs, whisked
½ teaspoon vanilla extract
A pinch of fine sea salt
Cooking spray

1. Place the chocolate, butter, and stevia in a microwave-safe bowl. Microwave for about 30 seconds until melted.
2. Let the chocolate mixture cool for 5 to 10 minutes.
3. Add the remaining ingredients to the bowl of chocolate mixture and whisk to incorporate.
4. Lightly spray a baking pan with cooking spray.
5. Scrape the chocolate mixture into the prepared baking pan.
6. Select Bake. Set temperature to 330°F (166°C) and set time to 15 minutes. Press Start to begin preheating.
7. Once the oven has preheated, place the pan into the oven.
8. When cooking is complete, the top should spring back lightly when gently pressed with your fingers.
9. Let the cake cool for 5 minutes and serve.

Cinnamon Apple with Apricots

Prep time: 5 minutes | Cook time: 15 to 18 minutes | Serves 4

4 large apples, peeled and sliced into 8 wedges
2 tablespoons olive oil
½ cup dried apricots, chopped
1 to 2 tablespoons sugar
½ teaspoon ground cinnamon

1. Toss the apple wedges with the olive oil in a mixing bowl until well coated.
2. Place the apple wedges in the perforated pan.
3. Select Air Fry. Set temperature to 350°F (180°C) and set time to 15 minutes. Press Start to begin preheating.
4. Once the oven has preheated, place the pan into the oven.
5. After about 12 minutes, remove from the oven. Sprinkle with the dried apricots and air fry for another 3 minutes.
6. Meanwhile, thoroughly combine the sugar and cinnamon in a small bowl.
7. Remove the apple wedges from the oven to a plate. Serve sprinkled with the sugar mixture.

Coconut Orange Cake

Prep time: 5 minutes | Cook time: 17 minutes | Serves 6

1 stick butter, melted
¾ cup granulated Swerve
2 eggs, beaten
¾ cup coconut flour
¼ teaspoon salt
⅓ teaspoon grated nutmeg
⅓ cup coconut milk
1¼ cups almond flour
½ teaspoon baking powder
2 tablespoons unsweetened orange jam
Cooking spray

1. Coat a baking pan with cooking spray. Set aside.
2. In a large mixing bowl, whisk together the melted butter and granulated Swerve until fluffy.
3. Mix in the beaten eggs and whisk again until smooth. Stir in the coconut flour, salt, and nutmeg and gradually pour in the coconut milk. Add the remaining ingredients and stir until well incorporated.
4. Scrape the batter into the baking pan.
5. Select Bake. Set temperature to 355°F (179°C) and set time to 17 minutes. Press Start to begin preheating.
6. Once the oven has preheated, place the pan into the oven.
7. When cooking is complete, the top of the cake should spring back when gently pressed with your fingers.
8. Remove from the oven to a wire rack to cool. Serve chilled.

Chapter 16 Staples

Lemon Anchocy Dressing
Prep time: 5 minutes | Cook time: 0 minutes | Makes about ⅔ cup

½ cup extra-virgin olive oil
2 tablespoons freshly squeezed lemon juice
1 teaspoon anchovy paste
¼ teaspoon kosher salt or ⅛ teaspoon fine salt
¼ teaspoon minced or pressed garlic
1 egg, beaten

1. Add all the ingredients to a tall, narrow container.
2. Purée the mixture with an immersion blender until smooth.
3. Use immediately.

Teriyaki Sauce
Prep time: 5 minutes | Cook time: 0 minutes | Makes ¾ cup

½ cup soy sauce
3 tablespoons honey
1 tablespoon rice wine or dry sherry
1 tablespoon rice vinegar
2 teaspoons minced fresh ginger
2 garlic cloves, smashed

1. Beat together all the ingredients in a small bowl.
2. Use immediately.

Baked White Rice
Prep time: 3 minutes | Cook time: 35 minutes | Makes about 4 cups

1 cup long-grain white rice, rinsed and drained
1 tablespoon unsalted butter, melted, or 1 tablespoon extra-virgin olive oil
2 cups water
1 teaspoon kosher salt or ½ teaspoon fine salt

1. Add the butter and rice to the baking pan and stir to coat. Pour in the water and sprinkle with the salt. Stir until the salt is dissolved.
2. Select Bake. Set temperature to 325°F (163°C) and set time to 35 minutes. Press Start to begin preheating.
3. Once the unit has preheated, place the pan into the oven.
4. After 20 minutes, remove the pan from the oven. Stir the rice. Transfer the pan back to the oven and continue cooking for 10 to 15 minutes, or until the rice is mostly cooked through and the water is absorbed.
5. When done, remove the pan from the oven and cover with aluminum foil. Let stand for 10 minutes. Using a fork, gently fluff the rice.
6. Serve immediately.

Paprika-Oregano Seasoning
Prep time: 5 minutes | Cook time: 0 minutes | Makes about ¾ cups

3 tablespoons ancho chile powder
3 tablespoons paprika
2 tablespoons dried oregano
2 tablespoons freshly ground black pepper
2 teaspoons cayenne
2 teaspoons cumin
1 tablespoon granulated onion
1 tablespoon granulated garlic

1. Stir together all the ingredients in a small bowl.
2. Use immediately or place in an airtight container in the pantry.

Poblano Garlic Sauce
Prep time: 15 minutes | Cook time: 0 minutes | Makes 2 cups

3 large ancho chiles, stems and seeds removed, torn into pieces
1½ cups very hot water
2 garlic cloves, peeled and lightly smashed
2 tablespoons wine vinegar
1½ teaspoons sugar
½ teaspoon dried oregano
½ teaspoon ground cumin
2 teaspoons kosher salt or 1 teaspoon fine salt

1. Mix together the chile pieces and hot water in a bowl and let stand for 10 to 15 minutes.
2. Pour the chiles and water into a blender jar. Fold in the garlic, vinegar, sugar, oregano, cumin, and salt and blend until smooth.
3. Use immediately.

Shawarma Seasoning
Prep time: 5 minutes | Cook time: 0 minutes | Makes about 1 tablespoon

1 teaspoon smoked paprika
1 teaspoon cumin
¼ teaspoon turmeric
¼ teaspoon kosher salt or ⅛ teaspoon fine salt
¼ teaspoon cinnamon
¼ teaspoon allspice
¼ teaspoon red pepper flakes
¼ teaspoon freshly ground black pepper

1. Stir together all the ingredients in a small bowl.
2. Use immediately or place in an airtight container in the pantry.

Garlic Tomato Sauce

Prep time: 15 minutes | Cook time: 30 minutes | Makes about 3 cups

¼ cup extra-virgin olive oil
3 garlic cloves, minced
1 small onion, chopped (about ½ cup)
2 tablespoons minced or puréed sun-dried tomatoes (optional)
1 (28-ounce / 794-g) can crushed tomatoes
½ teaspoon dried basil
½ teaspoon dried oregano
¼ teaspoon red pepper flakes
1 teaspoon kosher salt or ½ teaspoon fine salt, plus more as needed

1. Heat the oil in a medium saucepan over medium heat.
2. Add the garlic and onion and sauté for 2 to 3 minutes, or until the onion is softened. Add the sun-dried tomatoes (if desired) and cook for 1 minute until fragrant. Stir in the crushed tomatoes, scraping any brown bits from the bottom of the pot. Fold in the basil, oregano, red pepper flakes, and salt. Stir well.
3. Bring to a simmer. Cook covered for about 30 minutes, stirring occasionally.
4. Turn off the heat and allow the sauce to cool for about 10 minutes.
5. Taste and adjust the seasoning, adding more salt if needed.
6. Use immediately.

Buttery Mushrooms

Prep time: 8 minutes | Cook time: 30 minutes | Makes about 1½ cups

1 pound (454 g) button or cremini mushrooms, washed, stems trimmed, and cut into quarters or thick slices
¼ cup water
1 teaspoon kosher salt or ½ teaspoon fine salt
3 tablespoons unsalted butter, cut into pieces, or extra-virgin olive oil

1. Place a large piece of aluminum foil on the sheet pan. Place the mushroom pieces in the middle of the foil. Spread them out into an even layer. Pour the water over them, season with the salt, and add the butter. Wrap the mushrooms in the foil.
2. Select Roast. Set temperature to 325ºF (163ºC) and set time to 15 minutes. Press Start to begin preheating.
3. Once the unit has preheated, place the pan into the oven.
4. After 15 minutes, remove the pan from the oven. Transfer the foil packet to a cutting board and carefully unwrap it. Pour the mushrooms and cooking liquid from the foil onto the sheet pan.
5. Select Roast. Set temperature to 350ºF (180ºC) and set time to 15 minutes. place the pan into the oven. Press Start to begin preheating.
6. After about 10 minutes, remove the pan from the oven and stir the mushrooms. Return the pan to the oven and continue cooking for 5 to 15 more minutes, or until the liquid is mostly gone and the mushrooms start to brown.
7. Serve immediately.

Ginger-Garlic Dipping Sauce

Prep time: 15 minutes | Cook time: 0 minutes | Makes about 1 cup

¼ cup rice vinegar
¼ cup hoisin sauce
¼ cup low-sodium chicken or vegetable stock
3 tablespoons soy sauce
1 tablespoon minced or grated ginger
1 tablespoon minced or pressed garlic
1 teaspoon chili-garlic sauce or sriracha (or more to taste)

1. Stir together all the ingredients in a small bowl, or place in a jar with a tight-fitting lid and shake until well mixed.
2. Use immediately.

Creamy Grits

Prep time: 3 minutes | Cook time: 1 hour 5 minutes | Makes about 4 cups

1 cup grits or polenta (not instant or quick cook)
2 cups chicken or vegetable stock
2 cups milk
2 tablespoons unsalted butter, cut into 4 pieces
1 teaspoon kosher salt or ½ teaspoon fine salt

1. Add the grits to the baking pan. Stir in the stock, milk, butter, and salt.
2. Select Bake. set temperature to 325ºF (163ºC) and set time to 1 hour and 5 minutes. Press Start to begin preheating.
3. Once the unit has preheated, place the pan into the oven.
4. After 15 minutes, remove the pan from the oven and stir the polenta. Return the pan to the oven and continue cooking.
5. After 30 minutes, remove the pan again and stir the polenta again. Return the pan to the oven and continue cooking for 15 to 20 minutes, or until the polenta is soft and creamy and the liquid is absorbed.
6. When done, remove the pan from the oven.
7. Serve immediately.

Chapter 17 Dehydrate

Dehydrated Pineapple Slices
Prep time: 10 minutes | Cook time: 12 hours | Serves 6

1 pineapple, peeled, cored and sliced ¼ inch thick
1 tablespoon coconut palm sugar
2 teaspoons ground cinnamon
½ teaspoon ground ginger
½ teaspoon Himalayan pink salt

1. Toss the pineapple slices with the sugar, cinnamon, ginger and salt.
2. Place the pineapple slices in a single layer on three air flow racks. Place the racks on the bottom, middle, and top shelves of the air fryer oven.
3. Press the Power Button. Cook at 120ºF (49ºC) for 12 hours.

Cinnamon Orange Slices
Prep time: 10 minutes | Cook time: 6 hours | Serves 3

2 large oranges, cut into ⅛-inch-thick slices
½ teaspoon ground star anise
½ teaspoon ground cinnamon
1 tablespoon chocolate hazelnut spread (optional)

1. Sprinkle spices on the orange slices.
2. Place orange slices on the air flow racks. Slide the racks into the air fryer oven. Press the Power Button. Cook at 140ºF (60ºC) for 6 hours.
3. Remove when done, and if desired serve with chocolate hazelnut spread.

Peach Fruit Leather
Prep time: 15 minutes | Cook time: 6 hours 15 minutes | Serves 4

4 peaches, pitted and each peach cut into 6 pieces

1. Line three air flow racks with parchment paper. Place peach slices on parchment.
2. Slide the racks into the air fryer oven. Press the Power Button. Cook at 400ºF (205ºC) for 15 minutes.
3. Transfer the cooked peaches to a blender or food processor and blend until smooth.
4. Line a baking sheet with parchment paper and pour peach purée onto paper, spreading as necessary with a spatula into an even layer.
5. Slide the sheet into the air fryer oven. Press the Power Button. Cook at 130ºF (54ºC) for 6 hours or until leather is desired consistency.

Cinnamon Pear Chips
Prep time: 20 minutes | Cook time: 2 hours | Serves 2

2 pears
3 tablespoons cinnamon and sugar mixture

1. Line a baking pan with parchment paper.
2. Slice the pears very thin and lay them on the pan in a single layer.
3. Sprinkle them with the cinnamon and sugar mixture.
4. Slide the pan into the air fryer oven. Press the Power Button. Cook at 170ºF (77ºC) for 2 hours, turning pears over halfway through.
5. Transfer to wire rack to cool.

Dehydrated Zucchini Chips
Prep time: 10 minutes | Cook time: 3 hours | Serves 4

4 to 5 medium zucchini, thinly sliced
2 tablespoons olive oil
Garlic salt and black pepper, to taste

1. Toss the zucchini with the olive oil, garlic salt and pepper.
2. Lay in a single layer on the air flow racks. Slide the racks into the air fryer oven. Press the Power Button. Cook at 170ºF (77ºC) for 3 hours, until dry and crisp.
3. Store in a plastic container for up to two weeks.

Candied Bacon
Prep time: 10 minutes | Cook time: 4 hours | Makes 6 slices

6 slices bacon
3 tablespoons light brown sugar
2 tablespoons rice vinegar
2 tablespoons chilli paste
1 tablespoon soy sauce

1. Mix brown sugar, rice vinegar, chilli paste, and soy sauce in a bowl.
2. Add bacon slices and mix until the slices are evenly coated.
3. Marinate for up to 3 hours or until ready to dehydrate.
4. Discard the marinade, then place the bacon onto the air flow racks.
5. Slide the racks into the air fryer oven. Press the Power Button. Cook at 170ºF (77ºC) for 4 hours.
6. Remove from the air fryer oven when done and let the bacon cool down for 5 minutes, then serve.

Dehydrated Onions

Prep time: 15 minutes | Cook time: 9 hours | Makes 6 tablespoons dried minced onions and 1 tablespoon onion powder

1 medium onion

To dry the onions:
1. Prepare your onions by removing the skins, trimming the ends, and slicing into even sized pieces.
2. Separate the onion segments and spread them out evenly on the air flow racks in a single layer.
3. Slide the racks into the air fryer oven. Press the Power Button. Cook at 125ºF (52ºC) for 3 to 9 hours.
4. The timing will depend on the size of your onion pieces and moisture content. The dehydrated onions should be crisp and snap when your break them.
5. Let the dried onion pieces cool, crush into onion flakes, and package into airtight glass containers or process further into dried onion flakes and onion powder.

Pork Jerky

Prep time: 10 minutes | Cook time: 3 hours | Makes 35 jerky strips

2 pounds (907 g) ground pork
1 tablespoon sesame oil
1 tablespoon Sriracha
1 tablespoon soy sauce
1 tablespoon rice vinegar
½ teaspoon salt
½ teaspoon black pepper
½ teaspoon onion powder
½ teaspoon pink curing salt

1. Combine ground pork, sesame oil, Sriracha, soy sauce, rice vinegar, salt, black pepper, onion powder, and pink curing salt in a large bowl; mix until evenly combined. Cover and refrigerate for 8 hours.
2. Using a jerky gun, form as many sticks as you can fit on all three air flow racks. They will shrink almost immediately so you can put them close together and utilize the full length of the racks.
3. Slide the racks into the air fryer oven. Press the Power Button. Cook at 160ºF (70ºC) for 1 hour.
4. Remove racks from the air fryer oven and blot excess moisture with paper towels. Flip each stick and cook for 1 more hour.
5. Repeat step 4 for a total cook time of 3 hours. Transfer jerky sticks to a paper towel-lined baking sheet. Cover with another layer of paper towels and let sit out 8 hours for final drying. Repeat with any remaining jerky mix.
6. Transfer jerky to an airtight container and refrigerate for up to 30 days.

Strawberry Roll Ups

Prep time: 10 minutes | Cook time: 9 hours | Serves 2

2 cups fresh strawberries
½ lemon, juiced
3 tablespoons Splenda

1. Blend your strawberries, sugar and lemon juice until smooth.
2. Line the air flow racks with parchment paper.
3. Spread the fruit mixture evenly across the racks.
4. Slide the racks into the air fryer oven. Press the Power Button. Cook at 140ºF (60ºC) for 9 hours, or until it is no longer sticky.
5. Cut into slices and roll.
6. Store in an air tight container at room temperature for up to a month or in the freezer for up to a year.

Dried Hot Peppers

Prep time: 10 minutes | Cook time: 10 hours | Serves 2

10 hot peppers

1. Place the peppers on the air flow racks.
2. Slide the racks into the air fryer oven. Press the Power Button. Cook at 160ºF (70ºC) for 8 to 10 hours.
3. They should be very dry.

Beef Jerky

Prep time: 10 minutes | Cook time: 3 to 4 hours | Serves 8

12 ounces (340 g) top sirloin beef
1 garlic clove, minced
1 inch piece fresh gingerroot, peeled and grated
2 tablespoons reduced sodium soy sauce
1 tablespoon turbinado sugar
1 tablespoon chili paste (such as Sambal Oelek)
1 tablespoon rice vinegar

1. Using a sharp knife, thinly slice beef and place in a resealable bag.
2. In a bowl, combine garlic, ginger, soy sauce, sugar chili paste and rice vinegar; whisk well.
3. Pour marinade into bag, seal and place in the refrigerator for at least 4 or up to 24 hours.
4. When ready to cook, remove pieces of beef from a marinade and pat dry with a paper towel.
5. Place the beef on three air flow racks. Slide the racks into the air fryer oven. Press the Power Button. Cook at 160ºF (70ºC) for 3 to 4 hours.
6. Checking the jerky periodically for desired doneness. Allow to cool completely and then store in an airtight container.

Dried Mushrooms

Prep time: 30 minutes | Cook time: 4 hours | Makes 2½ quarts

4 to 5 pounds (1.8 to 2.3 kg) fresh mushrooms, washed, rinsed and drained well.

1. Rinse whole mushrooms well under cold running water. Gently scrub any visible dirt away without damaging the mushroom. Pat dry with paper towels if needed.
2. Break the stem off of each mushroom and slice into ¼ to ½ inch thick slices with a sharp knife.
3. Place the sliced mushrooms on the parchment-lined air flow racks.
4. Slide the racks into the air fryer oven. Press the Power Button. Cook at 170ºF (77ºC) for 4 hours.
5. Check the mushrooms after 1 hour and flip them over for even drying. Check the mushroom slices every hour.
6. As the mushroom slices dry, remove them from the air fryer oven and allow to cool on the racks or a paper towel.
7. Store dried mushroom slices in an airtight glass container.

Kiwi Chips

Prep time: 15 minutes | Cook time: 6 to 12 hours | Makes 10 to 12 slices

2 kiwis

1. Peel the kiwis, using a paring knife to slice the skin off or a vegetable peeler.
2. Slice the peeled kiwis into ¼ inch slices.
3. Place the kiwi slices on the air flow racks. Slide the racks into the air fryer oven. Press the Power Button. Cook at 135ºF (57ºC) for 6 to 12 hours.
4. These should be slightly chewy when done.

Dehydrated Strawberries

Prep time: 10 minutes | Cook time: 2 hours | Serves 4

1 pound (454 g) fresh strawberries

1. Line three air flow racks with parchment paper.
2. Wash strawberries and cut off stem ends. Cut strawberries into slices, about ⅛ inch thick.
3. Place sliced strawberries on the air flow racks. Space them so the pieces are not touching.
4. Slide the racks into the air fryer oven. Press the Power Button. Cook at 170ºF (77ºC) for 30 minutes. Use tongs to turn the berries. Cook for another 30 minutes. Repeat this until strawberry slices are leathery.
5. Allow the slices to cool completely. Transfer dried strawberry slices to an airtight container. They will keep up to 5 days.

Lemon-Pepper Salmon Jerky

Prep time: 20 minutes | Cook time: 3 hours | Serves 10

1¾ pounds (794 g) filet wild Alaskan salmon, skin on, bones removed
½ cup low sodium soy sauce
1 tablespoon lemon juice
1 tablespoon brown sugar
2 teaspoons mixed whole peppercorns
1 teaspoon lemon zest
½ teaspoon liquid smoke
½ teaspoon celery seeds
½ teaspoon onion powder
½ teaspoon garlic powder
¼ teaspoon kosher salt

1. Freeze salmon for 1 hour.
2. In the meantime, in a large bowl, combine the soy sauce, lemon juice, sugar, peppercorns, lemon zest, liquid smoke, celery seeds, onion and garlic powders, and salt.
3. Remove the salmon from the freezer and cut it into thin strips (about ½ inch), then place in the marinade. Cover and marinate for 1 to 3 hours in the fridge.
4. Remove strips and place on a plate, patting dry with a paper towel.
5. Place the salmon strips on three air flow racks in a single layer. Slide the racks into the air fryer oven. Press the Power Button. Cook at 170ºF (77ºC) for 3 hours, flipping over halfway through. Salmon is done when dried all the way through, but slightly chewy.
6. Store in a cool dry place in a sealed container.

Smoky Venison Jerky

Prep time: 30 minutes | Cook time: 4 hours | Makes 1 to 2 pounds

3 to 5 pounds (1.4 to 2.3 kg) deer roast
Hi-Mountain cure and jerky mix or another brand
3 to 5 teaspoons liquid smoke

1. Start by slicing your roast into thin strips, and removing any silver skin on each piece of the meat.
2. Lay it all out flat, and then mix up your seasoning per the box. Sprinkle on both sides of the meat, massaging it in.
3. Then transfer the meat into a bag and add in the liquid smoke. Massage bag.
4. Store in the fridge for 24 hours to let it marinade and cure.
5. Lay the jerky out on the air flow racks, don't let the pieces touch.
6. Slide the racks into the air fryer oven. Press the Power Button. Cook at 160ºF (70ºC) for 3 to 4 hours.
7. Make sure to flip and randomly check, and remove the meat when it is cooked to your texture liking.

New meal; fresh start. -Chapter 17 Dehydrate|175

Appendix 1 Measurement Conversion Chart

VOLUME EQUIVALENTS(DRY)

US STANDARD	METRIC (APPROXIMATE)
1/8 teaspoon	0.5 mL
1/4 teaspoon	1 mL
1/2 teaspoon	2 mL
3/4 teaspoon	4 mL
1 teaspoon	5 mL
1 tablespoon	15 mL
1/4 cup	59 mL
1/2 cup	118 mL
3/4 cup	177 mL
1 cup	235 mL
2 cups	475 mL
3 cups	700 mL
4 cups	1 L

VOLUME EQUIVALENTS(LIQUID)

US STANDARD	US STANDARD (OUNCES)	METRIC (APPROXIMATE)
2 tablespoons	1 fl.oz.	30 mL
1/4 cup	2 fl.oz.	60 mL
1/2 cup	4 fl.oz.	120 mL
1 cup	8 fl.oz.	240 mL
1 1/2 cup	12 fl.oz.	355 mL
2 cups or 1 pint	16 fl.oz.	475 mL
4 cups or 1 quart	32 fl.oz.	1 L
1 gallon	128 fl.oz.	4 L

WEIGHT EQUIVALENTS

US STANDARD	METRIC (APPROXIMATE)
1 ounce	28 g
2 ounces	57 g
5 ounces	142 g
10 ounces	284 g
15 ounces	425 g
16 ounces (1 pound)	455 g
1.5 pounds	680 g
2 pounds	907 g

TEMPERATURES EQUIVALENTS

FAHRENHEIT(F)	CELSIUS(C) (APPROXIMATE)
225 °F	107 °C
250 °F	120 °C
275 °F	135 °C
300 °F	150 °C
325 °F	160 °C
350 °F	180 °C
375 °F	190 °C
400 °F	205 °C
425 °F	220 °C
450 °F	235 °C
475 °F	245 °C
500 °F	260 °C

Appendix 2 Air Fryer Cooking Chart

Beef

Item	Temp (°F)	Time (mins)	Item	Temp (°F)	Time (mins)
Beef Eye Round Roast (4 lbs.)	400 °F	45 to 55	Meatballs (1-inch)	370 °F	7
Burger Patty (4 oz.)	370 °F	16 to 20	Meatballs (3-inch)	380 °F	10
Filet Mignon (8 oz.)	400 °F	18	Ribeye, bone-in (1-inch, 8 oz)	400 °F	10 to 15
Flank Steak (1.5 lbs.)	400 °F	12	Sirloin steaks (1-inch, 12 oz)	400 °F	9 to 14
Flank Steak (2 lbs.)	400 °F	20 to 28			

Chicken

Item	Temp (°F)	Time (mins)	Item	Temp (°F)	Time (mins)
Breasts, bone in (1 ¼ lb.)	370 °F	25	Legs, bone-in (1 ¾ lb.)	380 °F	30
Breasts, boneless (4 oz)	380 °F	12	Thighs, boneless (1 ½ lb.)	380 °F	18 to 20
Drumsticks (2 ½ lb.)	370 °F	20	Wings (2 lb.)	400 °F	12
Game Hen (halved 2 lb.)	390 °F	20	Whole Chicken	360 °F	75
Thighs, bone-in (2 lb.)	380 °F	22	Tenders	360 °F	8 to 10

Pork & Lamb

Item	Temp (°F)	Time (mins)	Item	Temp (°F)	Time (mins)
Bacon (regular)	400 °F	5 to 7	Pork Tenderloin	370 °F	15
Bacon (thick cut)	400 °F	6 to 10	Sausages	380 °F	15
Pork Loin (2 lb.)	360 °F	55	Lamb Loin Chops (1-inch thick)	400 °F	8 to 12
Pork Chops, bone in (1-inch, 6.5 oz)	400 °F	12	Rack of Lamb (1.5 – 2 lb.)	380 °F	22

Fish & Seafood

Item	Temp (°F)	Time (mins)	Item	Temp (°F)	Time (mins)
Calamari (8 oz)	400 °F	4	Tuna Steak	400 °F	7 to 10
Fish Fillet (1-inch, 8 oz)	400 °F	10	Scallops	400 °F	5 to 7
Salmon, fillet (6 oz)	380 °F	12	Shrimp	400 °F	5
Swordfish steak	400 °F	10			

Vegetables

INGREDIENT	AMOUNT	PREPARATION	OIL	TEMP	COOK TIME
Asparagus	2 bunches	Cut in half, trim stems	2 Tbsp	420°F	12-15 mins
Beets	1½ lbs	Peel, cut in ½-inch cubes	1 Tbsp	390°F	28-30 mins
Bell peppers (for roasting)	4 peppers	Cut in quarters, remove seeds	1 Tbsp	400°F	15-20 mins
Broccoli	1 large head	Cut in 1-2-inch florets	1 Tbsp	400°F	15-20 mins
Brussels sprouts	1 lb	Cut in half, remove stems	1 Tbsp	425°F	15-20 mins
Carrots	1 lb	Peel, cut in ¼-inch rounds	1 Tbsp	425°F	10-15 mins
Cauliflower	1 head	Cut in 1-2-inch florets	2 Tbsp	400°F	20-22 mins
Corn on the cob	7 ears	Whole ears, remove husks	1 Tbps	400°F	14-17 mins
Green beans	1 bag (12 oz)	Trim	1 Tbps	420°F	18-20 mins
Kale (for chips)	4 oz	Tear into pieces, remove stems	None	325°F	5-8 mins
Mushrooms	16 oz	Rinse, slice thinly	1 Tbps	390°F	25-30 mins
Potatoes, russet	1½ lbs	Cut in 1-inch wedges	1 Tbps	390°F	25-30 mins
Potatoes, russet	1 lb	Hand-cut fries, soak 30 mins in cold water, then pat dry	½-3 Tbps	400°F	25-28 mins
Potatoes, sweet	1 lb	Hand-cut fries, soak 30 mins in cold water, then pat dry	1 Tbps	400°F	25-28 mins
Zucchini	1 lb	Cut in eighths lengthwise, then cut in half	1 Tbps	400°F	15-20 mins

Appendix 3 Index

A

Air Fried Tofu Sticks 32
Almond, Coconut, and Apple Granola 15
Apple Bake with Cinnamon 169
Apricot Brioche with Croûtes Fraîche 159
Artichoke and Mushroom Frittata 21
Arugula and Prosciutto Pizza 105
Asiago Balls 134
Asparagus Casserole with Grits 111
Asparagus Frittata with Goat Cheese 117
Asparagus Strata with Havarti Cheese 21
Avocado and Egg Burrito 12
Avocado and Tomato Wraps 119
Avocado Chips with Lime 152

B

Baby Back Ribs with Paprika Rub 143
Bacon and Egg Wraps with Salsa 122
Bacon-Wrapped Herb Rainbow Trout 64
Bacon-Wrapped Pork Hot Dogs 49
Bacon-Wrapped Sirloin Roast 141
Baked Avocado with Eggs and Tomato 16
Baked Eggs with Kale Pesto 19
Baked Fries with Bacon and Eggs 11
Baked White Rice 171
Balsamic Asparagus 39
Balsamic Cherry Tomatoes 134
Balsamic Chicken Breast with Oregano 93
Balsamic Chuck Roast 142
Balsamic Duck Breasts with Orange Marmalade 93
Balsamic Ginger Scallops 77
Balsamic Italian Sausages and Red Grapes 47
Balsamic Prosciutto-Wrapped Pears 148
Balsamic Shrimp with Goat Cheese 73
Balsamic Turkey with Carrots and Snap Peas 83
Balsamic-Glazed Beets 37
Banana Carrot Muffin 22
Banana Chocolate Bread with Walnuts 17
Barbecue Drumsticks with Vegetable 83
Barbecue Turkey Burgers 91
Basil Scallops with Broccoli 80
BBQ Cheese Chicken Pizza 157
BBQ Chicken with Mustard Rub 140
BBQ Kielbasa Sausage 49
Beef and Bean Casserole 112
Beef Burgers with Korean Mayo 126
Beef Burgers with Seeds 125
Beef Jerky 174
Beef Meatloaf with Roasted Vegetables 48
Beef Meatloaves with Spinach 58
Beef Ravioli with Parmesan 57
Beef Rump with Red Wine Gravy 44
Beef Steak and Bell Pepper Rolls 123
Bell Pepper and Carrot Frittata 15
Bell Pepper and Ham Omelet 12
Blackberry Cobbler 167
Blueberries Quesadillas 19
Blueberry and Peach Crisp 162
Blueberry Cake with Lemon 22
Bourbon Sirloin Steak 55
Breaded Artichoke Bites 156
Breaded Asparagus Fries 39
Breaded Brussels Sprouts with Paprika 42
Breaded Calf's Liver Strips 62
Breaded Catfish Nuggets 72
Breaded Crab Cakes 68
Breaded Fish Sticks 72
Breaded Pork Loin Chops 54
Breaded Zucchini Chips with Parmesan 26
Breaded Zucchini Tots 148
Breakfast Raisins Bars 15
Breakfast Sausage Quiche 14
Brie Pear Sandwiches 155
Broccoli and Red Pepper Quiche 14
Broiled Lemony Salmon Steak 64
Brown Rice Porridge with Dates 18
Brown Rice Quiches with Pimiento 16
Brown Sugar Acorn Squash 40
Brown Sugar-Mustard Glazed Ham 53
Buttermilk Chocolate Cake 128
Buttermilk-Marinated Chicken Wings 156
Butternut Squash and Arugula Pizza 105
Butternut Squash and Parsnip with Thyme 31
Butternut Squash with Goat Cheese 29
Buttery Chicken with Corn 95
Buttery Eggplant and Tomato with Freekeh 38
Buttery Mushrooms 172

C

Cabbage and Prawn Wraps 121
Cajun Beef and Bell Pepper Fajitas 122
Cajun Catfish Cakes with Parmesan 75
Cajun Cod Fillets with Lemon Pepper 74
Candied Bacon 173
Carrot and Mushroom Spring Rolls 120
Carrot Chips 153
Carrot, Tofu and Cauliflower Rice 34
Catfish Fillets with Pecan Crust 64
Catfish, Toamto and Onion Kebabs 69
Cauliflower and Okra Casserole 110
Cauliflower Casserole with Pecan Butter 114
Cauliflower with Teriyaki Sauce 25
Cayenne Green Beans 34
Cayenne Prawns with Cumin 72

Cheddar and Egg Frittata with Parsley 115
Cheddar Bacon Casserole 14
Cheddar Baked Potatoes with Chives 146
Cheddar Black Bean and Corn Salsa 157
Cheddar Breakfast Sausage Scones 12
Cheddar Broccoli and Carrot Quiche 117
Cheddar Broccoli Casserole 115
Cheddar Broccoli Gratin 40
Cheddar Chicken and Broccoli Divan 116
Cheddar Chicken Empanadas 125
Cheddar Chicken Sausage Casserole 110
Cheddar Hash Brown Casserole 18
Cheddar Mushrooms with Pimientos 146
Cheddar Pastrami Casserole 112
Cheddar Sausage Balls 148
Cheddar Turkey Burgers with Mayo 87
Cheese and Bacon Muffin Sandwiches 10
Cheese and Egg Quiche 116
Cheese Tomato Pizza with Basil 104
Cheesy Chicken Tenders with Veggie 84
Cheesy Eggplant with Chili Smoked Almonds 29
Chicken and Broccoli Casserole 114
Chicken and Butternut Squash Pizza 101
Chicken and Cabbage Wraps 118
Chicken and Cheese Sandwiches 97
Chicken and Pepper Baguette with Mayo 85
Chicken and Veggies with 'Nduja 89
Chicken Breakfast Sausages 16
Chicken Breast in Mango Sauce 81
Chicken Drumsticks with Green Beans 100
Chicken Gnocchi with Spinach 99
Chicken Kebabs with Corn Salad 98
Chicken Pot Pie 82
Chicken Roast with Mustard Paste 138
Chicken Thighs with Cabbage Slaw 88
Chicken Thighs with Cherry Tomatoes 98
Chicken Thighs with Mirin 84
Chicken Thighs with Peppers 91
Chicken with Brown Sugar Brine 144
Chicken Wraps with Ricotta Cheese 120
Chicken, Vegetable and Rice Casserole 92
Chickpea and Mushroom Wraps 123
Chickpea and Spinach Casserole 113
Chickpea-Stuffed Bell Peppers 33
Chili Chicken Fries 92
Chili Tomato with Herbs and Pistachios 30
Chocolate Blueberry Cupcakes 162
Chocolate Cake with Blackberries 166
Chocolate Chip Brownies 168
Chocolate Macaroons with Coconut 131
Chocolate S'mores 169
Chocolate-Glazed Donut Holes 129
Chorizo Pizza with Piquillo Peppers 102
Chuck and Sausage Meatballs 57
Cider-Bourbon Glazed Pork Loin Roast 52
Cinnamon Apple Chips 151
Cinnamon Apple Fritters 163

Cinnamon Apple Turnovers 23
Cinnamon Apple with Apricots 170
Cinnamon Churros 134
Cinnamon Orange Slices 173
Cinnamon Peach Wedges 157
Cinnamon Pear Chips 173
Cinnamon Pineapple Rings 167
Cinnamon Rolls with Brown Sugar 20
Citrus Carrots with Balsamic Glaze 42
Citrus Pork Ribs with Oregano 54
Clam Appetizers 64
Coconut Curried Fish with Chilies 77
Coconut Orange Cake 170
Cod Fish Tacos with Mango Salsa 119
Coffee Cake with Pecan 10
Colby Pork Sausage with Cauliflower 55
Corn Casserole with Bell Pepper 110
Corn Casserole with Swiss Cheese 43
Corn Frittata with Avocado Dressing 13
Crab and Fish Cakes 76
Crab Cheese Enchiladas 65
Crab Ratatouille with Thyme 75
Cream Cheese and Crab Wontons 121
Cream-Glazed Cinnamon Rolls 133
Creamy Grits 172
Crispy Cream Cheese Wontons 127
Crispy Fish Fillet 67
Cumin Fried Chickpeas 154
Cumin Tortilla Chips 150
Curried Cauliflower with Cashews 36
Curried Chicken and Brussels Sprouts 96
Curried Halibut Fillets with Parmesan 67
Curried King Prawns with Cumin 79
Curried Pork Sliders 124
Curried Prawns with Coconut 74
Curried Shrimp and Zucchini Potstickers 118

D

Dehydrated Onions 174
Dehydrated Pineapple Slices 173
Dehydrated Strawberries 175
Dehydrated Zucchini Chips 173
Deviled Eggs with Mayo 153
Dijon Hake Fillets with Garlic Sauce 72
Dijon Pork Tenderloin 49
Dijon Turkey Breast with Sage 85
Dijon Turkey with Carrots 89
Dijon-Honey Pork Tenderloin 58
Dijon-Rosemary Chicken Breasts 81
Dill Pickles with Buttermilk Dressing 130
Double Cheese Roasted Asparagus 30
Double-Cheese Clam Pizza 106
Dried Fruit Stuffed Pork Loin 136
Dried Hot Peppers 174
Dried Mushrooms 175
Duck Breast with Potato 89

E-F

Easy Nutmeg Butter Cookies 159
Escarole and Radicchio Pizza with Walnuts 101
Fish Fillet with Poblano Sauce 67
Fish Fillet with Sun-Dried Tomato Pesto 70
Five-Spice Turkey Thighs 93
Flank Steak and Bell Pepper Fajitas 53
Flounder Fillet and Asparagus Rolls 68
Flounder Fillets with Lemon Pepper 78
French Toast Sticks with Strawberries 23
Fried Bacon-Wrapped Scallops 80
Fried Breaded Scallops 79
Fried Pickle Spears with Chili 150
Fried Scallops with Thyme 80

G
Game Hens with Cucumber Salad 97
Garlic Bell Peppers with Marjoram 28
Garlic Broccoli with Parmesan 41
Garlic Butternut Squash Croquettes 40
Garlic Calamari Rings 80
Garlic Chicken Wings 91
Garlic Duck Leg Quarters 93
Garlic Eggplant Slices with Parsley 33
Garlic Fried Edamame 154
Garlic Nuggets 132
Garlic Pork Belly with Bay Leaves 45
Garlic Pork Leg Roast with Candy Onions 60
Garlic Potatoes with Heavy Cream 39
Garlic Potatoes with Peppers and Onions 16
Garlic Ratatouille 25
Garlic Tofu with Basil 37
Garlic Tomato Pizza Sauce 103
Garlic Tomato Sauce 172
Garlic Turnip and Zucchini 24
Garlic Zucchini Crisps 43
Garlic Zucchini Sticks 40
Garlic-Lime Shishito Peppers 42
Garlicky Cabbage with Red Pepper 43
Garlicky Oregano Chicken with Chipotle Allioli 90
Garlicky Whole Chicken Bake 94
Ginger Apple Wedges 152
Ginger Pork Shoulder in Shaoxing Wine 46
Ginger Shrimp with Sesame Seeds 149
Ginger-Garlic Dipping Sauce 172
Ginger-Pepper Broccoli 32
Glazed Chocolate Cake 164
Glazed Sweet Bundt Cake 161
Gochujang Beef and Onion Tacos 118
Golden Potato, Carrot and Onion 31
Greek Potatoes with Chives 42
Green Chiles and Cheese Nachos 147

H-I
Half-and-Half Cinnamon Rolls 17
Halloumi Zucchinis and Eggplant 24
Ham and Pineapple Pizza 104
Ham with Dijon Bourbon Baste 142
Herb Buttery Turkey Breast 90
Hoisin Pork Butt with Veggies Salad 50
Hoisin Roasted Pork Ribs 54
Hoisin Scallops with Sesame Seeds 79
Honey Apple-Peach Crumble 165
Honey Baby Carrots with Dill 34
Honey Cashew Granola with Cranberries 19
Honey Halibut Steaks with Parsley 68
Honey Roasted Grapes with Basil 147
Honey Snack Mix 150
Honey-Glazed Peach and Plum Kebabs 161
Horseradish Green Tomatoes 157
Hush Puppies with Jalapeño 152
Italian Rice Balls with Olives 156
Italian Sausage and Bell Pepper Pizza 108

J-K
Jalapeño Poppers with Cheddar 147
Jalapeño Turkey Sliders with Chive Mayo 126
Juicy Bacon and Beef Cheeseburgers 47
Jumbo Shrimp with Dijon-Mayo Sauce 73
Kale and Egg Frittata with Feta 111
Kiwi Chips 175

L
Lamb Hamburgers with Feta Cheese 123
Lamb Leg with Herb Yogurt Sauce 52
Lamb Leg with Root Vegetable 44
Lamb Shoulder with Lemony Caper Relish 46
Lemon Anchocy Dressing 171
Lemon Chicken with Oregano 100
Lemon Crab Cakes with Mayo 79
Lemon Pork Loin Chop with Marjoram 51
Lemon Ricotta with Capers 150
Lemon Shrimp with Cumin 77
Lemon Tilapia Fillets with Garlic 69
Lemon-Pepper Chicken Wings 147
Lemon-Pepper Salmon Jerky 175
Lemony Shrimp with Arugula 68
Lemony-Honey Roasted Radishes 27
Lime Sweet Potatoes with Allspice 41
Low-Fat Buttermilk Biscuits 10

M-N
Mackerel with Mango and Chili Salad 66
Maple Banana Bread Pudding 20
Maple French Toast Casserole 19
Maple Garlic Brussels Sprouts 43
Maple Oats and Nuts 11
Maple Pecan Tart 129
Maple Turkey Breast with Rosemary 94
Marinated Catfish Fillet 66
Marinated Coconut Chicken with Pineapple 84
Mediterranean Baked Fish Fillet 67
Mexican Beef and Chile Casserole 113
Mexican Brownie Squares 161
Mexican Sirloin Steak and Pepper Fajitas 61
Mint-Roasted Boneless Lamb Leg 53
Minted-Balsamic Lamb Chops 49
Mixed Berry Bake with Almond Topping 163

Mixed Berry Crisp with Cloves 168
Moroccan Roasted Veggies with Labneh 31
Mozzarella Chicken Breasts with Basil 94
Mozzarella Chicken Taquitos 122
Mozzarella Meatball Pizza 103
Mozzarella Rice Arancini 128
Mozzarella Sausage Calzones 61
Mozzarella Tomato Salsa Rounds 14
Mozzarella Tomato-Stuffed Squash 38
Mozzarella Walnut Stuffed Mushrooms 25
Muffuletta Sliders with Olive Mix 158
Mushroom and Beef Casserole 112
Mushroom and Sausage Empanadas 153
Mushroom and Spinach Frittata 21
Mushroom and Spinach Pizza 109
Mushroom and Spinach Pizza 109
Mustard Lamb Shoulder 138
No-Knead Pan Pizza Dough 102
Nut-Crusted Pork Rack 51
Nutmeg Apple Chips 154

O-P

Old Bay Crab Sticks with Mayo Sauce 76
Old Bay Fried Chicken Wings 153
Old Bay Shrimp with Potatoes 74
Olive and Basil Stromboli with Garlic 131
Onion-Stuffed Mushrooms 25
Orange Beef and Broccoli with Sriracha 59
Orange Honey Glazed Ham 141
Orange Scones with Blueberries 23
Orange Shrimp with Cayenne 71
Orange-Glazed Whole Chicken 86
Oregano Eggplants with Chili Anchovy Sauce 37
Oregano Stuffed Chicken with Feta 82
Paprika Hens in Wine 88
Paprika Hens with Creole Seasoning 100
Paprika Lamb Chops with Sage 45
Paprika Nut Mix 154
Paprika Polenta Fries with Chili-Lime Mayo 149
Paprika Potato Chips 151
Paprika Pulled Pork Butt 137
Paprika Tiger Shrimp 77
Paprika Tilapia with Garlic Aioli 71
Paprika Whole Chicken Roast 95
Paprika-Oregano Seasoning 171
Parmesan Bruschetta with Tomato 155
Parmesan Brussels Sprouts 26
Parmesan Cauliflower with Turmeric 145
Parmesan Corn on the Cob 41
Parmesan Crab Toasts 151
Parmesan Eggplant Hoagies 121
Parmesan Fennel with Red Pepper 35
Parmesan Fish Fillets with Tarragon 75
Parmesan Green Bean Casserole 111
Parmesan Ham and Egg Cups 11
Parmesan Snack Mix 151
Parsley Shrimp with Lemon 75

Peach and Apple Crisp with Oatmeal 164
Peach and Blueberry Galette 163
Peach Chicken with Dark Cherry 96
Peach Fruit Leather 173
Peanut Butter Bread Pudding 166
Pear Pizza with Basil 106
Pecan Pie with Chocolate Chips 169
Pepper-Stuffed Portobellos 27
Pepperoni Pizza Bites with Marinara 145
Pepperoni Pizza with Mozzarella 103
Peppery Sausage Casserole with Cheddar 116
Perfect Upside-Down Chicken Nachos 86
Pigs in a Blanket with Sesame Seeds 131
Pineapple Sticks with Coconut 165
Poblano Garlic Sauce 171
Porchetta with Lemony Sage Rub 136
Pork and Cabbage Gyoza 126
Pork and Pineapple Kebabs 48
Pork and Turkey Sandwiches 155
Pork and Veggie Kebabs 56
Pork Butt withCoriander-Parsley Sauce 50
Pork Chop Roast with Worcestershire 55
Pork Chops and Apple Bake 56
Pork Chops with Lime Peach Salsa 51
Pork Chops with Pickapeppa Sauce 53
Pork Chops with Sour Cream and Dill Sauce 56
Pork Cutlets with Aloha Salsa 58
Pork Egg Rolls with Vinegar Dipping 130
Pork Jerky 174
Pork Loin Chops with Butternut Squash 63
Pork Loin Roast with Brown Sugar Brine 138
Pork Meatballs with Scallions 62
Pork Momos with Carrot 125
Pork Sausage Ratatouille 60
Pork Tenderloin with Rice 63
Pork, Squash and Pepper Kebabs 62
Potato and Asparagus Platter 28
Potato and Chorizo Frittata 113
Potato Samosas with Mint Chutney 127
Potato Shells with Cheddar and Bacon 27
Potato Taquitos with Mexican Cheese 124
Pro Dough 102
Prosciutto and Bacon Pizza 108
Prosciutto and Fig Pizza 105
Prosciutto Tart with Asparagus 59
Pumpkin Pudding with Vanilla Wafers 160

R

Red Chili Okra 24
Rhubarb with Sloe Gin and Rosemary 159
Rice and Olives Stuffed Peppers 28
Rice Pudding with Quince Jelly and Blackberry 160
Ricotta Margherita with Basil 106
Ricotta Pork Gratin with Mustard 117
Ricotta Spinach and Basil Pockets 120
Risotto Croquettes with Tomato Sauce 132
Roasted Bell Peppers with Burrata and 'Nduja 32

Roasted Mushrooms with Garlic   146
Roasted Potatoes with Rosemary   41
Roasted Veggie Rice with Eggs   32
Roasted Veggie Salad with Lemon   36
Roasted Veggies and Apple Salad   35
Roasted Veggies with Honey-Garlic Glaze   36
Rosemary-Balsamic Pork Loin Roast   54
Rum-Plums with Brown Sugar Cream   160
Rump Roast with Bell Peppers   48

S

Salmon Fillet with Spinach, and Beans   65
Salmon with Cucumber Sauce   70
Satay Chicken Skewers   86
Sausage and Onion Rolls with Mustard   145
Sausage French Toast Casserole with Maple   13
Sea Bass Stuffed with Spice Paste   69
Sea Bass with Asian Chili Dressing   65
Sesame Balsamic Chicken Breast   91
Sesame Green Beans with Sriracha   39
Sesame Kale Chips   155
Shawarma Seasoning   171
Sherry Lamb Leg and Autumn Vegetable   45
Sherry Tilapia and Mushroom Rice   66
Shrimp and Artichoke Paella   73
Shrimp and Spinach Frittata   18
Shrimp and Veggie Patties   73
Shrimp and Veggie Spring Rolls   78
Shrimp Kebabs with Cherry Tomatoes   78
Shrimp Salad with Caesar Dressing   71
Shrimp Scampi with Garlic Butter   76
Simple Chicken Cordon Bleu   83
Simple Pizza Dough   101
Sirloin Roast with Porcini-Wine Baste   139
Smoked Paprika Chicken Burgers   124
Smoked Paprika Lamb Leg   139
Smoked Paprika Vegetable with Eggs   29
Smoky Venison Jerky   175
Sour Cherry Brioche Pudding   166
Spareribs with Paprika Rub   137
Spice Cake with Creamy Frosting   169
Spicy Pepper Steak   57
Spinach and Egg Florentine   20
Spinach and Mushroom Frittata   112
Spinach and Shrimp Frittata   110
Spinach Calzones with Mushrooms   158
Spinach-Stuffed Beefsteak Tomatoes   26
Spring Pea Pizza with Ramps   107
Sriracha Shrimp with Mayo   135
Steak with Brandy Peppercorn Sauce   47
Strawberry Pizza   107
Strawberry Roll Ups   174
Stuffed Bell Peppers with Cream Cheese   34
Stuffed Peppers with Cheese and Basil   24
Stuffed Tilapia with Pepper and Cucumber   70
Sugar Roasted Walnuts   148
Sweet Banana Bread   10
Sweet Potato and Spinach Burritos   119
Sweet-and-Sour Chicken Breasts   87
Swiss Chicken and Ham Casserole   111
Swiss Ham Mustard Pastries   17

T-V

Tasty Meat and Vegetable Loaf   96
Teriyaki Chicken   143
Teriyaki Chicken Thighs   81
Teriyaki Roasted Chicken with Snow Peas   82
Teriyaki Sauce   171
Teriyaki-Glazed Pork Ribs   59
Teriyaki-Marinated Shrimp Skewers   133
Thyme Pork Chops with Carrots   55
Tilapia and Rockfish Casserole   115
Tomato and Black Olive Clafoutis   30
Tomato and Olive Quiche   113
Tomato-Stuffed Portobello Mushrooms   26
Tuna Melts with Mayo   149
Turkey and Cauliflower Meatloaf   95
Turkey and Mushroom Meatballs   85
Turkey and Pepper Hamburger   122
Turkey Breast with Strawberries   87
Turkey Casserole with Almond Mayo   114
Turkey Meatloaves with Onion   96
Turkey Scotch Eggs with Rosemary   99
Turkey with Thyme-Sage Brine   144
Turkey-Stuffed Peppers with Cheddar   99
Turkey-Wrapped Dates and Almonds   152
Vanilla Baked Peaches and Blueberries   168
Vanilla Banana Bread Pudding   13
Vanilla Banana Cake   128
Vanilla Blueberry Cobbler   18
Vanilla Butter Cake   135
Vanilla Cheese Blintzes   133
Vanilla Chocolate Cake   170
Vanilla Chocolate Chip Cookies   165
Vanilla Coconut Cookies with Pecans   162
Vanilla Fudge Pie   167
Vanilla Pancake with Mixed Berries   22
Vanilla Pancake with Walnuts   15
Vanilla Pound Cake   165
Vanilla Ricotta Cake with Lemon   167
Vanilla Walnuts Tart with Cloves   164
Veggie and Oat Meatballs   33
Vinegary Chicken with Pineapple   88
Vinegary Pork Schnitzel   60

W-Z

Whiskey-Basted Prime Rib Roast   140
White Chocolate Cookies with Nutmeg   168
Whole Duck with Cherry Sauce   92
Whole-Wheat Blueberries Muffins   22
Worcestershire Ribeye Steaks with Garlic   63
Zucchini and Spinach Frittata   115
Zucchini and Summer Squash Pizza   104
Zucchini Pizza with Pistachios   107
Zucchini Quesadilla with Gouda Cheese   35

CPSIA information can be obtained
at www.ICGtesting.com
Printed in the USA
LVHW101416070321
680811LV00006B/57

9 781637 335482